Coester, Alfred
Lester

The literary his-
tory of Spanish
America

THE LITERARY HISTORY OF SPANISH AMERICA

THE
LITERARY HISTORY OF
SPANISH AMERICA

BY

ALFRED COESTER, Ph.D.

PROFESSOR OF SPANISH AMERICAN LITERATURE
IN STANFORD UNIVERSITY
MEMBER HISPANIC SOCIETY OF AMERICA

SECOND EDITION

New York
COOPER SQUARE PUBLISHERS, INC.
1970

Originally Published 1928
Published 1970 by Cooper Square Publishers, Inc.
59 Fourth Avenue, New York, N. Y. 10003
Standard Book No. 8154-0356-9
Library of Congress Catalog Card No. 70-132942

Printed in the United States of America

TO
BELLE HAVEN
MY WIFE

PREFACE

LATIN AMERICA and the United States resemble two
neighbors who have long lived side by side, each too busy
with private matters to take more than an indifferent if
not hostile interest in the other. Recently we North
Americans have been taking a broader interest in our
neighbors. The building of the Panama Canal has directed our attention to the south. We have discovered
that those vast unknown regions are inhabited by human
beings worthy of being better known though their character differ widely from our own.

So great is our lack of acquaintance with our southern
neighbors that few can say with ex-President Taft:—
"I know the attractiveness of the Spanish American; I
know his highborn courtesy; I know his love of art, his
poet nature, his response to generous treatment, and I
know how easily he misunderstands the thoughtless
bluntness of an Anglo-Saxon diplomacy, and the too frequent lack of regard for the feelings of others that we have
inherited." (*The Independent*, Dec. 18, 1913.)

What ex-President Taft thus writes from personal
experience, it is possible for others to learn by reading the
books written by Spanish Americans. The main characteristics and trend of the Spanish-American mind are
revealed in his literature.

But shall we call Spanish-American writings literature?
A professor in Argentina wished a few years ago to estab-

lish a course for students in Spanish-American literature.
The plan was opposed by Bartolomé Mitre, ex-President
of the republic and himself a poet and historian of the first
rank, on the ground that such a thing did not exist. He
held the view that mere numbers of books did not form a
literature; though united by the bond of a common
language, the printed productions of Spanish Americans
had no logical union nor gave evidence of an evolution
toward a definite goal. On the other hand, he admitted
that their "literary productions might be considered, not
as models but as facts, classified as the expression of their
social life during three periods, the colonial epoch, the
struggle for freedom, and the independent existence of the
several republics."

Such is the general plan adopted for this book. The
conditions of life during the colonial period and the common aim of the different countries during the revolutionary
epoch gave a certain similarity to their literary productions. Freedom won, however, each country pursued its
own course in literature as in politics.

These two are interdependent. Literature is often
meaningless without an understanding of contemporary
politics. Everywhere the literary expression of politics is
found in journalism. In Spanish America it is found also
in verse and fiction. So the broad lines of politics have
been taken in this book as a guide through the maze of
print.

The judgment which one renders on the value of Spanish-
American literature depends entirely on the point of view
with which the critic approaches its study. If he considers
it a branch or sub-order of Spanish literature, he will reach

conclusions similar to those of the late Marcelino Menéndez y Pelayo in his *Historia de la Poesía Hispano-americana*.
To him as a Spaniard the exuberance of American patriotic verse is not only detestable but bad literature. To
his mind only those productions have worth which ap-
proximate the standard set by Spanish classics.

Another critic has observed the frank imitation of
French models. It is true that Spanish-American writers
in their eagerness to reject Spain have taken France
as the intellectual leader of their Latin America. The
term Latin-American republics which they prefer has the
justification of permitting the inclusion of Portuguese-
speaking Brazil and an easy absorption of the numerous
Italian element of Argentina. Moreover, it makes possible
a claim of kinship with admired France. But a critic who
attempts to set forth the literature of Latin America
wholly on the basis of its relation to French literature will
miss both its significance and its originality.

Both spring from the history and language of the Latin-
American republics. The language of Spanish America is
not only permeated with terms and expressions taken from
its daily life but also differs in pronunciation and structure
from the Castilian even more than the English of North
America from the educated speech of England. As to the
originality of Spanish-American literature it lies chiefly in
the subject-matter, in its pictures of natural scenery and
social life.

From the moment of their discovery of America the
Spaniards were amazed at the great rivers, the lofty
Andes mountains, the luxuriance of tropical vegetation.
And when they expressed their amazement in literary

form, Virgil was their model. To the participants in the conquest of the new world their enterprise resembled the deeds of knight errantry related by Ariosto. So in imitation of his art they often wrote down the story of their exploits in poems in which truth sometimes paid tribute to form. In the nineteenth century, when the reconstruction of the past became the popular literary fashion under the influence of romanticism, the legends of the colonial period supplied the poet with ample material. Later, when naturalistic fiction came into vogue, ambitious followers of Zola in Spanish America found ready at hand a novel type of society to portray. Thus the form of Latin-American literature has been imitative while the matter is original.

For an English-speaking American then who desires a better acquaintance with the mentality of his Spanish-American neighbors this book will offer a guide. The literature of Brazil written in Portuguese and so rich as to require a volume almost as large as the present for its adequate exposition, is therefore not included. The reader, aware at the outset that he has before him an extremely provincial type of literature, will not expect great masterpieces. On the other hand, he will learn what effect has been produced on the transplanted Spaniard by living on the great plains of Argentina. He will better comprehend the difference between the sober energetic Chilean and the fun-loving Peruvian or the passionate Venezuelan. He will understand why there have been so many revolutions in Mexico. The anecdotes of poets' lives and the tragic stories of men who have lived and died for an ideal will inspire him with greater respect for a country which like

Cuba struggled a whole century for its freedom. Even the names of the various writers, the constantly recurring José María, Joaquín, Manuel, will impress him with the deeply religious sentiments of these peoples.

The difficulty of preparing this book has been great. Only two really valuable collections of works by Spanish-American authors exist in this country, one in the library of the Hispanic Society of America, the other in the library of Harvard University. Both are far from being complete, but fortunately they supplement each other. Histories of the literatures of the several countries have been written by natives only of Argentina, Venezuela and Uruguay, and these are defective in many ways. The dates of the births and deaths of the writers, for example, are not always given. Spanish Americans in treating the literatures of their own countries usually include a consideration of historical writings, but the limits of this book allow only a casual mention of the most important works of purely historical or scientific content. Periodicals, on the other hand, have demanded attention because, as the means of immediate publicity for literary endeavor, they have often played a considerable rôle in literary history and now supply the investigator with much material.

On account of the character of his sources of information, not always reliable, the author of the present volume may have wrongly estimated the work of any given writer or even omitted mention of some whom a compatriot may deem important. Any grievous errors either of judgment or of omission should therefore be condoned.

The author wishes here to thank for their kind assistance in various ways Señor Paul Groussac, the learned librarian of the national library at Buenos Aires, Señor Carlos de Velasco, editor of the excellent review *Cuba Contemporanea*, Señor Pedro Henríquez Ureña, critic and formerly professor at the University of Mexico, Señor Max Henríquez Ureña, poet and essayist, Doctor Gonzalo Picón Febres, novelist and advocate of Americanism in literature, the late Dr. W. R. Martin, librarian of the Hispanic Society of America, and Professor E. C. Hills. To J. D. M. Ford, Smith professor of literature in Harvard University, the author is indebted for the suggestion which led to the writing of this book.

ALFRED COESTER.

NEW YORK, 1916.

PREFACE TO THE SECOND EDITION

As this book was being finished in the first year of the great war certain information about writers of the day was not available which has since come to the author's knowledge. During the eleven years which have passed since publication, the modernista movement has come to an end and a new generation of poets and novelists has risen to prominence. In preparing this second edition it was thought best to rewrite a portion of Chapter XIV as well as to discuss the younger writers. All the new matter has been placed together in Chapters XV and XVI.

A. C.

STANFORD UNIVERSITY, 1927,

CONTENTS

xiii

THE LITERARY HISTORY OF SPANISH AMERICA

LITERARY HISTORY OF SPANISH AMERICA

CHAPTER I

THE COLONIAL PERIOD

SPANISH enterprise on the American continent had for its participants the nature of a conquest. Trained on the battle fields of Italy under leaders who had assisted Ferdinand of Aragon to expel from Spanish soil the last of the Moorish invaders, they carried across the Atlantic the ideals of the successful soldier. A mere handful of them so well protected by steel armor against the weapons of the natives and so able to inspire terror in their opponents by means of their horses and the flash and roar of their musketry was enough to win an empire. When a common Spanish soldier could rise to the possession of immense wealth and hold sway over millions of human beings, a new world had certainly been discovered. To Spaniards no other name was so fitting for this continent as that by which it was constantly called, "el Nuevo Mundo," The New World.

They were not actuated, however, merely by the lure of gold. A religious fanaticism carried them like crusaders into unknown dangers. Wherever they went their first care was to plant the cross. So early as Columbus' second voyage thirteen monks sailed with him for the purpose of converting the natives to Christianity. Thus the monastic establishment became an integral part of every considerable Spanish settlement. To the honor of the monks and priests be it said that, having the natives as their especial care, they made heroic efforts to protect the poor wretches from the rapacity of the seekers after gold.

Columbus selected for permanent settlement on account of its gold mines the island which he named Hispaniola, now called Santo Domingo or Haiti. For many years it received a considerable immigration of men of substance coming to America with their families, though many later proceeded farther west. After the discovery of the mainland the two most important centers of Spanish civilization in America became Mexico City and Lima, La Ciudad de los Reyes, as it was named by its founder Francisco Pizarro, the conquistador of Peru.

The Aztec city of Tenochtitlan, developed and extended under the more pronounceable name of Mexico, was established by Hernán Cortés as the capital of Nueva España. The name Mexico for the whole country was not adopted till after the separation from Spain. New Spain or Mexico on account of its geographical situation, its climate, its greater proximity to the mother country possessed during the golden period of Spanish literature a high degree of culture. From those bibliographical manuals in rhyme, Cervantes' *Viaje de Parnaso* and Lope de Vega's *Laurel de Apolo*, written respectively in 1614 and 1630, one may learn how numerous were the versifiers and the dramatists who practiced the poetic art on both sides of the Atlantic.

Peru also received a full contingent of men of letters, but on account of its greater wealth in gold and silver there were attracted thither more purely adventurous spirits. Among them were men of the highest Spanish nobility. And a transfer in a governmental position from Mexico to Peru was apparently regarded as a promotion.

The government of the Spanish dominions in America was entrusted to viceroys assisted by a court or audiencia composed of several judges. At first Nueva España and Peru were the only viceroyalties, for outlying regions were administered by a member of the audiencia. It is needless to say that the holders of such responsible positions were men of education and culture. For their own entertainment the viceroys, if not always poets themselves as was sometimes the case, encouraged at their courts the production of literature.

Even the first explorers were often men of literary attainments. The letters of Columbus and the reports of Cortés to their monarchs are well known. Similar *cartas de relación* were returned to Spain from almost every expedition, so that few events in history have been more fully covered by a written record than the Spanish conquest of America. These accounts of exploration and adventure have value not only as historical documents of prime importance but as literary productions. With due allowance for differences in style and point of view one may say that their writers had as keen an appreciation of sensational effect as any modern war correspondent.

Close at the heels of the men at arms came friars who made it their business to gather at first hand materials for their writings. The most famous of these is Fray Bartolomé de las Casas whose *Historia de las Indias* was written especially for the purpose of voicing an indignant protest against the treatment of the Indians at the hands of his fellow countrymen. Other historical compilations, like the narratives of the conquistadores, are so numerous that a consideration of them is beyond the limits of this book. They cover practically every phase of Spanish settlement.

Another class of writers, some of whom were members of religious orders, consisted of men born in America who wrote with enthusiasm for love of their native soil. Special interest attaches to those who had in their veins blood of the conquered races. Having learned from their mothers the native language and moods, they were able to penetrate beneath the surface of the aboriginal mind and traditions. In Peru the Inca Garcilasso de la Vega (1540–1616) owed his title to his ancestry, his mother being of the blood royal, granddaughter of Tupac Yupanqui and niece of Huayna Capac, and his celebrity to his *Comentarios reales*, published as written in two parts in 1609 and 1616. As history the book is not absolutely reliable, but as entertaining literature it is unsurpassed by any other of the histories of Peru. Moreover, it presents within certain limits the native point of view of the conquest, with many details of history and manners which only a person with such an ancestry could give.

A somewhat similar position in the history of Mexico was held by Fernando de Alva Ixtlilxochitl, a lineal descendant of the royal line of Tezcuco, who was employed by the viceroy as an interpreter. The results of his researches in native history, made early in the seventeenth century, were contained in various volumes of which the most important was entitled *Historia Chichimeca*. The subject of aboriginal writers in Mexico alone requires however several books for its complete exposition.

Education and culture in America were fostered by two actions of the Spanish authorities, the establishment of universities and the introduction of the printing press, both the care of the clergy. The first book printed in America was the *Breve y Compendiosa Doctrina Christiana en lengua mexicana y castellana*, 1539, by Fray Juan de Zumárraga, first bishop of Mexico. By a strange coincidence the first universities in America were both authorized by Charles the Fifth in the same year, 1551, to be established in Mexico and Lima.

The printing of a book in the Spanish colonies was not a matter to be lightly undertaken, for it was a costly operation. It was therefore enjoyed only by authors with money or wealthy patrons. For that reason many a poem of the early period has remained in manuscript. Recent interest in colonial history has brought to light some of these manuscripts. Doubtless many more still lie forgotten in the dust of some library of Europe or America. One curious result of the expense attending the manufacture of a book is the fact that some of the best executed works, printed on the finest paper, and handsomely bound, are the most worthless from the point of view of literature. They contain the verses of occasion produced and recited at the exercises held to commemorate the death of a monarch, the birth of a prince, or the induction into his office of some viceroy. Concerning the history of the printing in Spanish America certain bibliographers have performed a notable service, and recorded every printed work.

The sixteenth century was preëminently a period when

the love of adventure possessed the souls of men, and the literary expression of that spirit in its most artistic form is the *Orlando furioso* of Ariosto. In its complete form the poem was published in 1532, one year before the author's death. By the middle of the century not only did metrical translations begin to appear in Spain but original heroic poems in the same metrical form became the fashion. Acknowledged by every critic to be the most successful of these epical compositions was Alonso de Ercilla y Zúñiga's poem, *La Araucana*, based on personal adventures in Chile. This was the first work of real literary merit composed in America.

In our review of literature during the colonial period of Spanish America it is necessary to omit consideration of purely historical records. Yet histories of course make up the bulk of what was written about America and in America at this time. And even when the writer thought to embellish his story by putting it in metrical form, its value lies more in the historical facts than in its literary qualities. But the *Araucana* stands apart from the other poems of the same type both in its intrinsic worth and in its influence on Spanish-American literature even during the nineteenth century. Regarding it the Spanish literary historian Ferrer del Río says, "It would be difficult to find a livelier impression of the Spanish sixteenth century, the great passions of Charles V and Phillip II, war, daring navigation, distant conquests, a love for the unknown and for adventures, religious sentiment and veneration for the sacred objects of worship."

Alonso de Ercilla y Zúñiga (1533–94) was born in the same year that Ariosto died. The translations of the

Orlando furioso became popular in Spain just before Ercilla set out for America. In fact Ercilla referred to Ariosto as one of his models; the imitation, however, was more general than particular, for Ercilla's episodes were chiefly historical facts, rather than poetical inventions. At the outset of his poem he announces that he does not intend to sing of ladies, love and chivalrous deeds which is quite contrary to Aristo who makes them the argument of his poem. Moreover, Ercilla in dedicating his work to Phillip II assured his monarch that it was a true relation; and to give weight to this assertion stated that the book was written in part during the war in Chile "often on leather for lack of paper and on bits of paper sometimes so small that they contained not more than six lines."

Of highborn parentage Ercilla was attached at the age of fifteen to the suite of the prince Phillip and accompanied him in 1548 when he went to take possession of the duchy of Brabant. He traveled with the prince over Europe for the next six years and was with him in England in 1554 when Phillip married Mary Tudor. In England Ercilla made the acquaintance of Gerónimo de Alderete, just appointed adelantado of Chile, who was to sail with the new viceroy of Peru, Andrés Hurtado de Mendoza. Ercilla, eager for the adventures in prospect, because news of the rebellion of the Araucanian Indians had reached Spain, joined the expedition and arrived at Lima in 1556. As the adelantado Alderete died on the way, the viceroy appointed his son Don García to lead the army which should restore peace in Chile. After the war had been in progress for some time Ercilla had an unfortunate quarrel with a companion, Juan de Pineda. The facts are very obscure, but for some reason Don García believed that the two men were conspiring against his authority. He condemned them both to be beheaded and the men were already on the scaffold before Don García was persuaded to relent and commute their punishment to imprisonment. Not long thereafter Ercilla was released and allowed again to take part in the war. But he cherished such resentment against Don García that he managed to leave Chile and return to Spain in 1562. There he found favor again with Phillip and high employment in business of state. In 1569 he published the first part, consisting of fifteen cantos, of his poem *La Araucana*. The second part in fourteen cantos he completed in 1578 and the third part of eight cantos in 1590.

The plan of the poem is to narrate in strictly chronological order events in Chile. The first twelve cantos deal with the raids of the Indians on the Spanish settlements and the numerous reprisals which occurred before Ercilla's arrival. As Ercilla wished to minimize Don García de Mendoza's part in the war the heroes of the poem are not the minor Spanish leaders whom he occasionally mentions but the Indian chiefs. The most attractive of these is the young Lautaro. In depicting his life Ercilla, with a poetic defense of the rôle of love in human life, probably by way of apology for changing his intention not to sing of ladies, introduces the reader to Guacolda, Lautaro's beautiful wife. Lautaro is surprised at night by her side and slain. After his death the most important of the various Araucanian caciques is Caupolicán. Of the Spaniards a certain common soldier Andrea and Ercilla himself play the most prominent rôles. In fact

Ercilla might be called the hero of the poem if one takes into account the amount of space devoted to his personal adventures.

On the other hand, the poem contains certain long digressions from the main narrative. In part two by the machinery of a personal interview of the poet with the Goddess Bellona contemporary events in Europe, especially Phillip's victories in Flanders, are recited. Even the naval victory of the Spaniards over the Turks at Lepanto, though subsequent in time to the period of the poem, is described as it was revealed to Ercilla through the agency of a magic ball belonging to an old magician whom he met in the mountains. In the third canto there is a long digression about Dido. Ercilla is requested by some soldiers to relate the true story of the famous queen who in his opinion has been much maligned.

To the modern reader these digressions are blemishes, but at the time of the publication of the poem they very likely assisted in making it popular. The victories of their king and the naval fight at Lepanto were events of which the Spaniards were pleased to read stirring and poetic accounts. Against the background of the distant war in Chile they were enhanced as by perspective. The book, immediately and immensely popular, passed through more editions than any Spanish book of the century. The eloquent speeches which Ercilla put into the mouths of both Spaniards and Indians met the taste of his day. The same may be said of the realistic details of battles and other adventures, so realistic at times as to be gruesome and repugnant, for Ercilla's descriptive power was very great. On the other hand, the poem lacks certain elements of general human interest so that it is not very attractive to-day. It is too intensely Spanish in sentiment.

Its local Chilean setting, however, has brought great popularity in Chile. Towns and localities have been named after the Indian heroes. In their war for independence Chilean orators and poets used to call themselves "sons of Caupolicán." The first war vessel of the Chilean navy was named "Lautaro." Episodes and incidents from the *Araucana* which is held to be almost a national poem, have been the inspiration of poems, novels and plays.

After Ercilla's death a certain Diego de Santistevan Osorio, of whom nothing beyond what he tells of himself is known, published at Salamanca in 1597 a poem, *La Araucana, Quarta y Quinta parte en que se prosigue y acaba la historia de D. Alonso de Ercilla.* The adventures related appear to be wholly imaginary combats between the Indians and the Spaniards.

Another poem, *Arauco Domado*, treating the same events in some sixteen thousand verses divided into nineteen cantos, was printed at Lima in 1596. The author was a native-born Chilean, Pedro de Oña, the son of a Spanish captain fighting the Indians in southern Chile. He was sent to the University of San Marcos in Lima in 1590. Two years later he took part in an expedition to Quito to quell an uprising. From this campaign he returned with much historical material and possibly the idea of putting into verse the deeds in the same region of Don García Hurtado de Mendoza.

In his poem Pedro de Oña declared himself an imitator

of Ercilla but made no pretension of competing with him. The *Arauco Domado* is in no sense a continuation of the *Araucana* but a new version of the historical facts contained in the second part of the latter poem. The narrative begins with the sending to Chile of his son, Don García, by the viceroy Don Andrés Hurtado de Mendoza. While Ercilla had written mainly about the Indians with slight reference to Don García, Pedro de Oña desired to repair this injustice by relating the personal exploits of the Spanish commander. To emphasize the part played by that nobleman, Pedro de Oña did not hesitate to violate either unity of plan or chronological order. His main narrative concerned the preparations of the savages for an attack on a Spanish fort and its successful defense by Don García. The latter's subsequent acts as viceroy of Peru in subduing a rebellion in Quito and in repelling the raid of the English admiral, Richard Hawkins, were introduced into the poem through the agency of the witch, Quidora, and the machinery of a dream. Though the love affairs of the Indians were fictions of the poet who invented them to relieve the strain of continuous warfare, the descriptions of their customs and those of the colonists have historical value. The poetic idyll of Caupolicán and Fresia and the adventures of Tucapel and Gualeva are interesting. Regarding the author the poem reveals little but his serious and religious disposition.

Pedro de Oña remained to the end of his days a diligent versifier. There exist from his pen a couple of sonnets; a canción of some length in which the river Lima addresses the river Tiber on the virtues of Fray Francisco Solano

of Lima who after his canonization was made patron
saint of Santiago de Chile in 1633; a second herioc poem,
El Vasauro, found in manuscript in Madrid by Barros
Arana, on the deeds of Don Andrés de Cabrera; and a mystical religious poem in six thousand verses divided in twelve
books on the life of Ignatius de Loyola, *El Ignacio de
Loyola.* Apparently the Jesuits requested Oña to compose
this poem in honor of the founder of their society. No
commission could have been more agreeable to the pious
character of the poet as is partly shown by the care which
he bestowed on the versification and the ornate rhetoric.
Printed in Seville, 1636, the poem contributed to the
author's reputation far more than the *Arauco Domado.*
Lope de Vega in his *Laurel de Apolo* referring to this poem
puts the serious lyre of Pedro de Oña "alone among the
swans of the Indies." Posterity may well consider Pedro
de Oña as the foremost poet in Chile during colonial
times.

Another poem produced under the stimulus of the
prevailing fashion for heroic poems was found by Barros
Arana in Madrid without title and name of author. The
learned historian of the colonial literary history of Chile,
José Toribio Medina, argues that the author was an
unknown Juan de Mendoza mentioned by Alvárez de
Toledo. The poem after giving a summary of Chilean
history relates many minor events which occurred at the
end of the sixteenth century. Though the reader's interest
is rather harassed by the multiplicity of unconnected
happenings, the central fact of the troubled state of the
Spanish settlements stands out clearly.

Hernando Alvárez de Toledo was another Spanish

warrior and colonist who pleased himself by the versification of his personal adventures.   He left Spain in 1581
in company with the famous governor Alonso de Soto-
mayor, who after an unlucky voyage, landed in Brazil
and reached Chile by crossing the Argentine pampa
and the Andes.   The fifteen thousand verses of Alvárez'
Purén Indómito composed entirely without poetical inventions or fictions form a rhymed chronicle of his own
feats of arms or those which he had heard in detail from
his companions.   To him the Indians are merely wily
and treacherous enemies.   Yet he gives many details
about their habits, dress, adornments, ceremonies, method
of fighting and the relations between them and the Spaniards.   At times he puts into the mouths of the natives
words about truth and the nature of God which are a
satire on the actions of bad Spaniards.   So great is his
adherence to fact that his statements are given full historical value by the historian Ovalle.   The latter credits a
portion of his history to the *Araucana*, another poem by
Alvárez which has been lost.

Personal adventures formed the substance of another
long poem printed at Lima, 1630, entitled *Compendio
historial de Chile* by Melchor Xufre del Águila (1568–1637).
The author boasted that he had come out at his own expense.   In the same year, 1581, in which Don Garcia Hurtado de Mendoza was made viceroy of Peru, Xufre went
to Chile to seek adventures in the war.   He got nothing
but a broken leg and loss of property.   So he determined
to retire to a life of leisure in the country and write an
account of his experiences.   His book has lent to it some
historical value by a long letter preceding the poem by

way of introduction from Luis Merlo de la Fuente, captain general of Chile, who outlines the events of his administration from 1606 to 1628.

In prose, if one omits works written with a serious purpose, few attempts at literature are to be found. Of these few one, *Cautiverio feliz*, by Francisco Nuñez de Pineda y Bascuñan (1607–82), was the most popular and widely read book of colonial times in Chile. The author, the son of a soldier much feared by the Araucanians, was placed by his father in a company of Spanish infantry which was called in 1629 to put down an outbreak of the Indians in southern Chile. The young man was one of a detachment attacked by overwhelming numbers and was taken prisoner with the few survivors. When the Indians learned his parentage, they were greatly delighted by their capture. Their leader Maulican determined to keep him alive though the other leaders wished to put him to death by torture. Bascuñan remained in captivity seven months before he was ransomed. In his old age he wrote the story of it, leaving the manuscript to his children. Though the narrative was intended for history, it was written almost in the style of a novel. The reader is kept in dramatic suspense to the end wondering whether the good intentions of Maulicán will prevail against the desires of those who seek the captive's death. The book, moreover, is a mine of curious facts about the Indians.

The romantic interest felt by some toward the natives appears in a strange book, *Restauración de la Imperial y conversión de almas infieles*, by Fray Juan de Barrenechea y Albis, written in 1693. Medina classifies it as a novel. It is a fiction concerning Rocamila, the beautiful daughter

of the Araucanian chief Millayan. Of her many lovers
the most favored was Carilab. Their wedding, however,
is postponed and their relations greatly troubled by the
war with the Spaniards and the multiplicity of adventures
which happen to them. The good friars and their efforts
to Christianize the Indians claim a part of the narrative.

The habit of versifying history into which was incorporated one's personal adventures, possibly encouraged
by the popularity of Ercilla's poem, became widespread
in other centers of Spanish settlement than Chile. Most
of these compositions have been held in light esteem, on
the one hand by historians as untrustworthy and on the
other by writers on literature as prosaic. Apparently
the more prosaic the versification the more accurate was
the narration. In this respect the extreme is represented
by Gaspar de Villagrá's *Conquista del Nuevo Mundo*, published in 1610, a rhymed chronicle of the attempt by
Juan de Oñate to settle in the country now called New
Mexico about the year 1598. Whatever the opinion elsewhere, natives of the respective countries in which the
scenes of these historical poems were laid have regarded
them highly. To the local poet they have proved a constant source of inspiration. To the local historian they
have supplied invaluable details of genealogy and local
history.

Juan de Castellanos for this purpose contributed the
most important document of all. His *Elegías de Varones
ilustres de Indias* consisting of some 150,000 lines is the
longest poem of its kind in any language. The first part
only was printed during the life of its author, but the

remainder appears to have been known though not printed complete till the nineteenth century. Part one, published in 1589, dealt with the voyages of Columbus and the early conquests and settlements of the Caribbean islands and the region near the mouth of the Orinoco, as well as the adventures of the infamous Lope de Aguirre. The author had already written part of his chronicle when a friend persuaded him to rival Ercilla by versifying it. The judgment of posterity believes he might better have stuck to prose. Nevertheless Juan de Castellanos possessed such an astonishing ability in versification that he wrote occasional passages of real merit, so that from the point of view of poetry his poem may be given second place among versified chronicles. The second, third and fourth parts treat minutely the history of Nueva Granada and a part of Venezuela, with less attempt at poetic embellishment as they approach the end.

Inferior in poetic qualities but priceless for its information because no other records of the events of which it treats has come down to us is *La Argentina y conquista del Río de la Plata, con otros acaecimientos de los reinos del Perú, Tucumán y estado del Brasil,* published at Lisbon, 1602, by Don Martín del Barco Centenera. The author was a soldier who took part in the expedition led by Juan Ortiz de Zárate into the interior of the Argentine. The poem is also valuable for biographical matter concerning Juan de Garay, the founder of Buenos Aires. As its title indicates the poem lacks unity of subject-matter and it is overloaded with fairy tales of golden kingdoms and marvelous voyages. Redolent of the pampa, however, are his descriptions of the life of the savages, their method of hunting the wild ostrich with bolas, and the anecdotes of their relations to each other and to the Spanish settlers. Some of his love stories and episodes furnished excellent material to later poets.

In Mexico the deeds of Cortés found their epic poet in Antonio de Saavedra Guzmán who published his *Peregrino Indiano* in twenty cantos of octaves in 1599. The author says of himself that he was corregidor of Zacatecas and that he spent seven years in collecting his material for a true history. As to his value the historian Prescott, who took a few details from his descriptions, estimated it in this wise, "Saavedra came on the stage before all that had borne arms in the conquest had left it." While Saavedra's story is mainly an account of military exploits from the moment of Cortés' departure from Cuba to the capture of the city of Mexico after the building of the ships in the lake, he does not neglect the amours of the leaders with the native women. The book has the additional bibliographical interest of being the first printed by a person born in Mexico.

Saavedra's poem was neither the first nor the last on the same subject. Contemporaries praised highly the lost work of Francisco de Terrazas, whose sonnets show real poetical feeling. The son of one of Cortés' most trusted officers, he is the first native-born Mexican poet. A few octaves that have been preserved of his *Nuevo Mundo y Conquista* show that Terrazas was especially skillful in depicting idyllic love scenes. Another rhymed chronicle, the *Mexico conquistada* of Juan de Escóiquiz has been dismissed by an eminent critic as "intolerable." On the other hand, the versification of Gabriel Lasso de la Vega's *Cortés Valeroso*, published in 1588 with three additional cantos in 1594, is praised. And even better from the same point of view is the *Hernandia* of Francisco Ruiz de León though the matter of the poem printed in 1755 is little more than the versification of Antonio de Solís' famous history of the conquest of Mexico.

In Peru, contemporary with the rich historical literature dealing with the conquest, were written many short poems on various events. Pizarro's exploits were related in a poem of eight cantos which, however, was not printed before 1848. In that year a bookseller of Lyons discovered the manuscript in the library of Vienna. Another longer manuscript poem in twenty cantos has for a title *Armas Antárticas, hechos de los famosos Capitanes españoles que se hallaron en la conquista del Perú.* Judging from such extracts as he had seen the Spanish critic Menéndez y Pelayo rated its poetic qualities higher than those of the more fortunate *Lima Fundada o Conquista del Perú* printed in 1732 for its author Pedro de Peralta Barnuevo, the poet laureate of the viceroys of his day.

These historical or heroic compositions on American topics, so ambitiously termed epic poems by their authors, form only a branch of the same tree which was flourishing so lustily in Spain at the same period. An occasional poem treating an event in Spanish history even saw the light in America. Another thriving branch was the sacred epic ramifying into poems on the lives of saints and noted churchmen. Of the many poems in Spanish on the life of the Saviour the most excellent in all respects was *La Cristiada* published in 1611 by Fray Diego de (H)Ojeda who wrote its eloquent octaves in a convent of

Lima. And in this outpouring of heroic verse what was more natural than that many a friar in America should desire thus to glorify the life of the founder of his order? Poems in many cantos on the life of Ignatius de Loyola, founder of the Jesuits, are especially numerous. Earlier than that by Pedro de Oña, already mentioned, was one by a friend of his, Luis de Belmonte, *Vida del Patriarca Ignacio de Loyola*, published in Mexico in 1609 and dedicated to the Jesuit fathers of Nueva España. The Dominicans, not to be outdone by others, wrote in heroic verses the life of their celebrity, the Angelical Doctor, Thomas Aquinas. As if symbolic of his great learning the most peculiar of these poems entitled *La Thomasiada*, was composed by Fray Diego Saenz Ovecurri and published in Guatemala, 1667. The poem aimed to be not only a biography but also a treatise on the art of poetry and a sort of encyclopedia in rhyme of matter taken from the works of the learned doctor. In the part relating to the art of poetry, examples of the most extravagant experiments in versification abound.

Of the lives of saints in heroic verse, two especially achieved a certain reputation. The Gongorist title, *La eloquencia del silencio. Poema heroyco, vida y martyrio del Gran Proto-Martyr del sacramental sigilo, fidelissimo custodio de la Fama, y protector de la Sagrada Compañia de Jesus, San Juan Nepomuceno*, is indicative of the style of the contents of this poem by a Mexican jurist Miguel de Reyna Zevallos, published in 1738. The other is far more interesting, *Vida de Santa Rosa de Lima y Patrona del Perú* by Luis Antonio de Oviedo y Herrera, Conde de la Granja, published in 1711. It is interesting not only because it relates the life of the most popular saint of America, Santa Rosa de Lima (as a measure of her popularity may be taken a certain bibliographical list of 276 works referring to her), but also because it contains entertaining descriptions of the country near Lima, of the raids of Drake and Hawkins on the Peruvian coast, and many other curious anecdotes of the life of the colony.

In the matter of lyric verse there were numerous practitioners of it at all periods in America. Students of Spanish literature will remember that following the manner of the poet-soldiers who brought back to Spain from Italy the new forms there arose in Seville a school of versifiers. A leading member of the school, Gutierre de Cetina, found his way to Mexico where in 1554 he was severely wounded by a jealous lover who mistook him in the dark for the object of his suspicions, a wound from which the unlucky poet probably died three years later. Another Sevillan poet who spent some time in Mexico was Juan de la Cueva. Among his literary remains exists an interesting description in tercets of the city of Mexico. So numerous in fact were poets among the adventurers in Mexico that at a poetical contest in 1585 no fewer than three hundred (?) took part according to the testimony of one of the winners.

The latter was Bernardo de Balbuena (1568–1627) who in later life became Bishop of Puerto Rico. And for the feeling which his works show for the tropical luxuriance of America he may be termed the first in point of time of American poets. Balbuena's most important poem, *La Grandeza Mexicana*, originally printed in Mexico in 1604, and many times reprinted, even in the nineteenth cen-

tury, sets forth the beauties and wonders of Mexico, its
wealth in precious metals and jewels, the strange costume
of its inhabitants, its fiery horses, the rich fabrics brought
thither in transit from China and the Philippine Islands.
The poem is written in tercets and divided into nine parts.
In 1608 he published *El Siglo de Oro en las Selvas de
Erifile*, a pastoral novel in prose and verse, the latter
consisting of twelve eclogues in imitation of Theocritus,
Virgil, and Sannazaro. For its value as a monument of
Spanish literature the Spanish Academy made a special
edition of it in 1821. No less ambitious was Balbuena in
vying with Ariosto in his longest poem *El Bernardo o la
Victoria de Roncesvalles* in twenty-four cantos. In one of
them the hero is conveyed to Mexico where the Tlascalan
wizard reveals to him the future conquest of Mexico.

Of Spanish versifiers who visited Lima about the beginning of the seventeenth century the names of those
known to Cervantes and Lope de Vega are very numerous.
In real poetic worth a certain anonymous poetess who
corresponded in rhymed epistles with Lope de Vega, signing herself "Amarilis," excelled the rest. And no speculation as to the identity of the lady has proved successful.
At the court of the viceroys who were themselves of the
highest Spanish nobility were many individuals of noble
rank. And the customs of their gay society demanded
much scribbling of verses as well as dramatic representations. The Prince of Esquilache, viceroy from 1615 to
1622, himself possesses a place in Spanish literature as a
poet of the second rank, author of epistles and sonnets in
the manner of Argensola and of an epic poem *Nápoles
recuperada*. His own works contain no references to his

sojourn in the new world, but it is known that he maintained a sort of literary academy in his residence.

Of books of verse produced during colonial times a few deserve mention. The *Primera parte del Parnaso Antártico de obras amatorias* by Diego Mexia was printed in 1608. The title refers to a very praiseworthy translation of Ovid's *Heroides* which the author, as he himself relates, made in a long journey from Lima to Mexico. The prologue to his book is interesting for the references to his journey.

The *Miscelanea austral* printed in Lima in 1603, though primarily a series of forty-four colloquies by its author, Diego de Avalos y Figueroa, on all sorts of subjects of most diverse character, love, jealousy, music, horses, the origin of rings, contains many verses by others as well as a long poem in six cantos, *La Defensa de Damas*, in which Diego de Avalos attempts to refute by anecdotes those who write ill of ladies.

A sort of anthology *Ramillete de varias flores poéticas recogidas* by Jacinto de Evia, a native of Guayaquil, offers an idea of the state of poesy in 1675. At that date Gongorism was the fashion in Spain and Evia's Sevillan master of rhetoric, Antonio Bastidas, whose own poems are really the best in the book, had taught him the secret of preciosity. The third poet whose lines appear here was a native of Bogotá, Hernando Domínguez Camargo. As a sample of his conceits may be taken some verses in which he compares the water of a certain cascade to a bull or to a stallion about to be dashed to pieces against the rocks. Domínguez Camargo was the author also of a Gongorist poem on the life of Ignatius of Loyola. The *Ramillete* is a curious book whose verses of occasion, sonnets and inscriptions, and extracts in artificial prose convey a lively idea of life in Ecuador.

Books of verse very popular in Lima, if one can judge by the number of manuscript copies which seem to have existed, were the *Diente del Parnaso* and *Poesías varias* of Juan del Valle y Caviedes. Their interest lay in the sparkling Andalusian wit of the author's lines. He was born the son of a Spanish merchant and had been sent at about the age of twenty to Spain where he remained three years. On his return to Lima about 1681 he fell sick as the result of dissipation. He whiled away his convalescence by writing satiric verses on his doctors whom he lampooned by name. His verses circulated in manuscript and were undoubtedly increased in number by other wits who put their smart and possibly obscene productions under his name. It is noteworthy that at such an early period the characteristic ot later Peruvian literature, its gayety and humor, thus made its appearance.

At the close of the seventeenth and the opening of the next century there were born in Peru several men of re- markable mental equipment who deserved to have fallen on an epoch more propitious in inspiration. By that date the ravages of Gongorism were at their height in Spanish literature and precisely by a defense of Góngora, *Apol- ogético en favor de D. Luis de Gongora*, published in 1694 has the learned doctor Juan de Espinosa Medrano distin- guished himself. The book is a creditable piece of literary criticism and gives evidence of the ability of a man who at fourteen years of age composed autos and comedies and at sixteen filled a professorial chair in the university of Cuzco where he taught all his life, beside being connected with

the cathedral in various capacities. He left behind also
volumes of sermons and theological works. A poem of his
El Aprendiz de Rico which draws a moral from the con-
demnation and death of a silver miner for counterfeiting
coin throws an interesting light on a phase of existence
in that ancient capital of the Incas.

The doctor of Cuzco was not, however, such a marvel
of encyclopedic knowledge and literary accomplishment as
Pedro de Peralta Barnuevo Rocha y Benavides. Of his
heroic poem *Lima Fundada* mention has already been
made. He was by profession professor of mathematics in
the university of Lima and made some astronomical
observations on eclipses the results of which he published.
In fact his works, including his scientific essays on military
and civil engineering, on metallurgy, on navigation, on
history, number no less than forty-eight between 1700 and
1740. Beside being several times rector of the university
he was the poet laureate of the viceroy. For that reason
his name appears on the many volumes of verses which
record the feasts and funerals of the period. He wrote
likewise several pieces for the stage beside a meritorious
adaptation of Corneille's *Rodogune*. His contemporary
the Spaniard P. Feijoo reckoned him the equal of the most
erudite men of Europe.

The custom of celebrating public events by issuing
volumes of bombastic and laudatory verses was not confined to Peru but was practiced in Mexico too. And in
general the bulk of Mexican verse is not only greater but
on account of a few artificers it ranks better in quality. A
stimulus to such abundant production was the custom of
poetic contests.

One of the best poems of the seventeenth century was so much admired that numberless imitations and glosses of it were written and it is to-day pleasant reading, *Canción a la Vista de un Desengaño*, by a Jesuit Father Matías de Bocanegra. It is divided into six parts on the following theme: A young monk is listening to the song of a linnet. The bird would not sing in a cage he is sure. Just so the loss of his liberty irks him and he complains. He decides to break his vows and enter the world. Before he can carry out his determination he is confounded to see a falcon seize and rend the linnet. The thought comes to him that if the weaker bird had been protected by a cage it would not have suffered death. It died because it was free. The moral of this lesson prevents the young monk from breaking his vows.

One wishes that more of the verse by friars had been written with such poetic simplicity of expression rather than in the tedious conceits of such poems on set religious topics as appear in the book entitled *Triumpho parthénico que en glorias de María Santissima inmaculadamente concebida celebró la Pontífica, Imperial, y Regia Academia Mexicana etc. . . . . Describelo D. Carlos de Sigüenza y Góngora, Mexicano, y en ella cathedrático propietario de Mathemáticas. En Mexico 1683*. The professor in his poetic style, even in his earlier poem published in 1668, *Primavera Indiana, Poema sacro-histórico, idea de María Santissima de Guadalupe*, lived up to the tradition of his maternal name of Góngora. This poem narrated in seventy-nine royal octaves the story of the appearance to the baptized Indian Juan Diego of our Lady of Guadalupe. Since the building of the church on the spot desig-

nated by her radiant apparition, the native religion materially declined.   The present rich edifice dedicated to
the patron saint of Mexico was built during the lifetime
of Sigüenza y Góngora (1645–1700).   As a cyclopedic
scholar he was only equalled in America by the Peruvian
doctor Peralta de Barnuevo.   Sigüenza made many
scientific and archæological studies.   Useful is his study
of the Aztec calendar which he investigated for the purpose of establishing the chronology of that people.   From
his pen came numerous works on mathematics and as-
tronomy which must be respected for their learning though
they bear such titles as a certain *Belerofonte matemático
contra la Quimera astrológica.*

Toward the end of the seventeenth century a real poetic
genius saw the light in Mexico.   Being a woman and a
poetess she was styled in accord with the bombast of
the time "la Musa Décima mexicana," that is to say
"the Tenth Muse a Mexican woman."   She was born
Juana Ines de Asbaje y Ramírez de Cantillana (1651–95).
At seventeen years of age she became a nun, assuming
the name Sor Juana Inés de la Cruz by which title she
has since been known.   She was possessed of the most
intense intellectual curiosity.   At one time she had gathered in her cell a library of no less than four thousand
volumes.   Her fame in worldly learning and in profane
literature causing the Bishop of Puebla some worry, he
wrote her a letter over the signature of "Sor Philotea de
la Cruz" beseeching her as an admiring sister to have a
care for her soul.   She replied in a letter which the bishop
had printed with the title of *Carta athenogorica.*

Its theme was a defense of the education of women,

but its interest to the world now consists in the biographical details concerning the writer. Very little else is known. She learned to read at the age of three. At eight she composed a loa in honor of the holy sacrament. At about the same time she begged her parents to send her up to the University of Mexico dressed as a man. However she had to content herself with twenty lessons in Latin in which language she acquired proficiency by her own unaided efforts. Becoming a maid of honor to the vicereine of Mexico, she was "tormented for her wit and pursued for her beauty," until she took the veil in the convent of San Gerónimo. From that moment her cell was her study. A certain superior at one time forbade her to use her books. She obeyed for three months but though she neglected her books she "studied all the things which God created." Though in her reply to the admonition of Sor Philotea, she defended her course of life, yet she was moved to sell her books and devote her mind to acts of piety. Shortly thereafter she died a victim of an epidemic.

Her collected literary works fill three volumes. The first was printed in 1698 with the florid title *Inundación Castálida de la única poetisa, musa décima, sor Juana Ines de la Cruz.* The third volume published after her death was entitled *Fama y Obras póstumas del Fenix de Mexico, décima musa, poetisa americana, sor Juana Ines dela Cruz.* Some of her productions were printed separately, as the verses indited in celebration of the arrival of the Conde de Paredes as viceroy, and called *Neptuno alegôrico, océano de colores, simulacro político.* Sor Juana wrote not only verses but plays. For the Condesa de Paredes she

composed an *Auto sacramental del Divino Narciso, por
alegorias.* Like their titles these compositions are Gon-
goristic. In fact her contemporaries praised her most
highly for her most obscure compositions. On the other
hand, she wrote many poems instinct with sincere feeling
and unclouded by the pedantic taste of the epoch. Her
lyrics suggest that her passionate temper was not always
stirred solely by mystical love nor by feigned jealousy.
Those verses of hers which have been best remembered
were satirically directed against the detractors of women,
foolish men who are to blame for the very faults in women
that they censure. As for her rank in the world of letters,
after the Cuban Gertrudis Gómez de Avellaneda, the
second place among women of American birth who have
written in Spanish may be rightfully accorded to Sor
Juana Ines de la Cruz.

Her death was followed by the literary sterility of the
eighteenth century. The only Mexican writer of Castilian worthy of mention in this period was Francisco
Ruiz de León whose *Hernandia* was a last effort to write
epic poetry on the subject of the conquest of Mexico. He
was the author of a devout poem in three hundred and
thirty-three décimas with the alluring title *Mirra dulce
para aliento de pecadores.* The mainstay of literature,
the friars began to neglect the vernacular for Latin. Of
these Latinists there is a formidable list. A certain
Jesuit father Rafael Landívar is the only one sufficiently
original to have left behind any literary influence. A
long poem in fifteen books, *Rusticatio mexicana,* in the
style of the Georgics of Virgil, set forth the natural beauties and wonders of America. Descriptive poetry of this

sort, beginning with Balbuena's *Grandeza mexicana,* has
a long history in America. Parts of Landívar's poem
were not only translated by some into Spanish but were
imitated by others.

Ruiz de Leon's *Mirra dulce* by some peculiar chance
happened to be one of the first books of verse printed in
Bogotá. Colombia was not an especially fertile field for
the cultivation of letters. Contemporary with Sor Juana
and inditing verses to her was a certain Francisco Alvárez
de Velasco y Zorrilla. And in prose there exist two books
which the Colombians are proud to exhibit as productions
of their early literary history, *Sentimientos Espirituales*
by a nun Francisca Josefa de la Concepción, known also
as the Madre Castillo and an autobiography, *Vida de la
venerable Madre Castillo.*

In the neighboring territory of Ecuador poetic and
literary activity seems to have been a little greater. A
Jesuit father, Juan de Velasco, himself the author of an
interesting *Historia del reino de Quito,* preserved the
verses of his contemporaries which he prepared for the
press in a miscellany in six volumes, entitled *El Ocioso de
Faenza.* The best of these poems show a real feeling for
nature.

One activity of the friars should by no means be overlooked. They interested themselves keenly in the native
languages for the purpose of teaching the aborigines the
gospel of Christ. Grammars and dictionaries, catechisms
and books of devotion in the native tongues abound.
And stranger still there exist plays, many of religious
character whose intent is obvious. The friars, finding in
the native dances something of a dramatic character,

from the first made use of this rudimentary drama to further their efforts in converting the Indians. It was an easy matter to turn into the native tongues the religious plays or autos of which the Spaniards were so fond for their own edification. But secular plays were also adapted. Three plays of Lope de Vega are said to have existed in a Mexican dialect, Nahuatl. To literary historians a certain drama in the Peruvian or Quechua language, *Ollantá*, has long presented a problem of interest.

The argument of the play is briefly as follows: Ollantá (or Ollantay) is a chief of lowly birth who meets parental opposition in his love for Cusi-Coyllur (Joy-star), daughter of the Inca. Her father dismisses the young man's suit with anger. The Andean mountaineers among whom Ollantá has taken refuge make him their king, with Ollantay-Tambo as his stronghold. After a few years the old Inca dies and his son Ima-Sumac reigns in his stead. The ten-year-old daughter of Ollantá and Cusi-Coyllur appears on the scene as an inmate of the convent where the elect virgins of the sun reside in Cuzco. She discovers that her mother is kept there a prisoner. By treachery Ollantá is bound in chains and brought before the Inca. The latter however pardons him. At that moment Ima-Sumac rushes into the Inca's court and tearfully relates the cruelties inflicted on her mother in prison. The Inca and Ollantá go to the convent of the elect virgins. Both recognize Cusi-Coyllur who is released by the command of the Inca and given in marriage to Ollantá.

It was formerly believed that this play was a relic of a Quechuan literature. The early Spanish historians, notably the Inca Garcilasso de la Vega testified that a rude form of drama existed among the Peruvians. But investigation has revealed not only that the rhetorical structure of Ollantá is that of a Spanish drama but also it is written in meters peculiar to Spanish, such as redondillas, quintillas and décimas. Much printer's ink has been shed over this play and its authorship. The last and most thorough study of it, that of Prof. E. C. Hills, seems to show that a certain Antonio Valdes, parish priest of Tinta, who produced it with great pomp between 1770 and 1780, was its author.

Other clergymen familiar with the native tongue used the drama to assist their religious teaching. The learned doctor Juan de Espinosa Medrano, was the author of an *Auto sacramental del Hijo Prodigo* in which the scriptural story of the prodigal son is edifyingly set forth with realistic details. Another considerable play in the Quechua language has for title *Usca Paucar*, by an unknown author. The dramatic quality of this play is meager, but its theme shows that it was intended to urge upon the natives the veneration of the Virgin at the chapel of our Lady of Copacabana.

This church stood on the south shore of Lake Titicaca where the aborigines had a sanctuary before the coming of the Spaniards. To adorn their mission the Augustinians by whose care it was maintained, brought from Spain an old painting of the Virgin. This way of converting the natives was similar to that pursued in Mexico at the establishment of the church of our Lady of Guadalupe. And while the relative greater importance of the latter has evoked more devotional verse, our Lady of Copaca-

bana had the signal honor of being staged in a play by
Calderón, *La Aurora en Copacabana*, who drew his argument either from a poem *El Santuario de Nuestra Señora
de Copacabana*, by Fray Fernando de Valverde, or a prose
narrative of the mission of the Augustinian fathers.

The history of the drama in Spanish America, apart
from the loas and allegorical pieces produced to celebrate
some viceroy's arrival, is obscure. The thorough establishment of the theater in Mexico is plain, however, from
Balbuena's testimony, who refers to the production of
"new comedies every day." Among the Spanish poets
who sought fortune in America were several dramatists,
as Juan de la Cueva and Luis de Belmonte Bermudez.
One of the most famous of the Spanish dramatists of the
golden period was on the other hand born in Mexico,
Juan Ruiz de Alarcón (died 1639). Though contemporary
with Lope de Vega, his plays were distinguished from
the latter's by a greater care for form and a more careful
psychological analysis of the characters. Alarcón's sober-
ness and the epigrammatic quality of his style were, in
the opinion of a recent critic, Pedro Henríquez Ureña,
the contributions of his Mexican birth. The high altitude
of central Mexico seems to tone down the native exuberance of the Andalusian. It is possible too that Alarcón
learned the dramatic art in Mexico where two of his published comedies, *El semejante a sí mismo* and *Mudarse
por mejorarse*, may have been written, since they abound
in expressions peculiar to Mexico.

A dramatist whose whole career was spent in Mexico,
though he was probably born in Spain, was Fernán González de Eslava. His works have been preserved in a

book printed in 1610, years after his death, with the title, *Coloquios espirituales y Poesias sagradas*. Though the form of his plays is mainly the allegorical, he introduces in the dialogue an endless series of everyday characters whose language, full of idioms and even vulgarisms, reveals as no other book the speech current in Mexico at that period.

The colonial history of Spanish America is faithfully mirrored in its literary productions. The prose narratives and the heroic poems picture the period of discovery and conquest during the sixteenth century. As the viceroys' courts become more important in the seventeenth century poems of occasion represent the secular side of life, while the friars' interests are revealed in devotional writing in verse and prose, in dramas intended for instruction, and in miscellaneous works in both the vernacular and Latin concerning the activities of their orders. At the beginning of the eighteenth century a profound lethargy descends on colonial life which remains almost unbroken till the great upheaval of the revolutionary period in the early years of the nineteenth century.

There were, however, a few stirrings which broke the calm in the different countries. In Mexico the prerevolutionary awakening centers in Fray Manuel de Navarrete (1768–1809). This Franciscan friar endeavored to restore poetry by founding a literary society, the "Arcadia mexicana" and by writing anacreontics of shepherds and shepherdesses in the style of the Spanish poet Meléndez, but without a hint of sensuality. His eclogues were written on the other hand after the manner of Garcilaso de la Vega. Navarrete displayed more originality, or at least a personal note, in his religious verse. As his style was fluent and musical he attracted admirers who followed him in his classicism. But they lived to witness the revolution and wrote under its inspiration their more important pieces. The poetic style of the Mexican revolutionary poets is rather better than those of other regions, a fact to which Navarrete's influence may have contributed.

Over South America a wave of scientific investigation in all departments of natural history and physical geography spread during the last half of the eighteenth century. In Bogotá, the capital of the new viceroyalty of Nueva Granada established in 1740, a botanist and scientist of the first rank, José Celestino Mutis, a Spaniard, began his teaching in 1762. A whole generation of enthusiastic students were trained in his classes. The most brilliant of them was Francisco José Caldas who became the master's successor. Caldas, as one branch of his studies, formed a herbarium of five to six thousand plants of this region of America, accompanied by an exhaustive account of the different altitudes and localities where each plant throve. As director of the astronomical observatory he made many useful studies of various character some of which he made public in a special periodical *El Semanario de la Nueva Granada*. To this journal many contributed both scientific articles and even verses. And it was this little group of lovers of science who first conspired against the hegemony of Spain. Some of them were sent as prisoners to Spain while others, among them Caldas, met their death from the rifles of a firing party in 1816.

In Ecuador the scientific spirit as embodied in a skillful physician, Dr. Francisco Eugenio de Santa Cruz y Espejo, paid attention to the subject of education. In 1779 he put into circulation his *Nuevo Luciano o despertador de ingenios*. It was a critical satire in dialogue form which exposed the evils of the prevailing system of education. Later Dr. Espejo satirized personally the Spanish colonial minister, an exploit which cost him a year in prison and banishment to Bogotá. There his writings assisted in preparing the revolution.

In Peru science was fostered by the viceroy Francisco Gil de Taboada, who had been an admiral in the Spanish navy. He permitted the establishment of a society "Los Amantes del Pais" and the publication, 1791, of a journal *El Mercurio peruano* which was mainly devoted to scientific topics. The editor and most learned contributor was Dr. Hipólito Unánue, professor of medicine in the university.

But the most celebrated literary production of this epoch in Lima was at the opposite pole of seriousness and respectability. The name of the book which has been many times reprinted was *Lima por dentro y fuera* by "Simon Ayanque," a pseudonym of Esteban de Terralla y Landa. The author was an Andalusian who eked out a living by writing verses of occasion. In 1792 he published his satire of the types of individuals in Lima. The title-page of the book gives a hint of the levity and even the obscenity of some of its seventeen romances. The ecclesiastical authorities considered suppressing it but such action was not necessary to complete its popularity. Its literary value, even as a provocative to laughter, has been unanimously denied by critics, but its ready sale both to contemporaries and to later generations, especially in a certain edition embellished by colored drawings, testifies to an element of truth in its portraiture.

Satire of the authorities was about the only method by which discontent at this time could express itself. In Chile a mock epic *La Tucapelina*, which for the personal safety of its author circulated in manuscript, burlesqued the captain general and his deputies for their part in the restoration of a church at Tucapel in 1783. This poem and certain others descriptive of disasters in Chile seem now at least to echo rumblings of the approaching storm of revolution.

Across the Andes from Chile on the shores of the Atlantic the eighteenth century witnessed the rapid growth of the commerce of Buenos Aires. In 1776 the vast region now known as Argentina including most of modern Bolivia was established as a viceroyalty. To Juan José Vértiz, viceroy from 1778 to 1784, the city of Buenos Aires owed its first steps in transition from a wretched town to a modern capital. He founded all manner of public works, a system of street lighting, a college, a hospital, an orphan asylum, and even a theater. For the benefit of the orphan asylum he established a printing press so that the first book printed in Buenos Aires dates from his administration.

As the first rector of his new Colegio de San Carlos, Vértiz appointed Juan Baltásar Maziel (1727–88), an ecclesiastic of liberal tendencies and wide reading owning the best library of the city. Maziel was an interesting personality who wrote much in prose and verse. Two satirical sonnets of his brought him into conflict with a subsequent viceroy, the Marqués de Loreto, who summarily seized his person and transported him to Montevideo. Maziel died before the news of his own vindication by the Spanish king's order reached America. About Maziel there sprang up a literary circle.

His friend and defender in the controversy over the sonnets Manuel José de Labardén (1754–1809) was a man of unusual literary ability. His claims on fame are two, an ode *Al Paraná*, and a play *Siripo*, both the more remarkable as anticipating subsequent Argentine literature. The verses descriptive of the great river penetrating far to the interior were the first about the landscape from which so many later poets drew their inspiration. *Siripo* is a play treating the relations of the white men and the aborigines. It breathes of the pampa. The life of the pampa in the form of gaucho poetry makes the originality of Argentine verses and plays.

The story of *Siripo*, drawn from an early chronicle, was frequently rehandled by others. A young white woman, Lucía Miranda, in a raid on the settlements, was taken captive by the cacique Siripo. Her husband joined her in captivity. Siripo condemned him to death but offered him his life on condition that he marry into the tribe while Lucía became Siripo's bride. The pair refuse. Their faithfulness to each other so exasperated the savage that he had them put cruelly to death.

This drama was first represented in the carnival of 1789 and immediately brought its author renown. The play had been long written however for Labardén read some of the scenes at Maziel's house. Moreover, in his youth Labardén had been a student at Chuquisaca in upper Peru where he was on intimate terms with Valdes, the discoverer or author of the Quechua drama *Ollantá*. In Valdes' small collection of dramatic books Labardén had his only opportunity to learn the dramatic art. And it is possible that Valdes' reading of *Ollantá* gave Labardén the idea of writing *Siripo*.

Labardén's ode *Al Paraná* embellished the first number of the first periodical printed in Buenos Aires, April 1, 1801, *El Telégrafo mercantil rural político, económico, e historiógrafo del Rio de la Plata*. An outlet for the thoughts of the restless spirits whose education had been acquired in Vértiz' Colegio de San Carlos was thus supplied. After a year's successful publication its suppression was caused by the satires of a festive versifier. But the ground was prepared. Other papers followed. The means of publicity and the ability to write were at hand when in the first decade of the nineteenth century the idea of revolution spread abroad in this part of America which first successfully asserted its independence from Spain.

CHAPTER II

THE REVOLUTIONARY PERIOD

THE literature of the revolutionary period sprang directly from the hearts of men, a literature of occasion inspired by the hopes and aspirations of the colonials or the events of their warfare against the mother country. To comprehend its meaning then one must follow its production step by step under the stress of the mighty struggle.

Its forms were often rude and uncouth because literary models within reach of the writers were few. In Chile for example Camilo Henríquez patterned his verses on a single volume of the poems of Tomás Iriarte, the only book of poetry which he could find in Santiago. The scarcity of books in Spanish America was due in part to the obscurantist policy of the Spanish government. In the reign of Carlos IV, when a question arose concerning the chair of mathematics in the University of Caracas the king abruptly dismissed the matter by the dictum, "It is not expedient to educate the Americans." Education had fallen to a low plane in Spain itself so that the state of culture in the mother country was naturally reflected in the colonies.

The lack of books was aggravated by the scarcity of printing presses. Though printing presses were set up in Lima and Mexico in the sixteenth century, there were none in Havana before 1787 nor in Chile before 1811. To

Venezuela the first press was brought by General Miranda in 1806 as a weapon to spread the propaganda of revolt. Moreover, the importation of books was opposed by the authorities who believed them to be agents of sedition. In 1797 the royal audiencia of Venezuela, reporting on the revolutionary fiasco of that year, noted as one of the causes, "the introduction of papers from the foreign islands and the old world in spite of the vigilance of the authorities." But an interesting light is thrown on the quality of their vigilance or their intelligence by an anecdote concerning an importation of books into Chile. A set of such pernicious writings as the works of the French Encyclopedists was successfully passed through the customs by the simple expedient of affixing to the volumes theological titles.

The friction between Spain and her colonies had its roots in the disposition of the government to exploit the new world for the benefit both economically and administratively of the old. The Spaniards assumed and maintained a monopoly of the trade with the colonies. The latter were compelled to buy only Spanish goods or goods brought in Spanish ships. In the matter of administration immigrants direct from Spain were favored over the children of the second generation who were known as creoles (criollos). In fact the latter were generally excluded from office holding. Spanish officials were forbidden to marry daughters of the creoles. If sometimes royal favor lifted the ban, the lucky couple were transferred to another district than that of the bride's residence. Political disabilities had quite as much influence in preparing the colonial mind for revolt as the economic restrictions.

The form of government which the rebellious colonies set up was that of a democracy. But fundamentally their governments were oligarchic. A league of families in each country maintained in varying degrees the colonial system in which the great body of the people had little part. The years of turmoil, not yet ended in some countries, which followed the separation from Spain denote the struggle of the crowd to win its share in the government.

The distress and confusion in Spain caused by the Napoleonic invasion brought the colonials their opportunity. The condition of affairs was first made clear to America by the English attempt in 1806 to seize and hold the city of Buenos Aires. On account of the relations between France and Spain at that time, the captain general of the provinces of the river Plate was a Frenchman by the name of Jacques de Liniers. Though the English landed a body of troops under General William Beresford, and occupied the city, Liniers organized a large volunteer force which, ably seconding his few regular soldiers, succeeded in compelling the surrender of the invaders. The next year another English expeditionary army under General Whitelock met a similar fate after severe fighting in the streets of the city.

This successful defense of Buenos Aires had a remarkable effect on the minds of the citizens. In the first place it made them conscious of their collective strength. In the second place the innumerable ballads and verses which appeared in print extolling their deeds of valor filled their spirits with truculence and their imaginations with visions of glory. When the occasion offered in 1810 they were ready to see them realized in a fight against Spain.

The title "poet of the English invasions" has been conferred on Pantaleón Rivarola (1754–1821). But the poetic worth of his compositions like those of José Prego de Oliver, Fray Cayetano Rodríguez, and many other balladists, is slight. Rivarola's longest effort, *Romance heróico de la Reconquista*, was written for recitation to the accompaniment of the guitar, but it was a very prosaic detailed account of the fighting. Greater artistic merit may be claimed for the *Triunfo Argentino* of Vicente López y Planes (1784–1856) who served as captain in a famous company called "Los Patricios." This ballad has vigor of movement and at times almost epic interest. López' celebrity rests however on his national hymn adopted as such by the national assembly in 1813.

The part played by the volunteers from Montevideo in retaking Buenos Aires from the English was set forth in an allegorical drama, *La Lealtad mas acendrada y Buenos Aires vengada*, by Juan Francisco Martínez, a native of Uruguay. The two cities are represented as nymphs dwelling in a forest. Montevideo, inspired and protected by Mars, undertakes the rescue of Buenos Aires from Neptune, the protector of the English.

For his part in the defense of Buenos Aires, Liniers was appointed viceroy. When Napoleon Bonaparte's brother Joseph became king of Spain, 1808, a revolt against the French broke out with violence in all Spain. The nationalist party wished to restore Ferdinand VII to power. In America riots occurred in the principal capitals and a "junta" or committee of citizens attempted to take over the powers of government "in the name of Ferdinand VII." These juntas were patterned after the central junta of Sevilla which was managing the rebellion in Spain. Consequently when it fell to pieces in 1810 the American juntas were left as it were hanging in the air. In Buenos Aires the situation was met by the gathering of an armed assembly. Liniers had been superseded as viceroy by Baltasar de Cisneros and a party in the assembly wished to make him president. This movement was defeated, and Cisneros withdrew to Montevideo. Henceforth the assembly ruled. The date of its first meeting, May 25th, has since been regarded as the Argentine national holiday.

One of the assembly's first acts, June 7th, 1810, was the establishment of a semiweekly official journal, *La Gaceta de Buenos Aires*. The director of this organ was also the secretary of the junta, Mariano Moreno (1778–1811). To the projects of this ardent democrat and the articles by which he urged them, the cause of the revolution in Argentina was greatly indebted. He brought about the establishment of the national library for which J. B. Maziel's books formed a nucleus. In the name also of liberty of thought he effected the establishment of a school of mathematics partly for training officers for the army. Finally as the Argentine people were preparing for national defense, he was sent on a diplomatic mission to England with full powers to conclude any international arrangement. But his feeble health broke down en route and he died at sea.

Preparation for the armed defense of Buenos Aires was largely entrusted to Manuel Belgrano (1770–1820). Rallying the young men under the colors sky-blue and white, now those of the Argentine flag, he made ready to meet the Spanish army advancing from Upper Peru. At the same time there was danger from the forces in Montevideo though the gaucho leader Artigas was besieging the city on the landward side assisted at sea by a daredevil Irishman, William Brown, in command of a few poor ships. Belgrano advanced to Tucumân, about eight hundred miles northwest of Buenos Aires. He had collected a goodly body of gauchos who on the day of the fight broke the strength of the Spanish army. Occurring in September, 1812, this battle resulted in such a victory that Buenos Aires was never again seriously threatened by a Spanish army. Belgrano proceeded toward Upper Peru but a year later was caught at a disadvantage and completely defeated in October of 1813. On his return to the city he was sent to Spain to try to arrange a settlement on the basis of autonomy for Argentina, but the Spanish government rejected his suggestions. On July 9th, 1816, a congress of the Argentine provinces in session at Tucumân formally declared themselves independent of Spain. Belgrano's services have never been forgotten by the Argentines. And a young poet, Juan C. Lafinur, who left the university to enlist in Belgrano's army, won fame for himself by certain elegies which he wrote at the time of the leader's death.

The student of the revolution must not forget that everywhere existed active partisans of Spanish interests. These loyalists had to be persuaded either by force or by rhetoric to join the revolution. To some the appeal was made through the press; to others by speeches in public meetings, by verses and patriotic songs. In Buenos Aires the poets vied with each other in writing a national anthem. Estéban de Luca, Fray Cayetano Rodríguez and Vicente López y Planes, each produced one which for a season enjoyed popularity. But in 1813 the national congress of which López y Planes was a member, decreed that his "*Marcha patriôtica* should be sung at all official festivals and that at dawn of the anniversaries of the 25th of May, the school children should meet in the public town square to salute the rising sun with the national anthem."

Beginning with the clarion call,

> Oíd, mortales, el grito sagrado,
> Libertad, libertad, libertad!

the song sought to arouse hatred of the oppressor and especially of certain leaders of the Spanish army, who, having been born in America, were called "vile." The several strophes were packed with allusions to recent events. In this close touch with reality the Argentine national anthem differed from those of other countries largely composed of abstract commonplaces. Certain phrases, such as "a new and glorious nation," "a lion bowed at her feet," and the term "argentino" recurring several times, caught the popular fancy. People had printed on their visiting cards designs to represent these notions. Its expressions of hatred for Spaniards were so ferocious that late in the nineteenth century, after futile efforts to substitute a milder hymn, the president of the republic decreed that only the first and last quatrains and the chorus which were free of offense should be sung at public celebrations. Its author, López y Planes, attained political prominence and late in life even became provisional president of Argentina.

The fierce hatred of the rebelling colonials has always been resented by Spaniards as unjust. They have specially ridiculed the colonial tendency to identify their own cause with that of the aborigines. How can the descendants of Spanish conquistadores refer to themselves, even in outbursts of patriotic song, as sons of the Inca? Though there is much sense in the Spanish point of view, yet the power of the appeal is evident. So thorough a student of Spanish-American history as Clements R. Markham, referring to the uprising of the Indians of Peru in 1780, says,—"From the cruel death of the last of the Incas may be dated the rise of that feeling which ended in the expulsion of the Spaniards from South America."

This historical event is known as the rebellion of Tupac Amaru. It will be remembered that after the Spaniards had thoroughly established their power in Peru, they made some slight provision for the welfare of the natives. A school, the Colegio de San Borja, for the Christian education of their young princes was opened in Cuzco. But the claimants to the throne of the Incas were cruelly treated. In 1571 the viceroy, Francisco de Toledo, second son of the Marqués de Oropesa, with the idea of stifling any future attempt on the part of the natives to rally around the person of an Inca, put to death on slight pretext the eighteen-year-old boy, Tupac Amaru, then the acknowledged head of the royal house. But one of the viceroy's own relatives married an Inca princess. A descendant of theirs in 1770, who had been educated in the Colegio de San Borja, successfully prosecuted his claim to the marquisate of Oropesa before the royal audiencia of Lima, which at the same time recognized him as the fifth in lineal descent from the Inca Tupac Amaru. Joining the prestige of this name which he assumed to that of his Spanish title, the new Inca set to work to bring about better conditions for the Indian population in Peru. Having exhausted during ten years of effort all legal means to attain his object, he stirred up the Indians to armed resistance. Their temporarily successful revolt soon met with defeat at the hands of the Spanish army. Not only was the Inca captured and cruelly executed but Indians everywhere were relentlessly hunted down. Including their reprisals on isolated white settlers and their own slaughter, no less than 80,000 people are said to have perished.

The story of this dreadful affair was undoubtedly used for political effect during the colonial struggle against Spain. An Argentine historian, Gregorio Funes (1749–1829) was the first to write a detailed account including it in his *Ensayo de la Historia civil de Buenos Aires, Tucumán y Paraguay*. The three volumes of this history published in 1816 and 1817 must be recognized as a scholar's effort to assist the revolutionary propaganda. Like Tacitus whom he took for a model Funes emphasized the errors of the government and the crimes of its agents. His story of the period preceding the revolution is brought to a climax with the rebellion of Tupac Amaru.

In the dedication, "A la Patria," Funes says: "The day was to arrive at last when the love of country would not be a crime. Under the old regime thought was a slave and the soul of the citizen did not belong to him. The scene was changed. We are now free men. The country demands its rights now from the beings it protects. . . .

As for me I dedicate to it the insipid fruit of this historical essay. At least it has the advantage of calling its ravagers to judgment. . . . Moreover the tyranny and the actions of those who have governed us will serve as documents to enable us to discriminate between the good and the bad and to choose the best."

Funes was born in the town of Córdoba, where is located the third oldest university in America. Besides attending its courses he was educated in Spain. Before his return to America, Carlos III appointed him a canon in the cathedral of Córdoba, of which he later became dean. Residing in his native town in 1810, he was one of the first to adopt the principles of the revolution. His fellow townsmen sent him to represent them in the first national assembly held in Buenos Aires. For a short time after the retirement of Mariano Moreno, Funes was editor of the *Gaceta*.

It was then that the idea occurred to him of writing his history. Despite its political purpose the work merits serious consideration as a history of the colonial period of the Argentine provinces. Its vigorous well-written prose makes it a worthy first of the long series of histories which form a leading characteristic of Argentine literature in the nineteenth century.

The *Gaceta* continued to be the chief means of voicing revolutionary aspirations, referred to collectively as the "dogma de Mayo." After Funes' brief editorship, its columns fulminated with the writings of Bernardo de Monteagudo (?–1825), one of the extraordinary personalities of the revolution in Spanish America. Of brilliant mind though of humble birth he was so vehement a revolutionist that he had been condemned to death and escaped the penalty five times before 1812. His articles in the *Gaceta* preached absolute social equality and the rights of man. To further his ideas he founded the "Sociedad Patriótica." But his doctrines were not pleasing to the so-called triumvirate which ruled the city, so they put a stop to the publication of the *Gaceta*. Monteagudo persisted in his utterances by starting a periodical of his own, *El Mártir o libre*, in which his expressions were even more violently extreme in favor of the "dogma de Mayo." Finally he was driven from Buenos Aires. During the years of the armed struggle he took part in the military operations in Chile. By 1821 he was in Peru in charge of the department of war. Again his writings preached liberty. Again he founded a Sociedad Patriótica to move a people sluggish to adopt revolutionary principles. After the final success of the revolution, Monteagudo died in Lima by an unknown assassin's hand. His writings consisting of articles and fiery speeches have been collected. His *Memorias* give interesting details of his unusual career, and a vivid picture of the times.

Contemporaneous with affairs in Argentina similar events were taking place in Chile. The interests of these neighboring countries have always been closely connected. Each has served at some time as a refuge for the political exiles of the other. And as the exiles have either been journalists or have taken up journalism as a means of support, their literatures have exerted a reciprocal influence.

The example of Buenos Aires in assuming the prerogatives of government in May, 1810, was followed in Chile by the establishment of a similar junta to govern in the name of Fernando VII. The date of its proclamation, September 18th, has since been considered the national holiday of Chile. The military situation was directed by three brothers by the name of Carrera, who corrupted the troops in garrison at Concepción. The first congress assembled in 1811. In April of that year occurred a royalist insurrection in Santiago. During the street fighting there appeared, encouraging the colonial soldiers, a friar, Camilo Henríquez (1769–1825), who was destined to be the most prominent person to support the war on the intellectual side. In the fight he was doubly conspicuous by reason of his garb unknown in Chile, a black gown decorated with a red cross on the left side of the breast. Though born a Chilean he had been sent to Peru to be educated by the friars of La Buena Muerte, an order which he entered. His militant action of April, Henríquez justified in a sermon on the anniversary of North American independence, July 4th, 1811.

This sermon was such an able argument in favor of the revolution that even in Buenos Aires it was ordered printed for distribution. The mental attitude of such a large portion of the better elements of the people, especially of the clergy, was so opposed to the revolution that Henríquez' determined stand in favor of it possessed great importance. As the intellectual champion of his party he was made the editor of the periodical, the *Aurora de Chile*, established as its organ. The first number appeared on February 13th, 1812. On July 4th, Henríquez uttered from its columns the first cry for independence in these words:

"Let us begin in Chile by declaring our independence. That alone can blot out the name of rebels which tyranny gives us. That alone can raise us to the dignity which belongs to us, give us alliances among the powers and impose respect on our enemies: and if we treat with them, it will be with the majesty proper to a nation. Let us take in short this indispensable step. Uncertainty causes our weakness and exposes us to disorders and dangers."

On the same date at a dinner given by the consul of the United States, Henríquez read one of the first of his compositions in verse, a *Himno patriótico*. From that time he endeavored to persuade by similar means, celebrating each victory over the Spanish arms by appropriate verses. In this he was joined by a man of somewhat greater literary ability, Bernardo de Vera y Pintado (1780–1827). Together on the occasion of the public rejoicing at the victory of José Miguel Carrera over the first army sent to Chile by the viceroy of Peru, Henríquez and De Vera, wearing liberty caps, sang in duet one of their original compositions.

De Vera, an Argentine by birth, had come to Chile to attend the University of Chile and had remained there as a practicing lawyer. At the very beginning of political unrest he had sprung into public notice because, previous to the establishment of the junta, he had been seized by the authorities and ordered for trial to Lima on a vessel waiting for him in the harbor of Valparaiso. Before his deportation, however, the revolutionary junta was established in Santiago. The mob assailed the prison where De Vera lay and releasing him escorted him in triumph through the streets. De Vera was then appointed secretary of the junta. He was associated also with Henríquez in the editing of the *Aurora de Chile*. Throughout his life he continued to be politically prominent. His most important literary work was the national hymn of Chile which he wrote in 1819. The first quatrain, expressing the idea that Chile would be either the tomb of the free or a refuge against oppression, was used as a refrain after each stanza. In 1847 it was felt that the sentiments of this hymn were too extreme and another national hymn was adopted in its place, though De Vera's hymn may still be heard at patriotic celebrations.

Toward the end of 1813 the military situation began to look black for the revolutionaries. Belgrano's Argentine army had been annihilated in upper Peru. A second Spanish army sent from Lima completely worsted the Chileans under Bernardo O'Higgins and Carrera at Rancagua on October 12th, 1814. A harsh period for patriots followed this reconquest of Chile. Those who escaped with their lives took refuge in Argentina. Henríquez went to Buenos Aires where he took a prominent part in a literary movement along dramatic lines which was going on there. O'Higgins and others joined a new patriot army then drilling beyond the Andes.

This army was the creation of José de San Martín (1778–1850). To his genius and hard work South America owes its independence. The son of a captain in the Spanish army stationed in Argentina, José had been taken to Spain at the age of eight for a military education. In the Spanish war for liberation from the domination of the French, he distinguished himself at the battle of Bailén and won the rank of lieutenant colonel. In 1812 he was induced by Carlos de Alvear, likewise of Argentine birth but belonging to a wealthy family of Buenos Aires, to accompany him to the land of his birth. On their arrival both assumed positions of prominence. San Martín was given command of a regiment of cavalry which speedily showed its mettle by beating a Spanish detachment. After Belgrano's defeat San Martín was put in general command of the Argentine army. He established a camp at Mendoza on the Argentine side of the Andes in September, 1814. Without confiding to anybody his ultimate purpose he succeeded in two years in collecting an army of four thousand men thoroughly equipped with arms, provisions and means of transport.

Early in 1817, this army began its passage of the Andes, a military feat which surpasses any similar thing in history. Napoleon's crossing of the Great St. Bernard is renowned; but this pass has an altitude of 7963 feet whereas that of the Andes lies at 12,700 feet above the sea with a steep descent of 10,000 feet to the plains of Chile. At such a height both man and beast suffer from the terrible mountain sickness to which many succumb. The Spanish forces in Chile were awaiting San Martín's army but by means of false reports he succeeded so well in keeping them in ignorance of his intended way of approach that his men were clear of the loftier mountains before the first clash of arms. The main battle occurred on February 12th, 1817, at the pass of Chacabuco. O'Higgins in command of the Chilean contingent carried out a flanking movement so that the result of the battle was the complete destruction of the Spanish army. Within forty-eight hours San Martín had entered Santiago. The dictatorship of the country,

which was offered him, was finally conferred on O'Higgins.
And the absolute independence of Chile from Spain was
proclaimed.

The next year the Spaniards made a supreme effort to
regain Chile. An army of veterans was sent from Lima.
At the first contact with the patriots at Cancha Rayada
they were victorious. But San Martín rallied the fugitives
on his reserves. On April 5th, 1818, was fought the battle
of Maipú which terminated Spanish power in Chile.

San Martín saw, however, the danger threatening American independence so long as the viceroy at Lima remained
in authority. Moreover the king of Spain was collecting a
vast army at Cádiz for an attack on Buenos Aires. After
the Argentine declaration of independence at Tucumán in
1816, the administrative control of the country had been
largely in the hands of Juan Martín de Pueyrredón, but
civil war had broken out and was paralyzing the country.
Nevertheless San Martín set to work to provide a navy and
transport ships for the purpose of assailing the viceroy in
Peru. In this effort he found invaluable assistance in
Lord Thomas Cochrane, Earl of Dundonald, an officer with
a brilliant record in the English navy but temporarily in
disgrace with the admiralty. Lord Cochrane's fleet set
sail with the combined Chilean and Argentine army on
August 21st, 1820. His first exploit was a surprise attack
with small boats on the largest Spanish vessel, the forty-
four gun frigate, "Esmeralda." His boarding party cut
her out at night from beneath the very guns of the forts
at Callao and added her to his own fleet. The army was
landed from the transports and, with but little fighting
because the Spaniards withdrew into the mountains,

entered Lima. San Martín organized a civil government and the independence of Peru was proclaimed on July 28th, 1821.

The Spanish army under the viceroy José de la Serna, some twenty thousand men, had not however been disposed of but was still capable of vigorous resistance. The honor of accomplishing its destruction was reserved for one whose name is even more famous in South American annals, the Liberator, Simón Bolívar. But before discussing his military career it will be advisable to consider the echoes in literature of these stirring events.

The only Peruvian poet whose name was connected with the revolution was Mariano Melgar (1791–1815), and he was not of Lima but of the provincial capital Arequipa. He was a teacher of mathematics in the local university and joined the corps of artillery among other Spaniards who associated themselves with an uprising of the Indian population under the cacique Pumacagua in 1813. General Ramírez operating under the orders of General Joaquin de la Pezuela, at that time facing Belgrano's army, overcame the ill-organized patriot army at the field of Humachiri. Pumacagua was hanged and the white officers including Melgar were shot. After the poet's death his papers were entrusted by his sister to a priest who piously destroyed the poems which he thought of seditious character. One of Melgar's political poems somehow preserved shows the vigor of the young man's mind. The lines depict the colossus of despotism falling beneath the blows of liberty to the amazement of mankind. His non-political poems reveal the delicacy of feeling of a real poet. They are mainly imitations of popular poetry described by the native word "yaraví," a sort of plaintive love song not dissimilar in form from the Spanish letrilla. Many later poets have tried their hand at writing "yaravíes." In honor of their patriot poet the citizens of Arequipa celebrated the centenary of his birth by erecting a statue of him in the public square.

In Lima the revolution found but few sympathizers. Consequently the literature shows rather the loyalist phase of the situation. The University of San Marcos for example published the poems and speeches delivered upon the occasion of General Pezuela's accession to the viceroyalty in 1816. The victories of the Spanish troops at Rancagua and in Argentina over Belgrano had their panegyrists. But life in Lima flowed on with all its colonial nonchalance so that the most characteristic literary productions were the festive verses of an easy-going priest, José Joaquín de Larriva (1780–1832), and his burlesque epic, La Angulada. With equal facility he could preach a sermon in praise of Pezuela in 1816 and eulogize Bolívar in 1826. Other versifiers too there were who maintained the traditional Peruvian love of jest.

The serious business of the revolution on the other hand continued to occupy all minds in Buenos Aires. A prolific versifier of political events was Fray Cayetano Rodríguez (1761–1823). His lines, though badly written, at times incarnate the spirit of the revolution of May. Two sonnets of his, Al 25 de Mayo, and a national hymn retained for a long time their popularity because they expressed a warm enthusiasm for liberty and a love of country. He was one of the first to improvise on the victory of Chacabuco when the news of it reached the city.

But the poet of greatest merit to follow in his verses the course of war was Esteban de Luca (1786–1824). His odes *A Chacabuco, Al Triunfo del Vice Almirante Lord Cochrane, Canto Lírico a la Libertad de Lima,* all brought him praise. The last was especially rewarded by a gift of books presented by the government. Somewhat different was his *Al Pueblo de Buenos Aires,* in which he exhorted the citizens to leave the town and devote their time to agriculture and the raising of cattle and horses. Beside being a poet Luca was an expert mathematician and metallurgist. As such he served his country in directing the cannon foundry which provided Argentina with artillery. He lost his life in a shipwreck in the Río de la Plata. This circumstance is commemorated by the greatest of Argentine poets, Andrade, in his *Arpa perdida,* of which the last stanza feigns that travelers may hear on quiet nights the sound of the forgotten poet's lyre.

The practice of writing patriotic poems was fostered by the custom prevailing in Buenos Aires of reciting them at evening parties. Two collections were printed, *La Lira argentina,* 1821, and *Poesías patrióticas,* 1822, the second by order of the government. The first includes compositions written during the English invasion, unfortunately without names of the authors. More useful to the student of literature is a collection printed in the *Revista de Derecho, Historia y Letras,* in 1898 and the following years with the title *Cancionero popular.* A characteristic of style, common to all the poems, a supposed embellishment but to modern taste a grave disfigurement, is the introduction of classical allusions or a mythological machinery, Greek gods in South America, a last sigh of Gongorism.

The mythological machinery was even more in evidence in plays of the period. The desire for dramatic entertainment excited by the recitation of patriotic verses was satisfied by the organization of a society, "La Sociedad del Buen Gusto," for the purpose of fostering the drama. The first meeting was held in July, 1817. Among the twenty-eight members were López y Planes, De Luca, and the Chilean refugee Camilo Henríquez. Colonel Juan Ramón Rojas was the managing director. The plays produced were either originals by the members of the society or translations from French or English because the director pushed his patriotism to the extreme of refusing to admit to the stage plays written by Spaniards. Rojas himself wrote the first drama given, *Cornelia Berorquia*, a tragedy of a young innocent girl condemned by the full tribunal of the inquisition. The scandal in Buenos Aires was tremendous. One lady who attended when asked about the play, said,—"To-night we cannot doubt that San Martín has passed the Andes and triumphed over the Spaniards in Chile."

Camilo Henríquez contributed his *Camila o la patriota de Sud América*. As this play was printed in a little volume, now a bibliographical rarity, it is possible to learn much about the sentiments and ideas of the period. The action of the drama takes place on the banks of the river Marañón a few months after the slaughter of the patriots of Quito. A family has fallen into the hands of an Indian chief who declares that the daughter Camila must become the bride of his prime minister. Camila objects because she holds dear the memory of her husband Diego, one of the patriots fallen as she supposes by the hand of Spanish murderers. The cacique insists on the marriage. When the so-called prime minister is presented, the whole affair proves to be a huge joke for the prime minister is no other than Diego. The chief purpose of the drama is to serve as a vehicle for Henríquez' ideas on education and tolerance in religion. He praises the Lancaster method of instruction as obviously advantageous. He lauds the industry and righteousness of the Quakers though "the burners hate them and would like to burn them all; perverse men have made the king of Spain believe that the burners are the pillars of his throne." A paper which the cacique hands his prime minister contains Henríquez' own program for the welfare of South America. "First: to remedy the depopulation of America and its backward condition in arts and agriculture, it is necessary to attract immigration by impartial, tolerant and paternal laws. Second: if America does not forget its Spanish prejudices and adopt more liberal principles, it will never escape from the rule of a Spain beyond the seas, wretched and obscure as European Spain."

Henríquez' tolerant religious principles were to bring him the wrath of the clerical party after his return to Chile. When his friends Bernardo O'Higgins and De Vera became influential, the one dictator, the other his secretary, they started a movement to invite Henríquez to Chile raising funds for his repatriation by popular subscription. There came with him Juan Crisóstomo Lafinur (1797–1824) who had been an intimate friend and acquaintance of his in Buenos Aires. Together they immediately began in the press the propaganda of their liberal ideas. But their attempts at reform came to naught for they met violent opposition from the clergy. The latter were fortuitously assisted by a disastrous earthquake, called by them an act of God, a demonstration of His anger at the impiety of the men encouraged by the dictator O'Higgins.

Lafinur died during the struggle as the result of a fall from his horse. He has a place in the history of Argentine literature by reason of his elegies on General Belgrano at the time of the latter's death in 1820. Though other specimens of his verse exist the three elegies so exalt the love of country that they keep alive the author's name.

Conditions in Buenos Aires about 1820 have been disclosed from a unique point of view in the dialogues of *Chano y Contreras* written by Bartolomé Hidalgo (1787–?). Jacinto Chano, the overseer of a cattle ranch, converses with his friend the gaucho Ramón Contreras. The latter reviews somewhat pessimistically the advantages gained by the revolution. The poor still remain poor, though a few men in power are able to "spend money like rice." Chano says he has learned that before the law, he is the equal of any man. "Yes," replies Contreras, "but there are difficulties in the practice," and relates the contrast in the punishment of a rich man guilty of a notorious crime and that of a poor gaucho who for some trivial offense received the limit of the law. The ironical vein maintained in the description of certain civic events is delightful.

Hidalgo's poems were a written imitation of the type of improvisation popular throughout Argentina. The custom brought from Andalusia of ballad recitation by an adept, or "payador," who, lightly strumming his guitar, begins to improvise in eight syllabled lines a narrative of some recent occurrence with original comments developed more widely on the pampas than elsewhere. The first to imitate in writing this popular poetry was J. B. Maziel in a ballad praising the viceroy's military exploits. Before Hidalgo it was used by Juan Gualberto Godoy (1793–1824) for political purposes. He kept a store far out on the plains where he is said to have sold verses to local payadores and published a paper *El Eco de los Andes* with satirical poems in gaucho style. But Godoy's work remained unknown till later writers made the gaucho type of verse one of the most original and entertaining features of Argentine literature.

Despite the importance of the victories won in the south by San Martín, the ultimate independence of South America was due to the assistance which came to him from the north. In large measure was it due also to San Martín's noble-minded and unselfish patriotism, rare in Spanish-American annals, which prompted him to self-effacement when that seemed the best course. When only his own withdrawal from the scene of active operations would assure the participation of Bolívar and his troops in destroying the Spanish army under the viceroy La Serna, the generous San Martín stood aside and even exiled himself from America.

Simón Bolívar (1783–1830) was the greatest military and political genius which the revolution in Spanish America produced. Though a wealthy landowner, he made common cause with the uprising in Caracas, Vene-

zuela, in April, 1810. Bolívar, Luis López Méndez, and
Andrés Bello were despatched as commissioners to secure the sympathy and material aid of Great Britain.
Bolívar's stay was short for he returned to Venezuela to
serve in the army of General Miranda which was defending the country from the Spanish forces. The latter
were successful in putting down the rebellion. Bolívar
fled while Miranda was taken prisoner and sent to Spain.
Bolívar then organized another army in Nueva Granada
and fought his way to Caracas which he entered on August 4th, 1813. The Spaniards, however, again won the
upper hand. In the bloody guerilla warfare which followed, the patriots accomplished little for several years.
In 1819, however, a foreign legion of 2000 trained soldiers,
mostly Irishmen, joined Bolívar. He learned that the
Spanish soldiers in Bogotá were to march to join those
in Venezuela. By a brilliant manœuvre, Bolívar led his
men over the windswept lofty paramo and effected a
union with the patriot army of Nueva Granada. He gave
battle to the Spaniards at Boyacá on August 7th, 1819,
and destroyed their army. After his return to Venezuela
Bolívar brought about the passage of a law by the revolutionary legislature erecting Venezuela and Nueva Granada
into the Republic of Colombia of which he was to be president. Turning then his attention to the Spanish forces re-
maining in Venezuela, he broke them at the battle of
Carabobo, June 24th, 1821. There now remained in South
America only that Spanish army which had retreated from
Lima at the approach of San Martín's forces.

Bolívar marched south by way of Popayán. Successful
in taking Quito in June, 1822, he added that province to

his new Republic of Colombia. The next month there took place in Guayaquil a famous conference lasting three days between Bolívar and San Martín. The details of this meeting have remained forever secret. But a letter written a month later by San Martín to Bolívar allows one to infer the reasons for San Martín's subsequent conduct. In it he says,—"My determination is irrevocably fixed. I have called the first Congress of Peru for the 20th of next month, and on the day after its opening I shall sail for Chile, convinced that my presence is the only obstacle which prevents your coming to Peru with the army under your command." San Martín evidently foresaw a civil war unless he gave way before Bolívar's immense personal ambition.

For two years the Spanish army avoided contact. On August 26th, 1824, Bolívar won the great victory of Junín. But the final surrender of the Spaniards was not made till December 7th, after the battle of Ayacucho, where the patriot army was commanded by Antonio José de Sucre (1793–1830). The next summer a general assembly of Upper Peru met and declared itself the Republic of Bolívia. General Sucre was elected the first president.

Bolívar's personal fortunes took him back to Caracas from which as his capital he attempted to administer the Republic of Colombia. Its extent, however, was so vast and its parts so diverse that after Bolívar's death, September 17th, 1830, it split up into the three republics, Venezuela, Ecuador, and Nueva Granada. The latter reassumed the same name Colombia in 1861.

Just as Bolívar's greatest campaign against the Span-

iards took place in Peru, so it was reserved for a native
of a Peruvian province, now a part of Ecuador, to compose the most remarkable poem written about his military success. So excellent is the classical finish of its style
that the Spanish critic Menéndez y Pelayo refers to José
Joaquín Olmedo (1784–1847) as, "one of the three or
four great Spanish-American poets, if not the first."

Bolívar requested Olmedo to write some verses in celebration of the battles of Junín and Ayacucho. In the
general's correspondence is found a long letter from
Olmedo dated January 31st, 1825, in which the poet
says:—"I regret that you recommend me to sing our
last triumphs. For a long time I have been revolving
that thought in my mind. Junín came and I began my
song; I should say I began to form plans. . . . Ayacucho
came and I awoke uttering a thunder, (Olmedo here al-
ludes to the opening lines of his ode) but I have made
little progress. Everything I produce seems poor and
inferior to the subject, I erase, tear up, correct; and
always it is bad. I have persuaded myself that my muse
cannot measure her strength with this giant. I was
proud because I expected to make a composition which
would bear me with you to immortality but I confess
myself downcast."

Olmedo did win by his ode the immortality which he
craved. Its opening peal of thunder,

> El trueno horrendo, que en fragor revienta
> Y sordo retumbando se dilata
> Por la inflamada esfera,
> Al Dios anuncia que en el cielo impera,

is an evident paraphrase of Horace's,

Caelo tonantem credidimus Iovem regnare: III, 5.

The poet then sees and describes the leaders as the battle begins. Suddenly the sword of Bolívar appears and eclipses all the warriors as the sun eclipses all the stars. Darkness comes on before the victory is complete; while the soldiers are singing hymns of triumph, a voice calls from on high in the heavens, the voice of the Inca, Huaina-Capac. They behold his illuminated figure as he reveals his personality. After recapitulating the horrors that had occurred on American soil since the conquest, he discloses the progress of the next fight at Ayacucho, describes the place of the battle and names the patriots who will distinguish themselves, especially the leader Sucre.

In regard to him Olmedo wrote, "Sucre is a hero, is my friend and deserves an ode for himself; at present enough immortality will fall to his share by being named in an ode dedicated to Bolívar."

The Inca continues by praising the new era of peace and prosperity that stands before, but urges on the Americans the necessity of union "in order to be free and never conquered." He is interrupted by the virgins of the sun who intone a hymn beseeching the continued protection of the sun as the ancient god of Peru. On the city of Lima the virgins make demand that she open her gates and receive Bolívar in triumph. At the close of the song the Inca and the virgins disappear behind a golden cloud.

As Bolívar was not himself present at the final victory the poet was obliged to connect the two battles in a manner that would not lessen the importance of Bolívar. Yet the means chosen, the apparition of the Inca, has raised a veritable critics' battle. Bolívar himself called

Huaina-Capac "the hero of the poem." Bello praises
the poetical device, while Miguel A. Caro ridicules the
words of the Inca who exclaims to the assembled patriots,
"You are all my children," and his offer to Bolívar as a
reward a place in heaven at his own right hand. But
Manuel Cañete sums up the criticisms justly. "We see
Olmedo rise to the clouds borne by inspiration and find
accents, if not superior to all, not inferior to any of our
best lyric poets, whenever he exclaims what has stirred
his heart. But he falls when he leaves the luminous
sphere of truth and sinks into the labyrinth of the artificial. The reader, however, forgets the defects of the
poem, thanks to the animation, the movement, the sublime
inspiration with which the author has succeeded in expressing and developing the idea."

The Liberator was evidently satisfied with Olmedo's
poem for he named him plenipotentiary of Peru in London,
for which city he left Guayaquil on August 5, 1825.
Cañete thinks it is unjust to Olmedo to attribute his appointment entirely to the poem, because Bolívar was a
good judge of men and he needed a superior person for
the mission.

The next year Olmedo published the poem in London
and Paris, with the title *La Victoria de Junín, Canto a
Bolívar*. In regard to it, Olmedo wrote to Bolívar: "The
canto is being printed with great elegance. It bears
the portrait of the hero; and a medallion representing the
apparition and oracle of the Inca in the clouds. The
canto needs all these externals in order to appear decently
among foreign peoples." It is interesting to note that the
plates of the Paris edition are in color and that the por-

trait of Bolívar which Olmedo termed "medianamente parecido" is the one which has been most widely reproduced.

Olmedo's sojourn in Europe was divided between London and Paris. He thus came into close intercourse with Andrés Bello and Fernández Madrid and his correspondence with them has been preserved. The former published in the second volume of the *Repertorio Americano,* Olmedo's poem, *A un amigo en el nacimiento de su primogénito,* as well as a critical notice by himself on the *Victoria de Junín.*

Olmedo did not, however, long remain in Europe. An intense love for his native province of Guayaquil characterized the man and greatly influenced the course of his life. As a student he lived in Lima where he obtained the degree of doctor of law. In 1810, he went to Spain to represent Guayaquil in the Cortes of Cádiz and was one of the members who refused to recognize Fernando VII until he swore to the constitution. Returning to his own country in 1814 he took an active part in political affairs and was elected to the Peruvian constitutional congress of 1822 in which he advocated a separate establishment for the provinces now known as Ecuador. Therein he was an opponent of Bolívar, but the Liberator's great victories turned him into an ardent admirer. Sent to Europe in 1825, he returned in 1828. Ecuador became a separate republic in 1830 and Olmedo was elected its first vice-president, an office which he soon resigned in order to become prefect of Guayaquil as he desired to live in that city. He continued active in politics until his death in 1847.

His poems are few in number for the reason that he wrote only when he felt inspired and took great care in their rhetorical finish. Amunátegui enumerates four translations and ten original compositions. Of the former the most important is a rendering of the first three epistles of Pope's *Essay on Man*. His first original poem is a *Silva a la muerte de María Antonia de Borbón, princesa de Asturias*, published in Lima, 1807. The poet represents the innocent princess as an expiatory victim chosen by God who is angry at the sins of the Spaniards. As God accepts the sacrifice, the poet urges his avenging angel to announce that God's wrath has been appeased and that the English who were preparing to attack Buenos Aires would be overthrown. As a note to this composition, Olmedo wrote: "Two months after this composition was written, ten thousand English attack the city of Buenos Aires and are beaten and obliged to surrender by its inhabitants."

His poem *Mi retrato*, 1817, gives us the portrait of a tall thin man with brown hair and eyes, a broad forehead, a large nose of which he is proud because therein he resembles the poets Virgil, Homer and Ovid, fine even teeth, a thin beard and a face much pitted from small-pox like the sky with the stars. His acquaintances describe him as agreeable in character with a large fund of knowledge which Olmedo himself ascribed to his own efforts rather than to his schooling.

The grandiloquent rhetoric of the *Victoria de Junín* was repeated in a poem which Olmedo composed in 1835 to *General Flores, Vencedor en Minarica*. As sheer rhetoric there are passages which are very fine, for example, the spirited description of the General's horse. As the subject of the poem is the victory of a partisan chief, the lines often strike the reader as bombast, especially when the poet urges the lofty peak of Chimborazo, king of the Andes, to bow his head because the victor passes.

Juan José Flores (1801–64) was not to be outdone in compliments. He also dabbled in verse-making and begins his *Ocios poéticos* with the line,

> ¡ Qué vida tan feliz, Omero mío!

He stars Omero and explains in a footnote: "Allusion to Olmedo, wherefore the H is suppressed."

Another poet to hail Bolívar's victories as worthy of great renown was the Colombian José Fernández Madrid (1784–1830), already referred to as one of Olmedo's friends in Europe. Some suspect that Fernández Madrid also owed his appointment as Colombia's minister plenipotentiary in London to his laudatory verses in which within the space of ten lines he compared Bolívar to all the great men of antiquity. In another passage the Peruvian Incas, raising their heads from the tomb, joyfully salute three times the great champion, while the volcanoes Pichincha and Chimborazo roar with indignation at the oppressors of America. Such hyperbolical exaggeration reveals the spirit of the times.

Fernández Madrid played an important rôle in the revolution in Colombia. A member of the first revolutionary junta organized in Cartagena de las Indias, 1810, he became the leader of the defense when the city was besieged by the Spaniards. He was also a member of the united provinces of Venezuela and Nueva Granada and

was named as their president in 1816 during the lowest
ebb of their military fortunes. Falling into the hands of
the Spanish forces, he saved his life by writing to the
Spanish general Morillo that he had accepted the presidency only in the king's interest. He was ordered deported to Spain but, on account of illness, he never went
beyond Havana, where he was soon set at liberty. After
Bolívar's successful campaigns, Fernández Madrid again
became prominent in politics. As confidential agent of the
republic of Colombia he was in Paris at the time of his
appointment to be her minister in London.

In this city he published a volume of his verses, 1828,
and two dramas, *Atala*, based on Chateaubriand's romance
of that name, and *Guatimoc*. These plays are specimens of
the enthusiastic attempt at play writing which flourished
in Bogotá during the revolution. Fernández Madrid, as
a versifier on occasional topics, is fluent and amusing.
"Hail, doubly hail, him who invented the hammock,"
he cries in the refrain to some stanzas in which he sings the
advantages of that blessing to humanity. To his friend
Andrés Bello, he sends some playful lines to accompany a
bottle of wine, "a dose of joy," at the baptism of the latter's infant daughter. As a patriotic poet Fernández
Madrid obtains a certain forcefulness by the use of epigrammatic balance. He sees Colombia rise from her
wounds, "majestic, full of wounds, but victorious; poor
but avenged, and independent." Though he execrates the
Spaniards for their crimes, yet he recognizes them as
brothers in blood and urges a spiritual union between
"the Hispanic lion and the American condor."

Two other Colombians who produced patriotic verses

worthy of mention were José María de Salazar (1785–1828) and Luis Vargas Tejada (1802–29). Salazar first exercised his poetic talents in *El Placer público de Santa Fe de Bogotá*, a complimentary poem to celebrate the arrival of the viceroy in 1804. In his student days he was one of the first to write original pieces actually produced on the stage in Bogotá. His *Soliloquio de Eneas* and *El Sacrificio de Idomeneo* materially assisted in the movement to restore the theater in that capital. Joining the revolutionary movement he became conspicuous as the author of the first national hymn of Colombia. Bolívar's victory at Boyacá called forth some stirring lines from his pen, for which Bolivar later rewarded him by appointment as the Colombian minister in Paris.

Luis Vargas Tejada was called by his fellow countrymen their André Chenier on account of the violence of his sentiments on liberty. These were expressed in tragedies written for the stage in Bogotá and especially in the tragic monologues *Catón en Útica* and *La Muerte de Pausanias*. The youthful poet thought to turn his fanatic politics into action by joining a conspiracy to assassinate Bolívar. He escaped the fate of his fellow conspirators by hiding in a cave for fourteen months. As he died insane from this experience a tragic interest was added to his poetical work.

Though Bolívar's exploits inspired so many patriotic lines, yet in his own country, Venezuela, there was little literary response to them. In fact conditions there were distinctly unfavorable to literary enterprise. Not only was the capital Caracas frequently the headquarters of the Spanish army, but the war was waged with absorbing and merciless bitterness throughout the country. Venezuela was, however, the birthplace of the greatest of all Spanish-American literary men, Andrés Bello (1781–1865). But the scene of his activity during the revolutionary epoch was London, far from the strife of arms.

Bello, from that viewpoint, was more largely interested in Spanish America as a whole. After the American republics had been firmly established he was invited to Chile, where his influence on matters of education and literature became tremendous. It seems almost as if he led the lives of two different men. In London to the age of forty-eight he eked out a narrow existence, always studying as though at school. In Chile for thirty-five years more he poured forth his accumulated wisdom for the benefit of the sons of his adopted country. The first period of Bello's life embraced the epoch of the separation of the Spanish colonies from Spain; the second their first efforts at the upbuilding of new nationalities.

Largely self-taught, the course of Bello's life is foreshadowed by his youth. He was both a precocious child and a constant reader. At the age of eleven he saved his pennies to buy a cheap edition issued in parts of Calderón's plays. At school he distinguished himself in Latin. He made there the acquaintance of friends who were to assist him in getting a start in life, especially the younger sons of the Ustáriz family, persons of wealth and culture. In their home where they had the habit of reading poems aloud after dinner, Bello found inspiration for his earliest verses, certain translations or paraphrases of Latin. Urged by his friends he undertook the study of both French and English. For the latter language he used as a text-book, Locke's *Essay on the Understanding.*

When he left school Luis Ustáriz obtained for him a position in the government office as undersecretary. In 1808 he was appointed secretary. As it was his task to translate the French and English letters, it fell to his lot that same year to be the medium through which the news of the fall of Carlos IV became known in Venezuela. He also played a part in the events which led to the uprising in Caracas on April 19th, 1810. As in the other Spanish colonies, there was established a junta or committee to govern ostensibly in the name of Fernando VII. The junta sent Bello as one of three commissioners, the other two were Luis López Méndez and Simón Bolívar, to London for the purpose of obtaining assistance for the revolution. But they received little encouragement from the British cabinet.

In Venezuela the revolution maintained itself until there occurred on March 26th, 1812, a severe earthquake on account of which many thousand persons in Caracas lost their lives. The royalist party, assisted by the priests who spread the idea that this event was God's punishment for rebellion, successfully prosecuted a counter revolution and restored Spanish rule. Bello was thus left stranded in London without money. Once even he came near being put in jail for his personal debts. Bolívar, a man of means, left London to work on his plans for the military accomplishment of independence for Venezuela. But Bello remained in London for nineteen years.

His friends aided him in finding means of support. The Spanish language being then fashionable in London, he obtained many private pupils. By 1814 he considered himself able to marry. His most influential friend at this

period was José Blanco White, a former Spanish priest of
Irish parentage, who had left his native Seville to settle in
London. He introduced Bello to Mr. Hamilton, Secretary
of State for India, to whose children he became tutor in
1816. Among his English friends were the philosophers
James Mill and Jeremy Bentham, and he is said to have
been employed at one time to decipher the latter's manuscript. From his intercourse with them, he may have
derived some of the ideas that guided his scientific studies.

During his sojourn in London, Bello was constantly
studying. First he learned to read Greek from the books
in the library of an English friend. His leisure time he
spent in the library of the British Museum. As results
of his study he published a modern Spanish rendering of
the *Poema del Cid* with accompanying notes and a study
of the *Cronique de Turpin*. Both of these show original
and sound critical thought. Next he made his version
of Berni's *Orlando Innamorato;* which Menéndez y Pelayo
terms the best translation in Spanish of any long Italian
poem. Moreover, he was deeply interested in educational
questions about which he published various discussions in
the *Repertorio Americano.* This was Bello's contribution
edited in company with the Colombian García del Río, to
the various periodicals in Spanish which appeared in
London during the revolutionary period.

A periodical in Spanish, *El Español*, had been founded
in London by Blanco White and conducted by him from
1810 to 1814. In 1820 the Guatemalan, A. J. de Irisarri
published a few numbers of *El Censor Americano* to
which Bello contributed. On his own account Bello
began, 1823, the *Biblioteca Americana,* which soon sus-

pended. Money to pay for such a publication even though well received in South America was slow and difficult to obtain.

Undaunted, however, he launched, 1826, a quarterly, *El Repertorio Americano* and continued it for four numbers. The editor's purpose is set forth in the first volume. "For years, lovers of American civilization have desired the publication of a periodical which would defend with the interest of their own cause the independence and liberty of the new states established in that new world upon the ruins of Spanish dominion." The contents of the periodical were, however, but slightly political. They comprised encyclopedic information on such topics as literary criticism, the orthography of the Spanish language, agriculture, science and education. Original poems formed one of its attractive features and here were first published Olmedo's poem, *En el nacimiento de su primogénito* and his translation of Horace's Ode XIV. Lib I; García Goyena's *Canto á la Independencia de Guatemala;* and a few poems of the Mexican Navarrete. The opening pages of the first number contained Bello's own masterpiece, a *Silva á la Agricultura de la Zona tórrida.*

Bello had conceived the idea of a vast poem to be entitled *América*. Of this he wrote its introduction, *Alocución á la Poesía,* and the *Silva* just mentioned. The latter puts him in the front rank of American poets and admits him even in the judgment of Menéndez y Pelayo to the category of those who have most artistically manipulated the Spanish language. In the former poem, which first appeared in the *Biblioteca Americana*, Bello invites the muses to leave Europe where an artificial culture, based on the power of gold, reigns preëminent and where nature is supreme and bestows on each its own peculiar beauty which the poet describes. In the silva to the *Agricultura de la Zona tórrida*, Bello presents the varied beauty of the tropics, its color, its rich perfume, the rare products of its cultivated fields, bounded by distant snow-capped mountains, and finally urges the possessors of this paradise to enjoy it in peace and union.

There is a certain resemblance between the two poems; the lists of plants and their epithets are almost identical, and an occasional line of the earlier is repeated in the later poem. Besides there are reminiscences of Virgil's *Georgics*. While Bello's poetry therein resembles other Spanish classicists, Menéndez y Pelayo finds him the possessor of an original note "not to be confused with any of his contemporaries. . . . He is a consummate master of poetic diction, learnedly picturesque, laboriously polished." His picturesque originality consists in appeals to the senses when he speaks of the "snowy fleece of the cotton," "the white jasmins of the coffee," "the living carmine of the flowers," epithets which seem to the critic to give a "strange flavor both Latin and American."

Bello's diplomatic activity continued during his entire sojourn in London. As a means of livelihood, however, its pecuniary return was uncertain even after the revolution was successful. In 1822 he accepted appointment as secretary for the legation of Chile, a place which he resigned in November, 1824, to become secretary for the legation of Colombia. Just before accepting this position he married his second wife, Isabella Dunn.

Though his old friend Bolívar was now president of

Colombia, Bello still received only a meager salary in irregular payments. He did not join the chorus of those who wrote fulsome verses to the Liberator, a fact which the latter probably resented, for there exists a letter written by Bolívar from Quito in which he says of Bello: "His coldness has kept us separated to a certain degree."

The truth may be that Bello's long residence in England, or his intellectual pursuits had subdued his native Venezuelan fire. The political odes which he wrote, *Himno de Colombia* and *Canción a la Disolución de Colombia*, lacked so much of the exaggerated rhetorical style then in vogue, that by the advice of his friend, Fernández Madrid, they were not published. The same chilliness of inspiration marks the ode, *Al 18 de Septiembre*, by which he signalized his arrival in Chile.

He was invited to Chile by President Prieto in 1829, who offered him the post of chief secretary for foreign affairs at a good salary, and an allowance of three hundred pounds for traveling expenses. From the day of reaching Chile Bello became closely identified with the intellectual movement of his adopted country, so that his career belongs with it rather than with his native Venezuela.

As the representative Venezuelan writer of prose during the revolutionary period, it is necessary to look to Simón Bolívar, however strange it may seem to think of the successful general, the Liberator, as a literary man. Yet in his speeches and his voluminous correspondence, recently edited by R. Blanco Fombona, he reveals an energetic style typical of the man. His speeches to his soldiers were apparently modeled after those of Napoleon with whom his contemporaries so fondly compared him. A fair example of them is the proclamation issued when he returned to Bogotá, on November 23rd, 1826:—"Colombians! Five years ago I left this capital to march at the head of the liberating army from the banks of the Cauca to the silver-bearing heights of Potosi. A million Colombians, two sister republics, have obtained independence in the shadow of our banners. And the world of Columbus has ceased to be Spanish. Such has been our absence."

CHAPTER III

In North America the course of the revolution was different from that on the southern continent. Of the two principal centers, Mexico and Cuba, the former emerged from the period as an independent republic, while the latter became a refuge for royalists. Moreover the Mexican revolution, unlike those occurring in South America, did not begin in the capital but in the provinces, and instead of originating with an intellectual class who fed its fires with argument and impassioned verse, the first outbreak in Mexico was the affair of provincials, many of them of pure Indian blood, led by a rural priest, Miguel Hidalgo. The literary expression of events was subsequent to them by many years. On the other hand, the greatest revolutionary poet, José María Heredia, whose unsurpassed verses were filled with burning inspiration and revolt, was a Cuban. In his country there took place nothing more than a mild conspiracy, easily suppressed, in which the poet was himself implicated. But Heredia during the impressionable years of youth lived and wrote in Mexico.

During the first decade of the nineteenth century there acted as viceroys of Mexico a succession of incompetent men whose chief aim in governing appeared to be the rapid

79

accumulation of personal wealth. Resentment at their
measures of taxation caused the formation of conspiracies
in various parts of the country, especially after the home
difficulties of Spain became known. One of these conspiracies was led by Ignacio Allende who organized military
forces in various towns assisted by the counsel and influence of Miguel Hidalgo, parish priest of the village
Dolores in the mining region of Guanajuato. Before their
preparations were completed, Allende learning that their
plans had been betrayed to the authorities, so informed
Hidalgo late one night. Undismayed, the latter replied,
"We must act at once, there is no time to lose." The
next morning, September 16th, 1810, a Sunday, Hidalgo,
instead of conducting the usual service, harangued the
men of the village from the church steps and bade them
follow him to liberty. This was the famous "Grito de
Dolores," the cry to arms, from which dates the revolution
in Mexico. The 16th of September is celebrated as the
Mexican national holiday.

Hidalgo's little band steadily increased in numbers as
they marched from village to village. A picture of Nuestra
Señora de Guadelupe served as a banner under which to
rally. In a week a horde of fifty thousand men, mainly
Indians, armed with improvised weapons and a few mus-
kets, had assembled. Their first objective was the city of
Guanajuato, a mining center, where in a strong warehouse
of stone, known as the "alhóndiga de granaditas," was
stored bullion to the value of $5,000,000. The place was
defended by five hundred Spanish troops. Though their
musketry caused great slaughter in the assaulting mob
crowded in the narrow streets, they were forced to yield

by the disparity in numbers. That night the town itself suffered pillage and burning such as has always marked revolutions in Mexico.

Then Hidalgo took up his march on the capital. The viceroy Venegas hastily collected such troops as he could. In the first encounters the royalist soldiers were defeated, but Hidalgo, being no soldier and his army a mob, was unable to take advantage of his successes. Instead of advancing steadily on Mexico city, he discouraged his forces by turning back. He occupied his time by trying to establish an organized government. He issued proclamations emancipating the slaves, restoring the land to the Indians, and calling a congress.

The royalist troops meanwhile were put under the command of Felix Calleja del Rey, an efficient soldier, who for his successes was later appointed viceroy. Calleja's army came into contact with Hidalgo's mob on January 17th, 1811, at the bridge of Calderón, where, favored by an extraordinary piece of luck, for the dry grass taking fire the flames and smoke were driven into the faces of the insurgents, Calleja completely routed the hosts of his opponents. A month later Allende and Hidalgo were taken prisoners, and after a formal trial were executed.

The direction of the rebellion fell to a friend and pupil of Hidalgo, also a priest and a younger man with a greater capacity for leadership, José María Morelos. He kept the field against the royalists until 1815 when he too was captured and executed. Among the exploits of these four years, one of the most famous was the defense of the city of Cuautla, from which after several months of siege, he and his forces succeeded in escaping. Morelos also carried out important plans for the organization of an insurgent government. A national congress was assembled which drew up a written constitution for Mexico. After Morelos' death the insurgents became mere marauding bands which were gradually hunted down.

In 1820 occurred in Spain the revolutionary movement making the liberal Cortes temporarily supreme. In Mexico the privileged classes of the city felt that the time had come for seeking independence. As military leader was selected Agustín de Iturbide, who had been one of the most active generals in the campaign against Morelos. Under pretense of putting down a rebel band then vigorous under Vicente Guerrero, he left the city with a few thousand soldiers which were later increased in number by the unsuspecting viceroy. At the proper moment Iturbide divulged to his troops his real intentions in which they acquiesced. On February 24th, 1821, he promulgated a manifesto, since known as the "Plan de Iguala." It declared for the absolute independence of Mexico, the Roman Catholic faith as the state religion, an absolute monarchy as the form of government with a member of the Spanish royal family for ruler, the maintenance of all existing institutions of property and privileges, the establishment of a junta to rule until the selection of a monarch and the support of the three guarantees of Independence, Religion, and Unity, symbolized respectively in the national colors, green, white, and red.

This revolution was entirely aristocratic and reactionary against the liberal tendencies at work in Spain. The privileged classes in Mexico were afraid of interference with their rights by the democratic Spanish Cortes which had won the upper hand in the contest with the King Fernando VII. Some Mexicans even proposed inviting the King to become Emperor of Mexico.

In consequence of the origin and character of the revolution, Iturbide met with little resistance. The garrisons of the provincial towns joined his forces. The main body of insurgents led by Guerrero agreed to the plan and the whole army entered Mexico city. A little later when a new viceroy Juan O'Donaju, sent by the Cortes, arrived, he found no soldiers to assist him. So he signed a treaty, for which the Cortes had given him authority, acknowledging the independence of Mexico. It is interesting to note that in this treaty of Córdova, signed in August, 1821, occurs the first instance of the use of the name Mexico to designate officially the whole country which the Spaniards from the time of its discovery had called Nueva España.

For a few months Mexico was governed by the junta presided over by Iturbide. Then in February of 1822, the latter by a coup d'état caused himself to be proclaimed Emperor of Mexico. The costly magnificence with which he set up his court and his various pretensions made him ridiculous and distrusted. It was not long before he was deposed and banished. The Mexican Congress established a federal republic of which Guadelupe Victoria, one of the leaders in Morelos' army, was elected the first president. A sentence of death was passed on Iturbide in case he should return to Mexico. The latter, apparently unaware of this decree, did land there in July, 1824, and in three days was shot without a trial.

About Iturbide and his fortunes clusters most of the

revolutionary literature. Typical is the vigorous ode *Al 16 de Septiembre de 1821*, by Andrés Quintana Roo (1787–1851). First it presents a picture of the Iberian triumph over the Mexicans led by Hidalgo. His example fires the noble soul of Morelos, but in spite of his efforts to achieve liberty for the Mexicans, fortune reserves the supreme glory for Iturbide, "whose name surpasses that of the others as much as the brilliance of the moon out-shines the numberless stars in the firmament."

Quintana Roo was a native of Yucatan and the Mexicans have commemorated his years of service to his country by naming a territory in that peninsula after him. In the same way states have been named for Hidalgo, More-los, and Guerrero. After Iturbide's fall, Quintana Roo edited various political journals in which he expressed in vigorous prose a high-minded position on public affairs. Verses by the Cuban poet Heredia exist praising Quintana Roo for daring to oppose certain arbitrary and tyrannical acts of the government. Quintana Roo's verses are well written for he was a student of prosody and published critical articles concerning it.

Another native of Yucatan, Wenceslao Alpuche (1804–41), struck in his odes a strongly patriotic note with almost epic intonation. His most famous one, *A Hidalgo*, reviews the bloody course of Mexican history; then after an apostrophe to liberty, Alpuche declares that Hidalgo, like Leonidas and Washington, was inspired by her. Realistically portraying Hidalgo's hour of death, he urges Mexicans to look on the hero's remains as he prophesies that from the ground fertilized by Hidalgo's blood will spring avengers. In a similar strain Alpuche

sang the death of Morelos, in his ode *Al Suplicio de Morelos*.

Morelos' most famous exploit, the escape from the
siege of Cuautla, was immortalized by Francisco Manuel
Sánchez de Tagle (1782–1847), who described it in his
poem *Romance Heróico de la Salida de Morelos de Cuautla*.
Being a city man Sánchez de Tagle was more especially
enthusiastic over Iturbide in whose honor he indited
several poems. In a political capacity he was associated
with that leader, for he was one of those who composed
the Declaration of Independence of the year 1821. As a
poet Sánchez de Tagle was prolific and is considered the
principal representative of classicism in Mexico. After
his death there was published by his son a volume of his
verse, mainly love lyrics and religious pieces in classical
style. One of his earliest poems in point of time consists
of verses of occasion to celebrate the erection in Mexico
of a statue of Carlos IV. The poet owed much to the
fact that he attracted the attention of the viceroy who
appointed him a professor in the university. The prominence of such a man in the revolution of 1820 shows how
different was its character from that of previous revolutionary efforts.

The admiration of Iturbide in its extreme form is revealed in the poems of Anastasio de Ochoa y Acuña
(1783–1833). His earliest writings were satiric and festive
lines and translations, especially of dramas. In 1813 was
produced his original drama *Don Alfonso*. The best of
his patriotic odes is *El Grito de Independencia*. In this
he compares Spanish tyranny to a cloud such as a shepherd
sees approaching with the destructive force of a whirl-

wind about to overwhelm his humble home. Like the
tempest are the misfortunes of Mexico where only a handful of patriots are fighting for liberty. But while Iturbide
lives there is hope, and in anticipation of his ultimate
success, the poet congratulates "the American Mars" on
his good fortune and triumph.

But Iturbide's assumption of the crown as Emperor of
Mexico aroused indignation and denunciation such as
was expressed in the ode *A Iturbide en su Coronación* by
Francisco Ortega (1793–1849). This ode deserves a
place as a classic invective against ambition. The poet
urges Iturbide to listen to the voice of patriotism and
turn aside from false ambition. His true glory lies in
having achieved the independence of a people and not
in occupying a throne. Ortega enjoyed the distinction
of having written an allegorical melodrama, *México
Libre*, which was produced as a part of the official celebration of the oaths of independence on October 27th, 1821.
In allegorical style Ortega wrote much other patriotic
verse, in which Liberty assisted by Mars and Pallas favors
America while Despotism and Discord are put to rout.
In the allegorical vein Ortega's longest poem is *La Venida
del Espíritu Santo*, to a large extent a paraphrase of the
first book of Milton's *Paradise Lost*, and yet worthy to
rank among the world's religious epics. The poem deals
with the opposition of Satan and his legions to the apostles.
The chief characters are Satan and St. Paul. The first
canto consists of a review of the forces of darkness in
which Moloch is represented by Huitzilopochtli, the war
god of the ancient Mexicans to whom their bloody human
sacrifices were made. Important episodes of the poem

are the triumph of St. Stephen, the conversion of St. Paul and the descent of the Holy Ghost upon the apostles, an event which Satan contemplates with scornful sneers.

One writer of prose who lived during the revolutionary period in Mexico deserves mention, José Joaquín Fernández de Lizardi (1774–1827). From 1812 to 1826, under the name of "El Pensador Mexicano," he was the champion pamphleteer of the revolution. In this capacity he defended the ecclesiastics who, stimulated by the example of Hidalgo, had supported the revolution by bearing arms. For his bold utterances he was thrown into prison by the viceroy Venegas in spite of that provision of the constitution of 1812 guaranteeing the liberty of the press. However, he was soon released. Then he gave forth his ideas upon the condition of Mexico and its needs by publishing in 1816 a picaresque novel, *El Periquillo Sarniento*.

This book, though written with a distinctly didactical purpose, is still read for the amusing character of the incidents. Like Gil Blas, the hero penetrates all classes of Mexican society, examining its virtues and vices, especially those which its author wishes to praise or flagellate. The title is a nickname, by explaining which the writer desires to discourage the habit of calling names. The hero's name Pedro had been turned by his schoolmates into Periquillo because he was sent to school dressed in a green jacket and yellow pantaloons, the colors of the plumage of the common Mexican parrot; and in order to distinguish this Pedro from another, the additional title Sarniento, derived from a malady which he suffered, was bestowed upon him. The practical result of his schooling at the hands of various ignorant teachers was to make him able to contend in sophistical argument. Beginning then his life career, he is, by turns, novice in a monastery, highwayman, jail-bird, barber and doctor.   In the course of his wanderings, he comes upon the corpse of a school friend hanging by the roadside, a warning to malefactors. The life of this friend, one of whose early adventures had been an attempt to seduce Pedro's sister, conveys the ordinary lesson of the bad end of the bad boy. Altogether the Mexican critic Altamirano considers this realistic novel to be "the most genuine representation of the period."

The "Pensador's" political writing becomes most interesting in *Las Conversaciones del Payo y del Sacristán*, in which are discussed with infinite irony and delightful jest "the advantages which have come to Mexico by the death of Iturbide."   These imaginary conversations issued between August and December, 1824, introducing various types of Mexican character and treating the serious problems which confronted society, are essential to any study of social conditions at that time.

Fernández de Lizardi published two other novels, *La Quijotita y su Prima*, 1819, and *Don Catrín de la Fachenda*, 1825, but in these the didactical motive has gained complete ascendancy for they are practically devoid of incident.   In the former a colonel instructs his daughter in the moral conduct of her life; the fact that such a preachment was widely read in several editions is perhaps illuminating in regard to the literary taste of the period. The title of the latter has contributed an epithet used in Mexico, to characterize the type of person represented by Don Catrín. A shorter book than either of these is

Noches tristes, in which the writer gives personal details of his imprisonment. Altogether "El Pensador Mexicano" is a name fondly remembered by his countrymen because it represents a typical personality of the period.

While revolution was setting Spanish America aflame, the island of Cuba became the place of refuge for loyalists. The immigration from Santo Domingo was the first to come. In 1795, the whole island had been ceded to the French, and immediately thereafter the negro insurrection raging in Haiti spread to Santo Domingo. In 1801, the negro leader Toussaint L'Ouverture captured the capital from which many of the leading families had already gone to Cuba. Among them were the parents of J. M. Heredia destined to be Cuba's greatest poet.

The loyalist immigrants contributed largely to the elements of culture in Cuba. An interest in literature among the men of Habana had led as early as 1790 to the establishment of a literary journal, *El Papel Periódico.* As the contributions to this paper were published anonymously it has been somewhat difficult to know much of their authors, but two names of poets surpassing the others have come down to posterity, Manuel de Zequeira y Arango (1760–1846) and Manuel Justo de Rubalcava (1768–1805).

De Zequeira rose to relatively high rank in the Spanish army and commanded the garrison of the fortress of Santa Marta in Nueva Granada when it was besieged by the colonial army. In private life he was a studious man whose influence and example was highly beneficial to Cuban letters. Of his poems, written in imitation of the classical style of the Spanish poets of the golden age, the

best is *La Batalla naval de Cortés en la Laguna de Mexico.*
This contains the striking description of the death of a
Spanish soldier, Pedro de la Barba, killed by the arrow of
a native. De Zequeira was also a graceful sonneteer,
but herein his work is not always distinguishable from
that of his friend De Rubalcava. So closely do their
peculiarities coincide that critics have been unable to
make certain which is the author of an admirable sonnet,
La Ilusión, in which all earthly glory is compared to the
fugacious glory of the dreamer. Though the sonnet has
been commonly assigned to Rubalcava, it first appeared
in the *Papel Periódico* over the pen name used by De
Zequeira. The latter wrote much religious verse also in
which is apparent the influence of the Mexican poet
Navarrete.

Such was the spirit of poetical production in Cuba
during the first twenty years of the nineteenth century
until there suddenly appeared a book of verse which thereafter became the inspiration of Cuban separatists. Its
author, José María Heredia (1803–39), has been called
by a Spaniard, "the compendium and epitome of all
enmity toward Spain." But Heredia regarded himself
as a Spaniard and refers in his verses to Spain as "tender
mother." As a partisan, however, of the liberals, who
supported in 1820 the revolution led by Rafael del Riego,
he wrote burning verses against "the oppressor of Iberia,"
and called Spain stupid because she consented to oppression and to the death of Riego. Heredia's language,
however, was later applicable to the political situation
in Cuba.

Heredia, moreover, was involved in the first attempt at

insurrection in Cuba, which occurred in 1823. He was a member of the society known as the "Soles de Bolívar," who plotted to obtain independence for Cuba through the assistance of Mexico and Colombia. Such a conspiracy of young hotheads in a society composed of loyalist refugees was predestined to failure. Besides, the relaxation of the Spanish commercial laws, incident to the political conditions of America, had brought great material prosperity to Cuba, and thereby an atmosphere not at all favorable to revolution.

But Heredia, though born in Cuba, had come to manhood in a more bracing moral environment. His father was a government official, who had acted as chief judge of the court in Caracas in the days when Venezuela was trembling under the tyranny of Monteverde. The elder Heredia felt such sympathy for the victims of official tyranny and in his capacity as magistrate showed such consideration for them that suspicion of complicity in the revolution fell on his own head. He was punished by being transferred to a lesser position in Mexico in which country he died in 1820. Of his father the poet wrote in a poem dedicated to his memory, "In your charge you took my education and never to others' hands entrusted my tender childhood. Love for all men, fear of God you inspired in me and hatred of atrocious tyranny."

After his father's death the young man went to Cuba to finish his studies in law and finally settled in the city of Matanzas as a practicing attorney. He took with him many of the poems which were to make him famous after their publication. Some of them probably circulated in manuscript and added fuel to the fires of revolt

which broke out in 1823. For his part Heredia was condemned by the audiencia of Cuba to perpetual banishment. He went to the United States, traveled about
there for a short time, then departed for Mexico where he
married, became a government official and lived there to
the end of his days. In 1836 he was permitted by the
Spanish authorities to return to Cuba for a brief visit of
two months, constantly harassed by annoying restrictions.
On account of the murmurs then circulating in the island
against the actions of the governor, the restrictions may
have been justifiable from the official point of view, but
in so far as they brought Heredia and his poetic utterances to the notice of Cubans they were unwise. Heredia
himself was far from thinking of inciting insurrection.
Suffering from ill health and a sort of moral dejection on
account of turbulent political conditions in Mexico, he
even gave expression to some thoughts which have been
widely published by Spaniards as a recantation of the
political beliefs which inspired his poems.

The first edition of his poems, printed in New York in
1825, contains practically all he ever wrote that people
care for. A comparison of it with the edition of Toluca,
1832, advertised to contain additional poems, shows that
the additions consist of a few occasional pieces, a philosophical dissertation in verse on immortality, and a
number of translations. In Mexico he first drew attention
to himself by writing for the papers and by the production
of certain tragedies largely adaptations from French,
the *Abufar* of Ducis, *Sila*, *Tiberio*, and *Los últimos Ro-
manos*. The tirades against tyranny which abound in
these dramas were quite to the taste of the Mexican public

and assisted materially in making the political fortune
of their author.

The New York edition has a preface in English which
cannot help exciting pathetic interest in the reader familiar with the circumstances. It is a sort of adver-
tisement designed perhaps to help along its sale, thus:
"The author has paid particular attention to the accents
to make these poems useful to Americans learning the
Spanish language. Nothing is better calculated to give
them a practical knowledge of the true pronunciation of
words than the habit of reading poetry. May they receive this little service of an exiled youth as an expression of gratitude for the asylum he has found in this happy
country."

Those poems of Heredia which are not political in character must be classed with that type of poetry more
noteworthy for its ideas than for its form. For that
reason they are susceptible of good translation into other
languages. At the same time his poems possess a subjective element revealing a passionate personality that
causes some critics to compare him with Byron and other
romantic poets. But there is nothing of the romantic
pose in Heredia's lines for his banishment had imbued
them with the note of sincerity. Heredia stands in personal touch with the elemental forces of nature in their
sublimest form. "Hurricane, hurricane, I feel thee coming," he cried; or to the sun, "I love thee, Sun: thou
knowest how joyfully I greet thee, when thou appearest
at the gates of the east." To the mighty falls of Niagara
he speaks in a familiar tone, "mighty torrent, hush thy
terrifying thunder; diminish a little the darkness that

surrounds thee; let me contemplate thy serene countenance and fill my soul with ardent enthusiasm."

Heredia's poems do not contain elaborate descriptions of nature. On the contrary he paints with a bold stroke, intent on producing a suitable background for the ideas which fill his soul. Take for example the poem *En el Teocalli de Cholula.* The poet seated in the ancient temple of the Aztecs watches the sun sink behind a volcano. Its snow-clad top seems to dissolve into a sea of gold. Darkness falls. The moon and the stars become visible. As the moon sinks behind the volcano, the shadow of the mountain, like a colossal ghost, strides across the plain till it envelops the poet and the whole world, though the vast form of the volcano is still outlined against the sky. The flight of time thus leaves no traces on this giant. Nevertheless the poet knows that according to the law of nature it must some day fall.

The flight of time seemed to be always present to Heredia's mind. The Aztec temple is now nothing but a desolate monument to the cruel pride of an extinct race. The majestic waters of Niagara run "like the dark torrent of centuries into eternity." It is such criticism of life, though commonplace at times, that gives Heredia's poetry a tinge of melancholy. Therein he resembles our own poet, William Cullen Bryant. And to Bryant we fortunately owe metrical translations of two of Heredia's greatest poems, the ode to the Hurricane and the ode on Niagara to which Heredia owes the appellation bestowed on him of "Singer of Niagara." The latter runs thus:

My lyre! Give me my lyre! My bosom feels
The glow of inspiration. O, how long

Have I been left in darkness, since this light
Last visited my brow! Niagara!
Thou with thy rushing waters dost restore
The heavenly gift that sorrow took away.

Tremendous torrent! for an instant hush
The terrors of thy voice, and cast aside
Those wide-involving shadows, that my eyes
May see the fearful beauty of thy face!
I am not all unworthy of thy sight,
For from my very boyhood have I loved,
Shunning the meaner track of common minds,
To look on Nature in her loftier moods.
At the fierce rushing of the hurricane,
At the near bursting of the thunderbolt,
I have been touched with joy; and when the sea
Lashed by the wind hath rocked my bark, and showed
Its yawning caves beneath me, I have loved
Its dangers and the wrath of elements.
But never yet the madness of the sea
Hath moved me as thy grandeur moves me now.

Thou flowest on in quiet, till thy waves
Grow broken 'midst the rocks; thy current then
Shoots onward like the irresistible course
Of Destiny. Ah, terribly they rage,—
The hoarse and rapid whirlpools there! My brain
Grows wild, my senses wander, as I gaze
Upon the hurrying waters, and my sight,
Vainly would follow, as toward the verge
Sweeps the wide torrent. Waves innumerable
Meet there and madden,—waves innumerable
Urge on and overtake the waves before,
And disappear in thunder and in foam.

They reach, they leap the barrier,—the abyss
Swallows insatiable the sinking waves.

A thousand rainbows arch them, and woods
Are deafened with the roar. The violent shock
Shatters to vapor the descending sheets.
A cloudy whirlwind fills the gulf, and heaves
The mighty pyramid of circling mist
To heaven. The solitary hunter near
Pauses with terror in the forest shades.

What seeks my restless eye? Why are not here,
About the jaws of this abyss, the palms—
Ah, the delicious palms,—that on the plains
Of my own native Cuba spring and spread
Their thickly foliaged summits to the sun,
And, in the breathings of the ocean air,
Wave soft beneath the heaven's unspotted blue?

But no, Niagara,—thy forest pines
Are fitter coronal for thee. The palm,
The effeminate myrtle, and frail rose may grow
In gardens, and give out their fragrance there,
Unmanning him who breathes it. Thine it is
To do a nobler office. Generous minds
Behold thee, and are moved, and learn to rise
Above earth's frivolous pleasures; they partake
Thy grandeur, at the utterance of thy name.

God of all truth! in other lands I've seen
Lying philosophers, blaspheming men,
Questioners of thy mysteries, that draw
Their fellows deep into impiety;
And therefore doth my spirit seek thy face
In earth's majestic solitudes. Even here
My heart doth open all itself to thee.
In this immensity of loneliness,
I feel thy hand upon me. To my ear
The eternal thunder of the cataract brings
Thy voice, and I am humbled as I hear.

Dread torrent, that with wonder and with fear
Dost overwhelm the soul of him that looks
Upon thee, and dost bear it from itself,—
Whence hast thou thy beginning? Who supplies,
Age after age, thy unexhausted springs?
What power hath ordered, that when all thy weight
Descends into the deep, the swollen waves
Rise not and roll to overwhelm the earth?

The Lord has opened his omnipotent hand,
Covered thy face with clouds, and given voice
To thy down-rushing waters; he hath girt
Thy terrible forehead with his radiant bow.
I see thy never-resting waters run,
And I bethink me how the tide of time
Sweeps to eternity. So pass of man—
Pass, like a noonday dream—the blossoming days
And he awakes to sorrow. I, alas!
Feel that my youth is withered, and my brow
Ploughed early with the lines of grief and care.

Never have I so deeply felt as now
The hopeless solitude, the abandonment,
The anguish of a loveless life. Alas!
How can the impassioned, the unfrozen heart
Be happy without love? I would that one
Beautiful, worthy to be loved and joined
In love with me, now shared my lonely walk
On this tremendous brink. 'Twere sweet to see
Her sweet face touched with paleness, and become
More beautiful from fear, and overspread
With a faint smile while clinging to my side.
Dreams,—dreams! I am an exile, and for me
There is no country and there is no love.

Hear, dread Niagara, my latest voice!
Yet a few years, and the cold earth shall close

> Over the bones of him who sings thee now
> Thus feelingly. Would that this, my humble verse,
> Might be, like thee, immortal! I, meanwhile,
> Cheerfully passing to the appointed rest,
> Might raise my radiant forehead in the clouds
> To listen to the echoes of my fame.

Even in the presence of the rushing waters Heredia yearns for love, an ever present desire with him. In the lines on his father's death he expresses the hope of finding consolation for his loss in "the arms of his beloved." In the matter of his beloved it is interesting to note the dedications of the two editions of his poems prepared by Heredia himself. In the edition of New York the honor of the first place is given to certain lines, "To a young lady who used to read my verses with pleasure." In the edition of Toluca these lines are replaced by a sonnet, "To my Wife," thus translated by James Kennedy.

> When yet was burning in my fervid veins
> The fieriness of youth, with many a tear
> Of grief, 'twas mine of all my feelings drear,
> To pour in song the passion and the pains;
> And now to thee I dedicate the strains,
> My wife, when love, from youth's illusions freer,
> In our pure hearts is glowing deep and clear,
> And calm serene for me the daylight gains.
> Thus lost on raging seas, for aid implores
> Of Heaven the unhappy mariner, the mark
> Of tempests bearing on him wild and dark;
> And on the altars when are gained the shores,
> Faithful to the deity he adores,
> He consecrates the relics of his bark.

The full intensity of Heredia's temperament is revealed

in the lines to the Hurricane. For some reason Bryant did not translate the last stanza of the poem, perhaps because it was too intense for the Puritan in him. It has been necessary then to add it in a prose form, because to Heredia this stanza was the climax to the rest. Though Bryant's translation is at times almost literal he paraphrased the opening cry, "Hurricane, hurricane, I feel thee coming."

> Lord of the winds! I feel thee nigh,
> I know thy breath in the burning sky!
> And I wait, with a thrill in every vein,
> For the coming of the hurricane!
>
> And lo! on the wing of the heavy gales,
> Through the boundless arch of heaven he sails;
> Silent and slow, and terribly strong,
> The mighty shadow is borne along,
> Like the dark eternity to come;
> While the world below, dismayed and dumb,
> Through the calm of the thick hot atmosphere,
> Looks up at its gloomy folds with fear.
>
> They darken fast; and the golden blaze
> Of the sun is quenched in the lurid haze,
> And he sends through the shade a funeral ray—
> A glare that is neither night nor day,
> A beam that touches, with hues of death,
> The clouds above and the earth beneath.
> To its covert glides the silent bird,
> While the hurricane's distant voice is heard
> Uplifted among the mountains round,
> And the forests hear and answer the sound.
>
> He is come! he is come! do ye not behold
> His ample robes on the wind unrolled?

Giant of air! we bid thee hail!—
How his gray skirts toss in the whirling gale;
How his huge and writhing arms are bent
To clasp the zone of the firmament,
And fold at length, in their dark embrace,
From mountain to mountain the visible space.

Darker—still darker! the whirlwinds bear
The dust of the plains to the middle air:
And hark to the crashing, long and loud,
Of the chariot of God in the thunder-cloud!
You may trace its path by the flashes that start
From the rapid wheels where'er they dart,
As the fire-bolts leap to the world below,
And flood the skies with a lurid glow.

What roar is that?—'tis the rain that breaks
In torrents away from the airy lakes,
Heavily poured on the shuddering ground,
And shedding a nameless horror round.
Ah! well-known woods, and mountains, and skies,
With the very clouds!—ye are lost to my eyes.

I seek ye vainly, and see in your place
The shadowy tempest that sweeps through space,
A whirling ocean that fills the wall
Of the crystal heaven, and buries all,
And I, cut off from the world, remain
Alone with the terrible hurricane.

Sublime tempest! As if filled with thy solemn inspiration,
I forget the vile and wretched world and raise my head
full of delight. Where is the coward soul that fears thy
roar? In thee I rise to the throne of the Lord; I
hear in the clouds the echo of his voice; I feel the
earth listen to him and tremble. Hot tears descend my
pale cheeks and trembling, I adore his lofty majesty.

The same fiery ardor is displayed in Heredia's political poems. Their chief sentiments are hatred of oppression and love of liberty. A series of sonnets on Riego, Rome, Cato, Napoleon, all express admiration for champions of human rights. Napoleon saved France from anarchy and made kings tremble; though he died abandoned on a lonely rock, his life exemplifies the fact that no oppression however strong is irresistible. Love of liberty is ever the poet's cry. In his earliest political composition, *La Estrella de Cuba*, written at the age of nineteen and probably circulated in manuscript among the conspirators of 1823, Heredia calls for sacrifice of this sort, "If the scaffold awaits me, upon its height my bleeding head will appear a monument of Spanish brutality."

When banished he indited an *Epístola a Emilia*, a gem of personal lyric verse. Homesick and longing for the "terrible sun" of Cuba, he wrote from the North: "I am free, but what cruel change! The winter's wind is roaring; upon its wings flies the piercing cold. The inert world suffers the tyranny of cruel winter. My ear hears not the voices of my friends but only the barbarous sounds of a foreign idiom. But it is not wearied by the insolent tyrant, nor the groan of the slave nor the crack of the whip which poisons the air of Cuba. At night when the light of the silent moon and the delicious perfume of the lemon invite to repose, a thousand thoughts of rage becloud my mind."

The political verse attains a climax in the closing lines of the *Himno del Desterrado:* "Cuba, Cuba, what life you gave me, sweet land of light and beauty! And am I to see thee again? How sternly the severity of my fate weighs on me to-day! Oppression threatens me with death in the fields where I was born. Cuba, at last thou shalt be free and pure as the air thou breathest, as the sparkling waves which thou dost see kissing the sand of thy shores. Though vile traitors serve him, the tyrant's wrath is vain, because not for naught between Cuba and Spain does the sea roll its billows."

Heredia's prophecy of September, 1825, was not fulfilled for nearly three-quarters of a century, but during that period his poems were a constant inspiration to Cuban patriotism. To this fact even the Spanish critic Menéndez y Pelayo testifies with bitterness in these words, "If his political activity does not equal that of other conspirators against Spain, because he took no part in an armed struggle, his literary influence was continuous and more effectual than any other because he surpassed all in talent."

As there is in Heredia something typical of Spanish Americans, his vague sensuality, his melancholia, his outbursts of hatred, his love of liberty, his poetry is doubly interesting. The ease with which he was able to express these different emotions made him indifferent at times to a classical finish in the form of his verse. In this he belonged to the romantic school. For an exact and comprehensive criticism of Heredia nobody has ever excelled that of the Spanish critic, Alberto Lista, who said after reading the first edition of his poems, "He is a great poet; the fire of his soul has passed into his verses and is transmitted to his readers."

Heredia must be classed with the revolutionary epoch though he stands alone among Cubans of that day. The Cuban struggle for independence was to fill the whole of the nineteenth century and therefore the whole of Cuban literature may be called revolutionary. On the other hand, in other Spanish-American countries the winning of independence was followed by a period of adjustment to new political conditions. As this adjustment varied with local conditions there sprang up local literatures which must be studied separately.

CHAPTER IV

ARGENTINA

AFTER separation from Spain the vast territory of the Argentine Republic, divided politically into provinces, was organized into a nationality by Bernardo Rivadavia. Under his dictatorship Buenos Aires became the capital of a centralized or unitarian republic. Against the supremacy of the city the provinces demanded a federal republic and rose in rebellion, fighting even among themselves. Moreover, it became necessary to assert Argentine sovereignty over the frontier province, now the independent republic of Uruguay, against the aggressions of the Portuguese from Brazil. The Uruguayans opposed an armed resistance to the claims of the Brazilians and were assisted by forces sent out from Buenos Aires. In the final battle at Ituzaingo, on February 20, 1827, the Brazilians were so decisively beaten that the question of sovereignty was settled, while a treaty between Argentina and Uruguay the next year conceded absolute independence to the latter.

An ode in celebration of this battle, *Al Triunfo de Ituzaingo*, is one of the best lyrical pieces of the Argentine poet Juan Cruz Varela (1794–1839). It is a long poem, relating rather minutely the course of the fight. In this respect it resembles the ballad chronicles which were inspired by the political events in Buenos Aires from the time of the bombardment of the city by the English. But

there is a swing to these verses of Varela's which puts him
poetically above his fellow balladists. Varela was not
only a journalistic champion of Rivadavia's administration but the poetic chronicler of all the occurrences of it,
writing odes on the foundation of the university, on the
hydraulic works ordered by the government, on the establishment of the philharmonic society. In spite of the
apparent dullness of such topics Varela infused them with
life. Especially praised is an ode on the liberty of the press,
for Varela was a fierce patriot. His fierceness reaches a
climax in an ode, *Al Incendio de Cangallo.* This was a
Peruvian village burned and razed by the Spaniards in
1822, an act which roused great indignation and is still
commemorated by the name of a street in Buenos Aires.
Varela called for "vengeance, pitiless vengeance, on the
Iberian tigers, the proud Spaniards, hateful race of the
execrated Attila." Such invective was as much to the liking of the author's contemporaries as it is unpleasant to
the Spaniards to-day.

The same hyperbolical and declamatory rhetoric made
popular two dramas by Varela, *Dido,* and *Argia,* written
for production before the Sociedad del Buen Gusto in
Buenos Aires. These were in some respects the most
original dramas produced through the influence of that
society for the promotion of the drama. In 1823 the
tirades in *Dido* created enthusiasm for their apt references
to the political situation. The same was true of *Argia*
a year later. This play was based on Alfieri's *Antigone,*
while *Dido* sometimes followed Virgil word for word. In
his later years Varela made a metrical version of the
Aeneid though only the first two books of the epic were

ever printed. Juan Cruz Varela deserves credit for his efforts in classic culture during the troublous times in which he lived.

The unitarian party to which Varela belonged was forced out of power and beaten in battle by the federalists under the leadership of Juan Manuel Rosas. This man, supported by the gauchos of the interior, finally succeeded in assuming absolute power. To his political opponents he was merciless. Calling them savages and confiscating their property for the benefit of his adherents, he organized a special body of police called the "Mazhorca" to hunt down and exterminate all unitarians. Many of those who escaped from his clutches into exile, since they were educated men, took up the fight against Rosas with pen as well as sword. For that reason Argentine literature until the latter's fall in 1852 is to a large extent a militant protest against that tyrant. Juan Cruz Varela's last poem, for example, rhetorically one of his best, *Al 25 de Mayo de 1838*, was directed against Rosas.

Before the worst days of Rosas' control there occurred an event of the first magnitude in the history of Spanish-American letters, the introduction of romanticism through the publication of Esteban Echeverría's poem *Elvira* in 1832. This date is noteworthy because it is the same year in which appeared the Duque de Rivas' *Moro espósito*, the first important production of Spanish romanticism. Argentina thus received directly the French type of romanticism whereas other countries absorbed the romantic spirit at second hand through the medium of Spanish works.

Nature in Argentina was to offer a fertile field for exploitation by romantic poets. Contemporary with Echeverría but dying too young to fulfill the promise of his early work was Florencio Balcarce (1815–39). His memory is kept alive by certain pieces through their evocation of national scenery and life. The song of the milkman, *El Lechero*, is fresh and natural. *El Cigarro* evoked the memory of the national hero San Martín then living in semi-exile in Europe. The poem depicts an old man smoking a cigar beneath the shade of an ombu tree. Philosophizing to his grandchildren, he finds that fame is like the ashes of his cigar, that old men are cast aside and despised like the butt of a cigar. There is something of the romantic spirit in Balcarce's poems and had he lived longer he might have been one of the ablest of Echeverría's disciples.

Esteban Echeverría (1805–51) at the age of twenty, went to Europe in search of educational advantages not to be found then in his native land. The study of literature appears to have been his chief occupation, the works of Shakespeare, Goethe and especially Byron. When in Bordeaux, a Swiss friend took him to see a representation of Schiller's *Kabale und Liebe*, which made a profound impression on his mind. Before his return to Buenos Aires, his interest in Byron's poetry led him to make a short visit to England in 1829. He arrived in Argentina, May, 1830. Warmly received there, he published a few gratulatory verses and then withdrew from public intercourse to work on a poem which was published in 1832, entitled *Elvira ó la novia del Plata*. The public was too violently agitated by politics to give much attention to this production, but his next volume of verse, *Los Consuelos*, made their author immediately popular.

Los Consuelos are short poems in the Byronic manner.
The romantic pose maintained throughout the collection
was new to readers in Argentina and delighted them.
The author explains the title by the words: "They solaced
my grief and have been my only consolation in days of
bitterness." The practice which he adopted from Byron
of heading each poem by a quotation gives an excellent
clue to their contents and character. For the entire collection he chose two lines from Auzías March which, after
quoting in the original Catalan, he gave in the Spanish
of Luis de León:

> Let no one see my writings who is not sad, or who at some
> time has not been sad.

From Byron he selected,

> Fare thee well! and if forever,
> Still forever, fare thee well!

to head the poem entitled *Lara ô la Partida.* The name
Lara was the poet's romantic disguise. Taken boldly
from Byron, it expressed the loneliness of heart that
characterized the original of the English poem. As Echeverría was hurt by the indifference of the public towards
his first volume, he withdrew from Buenos Aires to the
little village of Mercedes on the Rio Negro. The poem
Lara voices his adieu. After describing the departure
of the vessel, the poet is moved to sing because he "remembers the injuries of fate," he calls on hope and bids
good-by to love, but as his tears choke him, he is forced
to desist. The most original poem of the collection is,
El y Ella, a love dialogue which especially delighted the
young ladies of Buenos Aires. The form of this poem

departs from all classic standards as the strophes vary
in length from twenty-four lines to a single line of passionate utterance. The volume also contained several patriotic appeals which expressed the feelings of the public
at the moment and helped to arouse enthusiasm.

The success of this volume encouraged Echeverría to
bring out in 1837, *Las Rimas*. Besides short pieces it
contained a long poem, *La Cautiva*, which put into practice a doctrine previously expressed by the author, in a
note to *Los Consuelos*. Poetry, he declared, does not
enjoy in America the influence which it possesses in
Europe. "If it wishes to gain influence, it must have an
original character of its own, reflecting the colors of the
physical nature which surrounds us and be the most
elevated expression of our predominant ideas and of the
sentiments and passions which spring from the shock of
our social interests. Only thus, free from the bonds of
all foreign influence, will our poetry come to be as sublime as the Andes; strange, beautiful and varied as the
fertile earth, which produces it."

As a preface to *La Cautiva*, he wrote: "The main purpose of the author has been to paint a few outlines of the
poetical character of the desert; and in order not to reduce
his work to a mere description, he has placed in the vast
solitude of the pampa two ideal beings, or two souls
united by the double bond of love and misfortune. The
desert is our richest patrimony and we ought to try and
draw from its breast not only wealth for our well-being,
but also poetry for our moral pleasure and the encouragement of our literature." Thus Echeverría first expressed
a doctrine which Spanish Americans have generally felt

to be true and according to which, consciously or otherwise, they have produced in literature, whatever is really valuable.

The first scene of *La Cautiva* is laid in the camp of a band of Indians after their raid on a village of whites. Exhausted by their exertions and the drunken orgies of celebration, the savages fall asleep. The silence of the Argentine pampa creeps upon them and their captives. Most important of these is Brian, formerly a scourge of the Indians, now bound between two lances awaiting death by torture. His wife Maria, however, is not bound; for upon her the Indian cacique, Loucoi, had cast lustful glances. When sleep furnishes the opportunity, Maria plunges a dagger into Loucoi's heart. In the same way marking a bloody path through the band of sleeping savages, she reaches the spot where her husband is bound, cuts him loose and together they escape. But they are hardly gone before a band of horsemen surprise the camp, slay the Indians and free the captives; though to their sorrow, the rescuers are unable to find Brian and his wife. In the meantime the latter are straining limbs and nerves to put a great distance between them and their former captors. Brian, however, travels with difficulty on account of his wounds. As they are resting, they see a cloud of smoke swiftly approaching. The pampa is afire. Brian, scarcely able to stir, begs his wife to save herself; but she sturdily places her husband on her back, makes her way to the neighboring river, and swims to safety on the opposite bank. Such heroism, nevertheless, is vain for on the following day Brian is attacked by fever and dies. Maria sets out alone to cross the pampa, and soon meets a detachment of soldiers, who were searching for her and Brian. Of them she inquires deliriously for her son and though she herself had related his murder to her husband, she expires when the soldiers tell her that her son had been killed.

The literary significance of *La Cautiva* lies in its revolutionary departure in form from the classic Spanish ideal and the author's success in carrying out his purpose. The Argentine critic, J. M. Gutierrez, writes that "*La Cautiva* is a masterpiece, whose perspectives give the most complete idea of the sunburnt immensity of the pampa."

Echeverría, taking advantage of the prestige which his verses had brought him, plunged boldly into politics by launching a sort of secret society, "La Asociación de Mayo," in June, 1837, which had for its object to bring about the fall of Rosas. The main principles of the society were expounded by Echeverría in a pamphlet entitled *El Dogma socialista*. Despite the name the tone of the ideas was not so much socialistic as democratic after the manner of contemporary French writings.

When news of this secret society reached Rosas' ears, the dictator lost little time in sending his agents to suppress it. Echeverría took refuge in the country at some distance from the city. Then occurred a rising against Rosas among the landed proprietors in the south of the province of Buenos Aires. Being few in number they could not long withstand his soldiers though those who escaped after the battle which they fought took ship for Montevideo where they joined the forces of General Lavalle. The heroism of the unequal conflict inspired

Echeverría to compose a poem *La Insurrección del sud de la Provincia de Buenos Aires en 1839*. The poem is merely a rhymed chronicle of events. Whatever embellishments the author may have intended to make had to be omitted because he left the manuscript behind when the approach of Rosas' men caused his hasty flight. It was ten years before the manuscript was recovered and the poem published. Echeverría's second place of refuge was Montevideo.

In that city he was merely one of many refugees. As he suffered severely from an affection of the heart he was unable to take physical part in the armies that set out against Rosas. Moreover, he appeared to his fellows as a visionary. His pen, however, was not idle. Among his first poems were two of patriotic character published under the title of *Cantos a Mayo*. Then borrowing from Byron's *Parisina* the principal episode, that of the wronged husband who learns from his wife's lips as she talks in her sleep the story of her adultery and nevertheless flees from the room without carrying into effect his impulse to kill, Echeverría adapted it to an Argentine environment. First called *La Guitarra*, the poem was afterwards named from the guilty lady *Celia*. A very long continuation or sequel of this poem in eleven cantos and eleven thousand lines was published after the poet's death with the title *El Ángel caído*. Its literary value is correctly characterized by Menéndez y Pelayo thus:—"It is not the fall of an angel but the fall of a poet." The theme is a presentation of Don Juan in Argentine society, but he is not a person for he has become an abstraction expressing the author's moral and political ideas.

Better and more interesting at least in its descriptive part is another long poem, *Avellaneda*, intended to celebrate the heroism of a man by that name who died in the struggle against Rosas. The scene is laid in the province of Tucumán. In depicting its natural beauties Echeverría again demonstrated his principles concerning the Americanization of literature. The political element of the poem is of course less attractive.

These two peculiarities dominate all Argentine literature, and as Echeverría put them forth as a sort of theory of æsthetics, it may be said that his influence has prevailed during most of the century. The Americanization of literature which he advocated in a note to the *Cautiva* had a long and varied development in Argentina and found in other countries at the advent of naturalism a responsive echo. And his conception of poetry as a moral or civilizing agent became the literary creed of later romanticists.

The Argentines who fled from the tyranny of Rosas may be roughly divided into two groups, those who found refuge in Chile and those who preferred Montevideo. The story of the literary activities of the former in Chile on account of their undeniable influence in that country belongs with the history of Chilean literature. The exiles had to earn a precarious living by their pens, but they were personally more secure than their compatriots in Uruguay. The latter remained in the thick of the fight where a sudden shift of fortune would have thrown them into Rosas' hands. For nine years his army and fleet maintained a siege of Montevideo from 1841 to 1850. In the latter year General Urquiza deserting the tyrant brought his forces to join the league against him. In 1852 occurred the battle of Monte Caseros which terminated Rosas' power.

During the period of the great siege Montevideo was the center of Argentine letters, and their main theme anathema of Rosas. The foremost wielder of political invective was José Mármol (1817-71). At the age of twenty he found himself in prison as a conspirator. On the walls of his cell he scribbled in a quatrain his first denunciation of the tyrant in which he declared that the "barbarian" could never put shackles on his mind. The quatrain became Mármol's favorite vehicle of expression for his passionate hate. The sincerity, the variety, and the intensity of his quatrains rendered them famous. Making Rosas second only to Satan in his capacity for evil, they depict him more bloodstained than Attila or Nero, bloodguiltier than the Atridæ, bloodthirstier than a ravening tiger.

For the class of readers that prefer facts to objurgation Mármol prepared *Amalia*, in form supposedly a historical novel after the manner of Walter Scott, but more exactly a detailed account of Rosas' crimes so presented as to show the moral degradation of Buenos Aires. Many episodes are introduced solely for this purpose. For example, Rosas demonstrates to the crowd his democratic ideals by compelling his daughter to receive the kisses of a rum-crazed negro. The description of the state ball gives an opportunity to reveal the character of the persons who form Rosas' immediate entourage, their base flattery, the vulgar conversation of the ladies. The narrative part of the story concerns principally the acts of a Daniel

Bello, himself opposed to Rosas but protected in his operations because he is the son of one of Rosas' adherents. Though carrying on various intrigues and acting as a spy for those who are plotting in Montevideo for an uprising, Daniel remains unsuspected. When his friend Eduardo Belgrano ventures into Buenos Aires on a mission, Daniel is able to save his life even after Eduardo has been severely wounded and left for dead by the police by concealing him in Amalia's house. She is Daniel's cousin. She takes so much interest in the patient that she falls in love with him. The book ends with a description of their wedding night. Its festivities are interrupted by the police who break in for the purpose of arresting Eduardo and who kill him.

The novel *Amalia* met with a large sale in Europe. Menéndez y Pelayo explains this fact in his criticism. After pointing out that the story is so strange as to be unreal, that one involuntarily asks how such a social condition could endure so long, he says, "The interest of the narration is very great and one drops the book reluctantly."

Mármol further utilized his experiences and sensations as an exile in composing a long poem, *El Peregrino*. It is not complete, but many of the fragments possess great lyrical beauty. The main idea of the poem is that of a Childe Harold in South America. With descriptive passages concerning the clouds, the tropical sunset, the beauties of America, Mármol mingles the expression of his feelings, his love for his wife, his religious faith, his grief at the condition of his native land, the joy of loving even in the midst of grief.

The drama also tempted Mârmol. Little praise is accorded, however, to the two dramas which he wrote, *El Cruzado* and *El Poeta*. The latter deals with the love affairs of Carlos and Maria. Carlos, being a poet, is poor and therefore turned away from Maria by her father. Nevertheless the lovers continue to communicate even after Carlos is thrown into prison for writing political articles against the government. When Maria learns that Carlos is to be exiled, she prevails on her father to use his influence to secure the poet's release. In return she promises to marry Don Enrique. The fifth act of the play opens with the wedding ceremony. After the vows have been pronounced, Carlos appears at the house and gains entrance to Maria's room, where he succeeds in calling her for an interview. Reproached by her lover for inconstancy, she tells him that she has taken poison. Then Carlos obtains some of the same poison and swallows it. She dies in his embrace, but Carlos lives long enough to hurl curses at the unhappy father.

Another Argentine exile and knight of the pen in the struggle against Rosas was José Rivera Indarte (1814–45). At the early age of twenty-one, he suffered incarceration for the expression of his opinions. While in prison the reading of the Bible and Dante determined the style of his poems which he began to write then. After his release he took ship for North America. During the voyage he fell sick with an attack of smallpox. Being isolated and neglected, it was a marvel that he lived to reach Salem, Massachusetts. When news came to him of the emigration of his friends to Montevideo he set sail for that port where he began to write for *El Nacional*. His attack on

Rosas developed the thesis that it would be a saintly
action to kill the tyrant. His articles being largely descriptive of cruel deeds were published in book form under
the title *Rosas y sus Opositores* and had great influence
in shaping foreign public opinion. His poems, published
after his untimely death, from consumption contracted
during the shattered state of his health, contain some
political satires in the style of Mármol but without the
latter's force. His patriotic hymns of the Argentine emi-
grants and to Lavalle are more convincing. In his ode
on the battle of Caaguazu he introduced an apparition of
General Belgrano similar to the apparition of the Inca
in Olmedo's famous ode. But many of his poems are
Biblical paraphrases or imitations collected under the
title of *Melodias hebraicas*, which, however, are rather
prosaic without poetic fire.

Far better as poetry were the verses of Claudio Mamerto
Cuenca (1812–52), killed at the battle of Monte-Caseros
where Rosas was overthrown. He was a surgeon whom
circumstances had compelled to remain in Buenos Aires
as well as later to serve with the tyrant's army. His
reputation among the patriots, however, was saved by
the verses penned before the battle and found on his
body. After bitter denunciation they declared that the
hour of Rosas' purging had arrived. Cuenca's literary
remains were published in three volumes under the title
of *Delirios del Corazón*. Beside many lyrical pieces of
considerable inspiration he was the author of *Don Tadeo*,
a comedy of manners in five acts and a drama, *Muza*.

In the army that defeated Rosas there commanded the
artillery a young man of thirty, Bartolomé Mitre (1821–

1906), who afterwards proved himself to possess one of the strongest and sanest intellects in Argentina. A captain at the age of seventeen in the first siege of Montevideo, he rose rapidly in rank. The year 1848, however, found him in Chile where he showed that he could wield a pen as well as a sword by editing the *Mercurio de Valparaiso*. Among his companions in Montevideo he was known also as a poet.

What Echeverría said of Mitre's verses in 1846 is interesting: "His muse is distinguished among his contemporaries by the manly frankness of his sentiments and a certain martial quality." Now listen to Mitre's own comment when editing his poems in later days: "I love my verses because they reflect some of those intense sorrows and some of those solemn moments of the revolution against the tyrant Rosas. I have another reason for hating Rosas and the publication of these rhymes is my revenge. On account of him I have had to bear arms, travel the country, become a politician, and plunge into the stormy course of revolutions without being able to follow my literary vocation."

Mitre's poems were nearly all written before 1846. They possess high literary and lyrical qualities. In the elegies on the deaths of certain individuals, as General Lavalle, who had fallen in the civil war, there is a display of real feeling which surpasses that of his contemporaries. One of his anti-Rosas pieces became a popular song. The title *Inválido* refers to the old veteran who recites the story of his services to the country before begging "una limosna por Dios." The last stanza is the poet's own plaint in this wise:

La República Argentina
Bajo el yugo de un tirano
Pide al mundo americano
Una limosna por Dios!

One section of Mitre's *Rimas* is devoted to *Armonías de la Pampa*. Therein he shows himself a disciple of Echeverría by seeking inspiration in nature, or national customs. *El Ombú en medio de la Pampa* reveals a rare love for trees. *El Pato* describes a gaucho game by that name. In fact he is one of the first to attempt a poetical treatment of the Argentine gaucho by telling the legend of the famous Santos Vega. Again he sings *El Caballo del Gaucho* with all the enthusiasm and love for horses which he himself undoubtedly felt.

His reason for ceasing to write poems is interesting. He says: "At twenty years of age, I dreamed of immortal renown; the laurels of Homer robbed me of sleep. Soon I understood that I could not even aspire to live in the memory of more than one generation as a poet nor was our society sufficiently mature to produce a poet laureate."

Politics occupied Mitre after the return to Buenos Aires. In the fight of the city against the confederation in 1861, he led the city's military forces. Being successful he was proclaimed dictator of the new federation of which Buenos Aires became the undisputed seat of the government. To his wisdom and moderation was due the fact that the old bitter differences between the city and the provinces lapsed to the point of disappearance. In 1865 he led the Argentine forces in the war against Solano Lopez, dictator of Paraguay. In 1868 his term as president came to an end, and D. F. Sarmiento was quietly elected and inaugurated. Though Mitre was twice again a candidate for the presidency and leader of insurgent forces, his main business in life was literary.

In 1869 Mitre founded *La Nación*, to-day one of the leading newspapers in the country. His *Historia de Belgrano*, originally published in 1858, he improved and brought out in new editions. His monumental work, however, was *La Historia de San Martín*, printed in 1888. It was such a history as one great soldier could write of another.

During Mitre's administration as president there was much literary activity in Buenos Aires. Three literary journals, *La Revista argentina*, *El Correo del Domingo*, and *La Revista de Buenos Aires*, flourished. The last directed by Vicente G. Quesada and Miguel Navarro Viola was the official organ of an influential literary society, the Circulo literario, among whose members were numbered nearly everybody of prominence in the city. The study of Argentine history absorbed much of their attention, and occupied more than half the pages of the review.

A contributor was Luis L. Domínguez (1819–98), whose historical studies were later printed as *Historia argentina*, covering the period from the discovery of America to the beginning of the revolution against Spain. Among his fellow exiles in Montevideo he made himself remarked for his verses, especially those which he presented at the famous literary contest of 1841. In verses of a romantic type he quite caught the spirit of the master Echeverría. And a descriptive poem of his, *El Ombú*, has remained a classic of Argentine poetry. About that shade tree Domínguez made the whole of Argentine life revolve. The opening stanza of the poem, perhaps little more than a jingle, is known by heart by every school child.

> Cada comarca en la tierra
> Tiene un rasgo prominente:
> El Brasil su sol ardiente,
> Minas de plata el Peru,
> Montevideo su cerro,
> Buenos Aires, patria hermosa,
> Tiene su pampa grandiosa;
> La pampa tiene el Ombú.

Domínguez, during Mitre's administration, held important governmental positions and later rose to prominence in the diplomatic service of his country.

Another historical writer of the same group was Vicente Fidel López (1815–1903), son of the author of the Argentine national hymn. His *Manual de Historia argentina* became the standard text-book for schools. His place of refuge from the tyranny of Rosas was Chile where he was one of the Argentine journalists so influential in the literary history of that country. There he collected the material for some historical novels which were numbered among the first of the kind to be written by Argentines.

At one time a fellow exile with López in Chile was Juan Bautista Alberdi (1810–84), a most voluminous and influential Argentine writer. When a youth of fifteen he was given one of the public scholarships at the Colegio de Ciencias morales founded by Rivadavia whose foresight recognized the value of education in a democracy. Being a member of the Asociación de Mayo in 1837 he was obliged to seek safety from Rosas by flight. In Montevideo he completed his studies for the doctorate of law. At the same time he was active in journalistic work by writing humorous descriptive articles of manners and by contributing to the comic sheet, illustrated by caricatures, *Muera Rosas*, one of the many forms of attack on the tyrant. In 1843 Alberdi went to Europe on a ship named the "Eden" and in fantastic prose wrote out impressions of the voyage which he proudly published as a poem with the same name. But his enduring reputation is due to a critical examination of Argentine history and the suggestions for a suitable form of government for the country contained in his *Bases para la Organización de la República Argentina.*

This book was written in Chile after his return from Europe while the final campaign against Rosas was being waged by General Urquiza. When a congress met after Rosas' overthrow for the purpose of preparing a constitution for the republic, the *Bases* directed the otherwise conflicting and vague ideas of its members along logical lines so that Alberdi's suggestions became to all intents the constitution of the Argentine republic. A curious synchronism of events has been noted herewith. In May, 1851, General Urquiza declared his revolution against Rosas and began to prepare his campaign. In May, 1852, Alberdi's book came from the press. In May, 1853, the constitutional convention voted the constitution. The foreign reader should remember that May is the glorious month of Argentine history, for the twenty-fifth is the national holiday.

Argentina's indebtedness to Alberdi was recognized

two years later by a decree of the government to deposit in the national archives certain of his writings signed with his autograph and to print at public expense an edition of his works. Alberdi was entrusted with important diplomatic missions in Europe, but he did not always meet the views of his compatriots respecting their foreign policy. His later years were spent for the most part in Europe in the diligent production of political and economic writings.

Among the expatriated Argentines the one who became the most thorough man of letters was Juan María Gutiérrez (1809–78). With Echeverría and Alberdi he was active in the Asociación de Mayo and suffered three months' imprisonment in Rosas' jails before going into exile. Gutiérrez was initiated by Echeverría into his literary as well as his political ideals, for within a year after the publication of *La Cautiva*, Gutiérrez wrote *Los Amores del Payador*, a long poem closely following the master's doctrine of the Americanization of literature of which he remained an ardent advocate. In Montevideo in 1841, Gutiérrez distinguished himself by winning the first prize in a literary contest by an ode, *La Revolución de Mayo*. It is praised by Menéndez y Pelayo because it "departs greatly from the current vulgarity of the patriotic odes," though at the same time the Spanish critic is very impatient with the poet for his anti-Spanish expressions. Refinement and good taste, however, are the marks of Gutiérrez' poems.

In 1846 Gutiérrez published a collection of the poems written by Spanish Americans with the title of *América Poética*. Its purpose of attracting the attention of Europeans undoubtedly succeeded.   In the matter of taste in selection subsequent collections have not excelled it.

Gutiérrez passed a part of his period of exile in Chile and Peru where he materially broadened his knowledge of literature.   In Chile, he was one of the group of Argentine exiles who were prominent in writing for the newspapers.

After the fall of Rosas, Gutiérrez participated in politics.   He was a prominent member of the constitutional convention of 1853.   And as minister of foreign affairs he negotiated an important treaty with Spain.   Recognition of Gutiérrez' scholarship led to his appointment as rector of the University of Buenos Aires, a post which he held for many years.

Gutiérrez' interest in literary studies and his contributions to the *Revista de Buenos Aires* made it one of the most important reviews in America.   Afterwards printed in book form his *Bibliografía de la primera Imprenta de Buenos Aires* and the *Estudios biográficos y críticos sobre algunos Poetas anteriores al Siglo XIX* made his name widely known among scholars.   The presentation of a copy of the latter to George Ticknor was the origin of some interesting correspondence between the two men. To the end of his life Gutiérrez encouraged the production of literature, as is evident by the many introductions usually enthusiastic in tone which he wrote to accompany the volumes of younger men.   From 1871 to 1877 he conducted with V. F. López the *Revista del Río de la Plata* whose pages were the medium of publication for their literary and historical studies.

Among the enemies of Rosas the man who most nearly

approached positive genius was Domingo Faustino Sarmiento (1811–88). This fact is partly recognized in the epithet, "loco Sarmiento," by which Rosas' official journal in Buenos Aires was accustomed to refer to him. His individuality was as uncommon as his intelligence. From almost absolute indigence he rose by personal endeavor to be president of the Argentine Republic. His schooling was limited to a few years in a primary school, but he utilized every means falling to his command to extend his education. One of the books which came into his possession about the age of sixteen was the autobiography of Benjamin Franklin who thereafter became his model.

The vicissitudes of his career began at about the same age. Having been summoned to attend military drill by the governor of his province, he refused and soon thereafter joined an uprising against the party in power. As the result of this act, after barely escaping with his life, he found himself an exile in Chile.

The peculiarity of Sarmiento's politics resided in the fact that he was a provincial partisan of the citizens of Buenos Aires who were demanding a strongly centralized government with the city at the head. In fact after the return from his first exile, he became a member of a branch of Echeverría's Asociación de Mayo. On the other hand Rosas represented the federalistic theory which accorded practical autonomy to the provinces, each ruled by a governor. Though nominally appointed by the government at Buenos Aires, these governors were local political bosses or caudillos, who like bandit chieftains were able by personal strength to maintain their positions. Consequently risings in the provinces though theoretically in support of the centralizing tendencies of the unitarian party were really directed against the local caudillo. The results of such fights were usually decisive, because the defeated were slaughtered or driven into exile. Sarmiento belonged in the province of San Juan, situated just below the Andes mountains through whose passes he more than once journeyed into safety in Chile.

The full story of Sarmiento's participation in the fighting in his own country and his efforts to earn a living in Chile is needless here. In regard to the latter it is sufficient to say that teaching school and writing for the papers were the most important at the time and in their results on his subsequent life. His readiness to enter into a controversy and the biting character of his clever satire made him many enemies. But a Chilean politician, Manuel Montt, afterwards president of Chile, not only made use of his brilliant journalistic ability but also stuck by Sarmiento through thick and thin. Sarmiento's rôle, in the outburst of literary activity, which followed his criticism of Andrés Bello's poem on *El Incendio de la Compañia* is elsewhere discussed.[1]

This preceded the establishment of the University of Chile of which Bello was appointed the first rector, while Sarmiento was given a place in the faculty of philosophy and humanities. At the first session of the faculty, he read a paper proposing certain changes in spelling Spanish which were later adopted. Partly to Sarmiento's initiative as well as to Bello's scholarship is due the fact that, of all countries where Spanish is spoken, Chile has the credit of

[1] See page 198.

introducing reforms in orthography. Sarmiento also interested himself in the introduction in the primary schools of improved methods of teaching children how to read. And at the instance of Montt he was made the principal of the newly established normal school. By the year 1845, however, the political situation claimed all his time for the editing of *El Progreso* in support of his patron Montt. Then appeared as daily articles the substance of the book to which Sarmiento chiefly owes his literary fame, *Facundo o la Civilización y la Barbarie.*

This book, nominally the biography of Facundo Quiroga, the caudillo lieutenant of Rosas, performs for the latter's regime the same damnatory service as Mármol's verses. Perhaps it was even more widely known. As the articles were promptly reprinted in Montevideo, it is not impossible that they suggested to Mármol his treatment of Rosas in the celebrated novel *Amalia* published five or six years later. Facundo Quiroga had been active in Sarmiento's native province and it was to escape death at his hands that Sarmiento had first taken the road to Chile at the age of twenty. The tale of Quiroga's atrocities occupies only the central part of the book by way of illustration to the economic and political principles developed in the remainder. The opening chapters are devoted to a description of the Argentine country, both brilliant and masterful, and to the student of Argentine history indispensable. The concluding chapters give an exposition of Sarmiento's political ideas which undoubtedly assisted in raising him to the presidency of the republic.

The physical conditions of the Argentine, the isolation and primitive ignorance of the gaucho, his belief in force as the only means of overcoming the difficulties of life, his consequent contempt for a civilization based on intelligence, are the causes, according to Sarmiento, of social anarchy in that country. The gaucho thus typifies barbarism in strife with civilization exemplified by the city of Buenos Aires. Without the support of the local caudillos, such as Facundo Quiroga, a tyranny like that of Rosas would be impossible. But even Rosas face to face with the difficulties of government was obliged to practice unitarian principles, "though the label on the bottle said differently." The Argentine Republic without rivers and mountains to mark natural boundaries can "be only one and indivisible." So thought Sarmiento in 1845, but after wider experience from his travels in the United States he became a champion of the federal principle which finally prevailed in Argentina.

Sarmiento, believing that his book *Facundo* would open a way for him in Europe, desired to visit it. In this purpose he was assisted by his staunch friend Manuel Montt, who procured for him a commissionership ostensibly for the purpose of studying European schools with a view of finding possible reforms for Chilean schools. Throughout his European tour Sarmiento industriously made inspection of educational systems of which he published an interesting report, *De la Educación popular*. But from the point of view of literature his book published at the same time, *Viajes por Europa, Africa y América* is more important and interesting. The latter was widely reproduced in various journals. It consists of a series of brilliant pictures arranged to suit the political ideas of the writer but drawn with such clearness of detail that the

unbiased reader may examine them with pleasure. He
portrays France regenerated by its great revolution and
placed at the head of humanity; on the other hand, Spain
lies prostrate amid the artistic ruins of her former splendor; the future, however, belongs to the rising culture
of North America. The anti-Spanish character of this
book called forth a reply from a satirical writer, then
popular in Spain, Juan Martínez Villergas who attempted to counteract its effect by a pamphlet, *Sarmen-
ticido o a mal Sarmiento.* But putting aside the political reflections, Sarmiento's *Viajes* is of its kind good
literature.

After an absence of three years, Sarmiento returned to
Chile by way of North America and Cuba. Political
affairs in Argentina were beginning to look toward the
fall of Rosas. Sarmiento attacked him so vigorously in
the press, that Rosas called on the Chilean government to
forbid Sarmiento the right to continue his activity, a
request which was promptly refused. Sarmiento replied
by a pamphlet, discussing the form of government suitable
for the country after Rosas' fall. Sarmiento was plainly
endeavoring to make himself a central figure in any reconstruction of the government. To further this purpose he published, *Recuerdos de Provincia,* a series of
sketches and anecdotes about himself, his parents, relatives and friends. The student of literature must
recognize the lifelike quality of his characterization
equal in many respects to Addison's famous De Cov-
erley papers. To Sarmiento's numerous enemies, the
book seemed only another instance of the man's overwhelming vanity,—so great, according to the Chilean

Benjamin Vicuña Mackenna, that the whole pampa would not hold it.[1]

Accordingly when General José Urquiza, the caudillo of the province of Entre Rios, hitherto the strongest supporter of Rosas, raised the banner of revolt, Sarmiento joined his army. General Urquiza, however, after the victory at Monte Caseros, disappointed his followers by continuing on his own account the personal government of his predecessor. Sarmiento returned to Chile once more to engage in journalism. But his stay was short, for when Buenos Aires rebelled successfully against Urquiza, Sarmiento came again to the city. From 1855, he played a prominent part in politics. After the battle of Pavón where Mitre's defeat of Urquiza decided for all time the question of constitutional government for the Argentine, Sarmiento was sent to the outlying provinces as auditor general of the armies, a position which gave him great influence. It helped him to become governor of his native province of San Juan to which office he was elected in February, 1862. He became so arbitrary and independent that he worried the central government at Buenos Aires. President Mitre solved the difficulty by appointing him ambassador to Chile and later minister to the United States. While in the latter country in 1867 he was elected to the presidency of Argentina.

Sarmiento's administration was marked in the matter of progress by the completion of the railroad from Rosario to Córdoba, an event which was celebrated by an exposition in Córdoba. The President's journey thither was a continuous ovation because among the provincials, if

[1] "su vanidad no cabe en toda la Pampa."

not in Buenos Aires, he was popular. At his suggestion also a naval academy was founded and three vessels of war purchased. He caused to be put in effect the clause of the constitution calling for the establishment of a national Argentine Bank.

On the other hand, his administration was harassed by the outbreak in Entre Rios of two uprisings by the caudillo López Jordan who had assassinated the old leader General Urquiza. The second time Sarmiento proposed to deal with the outlaw in the manner followed in the United States at the time of Lincoln's assassination, namely, by putting a heavy price on the bandit's head. The proposition was rejected by the Congress and by public opinion on the ground that it was an inalienable right of a man of Spanish race to start a rebellion and therefore it would be wrong to treat him like a criminal. López Jordan replied to Sarmiento by hiring some Italian sailors to murder him, an attempt which happily failed. Sarmiento, on account of the rigidity of his character, was not popular, but his administration was certainly an era of progress.

Though Sarmiento retired from the presidency in 1874 he did not withdraw from public life. It is needless to follow his various activities here. It is sufficient to call attention to the fact that his interest in the cause of popular education was still predominant, and among other offices held by him he was the first national superintendent of Argentine schools, and effected many reforms. In recognition of the courtesies shown Sarmiento in the United States, especially in Boston, where he imbibed many of his ideas about schools from acquaintance with

Horace Mann, the Argentine government in 1913 presented that city with a statue of their great educator and former president.

The statue is also a symbol of the growth after his death of the appreciation by his countrymen of Sarmiento's services to his country. In his lifetime his advocacy of various North American ideas was resented and most of those whose adoption he forced were discarded. In the judgment of Paul Groussac, the able librarian of the National Library at Buenos Aires, Sarmiento is, in the Emersonian sense, "the representative man of the South American intellect"; and "the most genuine and enjoyable writer of South America, the rude and sincere colorist of his native plains."

Though the officially printed collection of Sarmiento's writings fill fifty volumes, his literary fame is based on those already mentioned. The characteristics of his style, its swift movement, his ability to select the striking detail or apt anecdote, may be partly illustrated by the following extract from the description of Argentina in the first part of *Facundo*.[1] Moreover, no better introduction could be given to a study of the development of the most original of all Spanish-American poetry, that pertaining to the gaucho.

There is another poetry which echoes over the solitary plains, the popular, natural, and irregular poetry of the gaucho. In 1840, Echeverría, then a young man, lived some months in the

---

[1] *Facundo* was translated by Mrs. Horace Mann and published under the title of *Life in the Argentine Republic in the Time of Tyrants*, Boston, 1868. The volume also contains other extracts from Sarmiento's writings, especially from the *Recuerdos de Provincia* dealing with his family.

country, where the fame of his verses upon the pampa had already preceded him; the gauchos surrounded him with respect and affection, and when a new-comer showed symptoms of the scorn he felt for the little minstrel, some one whispered, "He is a poet," and that word dispelled every prejudice.

It is well known that the guitar is the popular instrument of the Spanish race; it is also common in South America. The majo or troubadour is discoverable in the gaucho of the country, and in the townsman of the same class. The cielito, the dance of the pampas, is animated by the same spirit as the Spanish jaleo, the dance of Andalusia; the dancer makes castanets of his fingers; all his movements disclose the majo; the action of his shoulders, his gestures, all his ways, from that in which he puts on his hat, to his style of spitting through his teeth, all are of the pure Andalusian type.

The name of gaucho outlaw is not applied wholly as an uncomplimentary epithet. The law has been for many years in pursuit of him. His name is dreaded, spoken under the breath, but not in hate, and almost respectfully. He is a mysterious personage; his abode is the pampa; his lodgings are the thistle fields; he lives on partridges and hedgehogs, and whenever he is disposed to regale himself upon a tongue, he lassos a cow, throws her without assistance, kills her, takes his favorite morsel, and leaves the rest for the carrion birds. The gaucho outlaw will make his appearance in a place just left by soldiers, will talk in a friendly way with the admiring group of good gauchos around him; provide himself with tobacco, yerba mate, which makes a refreshing beverage, and if he discovers the soldiers, he mounts his horse quietly and directs his steps leisurely to the wilderness, not even deigning to look back. He is seldom pursued; that would be killing horses to no purpose, for the beast of the gaucho outlaw is a bay courser, as noted in his own way as his master. If he ever happens to fall unawares into the hands of the soldiers, he sets upon the densest masses of his assailants, and breaks through them, with the help of a few slashes left by his knife upon the faces or bodies of his opponents; and lying along the ridge of his horse's back to avoid the bullets sent after him, he hastens toward the wilderness, until having left his pursuers at a convenient distance, he pulls up and travels at his ease. The poets of the vicinity add this new exploit to the biography of the desert hero, and his renown flies through all the vast region around. Sometimes he appears before the scene of a rustic festival with a young woman whom he has carried off, and takes a place in the dance with his partner, goes through the figures of the cielito, and disappears, unnoticed. Another day he brings the girl he has seduced, to the house of her offended family, sets her down from his horse's croup, and reckless of the parents' curses by which he is followed, quietly betakes himself to his boundless abode.

And now we have the idealization of this life of resistance, civilization, barbarism, and danger. The gaucho Cantor corresponds to the singer, bard, or troubadour of the Middle Ages. The Cantor has no fixed abode; he lodges where night surprises him; his fortune consists in his verses and in his voice. Wherever the wild mazes of the cielito are threaded, wherever there is a glass of wine to drink, the Cantor has his place and his particular part in the festival. The Argentine gaucho only drinks when excited by music and verse, and every grocery has its guitar ready for the hands of the Cantor who perceives from afar where the help of his "gay science" is needed, by the group of horses about the door.

The Cantor intersperses his heroic songs with the tale of his own exploits. Unluckily his profession of Argentine bard does not shield him from the law. He can tell of a couple of stabs he has dealt, of one or two "misfortunes" (homicides) of his, and of some horse or girl he carried off.

To conclude, the original poetry of the minstrel is clumsy, monotonous, and irregular, when he resigns himself to the inspiration of the moment. It is occupied rather with narration than with the expression of feeling, and is replete with imagery relating to the open country, to the horse, and to the scenes of the wilderness, which makes it metaphorical and grandiose. When he is describing his own exploits or those of some renowned evil-doer, he resembles the Neapolitan improvisatore, his style

being unfettered, commonly prosaic, but occasionally rising to
the poetic level for some moments, to sink again into dull and
scarcely metrical recitation. The Cantor possesses, moreover,
a repertory of popular poems in octosyllabic lines variously
combined into stanzas of five lines, of ten, or of eight. Among
them are many compositions of merit which show some inspiration and feeling.

The character whom Sarmiento terms a 'cantor' was more
popularly known in Buenos Aires as a ' payador,' a name
derived from the verb ' payar ' meaning to improvise in
verse to the accompaniment of the guitar. As Sarmiento
intimates, the popular poetry of Argentina is a derivative
of the Andalusian of the Middle Ages and has a long popular development. The episodes related by the payador
reveal a certain epic quality tinged with Moorish sadness
but tempered by the Andalusian keenness for the satirical
and the comic. Frequent also is the intent to teach a
moral lesson; barbarous at times, for the purpose often
is to inculcate a spirit of rebellion.

B. Hidalgo and J. G. Godoy used the popular poetry
in dialogue form during the revolutionary epoch for the
propaganda of their patriotic ideas, but they did not make
a literary character of the gaucho. Among the first to
put the gaucho into cultivated literature was J. M. Gutiérrez whose *Amores del Payador* was written in February,
1838. It is worth while to note that this date is only a
year later than the publication of Echeverría's *La Cautiva*
and his suggestion regarding the utilization of Argentine
sources for the creation of a native literature. *Los Amores
del Payador* should be ranked high. It is the typical
gaucho legend. It is full of true poetical feeling. It is well
written in good Castilian. It is highly dramatic. The

reader is introduced to Juana who is waiting at the door
of her father's house for her lover, the payador. At last
he rides up mounted on his swift courser. As he is reciting
his amorous ditty, a rich suitor for Juana's hand appears.
The men's words bring on a fight. When Juana tries to
separate them she is mortally stabbed by the rich man
who is promptly killed by the payador. Over the corpse
of his beloved he sings the characteristic mournful gaucho
lament. Then covering her body with his poncho he
departs to take up again his wild life in the wilderness.

About 1844 were written Bartolomé Mitre's gaucho
poems. Among them is the first treatment of the legend
of Santos Vega, a gaucho who has been called the spirit
of "popular poetry incarnate in a Don Juan of the coun-
tryside." Santos Vega was a payador who died of grief
because he had been beaten in a contest with a young
amateur in the art of improvisation. Popular report
asserted that the stranger before whose skill the inspiration of Santos Vega had failed was no other than the
Devil. Ten years later after a more realistic representation of the gaucho was coming into vogue, Mitre published
the second edition of his poems accompanied by an introduction and notes. In them he wrote, "Primitive customs have had many singers but almost all have limited
themselves to copying them instead of giving them a
poetic character. So it is that, in order to make gauchos
talk, the poets have used all the gaucho idioms, thus
raising a jargon to the rank of poetry. Poetry is not the
servile copy but the poetic interpretation of nature."
These words are an excellent expression of the two lines
along which this class of literature developed.

During the revolutionary period the gaucho served as a mouthpiece for the opinions of Bartolomé Hidalgo to whose celebrated dialogues of Chano and Contreras reference has already been made. Their realistic form and popular idiom served as a model for Hilario Ascásubi (1807–75) whom, some, if not Mitre, have praised for his "faithful reproduction of nature." One of Ascásubi's earliest pieces was a dialogue between Chano y Contreras who are represented as serving together in the trenches before Montevideo and conversing on the past glories of the country.

Ascásubi was himself a soldier who had suffered imprisonment at the command of Rosas. After two years in a dungeon he learned that the order for his execution had been issued, but the connivance of his jailers afforded him an opportunity to escape from the prison by dropping over the wall into the moat. In Montevideo he was encouraged to write his patriotic verses by Florencio Varela, then the leading journalist of the city. At the latter's expense thousands of copies of one poem were printed and distributed to the soldiers in General Lavalle's army as they set out on their campaign against Rosas. This poem bore the title of *Media Caña del Campo*, the name of a favorite dance, and was written in a meter which allowed it to be sung to the tempo of the dance. Its spirited words were intended to hearten the soldiers by dwelling on the defeat of Rosas at the battle of Cagancha.

Florencio Varela (1807–48), younger brother of Juan Cruz Varela, won the admiration of his contemporaries by his energy and abilities. They sent him to Europe to enlist the assistance of England and France at the

opening of the great siege of Montevideo. There also
he made a favorable impression of his personality. After
his return his journalistic attacks on Rosas and his lieutenant Oribe were so fierce that they dispatched an assassin
who succeeded in his purpose one night at Varela's very
doorstep. Beside his political writing, Varela was the
author of some odes in the classical style on the hospital
of the Brothers of Charity, on anarchy and on peace, all
much praised by his friends. The lofty sentiments of
the poems reveal the noble character of the man.

With his encouragement Ascásubi continued to produce
his gaucho dialogues and letters. A favorite device of the
poet was the letter written by the gaucho Donato Jurao
to his wife narrating recent events or by Paulino Lucero
discussing the cruel deeds of Rosas such as the execution
of Camila O'Gorman and the priest Gutiérrez. (This act
was staged by the Uruguayan Fajardo.) These occasional pieces were afterwards collected in a volume and
printed with the title *Paulino Lucero* or "the gauchos of
the río de la Plata singing and fighting against the tyrants
of the Argentine and the Oriental Republics, 1839–51:
relating all the episodes of the nine years' siege which
Montevideo sustained heroically and unequally as well as
the combats which the gaucho patriots fought until the
tyrant J. M. Rosas and his satellites were laid low." As
the long sub-title promises, the book is a perfect mine of
facts, especially for the student of local manners and customs.

His success in political verse led Ascásubi to attempt
an ambitious reconstruction of the life of the gaucho at the
end of the eighteenth century. The title which he finally

gave to the collection of his sketches originally published in 1851, was *Santos Vega o los Mellizos de la Flor*. In this picaresque novel in verse the payador Santos Vega, "aquel de la larga fama," relates the life and criminal deeds of a famous gaucho outlaw who flourished between 1778 and 1808. In this manner the author finds opportunity to describe life on the estancias, its danger from the Indians, the rural customs and ideas, the good features of gaucho character as well as the evil and to celebrate the somewhat mythological Santos Vega himself.

After the fall of Rosas and the establishment of the rule of General Urquiza, Ascásubi began the publication of a periodical entitled *Aniceto el Gallo* from whose pages a gaucho by that name preached unitarian doctrines to the federalistic adherents of Urquiza. Many of his old poems against Rosas were reprinted. Though public interest kept the periodical alive for a year during 1853 and 54, not many political conversions have been attributed to the influence of Aniceto el Gallo.

Ascásubi's verses are so closely connected with contemporary events and can scarcely be read without constant reference to a glossary that they lack interest now, but to his friends he was a "second Beranger." In a degree the footnotes with which he provided the final edition of his poems are more interesting than the text.

When Mitre condemned the gaucho jargon in the theory of poetics prefaced to the second edition of his *Rimas*, he was preparing the way for a poet of the younger generation. Ricardo Gutiérrez (1836–96) published in 1860 a volume of poems which must have obtained Mitre's approval. The long poems contained therein, *Lázaro* and

La Fibra Salvaje, have been termed by enthusiastic admirers the most criollo of all Argentine poems. At the same time their expression of the passion of love is most intense. *Lázaro* is the tale of a gaucho disappointed in love. *La Fibra Salvaje* possesses the intensity of a gaucho tale at least as the title suggests. It depicts the despair of a lover, Ezequiel, who separated from Lucía, the object of his passion, becomes a monk when she marries another man. After several years the husband, Don Julio, comes in remorse to the monk's cell and, without knowing the latter's personal interest in the matter, confesses that he had sold his wife for gold to satisfy his passion for gambling. The monk is so inflamed with anger that he challenges Julio to fight. Julio is killed. Then Ezequiel lays aside his monk's garb to enter the army of San Martín in one of whose victorious battles he meets his own death.

Ricardo Gutiérrez became a physician. The experiences of his calling are revealed in many of his poems, for he constantly cries to God in prayer for consolation for the miseries which he witnesses. In 1880 he published a novel *Cristian.* The protagonist of that name is a student who, during his vacation on his brother's ranch, falls in love with his brother's wife to whom he discourses much of the soul. And finally like Werther commits suicide. The significance of Ricardo Gutiérrez lies in the fact that he penetrates the depth of the gaucho soul and reveals as no other of his countrymen its inner workings prompting to the deeds of violence so frequently described.

Poems in the gaucho jargon after the cessation of the publication of *Aniceto el Gallo* were next written by

Estanislao del Campo (1834–80). His first verses signed "Anastasio el Pollo" were ascribed to Ascásubi till the latter denied their authorship in a letter from Aniceto el Gallo congratulating Anastasio el Pollo upon his first efforts as a cantor. The best of Del Campo's early poems is the account of the battle of Pavón fought in 1861 which it will be remembered established the supremacy of the province of Buenos Aires in revolt under the generalship of Mitre against Urquiza. This poem gives a mock account of the battle as a report from the defeated general. Del Campo also wrote verse in a more elevated style; for example, his ode to America on a text taken from Mármol's lines that America prophesies liberty to the world is readable. Were it not however for one gaucho poem of his he would be speedily forgotten. At the suggestion of Ricardo Gutiérrez, to whom he dedicated his production, he composed and published in 1866 a long poem entitled *Fausto. Impresiones del gaucho Anastasio el Pollo en la representación de esta ópera.* And it is a masterpiece.

It is a masterpiece because, in retelling the story, in homely dialect, Del Campo has retained the literary values and pathos of the original and at the same time he paints the reflection of the tragedy in the gaucho's soul. The poem fulfills the demand of Mitre that the poet should treat his material in an artistic manner; yet it is filled with gaucho sentiment. The setting of the story, Anastasio el Pollo's breezy humor, his metaphorical comparisons drawn from his daily life are incomparable bits of realism. Its effectiveness is increased by the simple direct way in which the story proceeds.

In the opening lines of the poem the reader is introduced

to the gaucho Laguna riding along on his dappled pony, gay with trappings of silver, so heavy that he seemed to bear on him "a Potosí." Arriving at the river he had dismounted and was unsaddling his horse when he caught sight of a man's clothes. Then his horse neighed as a man on horseback came out of the river. Laguna recognizes his old friend Anastasio el Pollo. After they embrace, Laguna relates his recent adventures. He had been to the city to collect money due him for some wool but he had been greeted by excuses, "To-morrow. Come later. No money." El Pollo jests him on the amount of silver that he carries about. Laguna explains that he won it from a gambler, who had the insolence to accuse him of witchcraft. "According to his story you'd think the Devil and I —" "Hush! friend, the other night I saw the Devil. Cross yourself." Besought by his friend to relate the adventure, el Pollo, after fortifying himself by a drink from Laguna's flask, began.

Being near the theater Colón, he saw a crowd going in, so he paid his admission and went in too. After climbing a hundred and one steps he found his seat. Then the band began to play and the curtain went up. A doctor made known his weariness with life because he was in love with a little blond. In despair he called on the Devil who then appeared. Laguna doubts that it really was the Devil. "Half the city saw him," maintains el Pollo. The Devil then gave the doctor a glimpse of the blond. "Ah! she was as beautiful as the Immaculate Virgin." The Devil, before doing more for the doctor, insisted on his signing a contract, and when it was signed, laughed so that "it rang in my ears all night."

In this manner el Pollo narrates the story of the opera act by act. At the end of the tragedy he tells how Faust visiting the prison prayed. Then the wall opened and the girl's soul ascended to glory. Saint Michael brandishing his sword came down from among the clouds, before whom the Devil sank into the ground. "Lend me your handkerchief. My head sweats; how could you see such witchcraft?" cries Laguna. "I went about for four or five days with a headache," replies el Pollo.

The first edition of *Fausto* distributed twenty thousand copies, the proceeds of which were donated by the author to the military hospitals. But more popular still has been *Martín Fierro*, published in 1872, by José Hernández (1834–86). The author was a journalist in Buenos Aires, who founded the *Revista del Río de la Plata*. The editions of his poem, nearly tripled in length by a second part, *La Vuelta de Martín Fierro*, are still issued. As a measure of its popularity may be taken the fact that it used to be on sale in country groceries and the often quoted anecdote of the messenger sent to buy various supplies and "the latest part of *Martín Fierro*."

The poem relates in the language and manner of the gaucho, the story of Martín Fierro's misfortunes. Once a small farmer with wife and child, he was taken from them by a recruiting officer. The regiment into which he was drafted fights with the Indians. After a while he deserts and returns to his farm. He finds it without signs of life and the buildings burnt. So he becomes a "matrero," or gaucho outlaw, in company with one Cruz. Tired of being hunted by the police, Martín smashes his guitar as a sign of renouncing his ties with the white race and joins the Indians. *La Vuelta de Martín Fierro,* or his return to civilization, has less movement and long moralizing sermons by Padre Vizcacha. These however were not displeasing to its readers who found their own sentiments voiced by his words. The generation who received this poem understood it as a challenge to the government in Buenos Aires that was legislating for the country people without understanding their needs.

To others the poem symbolized the whole race of the gaucho who has now disappeared before the advance of the railway and European immigration. The truth of Hernández' representation was instantly recognized. Hernández was brought up in the country and thoroughly understood the physical conditions and the characters whose daily life, passions, pleasures, aspirations, and dreams he portrayed so minutely.

As literature *Martín Fierro* is ranked high by the Spanish critic, Miguel de Unamuno, who finds in it a commingling of the epic and the lyric. Further he says: "When the payador of the pampa beneath the shade of the ombu in the calm of the desert, or on a pleasant night by the light of the stars intones, to the accompaniment of his Spanish guitar, the monotone décimas of *Martín Fierro* and the gauchos listen with emotion to the poetry of the pampa, they hear, without being aware of the fact, the inextinguishable echoes of their mother Spain, echoes which with their blood and soul were bequeathed to them by their parents. *Martín Fierro* is the song of the Spanish warrior who, after having planted the cross in Granada, went to America to serve in the vanguard of civilization. Therefore his song is filled with the Spanish spirit; his language is Spanish, his idioms, his maxims, his worldly wisdom, his soul are Spanish."

With the popularity of *Martín Fierro*, the gaucho became the fashion. As a part of an evening entertainment or as a side show to a circus the payador flourished. A few professionals attained celebrity for their ready wit in improvisation for it was customary to pit against each other representatives of different provinces.

With less realism and more of the artistry demanded by Mitre, the gaucho next appeared in verse in the *Tradiciones Argentinas* of Rafael Obligado. These three brief poems are poetical interpretations of the Santos Vega legend. In the first a payador relates how the ghost of Santos Vega had played at night on a guitar accidentally left by a well. The second brings the famous gaucho to a ghostly love tryst. The third narrates the death of Santos Vega in contest with an unknown payador, to whom Obligado gives the symbolic name Juan Sin Ropa. According to the legend Santos Vega, the unexcelled, had succumbed only in a contest with the Devil; but this victor's name typifies the new immigration which has brought about the passing of the old conditions in the country. In the words of the poem, Juan Sin Ropa's song "was the mighty cry of progress on the wind."

Written with a like symbolism as if to mark the disappearance of the gaucho, at the close of the nineteenth century was published in 1899 the last recorded gaucho poem, *Nastasio*, by Francisco Soto y Calvo. It is the story of the death of old Anastasio, the gaucho, after a terrific hurricane had robbed him of his wife and children. Into this poem filled with the spirit of the pampa, the

author has attempted to concentrate the essence of all
the rich gaucho literature.

Two years later Soto y Calvo brought out a counter-
part to this poem in *Nostalgia* in which he portrays the
new life that has come into the country with the influx
of foreign immigration. An Italian immigrant, Vittor,
falls in love with a maid servant of native birth whose
employers take him as a farmhand. After their marriage
riches come to them as the reward of sturdy effort and
allow Vittor to put into execution his long cherished ambition of returning to Italy. But the couple are not happy;
they are homesick for the pampa (hence the title.) One's
country is where one is well off. The story would have
been better if its twelve thousand lines had been prose.

The prose treatment of the gaucho began about 1880,
when realistic fiction in the style of Zola was coming into
vogue. Eduardo Gutiérrez, making use of police reports,
filled the literary sections of the newspapers with the
exploits of notorious criminals so that Juan Moreira, the
assassin, and El Jorobado, thief, became household
names. But as M. García Merou points out, the romantic
payador Santos Vega has become a degenerate who
spends the intervals between his robberies in getting drunk.

But Eduardo Gutiérrez by adapting one of the episodes
of his novel *Juan Moreira* to pantomimic representation
in a circus opened another path in literature to the gaucho.
At first to fill the part in the pantomime real gauchos rode
their horses into the circus and strummed the guitar. Soon
spoken dialogue was added to their rôles. In this play
the brothers Podestá achieved a reputation and continued
it independent of the circus. Their success encouraged

them to stage *Martín Fierro*. Then original plays about gauchos were written both in Argentina and Uruguay. So to the present day the gaucho has kept the stage. And from this popular origin has developed a class of plays which represent the manners and speech of the lower classes.

Public enthusiasm over the productions of the popular poetry never hindered cultivation of verse along more classic lines. The poet called on to voice the sentiments of Buenos Aires at a public gathering in celebration of the establishment of the third French Republic in 1870 was Martin Coronado. He had attracted attention only the year before by the essentially virile tone and sparkling eloquence of his verses, a quality which made them very suitable for declamation. As a poet of occasion he practiced also the epigram and the jocose. But his most interesting poems are narrative pictures of dramatic events in contemporary life. In *Los Hijos de la Pampa* his heart beats in sympathy with the soldier who, wounded by the same bullet that had killed his horse, lovingly caresses the animal before dying. *Angela* is the story of a young woman whose conduct fits her name. At her wedding ceremony a woman appears to claim the prospective bridegroom as the father of a child in her arms. Angela recognizes a bow of ribbon in the woman's possession as one which she had herself given the man as a token of love. Removing her wedding veil and putting it on the woman, Angela compels the man to marry the mother of his child. Later Angela dies of a broken heart. In these narrative poems Coronado reveals himself as a disciple of Ricardo Gutiérrez. The two poets resemble each other also in their intensity of expression when treating the passion of love.

Coronado on the other hand essayed the drama in productions the most important since those of Mármol. *La Rosa Blanca*, 1877, dramatizes the efforts of a physician to cure a girl who had become insane through disappointed love. *Luz de Luna y Luz de Incendio*, played a year later, stages with great realism the days of Rosas. Cuitiño, a despicable villain and officer of the tyrant, appears at an evening party where he succeeds in getting his victim, young Emilio, to betray his unitarian sentiments, whereat he is arrested and taken to the barracks of the federal soldiers. The scene at the barracks gives opportunity for declamatory eloquence from Emilio. The drunken Cuitiño and his soldiers display the utmost brutality and thereby prepare the spectator for the killings in the last act.

These plays were partly the outcome of the efforts of a literary society, the "Academía Argentina," to promote the theater. The members proclaimed themselves disciples of Echeverría with the purpose of nationalizing literature on the model of *La Cautiva*. As a step in this direction they occupied themselves also in preparing a dictionary of expressions peculiar to Argentina. The member of this society who won the greatest name for himself as a poet was Rafael Obligado. One of his best poems, *Echeverría*, which may be taken as the manifesto of the society, turns on the idea:—

> Lancémonos nosotros sus hermanos
> Por la senda inmortal de Echeverría.

Obligado is a genuine poet with the truest feeling for

the intimate moods of nature. As his family was wealthy, he was able to spend his time observing her and putting into verse such impressions as he willed. His earliest long poem, *La Pampa*, written in 1872 under the direct imitation of his chosen master, is an ambitious attempt at word painting. But he was more successful in such gems as *La Flor del Seibo* and *El Nido de Boyeros*. The former is a letrilla composed to vie with the Cuban poet, Placido's *La Flor de la Caña* to which Obligado refers in the opening lines when he declares his belief that the inspiring Cuban beauty had no blacker or prettier eyes than a certain little Argentine maid. Perhaps the same little maid was the passionate, tender-hearted lass of the adventure with the birds' nest related in *El Nido de Boyeros*. The poet says he is acquainted with a girl of thirteen who likes to row about the river amusing herself by picking flowers. Whenever she sees him she haughtily threatens him with her fist. One day he saw her approach a nest of boyeros hanging over the water. When she tried to get it with a long stick she just missed it. Thereby losing her balance she was thrown to her seat in the boat. In anger she started to strike the nest, but the cries of the young birds deterred her. Instead she gently rocked the nest. While engaged in this motherly occupation she caught sight of the poet watching her. And thereafter when she passes him in her boat instead of threatening him, she rows quickly past with averted head.

Beside the breath of the pampa and the woodland fragance rare in Argentine poetry, Obligado's lines reveal tender human sentiments. The sense of personal loss through the death of loved ones has seldom been more exquisitely expressed than in *El Hogar Vacío*. And from *El Hogar Paterno* the reader discovers that the poet's love for his country is rooted in his love for his home. The total number of Obligado's poems is small, a fact which testifies to the care with which he wrote. At the same time he claimed a romanticist's freedom of treatment.

Partly from this and partly from his choice of subjects came about the most interesting episode of his literary career. One day he sent a challenge written in tercets to his friend Calixto Oyuela to debate in a *Justa Literaria* the old question of classicism and romanticism. Nothing averse, the latter, who had just been winning some prizes in Buenos Aires for his classic verses, replied in tercets accepting the challenge. In the same meter and form they reproached each other for what each one believed to be the other's shortcomings. Obligado thought that Oyuela was neglectful of the light of the present ideal and unmindful of the Andes. Oyuela replied that Obligado was irreverent of the past. Finally the poets agreed to submit their contest to an older poet, Carlos Guido y Spano, a man who inspired great respect and even affection in his contemporaries. In a genial letter, interesting to the student of literature in many ways, Guido y Spano replied in this strain.

The guitar is worth as much as the lyre. For a new world, new songs. But form must be considered. Obligado's exquisite *Flor del Seibo* would perish were it not preserved in a vase of fine crystal. Therefore the judge advises Oyuela to stop reading Homer and spend a few hours with Aniceto el Gallo and Martin Fierro. On the other hand, Obligado should go to Athens and Greece. Then the two poets will understand each other without need of his decision. Let them make truce and continue singing each in his own fashion.

Obligado referring to the ancient habit of presenting the victor of a poetic contest with a rose, sent to Oyuela his *Flor del Seibo*. The latter in acceptance complimented his adversary on possessing more true American savor than any other and advised that they make war on their common enemy, that literary pest, Gallic imitation.

To understand the significance of the *Justa Literaria*, it is necessary to consider certain minor movements in Argentine poesy. Even Echeverría believed that poetry was a sort of handmaid to morality and humanitarianism. A spiritualistic tendency of this kind easily joined itself to an undercurrent of classicism. And when about the year 1880 literary societies established contests in Buenos Aires to which they gave the old name of "juegos florales," the poems submitted to the judges were compositions on the classical or philosophical order.

Calixto Oyuela was a prize winner in these contests, in 1881 with his *Canto al Arte* and the next year with *Eros*. The latter is a very beautiful poem, distinguished on the one hand for its correctness of diction and classic spirit and on the other for the development of the sentiment which it expresses. The poet declares that love is the inspiration of all his verses. Every flower, the breeze, each wave of the sea, the last breath of evening, the shining stars, all nature speaks to him of love.

This poem is perhaps the fairest product of the purely classic school. In the same year in which it was written, died the man of whom the classicists believed themselves disciples, namely, Carlos Encina (1839–82). When nineteen years of age, he won first prize in a school contest by a *Canto lírico al Colón*. Later he wrote two poetical dissertations, *Canto al Arte* and *La Lucha por la Idea*. They comprise practically all his compositions in verse, for he became a teacher of mathematics and of philosophy along evolutionary lines. His poems are judged somewhat harshly by Menéndez y Pelayo on the ground that they are not poetic but are merely the versification of Hegelian and Spencerian ideas. How the Argentines regarded the poems has been told by Ricardo Gutiérrez. To them they opened a new course of æsthetics which was the religion of the new school.

Carlos Guido y Spano (1827–1918) was, however, the grand old man of the classicists. He was the one who gave them translations from the Greek and showed them by example what correctness of form meant. His sober and severe style was a development of his later days as one may discover by reading the verses published in the collection of 1871, *Hojas al Viento*. Here are revealed the same tenderness of feeling and the same breadth of sympathy which made him personally so beloved. Sympathy with the bereaved or the sufferer from injustice is the dominant note of his best poems.

Perhaps he inherited this trait from his father Tomás Guido, one of San Martín's generals at the battles of Chacabuco and Maipú, and an orator of renown. At any rate the poet relates in the autobiographical sketch prefixed to *Ráfagas*, a volume of collected newspaper articles, two notable instances of his own nobility of character. In 1851, his brother being sick in Paris, Carlos was sent by his parents to look after him. When he arrived he found his brother dead. Paris was in an uproar of revolution. Filled with democratic enthusiasm for justice the young Argentine fought behind the barricades. Luckily he came away alive, for in 1871 an opportunity offered for him to show the same spirit of disregard of self, to the benefit of his native city. Buenos Aires was being ravaged by an epidemic of yellow fever and it was necessary for a popular commission to fight the peril. As a member of it Carlos Guido y Spano distinguished himself by his activity.

Sympathy with a sister nation inspired him to his most ambitious poem, *México: canto épico*. When the French invaded Mexico in 1862, their army at first met with defeat. Guido's sentiments on this occasion are so vehemently expressed that the Mexican critic, Sosa, declares that one might easily suppose the author of the poem to be a Mexican. But Guido y Spano was equally moved by the injustice of an act when his own country was a participant. The result of Argentina's coalition with Brazil to oppress Paraguay is most pathetically signified in *Nenia*. This brief poem is one of the most precious gems of Argentine lyrism. It is the lament of a young Paraguayan girl who has lost her parents, brothers and lover by the ravages of the war. The lament begins and ends with an apostrophe to the urutaú, a native bird of sweetest song, perched on the yatay, a kind of palm tree.

> Llora, llora, urutaú,
> en las ramas del yatay;
> ya no existe el Paraguay,
> donde nací como tú.
> Llora, llora, urutaú.

No less affecting is the poet in rendering his personal feelings, whether it be to his mother, *A mi Madre*, or to a friend just bereaved by the death of her father, *Al Pasar*. Few poems depicting the awakening of a first love excel *En los Guindos;* the boy has climbed a cherry tree and as he tosses the fruit into the outspread skirt of his girl companion, his heart fills with emotion as he glimpses her charms.

It is easy to understand why Guido y Spano should have been selected by Oyuela and Obligado to decide their literary joust. With Oyuela he had in common a reverence for form, and with Obligado a love for the tender and sentimental. But their verses began to seem trivial to the public beside the grandiloquent outbursts of a poet who is generally regarded as Argentina's greatest poet, Olegario Victor Andrade (1841–82).

Before the juegos florales of 1880 he was scarcely heard of because he was on the wrong side in politics. He was one of the boys whom General Urquiza had ordered to be sent to school and to the university. He repaid his patron by dedicating to him a poem, *Mi Patria*, which won a prize in the school contest in 1856. But he lost favor the same year by marrying at the age of eighteen. He supported himself by writing for provincial papers. In 1860 he became private secretary to President Derqui, but as his government was soon overthrown, Andrade had no resource but to continue to write in the provinces. Though he once succeeded in securing a place in Buenos Aires, he lost it by espousing the cause of Urquiza against Sarmiento. In the following administration of Avellaneda he held a position in the custom house at Concordia, but was accused of negligence in administration, a charge from which he was later acquitted. With the advent of General Roca to the presidency in 1880, the provinces acquired a larger share in the government. Roca placed Andrade in charge of *La Tribuna* as chief editor of this government organ. And after his death, in 1883, President Roca assisted Andrade's widow by buying from her for the National Library the manuscripts of all his poems for sixteen thousand pesos, and by printing at national expense a fine edition of his poems. Moreover, President Roca paid Andrade the personal compliment of delivering an oration at his funeral.

Andrade's poems are characterized by a declamatory eloquence on patriotic topics and an exaggerated Americanism. They are didactic on the theory that the poet has a mission to preach to the multitude. Having been written within the space of five years when the man was about forty years old, they display a certain unity of conception which, despite their diversity of title, gives them additional force.

The first of this series of mature poems is *El Nido de Cóndores*, dated 1877. A condor's nest situated on a gloomy and precipitous cliff above a defile in the Andes, surrounded by a white band of snow, amid perpetual silence, has attracted the poet's attention. Musing he recollects the stirring events of which the nest of the condor witnessed in part at least, San Martín's passage of the mountains, the battles of Maipú, of Chacabuco, the disaster of Cancha Rayada.

The next poems are more personal, to General Lavalle, to San Martín, *El Arpa Perdida,* an elegy on the poet

Luca, singer of Argentine triumphs in revolutionary days, who was drowned in a shipwreck in 1824. Heroism, American heroism is ever his theme as in the ode, *Paysandú*, to the memory of the victorious Uruguayans.

In *Atlántida,* which won him a prize in the juegos florales of 1881, Andrade advanced to a more abstract and prophetic tone. This poem, dedicated to the future of the Latin race in America, begins with a summary of the history of that race. Rome, Spain, France, have each in its turn risen to leadership and fallen to decay. But in America are republics, the poet characterizes each in memorable lines, republics where life beats high and liberty will come to full fruition.

The poet's mission as a teacher and prophet is exalted in a *Canto a Victor Hugo.* To Andrade, the French poet seems greater than any of his predecessors, who have tried to uplift humanity, excelling Isaiah, Juvenal or Dante. He possesses the peculiar qualities which marked each of them. And he lives in France, "height where nests human genius." But in America, "new theater which God destines for the drama of the future, free races admire thee, Orpheus, who went down in search of thy beloved, sacred democracy. And across the seas, O setting star, the sons of the dawn salute thee."

Hugo replied to this effusion by nothing more than a few courteous words of thanks; whereby it was "ill paid," in the opinion of Menéndez y Pelayo. But Valera is uncertain whether Hugo was vexed at being called old and a setting star or whether the French poet was ignorant of Castilian and failed to understand the poem.

In *Prometeo,* the most transcendental of his poems,

Andrade wrote the spiritual history of the man of genius, of the thinker who strives for the good of the human race. We have perhaps an echo of Andrade's personal misfortunes. The setting of the poem is the same as in the tragedy by Æschylus. The Titan lies chained to the rocks, hurling his defiance at Jupiter and is pitied by the Oceanids. Aside from the words which the poet puts in the Titan's mouth, Andrade's innovation in the legend consists in the term which he puts to the suffering. When the Titan views the cross of Christ on Golgotha, he feels that he may die because another martyr is about to win the fight for the liberty of human thought and human conscience.

The Spanish critics are somewhat captious of Andrade's merits because his Americanism is distateful to them. To Valera the poet's expression "Latin race" is especially distressing. He thinks, however, that Andrade, given a better and wider education, might have excelled both Bello and Olmedo as he is superior in inspiration. What the Argentines think of Andrade has been well said thus: "He is the true national poet of the Argentines, because he reflects in his beautiful songs the aspirations of that young and lively democracy which frets itself in supreme longings for liberty, progress, and civilization, while it is the melting pot for the diverse elements of the Latin races from which will spring a new American type, destined to preside over an important evolution of the human species in the new world." [1]

Soon after Andrade was laid in his tomb, it witnessed a strange ceremony. A paralytic whose lower limbs had

[1] M. García Merou, *Recuerdos Literarios.*

been useless for ten years, was brought there for the purpose of paying honor to a fellow poet by laying on the
tomb a wreath which he, Gervasio Méndez (1849–98), had
won in a poetic contest.   For many years Méndez was a
pathetic figure in Argentine letters.   The poems sent
forth from his couch of suffering rang with no feigned
note of melancholy.   When he besought, in *Los Náufragos
del Mundo* the pity of the world upon the failures, or
urged in *Amor Celeste* the joy of religious consolation,
there sprang to mind the poet's own story.   Friends by
printing editions of his poems and assisting their sale
helped to keep him in the public mind.   Leopoldo Díaz
in a sonnet compared him to the bound and helpless
Mazeppa.   In a measure Méndez was a precursor of the
youthful poets whose pseudo-melancholy began in the
late seventies to be the fashion.   His first volume of
verses, printed in 1876, was greeted by the veteran critic
J. M. Gutiérrez with the enthusiastic cry that a real poet
had appeared in Argentina.

The early eighties witnessed in Buenos Aires a peculiar
recrudescence of French romanticism of the type of Alfred
de Musset.   The youths who prided themselves on writing
verses like the master sought also to imitate him in
manner of life.   They organized a society, the "Circulo
Cientifico Literario," to foster the production of poetry
by listening to each other's lines.   Translations of their
favorites, such as Gautier's *Albertus*, De Musset's *Rolla*
were interspersed with recitations in the original of the
most risqué passages of the same poets.   Making Murger
their model the young Bohemians indulged in much
horseplay not always devoid of Bacchanalian excesses.

The verses of some of these young men are interesting to read. Julio E. Mitre, president of the circle, imitating the elegies of Gautier sang that love was the sweetest of goods and the cruelest of ills. Adolfo Mitre (1859–84), took immense pains with the form of his verses melancholy in tone on gloomy topics. Alberto Navarro Viola (1856–85), possessed a wider literary and moral horizon in his poems on Giordano Bruno, Voltaire, and Moreau, though a series of twenty-five poems on the death of his mother, the memory of her kisses and his doubts after her death, gave forth the truest note. He also published an annual bibliography of literary works printed in Buenos Aires, which is now of real value to the student. To Luis S. Ocampo was due the introduction of orgiastic lines in the manner of Espronceda. Domingo Martinto strove for Parnassian elegance and succeeded so well that some of his poems might easily be taken for translations from the French.

Equally as careful in expression was Martín García Merou (b. 1862). His literary activities were many and various, including attempts at the Zolaistic novel in *Ley Social*. For a time he mystified his companions by publishing sane criticisms on their mad verses. To him we are indebted for an amusing and instructive account of the movement in his *Recuerdos Literarios*. Long connected with the diplomatic service of Argentina his graphic pen described the life of those countries in which he resided. More than fifteen volumes of verses, tales, and criticism bear his name. Another poet who began to write with these young men (his ode *El Descubrimiento de América* won a prize in 1882), but who lived longer than they and continued to write for twenty-five years was Enrique E. Rivarola. Among his later productions were realistic prose tales of life in Argentina.

All this poetic activity of the early eighties in Buenos Aires created an atmosphere favorable to the new ideas in literature, which were to spread from that center through the Spanish-American world till they affected even Spanish poets. The "modernista" movement, though originating in part with others, dates from 1888 with the publication of *Azul* by Rubén Darío. It is significant of the cosmopolitan character of the movement that its leader was a native of Nicaragua, who had come to Buenos Aires by way of the west coast of South America. On account of the world-wide influence of Rubén Darío and the modernista school they must be studied apart from the local poetry of Argentina.[1]

Lesser or younger followers of the movement than the galaxy of the great, those whose reputations have been mainly local, are Emilio Berisso, Eugenio Díaz Romero, Alberto Ghiraldo and Ricardo Rojas. Enrique Banchs, since 1907, has been perhaps the most prolific. In the monthly review *Nosotros*, now representing the best literary production of Argentina, find their opportunity for literary endeavor such writers as Juan Mas y Pi, Manuel Gálvez, and Alvaro Melian Lafinur.

Though fiction as a kind of literature in Argentina began with Mármol's *Amalia*, other novels made their appearance after the fall of Rosas. In the periodical *El Plata científico y literario*, founded in 1854 by Miguel Navarro Viola, a leading attraction was the historical novel *La*

[1] See Chapter XIV.

Novia del Hereje o la Inquisición de Lima, by Vicente Fidel López. The author attempted to depict society in Lima about the year 1578, when Peru was startled by the appearance off its coasts of the English admiral Francis Drake on his famous cruise in the Pacific ocean.

V. F. López, during his studies for his *Historia Argentina,* found material for another story entitled *La Loca de la Guardia.* Such was the name given to a crack-brained woman living near the passes of the Andes, who used to give information to the patriots of the movements of the Spanish armies. As her mental condition was said to be due to abuse from Spanish soldiers, López made a story out of the mystery of her life.

The periodical *La Revista de Buenos Aires* established in 1863 to which López contributed historical articles and J. M. Gutiérrez literary criticisms tried to encourage the production of fiction. The editors promoted an edition, sold by subscription, of the stories of Juana Manuela Gorriti de Belzu.[1] Though she had removed from Argentina in her childhood and spent her life in Bolivia and Lima, where she was a prominent figure in literary circles, the people of Buenos Aires were proud to claim her as a countrywoman. The sale in 1865 of the collection of her stories, *Sueños y Realidades,* was very successful. Ten years later visiting her native country she was received with a royal welcome, and another collection of her tales, *Panoramas de la Vida,* was brought out.

Another female writer of fiction to whom Gutiérrez called the attention of the public was Eduarda Mansilla de García who printed her work under the name of "Daniel."

[1] See page 257.

She published in 1860 *El Médico de San Luis*, a valuable picture of contemporary social conditions. The protagonist was an English doctor who had married in Argentina. The childish character of his wife is contrasted with that of his sister Jane, a practical woman to whose sternly Protestant mind the weaknesses of her foreign and Catholic sister-in-law, as well as the kind of education being given to her twin nieces is abhorrent. By this means the author made public her ideas on the education and social position of girls. Eduarda Mansilla wrote other novels, one of which, *Lucía Miranda*, dealt with the fortunes of that colonial heroine so attractive to Argentine novelists and dramatists since Labardén's play *Siripo*.

Romantic fiction gave way to realism about 1880. Eduardo Gutiérrez' tales of criminal gauchos mark a transition to the novels which were inspired by the appearance of Zola's works. For their novels his imitators found ample material in the cosmopolitan city Buenos Aires. On the one hand the influence on character and family life of the sudden acquisition of wealth afforded opportunity for naturalistic studies, and on the other the clash between the foreign immigrants and the native population presented dramatic contrasts.

Eugenio Cambaceres was one of the first to write in the naturalistic manner. His *Silbidos de un Vago*, 1882, was little more than sketches of life in the city and on the estancias. That and his next book *Música Sentimental* were greeted by adverse criticism because the freedom with which the relations between the sexes was treated shocked the public. When, however, in 1885 he published *Sin Rumbo* it had been educated sufficiently to appreciate the good points of the novel. This is the story of a man of the world who seeks in the country the restoration of his health undermined by dissipation. On the estancia he amuses himself by making love to a humble country girl. After a time he returns to the city. Once more tiring of fast living he goes back to the estancia where he finds that a son has been born to him. Paternal love awakens and makes a better man of him. Unluckily his little Andrés falls sick and dies whereat the father is so grieved that he commits suicide. The attraction of this novel lay in its detailed pictures of native life; a long journey on horseback across the sunlit pampa, night on the farm, the raging storm that turned dry brooks into torrents, the pathetic death of little Andrés. Moreover, the language of the characters, the jargon of the peasants and the slang of the city, with their familiar and picturesque expressions, added to the enthusiasm of the critics who hailed Cambaceres as the founder of the national novel.

His next, *En la Sangre*, 1887, developed the suggestion of the title by a study of the influence on national life of the admixture of Italian immigration. An Italian born in Buenos Aires and educated in its streets succeeds in marrying a wealthy girl by first seducing her. The fortune thus gained is lost in speculation and there is nothing left for Máxima but ill treatment from her ugly-tempered husband. The novel had a tremendous success as a serial in the columns of a daily paper.

Cambaceres, however, was not the first to study the foreign element in the metropolis. And in fact three novels which appeared in 1884 must have helped to prepare the public for his somewhat harsher naturalism.

Inocentes o culpables by Antonio Argerich related the fortunes of an Italian immigrant who rises from his beginning as a bootblack through various trades and marries above his station. The eldest son is a dissipated fellow who finally commits suicide, while the father is no better in his later years and ends in the asylum for the insane. *La Gran Aldea* by Lucio V. López (1848–94), son of V. F. López, depicted the whole life of the city, its politics, its morals, its social diversions. The youthful Blanca, married on account of her horror of poverty, to an old man, and Julio, for whom she has a guilty passion, are the principal characters. Sketched from life, the originals were known to the readers who took great delight in the personal allusions, the racy dialogue and the epigrammatic style.

The third novel of that year, *Fruto Vedado*, also a study of political and social life in Buenos Aires, was by a Frenchman whose abilities have won for him a prominent place in the life of the city.

Paul Groussac first drew public attention by this novel written more in the manner of Daudet than in that of Zola, though it is also the tale of a guilty love. But the hero Marcel is a hard worker whose passion for Andrea resembles more a blow of ill fortune than a bit of degeneracy, and when Andrea's blind husband discovers their fault, Marcel departs to start life anew in Africa. Groussac after the publication of this novel devoted his time to the cultivation of more serious literature, essays, bibliography and history. In 1893 he visited Chicago to deliver before the World's Folklore Conference an address on the Argentine gaucho. This and other essays were published

in a volume entitled *El Viaje Intelectual*. The description
of his long journey by way of the west coast of South
America and throughout the United States, *Del Plata
al Niagara*, printed in 1897, is the most interesting book of
travel from the South American point of view that I know.
Señor Groussac well deserved his appointment in 1885 as
librarian of the National Argentine Library in Buenos
Aires, a position which helpfully to students he still holds.
The monthly *La Biblioteca*, which he edited for two years
from 1896, contributed much to the diffusion of knowledge
concerning early Argentine literature.

The greatest Argentine novelist is Carlos María Ocantos,
who may be correctly termed the Balzac of his native
city. Following the latter's example he formed a bond of
union between his many novels by making the principal
characters members of the same family. By this device he
could lay the scenes not only in the present day but in the
past. For example, *Don Perfecto*, published in 1902,
written in the form of an autobiography of an old man,
gives many pictures of life in Buenos Aires as far back
as 1855. Ocantos' first novel, *León Saldívar*, printed in
Madrid in 1888 when the author was secretary there of the
Argentine legation, was greeted with applause. The
critic Ernesto Quesada, an Argentine essayist of power,
said that the novel realized in prose Echeverría's famous
dictum regarding the field of Argentine poetry.

León Saldívar is a rich young man who leads the ordinary life of elegant society in Buenos Aires. He courts
Lucía Guerra, whose father is a wealthy cattle raiser,
living six months of the year on his estancia and spending
the rest of the time in the fashionable life of the city.

The family's manners thus stand in ridiculous contrast with the refinement of their associates. The mother allows her ambitions to sacrifice her daughter to the wiles of a fortune-hunting Frenchman, who celebrates his marriage with Lucía by getting drunk at their wedding. A few months later the police appear at their house, guided by the man's wife from France. It seems he is an escaped convict whose deserted wife revenges herself by getting him sent back to prison. Lucía's wedding had so affected León that he fell sick with brain fever. When he recovers he determines to seek restoration of his health by a trip to Europe. Meeting Lucía accidentally he is about to refer to her misfortunes when she tells him that she is going to sail to Europe to join her husband called there because his aged mother was dying. Such indifference and levity of mind in Lucía puts an end to León's infatuation. When he reaches home he discovers that he is really in love with Cruzita, an orphan girl whom his mother had brought up. To marry her he postpones indefinitely his European trip.

The interesting pictures of native life, the carnival, parties, dances, the fashionable Progreso club, the summer sports, the wedding, are drawn from reality with a master hand. Ocantos applied his descriptive talent to the composition of a series of novels which now numbers a long list of titles. They treat the many phases of life in the Argentine metropolis. The important one of immigration, especially of Italians, receives due consideration, notably in one of the latest novels *El Peligro*, 1911.

The peculiarities of society in Buenos Aires from the feminine standpoint found an excellent interpretation in *Stella*, published anonymously in 1905 by "César Duayen," who afterward proved to be a well-known lady, Emma de la Barra. The keenness of observation displayed in this book, the accuracy of its details of wealthy families, and its pathos awakened a justly merited interest. While the story does not deal specifically with the question of the mingling of races in Argentina, the fact that its heroine, Alejandra Fussler, is the daughter of a Norwegian scientist who had married into a prominent family touches the problem. The child of the south had been unable to withstand the climate of the cold north and had died leaving two daughters. The novel opens with the arrival at her rich uncle's house of Alejandra bearing her little sister Stella, whose lower limbs are paralyzed. Her father had never returned from a scientific expedition to the Arctic. According to his instructions in that event she had come to Buenos Aires. Having inherited her father's talent, being well educated and showing in her disposition the northern strain in her blood, Alejandra proved very attractive to the men of the household, especially to Máximo, the bachelor brother of her uncle's wife, because she was such a contrast to the native women. Moreover, her womanly qualities in caring devotedly for the crippled Stella irresistibly drew the man of the world to her side. Máximo began to devote almost as much attention to Stella as Alejandra herself. Consequently when the poor child died, it was easy for Alejandra to accept Máximo's offer of marriage.

Conditions on the estancias and in the country villages have also formed the subject of numerous sketches and tales. Their realistic details lend them both attraction and power, though the author's choice of episode is often gruesome and sometimes revolting. Roberto J. Payró, Martiniano P. Leguizamón, Manuel Ugarte, Godofredo Daireaux, and Carlos Octavio Bunge have practiced with success this type of literature. Bunge and Ugarte have also attracted attention as essayists on matters of literature and public affairs.

The latest novels to win praise are *La Gloria de Don Ramírez*, 1911, by Enrique Rodríguez Larreta, which in most excellent style reconstructs a historical epoch of the Middle Ages in Spain; and *La Novela de Torquato Méndez* by Martín Aldéo, 1912. The latter is another study of wealthy society in Buenos Aires, and is specially recommended to those who wish to obtain a conception of the great cosmopolitan metropolis of the southern hemisphere.

CHAPTER V

In studying the literary productions of the República Oriental de Uruguay it is well to bear in mind the adjective in the official name of this country. It remains from the local term of Banda Oriental applied to the region before its establishment as an independent republic. After the struggle with Spain the emperor of Brazil laid claim to the country, but the political question was settled at the battle of Ituzaingo, where troops from Buenos Aires assisted. The capital, Montevideo, situated on the eastern side of the estuary of La Plata is a sister city to the capital of the Argentine Republic. Their intellectual life has been similar and their literary productions have appeared in the journals of either city according as political exigencies have dictated the residence of the author. Again their material wealth is based on the same industries, cattle and grain, so that conditions of life are much the same.

The patriarch of letters in Uruguay was Francisco Acuña de Figueroa (1790–1862). He was a monarchist, educated by the Jesuits, and his earliest verses were satires against the colonists who were fighting for independence. When they were successful he had to take refuge in Brazil. Later he was permitted to return. How well he became reconciled, is evident from the truly patriotic inspiration of the national hymn of which he is the author. His popularity as a literary man brought him such positions as treasurer general, director of the national library, and censor of theaters.

His verses, composed in the classic forms, sonnets, letrillas, odes, canciones, and décimas, fill twelve volumes in the collected edition of 1846, so arranged according to the explanation of the author, as to afford the reader an agreeable variety of matter. There is a little of all sorts, political, religious, praise of the bull-fight, congratulations on family events or election to office, epigrams on current gags, anecdotes or scandals. In explaining the liking of the Uruguayans for the poet, F. Bauzá [1] says:—"There is something local, characteristic, and peculiarly ours in his style, in his turns of expression, in all he has produced. On his pages may be observed the reflection of what is most habitual with us and what we like best."

It was natural that Acuña de Figueroa should be an opponent of the romantic school. So when the Argentine leaders of that school, Echeverría, Mitre, F. Varela, Rivera Indarte, Mármol, were refugees in Montevideo about 1844, he turned his sharp wit upon them. He satirized their peculiarities in a mock epic, entitled *La Malambrunada*, divided in three cantos. It relates the war which some old women begin in envy upon the young women. The first canto describes the congress of witches presided over by Satan before whom Malambrunada argues her case seeking their assistance. In the second canto the old women assemble under different standards. Falcomba strives to obtain the chief command. Voted

[1] F. Bauzá, *Estudios Literarios*.

down she opposes the plan to march at night and surprise
the young. The question being referred to a council of
thirty they approve the plan. The scene of the third
canto shifts to the young women. Venus has resolved
that they shall not be surprised. So she urges them to
choose a leader and prepare their forces. They elect
Violante to whom is given as a badge of authority a crown
of laurel interspersed with rubies. When Cupid sees her,
he cries out that she is more bewitching than Psyche.
Accordingly the old women fail in surprising the young
and when the armies meet in a plain, Venus guides Violante and her escort to the place where Malambrunada
has taken her stand. The old leader is beaten and killed.
The rest of the old women flee into a swamp where Satan
hides them by turning them into croaking frogs. In this
satire on the quarrel between the classicists and the
romanticists, the poet, to be sure, gives the victory to the
latter, but he makes their exaggerations and mannerisms
ridiculous by imitating their style and fantastic episodes.

While humor and Andalusian salt may predominate
in the verses of Acuña de Figueroa, it would be wrong to
suppose that he was incapable of a more elevated strain.
Few poems have been written more heart-stirring than
La Madre africana whose purpose was to put an end to
the African slave trade, at least that part of it which was
carried on in the ship Aguila flying the flag of Uruguay.
Very nobly and simply expressed are the feelings of the
woman who sees herself robbed of husband and children.
Very scornful are the words of the poet referring to the
"bravos who proclaim liberty and make slaves."

In spite of ridicule the young men in Montevideo fol-

lowed the romantic order.   The first in point of time was
Adolfo Berro (1819–41).   The amount and quality of
his work is all the more remarkable on account of the
shortness of his life.   His sympathies are with the fallen
and the downcast, the grief-stricken of all kinds.   And
true to the example of his master, Echeverría, he sought
also to exploit the poetic in native life, as in the ballad of
Yandubayu and Liropeya.   The young Indian and the
Spaniard Carvallo are wrestling in sport.   When the
maiden Liropeya reminds her lover that he must that
day fight for her possession with certain of her suitors,
he desists from the sport.   The Spaniard then treacherously kills him in order to make love to the maid.   She
indignantly rejects his advances, then suddenly consents
to follow him if he will dig a grave for Yandubayu.   While
the Spaniard is digging, she gets possession of his sword.
After he has finished his task and come for her, she kills
herself, bidding him to open another grave.

The same legend was used by Pedro P. Bermúdez
(1816–60) who turned it into a lyric drama, *El Charrua*,
in five acts and in verse which was produced with very
great success in Montevideo.   The title was derived from
the name of the tribe of aborigines found by the Spaniards
at their arrival in Uruguay.   Some of their peculiar qual-
ties, stubborn courage, taciturnity, and reserve, they
bequeathed with the strain of their blood to the present
inhabitants of that region.   Hence the poetic appeal met
with a certain atavistic response in the hearers of the
drama.   The action, laid in 1573, is slight, so that the production might better be termed a dramatic poem.   The
youth Abayuba adores the maid Lirompeya.   Her father,

Zapican, is willing to grant him her hand as soon as the lad has driven the Spaniards from the country. He calls together the chiefs who decide on war. Act three is devoted to the farewells of the lovers. In act four the Spanish captain Carvallo challenges Abayuba, but by guile he gets him as well as the maid Lirompeya into his power. The latter resists the captain's advances even though he announces to her the torture of her lover in prison. In act five Lirompeya succeeds in getting hold of Carvallo's dagger. Abayuba breaks from his prison and finds his beloved. After a love scene, she strikes herself with the dagger and hands it to the young man who follows her example by killing himself.

In lyric poetry the most successful romantic was Juan Carlos Gómez (1820–84). There is a personal note in his lines undoubtedly derived from the vicissitudes of his life. One feels that he is sincere when he sings his homesickness or rails at the evil of the world. He was by profession a lawyer, but during his many proscriptions from his native country he earned his living by journalistic work. He was one of the group who carried the romantic movement to Chile and was employed as a writer for the *Mercurio* of Santiago from 1845 to 1852. When he returned to his home he engaged in politics only to be obliged shortly to flee to Buenos Aires. There he became one of the leading journalists possessed of a trenchant, epigrammatic style quite in contrast with the vague, mournful tone of his verses. But he was not beloved in Montevideo, because he long waged a press campaign in favor of annexing the Banda Oriental to the Argentine Republic.

In spite of his sufferings at the hands of political tyrants, Gómez did not break forth in vituperation like Mármol, but expressed his emotions in poetical metaphor. *La Nube* is an example of this. In this poem he inquires of the cloud:—"Why weep upon the earth that does not deserve it? Its perfumes serve only to cover its evil." In many poems he finds comparisons between his personality and the sea, the sea that he had crossed so often, as a fugitive. He put himself also in a legend in six cantos dealing with an old man, *Figueredo*, who hates to see Uruguay under the domination of Brazilians. To the accompaniment of his guitar he sings to stir up his sons to a desire for emancipation. Finally he throws away the instrument, urging them to fight. Unfortunately in the first encounter through the fall of his horse the old man is taken prisoner and his sons are unable to rescue him. When he is liberated and permitted to return to his country, in a long apostrophe he refuses to do so because it is under the domination of Brazil.

Of the same period as Gómez but with decided classical leanings were Bernardo Prudencia Berro (1803–68), at one time president of the republic who met his death leading a revolution; Enrique de Arrascaeta a correct but cold rhymster; and Francis X. de Achá (1828–88).

While the Argentines were pouring out their diatribes against the tyrant Rosas, the Uruguayans found material for the drama in his rule. Francis X. de Achá wrote in verse *Una Víctima de Rosas*, then *La Fusión*, produced in 1851, the story of two friends separated by the civil war. Achá was a journalist and editor of *El Molinillo*, a satirical sheet. To this and to other papers he contributed many verses of a romantic type protesting against the civil war and various social evils. The fun-loving strain of his nature led him also to write comedies. *Bromas caseras* depicts in three acts the torments suffered by the husband of a jealous wife. In 1877 was represented his romantic drama, *Como empieza acaba*. Federico tricks Magdalena, the daughter of his partner, into marriage during the absence of her lover Carlos, who had been sent to Havana on business. Carlos, on his return, is found making love to the lady by her husband. They fight and Federico dies. But Magdalena refuses to marry, preferring the convent.

Another drama concerning Rosas, *Camila O'Gorman*, was written by Heraclio C. Fajardo (1833–67) and produced in 1856, with great success. This dealt with a particularly notorious act, the execution of a priest named Gutiérrez and a woman, Camila O'Gorman. In the play a platonic affection is shown to exist between Camila and the priest who is her piano teacher. A mutual friend, Lázaro, is arrested as a conspirator against Rosas. To save their friend's life by pleading with the tyrant, they go together to his house. Rosas is smitten with violent desire at the sight of Camila's beauty. During a momentary absence of the former, the friends refer their case to Manuelita, Rosas' angelic daughter. She promises to save Lázaro but warns that only flight can save Camila's virtue from the base purposes of her father. Act four discloses Gutiérrez, Lázaro, and Camila free but in the act of conspiring against Rosas. A certain Ganón who is himself in love with Camila leads the police to their resort. All escape the raid except Camila, but she is rescued later

by her friends. The love between Gutiérrez and Camila
ceases to be platonic. Ganón betrays their whereabouts
to the police. Arrested, they are shot according to the
orders of Rosas in spite of the pleadings of Manuelita.

Cursing Rosas in imitation of Mármol was also a poetic
diversion of Fajardo, but he did not do it quite so well as
his master. In other ways he won a reputation as a poet.
He won the gold medal in the certamen of 1858 by an ode
on *América y Colón*. Two years later he published a long
poem occupying over a hundred printed pages, *La Cruz de
Azabache* and in 1862 a volume of collected verse, *Arenas
del Uruguay*. The long poem treats the love affairs of a
poet, Helio by name. After a series of women, Ana, María,
Yola who deceives him, he meets Vitalia. The last he is
obliged to leave in order to take part in the war. As a
remembrance he takes with him a "cross of jet." Little
results from his participation in the war though he is
constantly dreaming of Vitalia. In the meantime, Yola
writes a lying letter to Vitalia saying all manner of evil
about Helio, among other things that he had left her. The
poem concludes with the death of Vitalia distressed by
the vision of a battle field on which vultures devour the
corpse of Helio.

The greatest figure in Uruguayan letters is undoubtedly
Alejandro Magariños Cervantes (1825–93). At the age
of twenty he was connected with the legation in Brazil.
A year later he started for Europe. While still a student
in Madrid he published his first novel, *La Estrella del Sur*,
which he had written in part during his voyage from
America. This was followed by two plays, *Percances
matrimoniales* and *Amor y Patria*. In 1852 he gave to the

world his poetic legend *Celiar* to which he owed his greatest fame. On somewhat similar lines was written in prose *Caramurú*, his best novel. In 1855 he returned to Uruguay where during the remainder of his life he enjoyed various public offices among which were those of rector of the university and senator. The volumes of collected verse, *Brisas del Plata*, 1864, and *Palmas y Ombúes*, 1884, were distinguished by their intense patriotism and local color.

The scene of *Celiar* is laid on a ranch belonging to Don Diego Sandoval, father of a pretty daughter. The social conditions are those of the eighteenth century. Don Juan de Altamira is the commander and tyrant of the town near the ranch. He makes love to Isabel, but her head and heart have no place for him, because the handsome and dashing gaucho, Celiar, fills them. She even snubs the proud Spaniard, who then pretends to give her up to his rival. Three days before their projected wedding there is brought to Celiar a letter asking him to come to the bedside of a dying uncle who had been a father to him in his childhood. Celiar sets out by moonlight, but well on the way his party is surprised by "Indians," of whom Don Juan is the leader. Don Juan stabs Celiar three times. Nobody dares denounce this act because the Spaniard is the legal representative of the king of Spain. He himself, however, is somewhat uneasy because Celiar's corpse disappeared. Another victim of Altamira is then introduced to the reader, a maid, Emilia. When she dies in child-birth her betrothed promises to avenge her wrongs on the Spaniard. So he flees to the Charruas, who at the moment are ravaging the white settlements

under a mysterious cacique Toluba. He is really Celiar.
The band descends upon the village where Don Juan commands and Celiar kills him. But Celiar and Isabel, who
are both injured, die in each other's arms.

Celiar is a novel in verse, written for the public in Madrid. Consequently the poet was obliged to make explanations of conditions, which mars the flow of his narrative. In *Caramurú*, however, prose allows the author
greater liberty of expression.

Caramurú is a gaucho, who has carried off Lia, the
daughter of a city lawyer, to save her from marrying a
man whom she dislikes. Moreover, he had saved her
life from a wild beast so that she has fallen in love with
him, but he maintains her in platonic affection, in a
covert in the woods. After her flight with him, Caramurú
enters a drinking place where other gauchos are discussing
the mysterious event. One of them remarks significantly
that he knows the abductor and the whereabouts of the
young woman. Caramurú fights with him and kills him.
When the other gauchos pursue the assassin through the
night, he eludes them by dropping off his horse, which
goes racing on, leading the pursuers far astray. Under
the name of Amaro our gaucho enters the service of a rich
Brazilian. In time he asks his employer to loan him a
large sum of money. The Brazilian promises him a large
reward, if Amaro will obtain a horse that can win a certain race. Now Amaro is aware that an Indian cacique
possesses an exceedingly swift horse, so he proceeds to
his camp. By a little trickery, by frightening the Indians
by big medicine, he succeeds in getting away with the
horse. When the day of the race is at hand the Indian

horse Dayman has for its only serious competitor, a noble animal, Atahualpa. The description of the horse race forms one of the most spirited passages in the book. Atahualpa exerts himself to the utmost, even bursting a blood vessel and falling close to the goal. As Amaro races by on Dayman, he is recognized by a soldier as the fugitive Caramurú. The latter is warned in time and again escapes by means of the speedy Indian horse. Soon after he learns that his hidden damsel is the daughter of Don Carlos Niger to whom he owes his life. Consequently, he brings her back to her father. This gives rise to a fight between Don Álvaro de Itapeby, to whom Lia was engaged, and Caramurú. They meet in single combat at the battle of Ituzaingo where Caramurú gives his adversary a mortal wound. As Don Álvaro lies dying in Caramurú's presence he discovers that the latter is his half brother, an illegitimate son of his own father. With his dying words he blesses the love of Caramurú for Lia.

Criticism has been made that this love affair during its existence in the forest was too platonic for reality. However that may be, Magariños Cervantes has succeeded in presenting an excellent picture of gaucho life and its ideals, love making, drinking, fighting and horse racing. No other man so completely dominates and incarnates the spirit of Uruguayan literature between 1840 and 1879. Therefore his admirers taking their cue from the identity of name are fond of referring to the author as the "Cervantes criollo."

In 1865 there was published in Montevideo *La Revista literaria* in which appeared the verses of Melchor Pacheco y Obes and Laurindo Lapuente. The former were given to the world by his widow. Their tone was melancholy and sentimental and are well exemplified by the poem *A una Cruz en medio del Campo* which Magariños Cervantes included in his excellent *Album de Poesías uruguayas*. It is like life this lonely cross and grave, according to the poet.

In contrast to Pacheco, Lapuente forgets himself in an exalted praise of liberty and America, and his heroes San Martin and Bolívar. In ringing verse he put such sentiments as this:—"Land of hope was America for the human race. In her heart God put a treasure more precious than the metal of her mines, which Spain filched from her—liberty."

These two poets terminate the first period of romantic poetry in Uruguay. After them the intensely personal note is greatly modified, for their successors in the next decade believed that poetry had a mission to put religion and philosophy within the reach of the people. Moreover, the younger generation were solicitous of form.

Of poets who came into notice during the seventies there are deserving of mention Washington P. Bermúdez, born in 1847, the son of Pedro P. Bermúdez, Victoriano E. Montes, Joaquín de Salterain, a well-known physician, and Antonio Lussich. The last was only one of a number of minor writers cherishing the tradition of the gaucho verse. As an exponent of gaucho literature Orosmán Moratorio (1852–98) distinguished himself in numerous ephemeral dramas. The most attractive at this distance of the poets in the above group is Montes. His *Tejedora de ñanduti*, the country lass who rejects the city wooer, touches the heart just as *El Tambor de San Martín*, the old soldier who recollects the glories of the war for independence, arouses enthusiasm.

Washington P. Bermúdez first attracted attention by reciting a heroic ode of his own composition, *Gloria a los Bravos*, referring to the successful defenders of Paysandú in the war with Brazil. But he could also write witty and satirical lines as shown by his compositions in the political journal, *El Negro Timoteo*. His greatest literary fame, however, like that of his father, rests upon a historical drama, *Artigas*. As a patriotic appeal to the Uruguayans this career of their national hero presented in four acts and many scenes with a final hymn to the national colors was a triumph. Though Bermúdez wrote other plays none met with like success.

Another dramatist dealing with the period of revolution was Estenilaso Pérez Nieto in *Apariencias y Realidades*. The patriotic sentiments in his drama are, however, incidental to the main action. This is laid in the camp of the famous "Thirty-three," that devoted band under the leadership of Lavalleja who demanded from Brazil in 1825 either liberty or death, and won the former. In the play the villain Carlos in order to ruin his rival Alberto brings the Portuguese into the camp in such wise as to throw suspicion on him. At the same time Carlos has secreted in Alberto's tent a young girl whom he himself had seduced and then brings upon the scene Elena, Alberto's fiancée. But both the Portuguese and the young girl accuse Carlos so that Alberto is cleared of the suspicion of treachery and reunited to his fiancée. This play greatly pleased the public of 1877.

The notion that poetry had a definite idealistic mission

had its stronghold in the society known as the "Ateneo del Uruguay." In its public meetings the veteran poet Arrascaeta announced the holy liberty of humanity; Luis Melian Lafinur cursed tyrants; and José G. Del Busto in his odes *A Grecia, A Polonia, El Ideal,* hurled Tyrtaean strophes at a people crushed under a despotic dictator. His epic romance *El Último de los Treinta y Tres,* a cry of indignation at the neglect of the last of these heroes dying in poverty, received great applause. Del Busto is the interpreter of the ideas and conscience of his country just before the revolution of 1886.

During this same period romanticism in Uruguay received an original bent from a poet who stands alone in his class and manner. Juan Zorrilla de San Martín, born in Montevideo in 1857, was sent to study in the University of Santiago de Chile. He returned home in 1877 with a printed volume of verses bearing the title of *Notas de un Himno* whose themes were mainly faith and love. He then began work on the masterpiece of Uruguayan literature, the long poem *Tabaré,* which he read in sections to the public as fast as it was written. When finally published it was composed of six cantos and more than forty-five hundred lines. At such length the poet recited the tragic love of Tabaré, the half breed Charrua Indian, whose Spanish mother had taught him to kiss the cross. The soft blue eyes of the mother, now dead, who used to sing to him, haunted his memory. So when brought a prisoner to the stockade of the whites he fell violently in love with Blanca, the sister of the Spanish commander, Don Gonzalo. After a while the love-sick

Indian is allowed to depart to his tribe. He arrives to find that the tribesmen are celebrating the funeral dance of their deceased cacique. A certain Yamandú persuades them to elect him their chief and then to celebrate his election by beginning an attack upon the settlement of the whites. Yamandú is the villain in the tragedy. He also has seen Blanca and to carry her off is for him a prime reason for the raid. The savages are successful. From the burning houses of the Spanish village Yamandú bears Blanca into the recesses of the forest. When Don Gonzalo discovers the disappearance of his sister, instantly attributing the raid to Tabaré, he organizes a posse in pursuit. In the meantime Yamandú waits beside the unconscious body of Blanca for her to recover from her swoon. Just as she opens her eyes she becomes aware of the struggling forms of two fighting men. Tabaré had followed Yamandú and there kills him. Tabaré then carries Blanca toward the settlement. Don Gonzalo meets them. Rushing at the Indian, in ignorance of the truth the Spaniard plunges his sword into Tabaré's heart. The poor savage is only too happy to die as Blanca weeps over him and embraces him. In the closing words of the poem: "The Indian is silent forever, like his race, like the desert, a tongueless mouth, a heavenless eternity."

Comparison of *Tabaré* with Longfellow's *Hiawatha* has occurred to many, but there is little similarity either in subject-matter or the spirit of the two poems. Critics almost scoffing at the possibility of so sentimental a savage have raised the question also of the likelihood of such a character as Tabaré. But Valera concludes his remarks on the poem with an ingenious argument in favor of its probability, because he believes in the all-compelling power of love.

The style in which the author has written is described by Valera[1] thus. After stating that Zorrilla de San Martín belongs to the school of Becquer, he says:—"The new thing in Juan Zorrilla is that, although Tabaré is a narration, in part of it he narrates and almost does not narrate. The poem seems a beautiful series of lyrics in which the action gradually unfolds. When the personages speak, one remains in doubt whether it is they speaking or the poet in whose spirit are brightly reflected the feelings and ideas which the personages have in a vague manner."

At the time when Zorrilla de San Martín was beginning his great poem *Tabaré*, occurred the dedication of a monument to Uruguayan independence in the Plaza de la Florida. Zorrilla de San Martín was called upon to write a poem befitting the occasion. He read his ode *La Leyenda Patria* which won the greatest applause ever given to a similar bit of literature and which since that day has been declaimed till people are tired of it. Somewhat classical in form and slightly reminiscent of Olmedo, the ode develops the poet's ideas in pictures and visions of his country's history. He sees the country prostrate under the invader, the heroism of the Thirty-three, the great battles of Sarandí and Ituzaingo and the possibilities of the future.

The publication of *Tabaré* brought its author such fame that he was sent to Europe first as envoy to the Holy See and then as minister to France and Spain. He has published his impressions of travel in *Resonancias del Camino*.

[1] J. Valera, *Cartas americanas*, 2a serie.

Lately he gave to the world a historical monograph, *La Epopeya de Artigas*, written in poetic style.

After the passing of the romantic epoch the composition of verse developed as elsewhere from Becquer to the decadent school. Luis Piñeyro del Campo began publishing verses as early as 1875, but his finest work appeared much later. *El Último Gaucho* is a long poem descriptive of country life in which the contrast between the new conditions and the old is made artistically manifest. The grandfather sits by as the cart is being loaded to depart for the day's work. He had been a soldier and taken part in the great events of the past. To see his grandsons engaging in such labor and enjoying the fruits of peace makes him weep. After the cart is gone he falls into a delirium in which he rehearses his deeds, and demands his horse and lance. As the locomotive on the railway whistles and rumbles by the old man dies, a symbol of the primitive life fast yielding before the progress of civilization.

Rafael Fragueiro at the time of the publication of his first volume of poems, *Recuerdos Viejos*, 1887, posed as the poet of poets attempting to practice in life the exaggerations and artificialities which he put into his verses. He was the first becquerista. After a romantic marriage he went to Buenos Aires, where he became a professor and forgot the production of verse for a time. When he began writing again it was in the prevailing decadent manner.

In Buenos Aires lives another poet and professor of Uruguayan birth, Victor Arreguine. He began rhyming in the becquerista manner, but his latest poems were in the style of Verlaine. The title of one of the best, *La Vejez de Venus,* is suggestive of its character, decadent, artificial, polished and beautiful.

More national in character were the poems of Santiago Maciel (born 1867). His first volume, *Auras primaverales,* 1884, contained a notable poem on the war between Chile and Peru. In 1893, he published *El Flor del Trébol,* a long poem redolent of Uruguayan fields. The first canto describes the happiness of a country lass in love. She is rudely awakened from her dream by the call to arms which takes her lover away. The second canto recites various incidents that occurred during the days of his presence and whose recollection cheers her in his absence. The third canto opens with a message which she has received from her lover. He tells her that a severe fight is impending and that he expects to die. One afternoon as she is absorbed in melancholy revery, she catches sight of a horseman pursued by another. The foremost is her lover, overtaken by his pursuer and killed so that he falls at her feet. A poem so characteristically national as this is pleasant reading.

A prolific writer of verse in various manners is Carlos Roxlo. He is classed as an eclectic poet with reminiscences of Becquer and Campoamor, of De Musset and the Mexican Flores. This is not surprising because he is a thorough student of literature, and in this respect has deserved the greatest praise from all those who love Uruguayan letters. His *Historia crítica de la Literatura uruguaya* is a monumental work.

The only other person who has treated the same subjects is Francisco Bauzá whose essays *Estudios Literarios,* were really incidental to his main interest, the political history of Uruguay. He wrote also a few poems and was noted as an orator.

The development of the novel in Uruguay owes something to Carlos María Ramírez (?–1898), important in the history of his country as a lawyer, publicist, orator and politician. His *Amores de Marta* is a romantic story, while the unfinished tale *Los Palmares* is redolent of Uruguayan fields and perhaps set the example for later novelists who picked their themes from national events.

Asociated with Ramírez, at least in exile, was the greatest of Uruguayan novelists, Eduardo Acevedo Díaz. Attacking the government in 1875 with trenchant pen for its attitude toward the freedom of the press, he was arrested and banished. In his place of refuge, Buenos Aires, he produced his first novel, *Brenda*, which remained his own favorite and has a wider appeal than his more powerful nationalistic tales. The general plan of *Brenda* is romantic in type, but the story abounds in realistic episodes.

The title is derived from the name of the heroine of the novel. She is the adopted daughter of the rich Señora de Nerva, who desires that Brenda should become the wife of her physician, Doctor Lastener de Selis. But Brenda is in love with Raúl Henares. This gallant young man had saved the life of a certain Areba Linares who thereupon had fallen in love with her savior. Consequently she assists the Señora de Nerva in her efforts to marry Brenda to Doctor De Selis, by disclosing a fact of which she had been an eyewitness, namely, that Raúl Henares was the unknown man who during the last civil war had killed the colonel Pedro Delfor, Brenda's father. Even this disclosure has little effect on Brenda's feelings either toward her lover or toward De Selis whom she hates because he had refused to attend professionally on her dying mother. In spite of the Señora de Nerva, the lovers continue to communicate through the negro gardener Zambique, whose faithfulness unto death forms one of the most pathetic and interesting episodes of the story. The great obstacle to the lovers' complete happiness is removed by the death of the doctor in a duel with a friend of Raúl. Then Señora de Nerva dies of her chronic malady. And after a year of mourning, Brenda and Raúl are married.

Acevedo Díaz returned from exile in time to take part in the important affair in 1886, known as the revolution of Quebracho. The result being disastrous for his party he again took refuge in Buenos Aires. His experiences of campaigning as a rebel he applied in writing a series of semi-historical novels dealing with the adventures of a family during the wars for independence won at Sarandí, in 1825. The first of these, *Ismael*, was published in 1888, followed by *Nativa* and then by *El Grito de Gloria*.

The shortest of these is *Nativa* which is little more than one episode taken from the series making up the whole story. Nata and Dora are sisters, girls from the city living on the estancia of the "Three Ombúes." On this estate is a ruined house where José María Beron, a patriot officer wounded by the Portuguese, has taken refuge. Being young and a hero he is very interesting to the girls. He prefers Nata, which fact so oppresses Dora that she commits suicide by drowning herself in a pool. Shortly thereafter the Portuguese approach so that Nata is obliged to depart, leaving her wounded lover among the troops who occupy the estancia. This young officer is a leading character in *El Grito de Gloria*. He meets death heroically at the battle of Sarandí from where his corpse is carried to be interred beside Dora.

The strength of this trilogy of novels consists not only in the vivid pictures of landscapes and manners, but also in the characterization, wherein the author approaches the contemporary naturalism of Carlos Reyles. In fact in discussing the trilogy one must consider the personages rather than the plots. Ismael is the personification of the gaucho of the period with his bravery, vices, crimes and prejudices as he contributed to the foundation of Uruguayan nationality. Cuaró, the Charrua Indian, is a type taken from nature. Another element of this variegated society is exemplified by the half-breed girl, Jacinta, who rides with the soldiers, furnishing them with female companionship, cooking their meals, fighting among them like a man, and dying a heroic death in protecting the body of José María after his fall.

The significance of *Ismael* as a work of art is set forth by the eminent journalist Alberto Palomeque, an associate of Acevedo Díaz in his first exile. His publication of the review *Vida Moderna* was a real service to Uruguayan letters. In the issue for May, 1901, he says: "*Ismael* is a hymn to blood. On every page is breathed hatred and blood. The author believes that in the shedding of blood is the law of all human progress. In this book is the explanation of all our misfortunes. A society founded in hatred, in slaughter, in blood, in violation of the family, in attacks on property, in terror imposed by a vulgar caudillo who is master of lives and estates, must continue to suffer." And in similar vein concerning *Soledad*, the last novel by Acevedo Díaz, he continues. "Soledad is the mistress of her father's murderer. Thus from an assassin springs the germ of native society. Soledad will have children by a bandit. On every side blood, crimes, seduction, children of assassins. Our nationality will have for basis crime, vagabondage and unstable abode, a sad heritage."

When the naturalistic movement reached Uruguay, the example of Acevedo Díaz directed attention to the gaucho and country life in general as a source for novels and tales. Manuel Bernárdez, born 1867, was one of the first to publish excellent realistic stories. Mateo Margariños Solsoña wrote not only short stories but practiced the novel. His *Las Hermanas Flammary* appearing in 1893 followed the methods of Zola almost to the point of direct imitation. Through the efforts of her mother, Elvira Flammary is married to Mauricio Castaigne, but her older sister is more attractive. Margarita's marriage, however, fails to materialize, so she casts envious eyes upon her sister's complaisant husband. Elvira's illness favors the dénouement, and as the illness develops into a chronic malady after the mother's death, the household settles down into a three-cornered affair. Another practitioner of the realistic tale was Javier de Viana. His gauchos are degenerate sons and his women vile creatures.

The master of these naturalists is undoubtedly Carlos Reyles. Living on a vast cattle ranch which he inherited, he found time not only to develop his property scientifically but also to imitate the literary methods of the French and Spanish novelists whom he admired. *Beba*, which he published in 1894, marked a new path in the literature of Uruguay. The action of the story begins at the Estancia of El Embrión. Its owner, Gustavo Ribera, is a reformer in the methods of agriculture. So many are his innovations, such as the substitution of iron plows for the old wooden ones, the use of horse rakes and tractor engines, scientific treatment of drying fodder, that his peons think him crazy. He is specially interested in classifying his cattle and in improving the breed. Growing up on the estate is his dead sister's child Beba. When she arrives at a marriageable age she marries Rafael Benavente, a broker in the city. Living there bores her as much as her husband's mode of life for he is indolent, without ambition, and given to drink and the pursuit of pleasure. By and by the couple visit the estancia. Rafael to cure his ennui keeps soaked with liquor, but Beba rejoices at every moment spent in the open. She passes her time with her uncle whose manly strength and skill she admires to the disadvantage of her husband. One day she falls in with an old woman who tells her the secret of her birth, a love child. The phrase works in her mind till in a moment of mad adoration she gives herself to Gustavo. The weak husband merely cries when he hears the facts from his wife's mouth. The lovers continue on the farm for a time. One day Gustavo in Beba's presence angrily kills his best stallion on account of defects in his progeny. Soon thereafter Rafael and Beba return to the city. In course of time Beba has a child, but it is still born and a monster. The crossing of blood relatives which Gustavo had studied so scientifically in his cattle asserts itself as a principle of human mating. Beba, remembering the scene with the stallion, feels that Gustavo will despise her. Consequently she winds a heavy work chain about her body and leaps into a deep pool of water.

Reyles' next production consisted of three short stories on the theme of adultery. Of these *Primitivo* is the most striking in plot. In 1910 he published *La Raza de Cain*. While this novel mainly consists of a study of the base spirit of Cacio, the evil habits and manners of a certain class of wealthy society are cruelly bared to inspection. Cacio is a poor devil whom the rich Arturo Crooker met at college. There he bullied him physically and domineered over him with his money. Their relations continue in business, and in society on the same footing. They fall in love with the same woman, Laura. Arturo wins her. Cacio is like Cain always beaten by Abel and he exclaims, "The happiness of others irritates me." One day he slips poison into a cup of milk given to Laura and stolidly watches her die.

In the theater the naturalistic movement has been well represented by Samuel Blixen (1869–1909) and Victor Pérez Petit (born 1871). Blixen's plays bear titles borrowed from the seasons, *Primavera*, *Otoño*, and *Invierno*. That the names should suggest the development which takes place in the characters of the plays is plainly the author's intention. In *Primavera*, the widow Emilia, cold of heart, listens to the amorous solicitation of Bonafacio with increasing interest till she glows with passion. *Otoño* was the most successful of the series. In this play Máximo, fifty years of age, attempts to win Celeste, a maid of forty of angelical character. She listens, hesitates, and finally consults her young nephew and niece to whom she is a foster mother. When the latter begs her not to go away, Celeste refuses the offer of marriage on the ground that, by accepting it, she would be a bad mother to the children whom she has cared for and taught to love her. This play pleased the same public which laughed at *Invierno*. The principal character of the latter is an old man of eighty-four who wishes to marry his granddaughter to an individual whom she dislikes. He is brought to terms by his aged wife who makes plain to him that he has lost the fortune which made him proud.

Victor Pérez Petit has been a very industrious man of letters in several fields. He came into notice through his literary studies, one of Zola and others published in a volume entitled *Los Modernistas*, 1903, concerning such men as Verlaine, D'Annunzio, Strindberg, Nietzsche, and Tolstoi. Then he tried his hand at realistic tales of which *Gil* is the most important. It is the study of the reassertion of atavistic instincts in the son of a murderer and prostitute. This boy is picked up from the gutter and given a home by a wealthy man, but the depravity in his nature comes to the surface at the age of puberty when he attacks and kills his benefactor's young wife. In 1907, Pérez Petit published a volume of sonnets, *Joyeles Bárbaros*, written in apparent imitation of Leconte de L'Isle. Throughout the decade he wrote plays from time to time of which he printed two volumes in 1912.

The plays show considerable variety in both theme and treatment. *Cobarde*, for example, is a drama of national manners. It concerns Pedro who loves Natividad, the daughter of Gil Grajales, a prosperous Spanish immigrant. He wishes his daughter to marry Rampli, an Italian, because, in his opinion, only foreigners in Uruguay are men in that country, where the natives are idle fellows given to boasting and singing to the accompaniment of the guitar. Just before a party Natividad makes Pedro swear that whatever happens he will not fight with her father. When Gil sees the despised Pedro dancing with his daughter, he interferes with a shower of insults. Pedro draws his dagger but Natividad calls on him to keep his oath. Like a coward he slinks away. His father Anastasio, however, takes up the quarrel and kills Gil. For a time the assassin eludes the police. When his whereabouts become known to them through the activity of Rampli, Pedro again appears on the scene. By fighting the police in a mad attempt to free his father, Pedro proves, even though he dies in vain, that he is no coward.

In other plays Pérez Petit makes adultery the pivot about which the action revolves. *El Esclavo-Rey*, called a comedy, depicts the degradation of a poor clerk who not only neglects his family but also steals for his mistress. *Yorick*, on the other hand, is a tragedy revealing the mental tortures of a pair of adulterers. Yorick is the young son of Adelina whose husband, a banker, had committed suicide after his bankruptcy. She might have saved him the bankruptcy had she used her influence; but, knowing his intention to shoot himself, she preferred to let him die because she was infatuated with a certain Doctor Lazlo. Yorick is sent to Europe to complete his education. On his return he finds his mother living in Lazlo's house. At first Yorick is not suspicious and even

makes love to Clara, the doctor's daughter. Objections
to his love-making somehow excite his curiosity about his
mother's position in that house. Though he questions
her, he learns little till he surprises her and the doctor in
a compromising situation. Then the truth flashes upon
him. Yorick knows that his father's life might have been
saved had Lazlo loaned him money. So Yorick determines to revenge his father by taking advantage of Lazlo's
great love for Clara. Unless the doctor will instantly go
out and shoot himself, Yorick will reveal the whole dis-
graceful story to the daughter. And she is coming to a
conference directly. Lazlo leaves Yorick. Clara enters.
While she is inquiring for her father, a pistol shot rings out.

It is significant of the power and originality of Uruguayan literature that it gave to the modernista movement not only dramatists like Pérez Petit and a review so
excellent as *Vida Moderna*, essentially national, however,
in their meaning, but also that it produced a poet like
Julio Herrera y Reissig and the critical essayist, José
Enrique Rodó. The poet rose so far above his local sur-
roundings that the value of his work was not fully appreciated until the modernista movement began to be studied
as a whole. And Rodó is universally acknowledged by
Spanish Americans as an intellectual leader.

CHAPTER VI

From the point of view of general education Chile, at the close of the revolution, was one of the most backward of the young American republics. The question of filling the need for education became a political dispute between the party of the oligarchs, supported by the clergy, and the liberals. The former composed largely of the adherents of a few wealthy families have up to the present given Chile a more stable government than that enjoyed by the other republics; but the liberals have from time to time been able to obtain many concessions. With their efforts at democratization the history of literature in Chile, no less than her political history, is concerned.

In 1828, the liberals happening to be in power, they promulgated a new constitution. At this time there was in Chile a remarkable Spaniard, José Joaquín de Mora (1783–1864), whose adventurous life led him over South America, and whose *Leyendas Españolas* later found an imitative echo in American literature. President Pinto is said to have taken his advice in preparing the liberal constitution. At any rate he encouraged Mora, made a citizen of the republic by special act of Congress, to attempt educational reform in Chile by opening a school known as the Liceo Nacional de Chile. Mora also defended the interests of the liberal party by editing *El Mercurio chileno*. He established a literary society, wrote poems and even produced a play, *El Marido ambicioso*, based on French models. But his ascendency was short lived, for in 1829 the conservatives returned to power under the presidency of Joaquín Prieto and his prime minister, Diego Portales.

By them Andrés Bello was invited to Chile to serve as a counterweight to Mora. To Bello was entrusted the editorship of the government organ *El Araucano*, which position Bello held for more than twenty years. In this journal he had ample opportunity to foster an improvement in the literary taste of the Chilean public. To Bello's training in education were entrusted the sons of the leading families. On the other hand, Mora's school was closed by governmental action and the man himself driven from Chile in 1831.

Bello's school, El Colegio de Santiago, was held in his own house. He conducted his instruction by original methods, graphically described thus by one of the pupils:[1] "The study of language was a complete course on philology, which comprised everything from general grammar and the history of the Castilian language down to the most minute questions of Castilian grammar. The professor followed his ancient custom of writing his texts as he taught them. His treatise on conjugation and the most interesting chapters of his Spanish grammar were discussed in those long pleasant conferences with his pupils. He never explained, but conversed, beginning always by expounding a question in order to discourse on it to his pupils. In these conversations he was the one who talked, at the same time almost always smoking a Havana cigar.

[1] J. V. Lastarria, *Recuerdos literarios*.

His lecture hall was his library and all his references to authors were made by the pupils under the direction of the master."

In this manner were trained a body of young men who were ready in 1842 to defend their country in a literary controversy against the Argentine journalists who had taken refuge in Chile. Fleeing from the tyranny of Rosas, they had brought with them the spirit of the romantic movement in literature taught them by Esteban Echeverría. And they did not hesitate to criticise adversely the state of Chilean literature.

The first opportunity for this was offered by the publication in 1841 of Andrés Bello's poem *El Incendio de la Compañia*. Inspired by the destruction by fire of the principal church left by the Jesuits in Santiago, the poem was written in quintillas in the classical style and may be accounted one of the most interesting of Bello's minor productions. The poet as a spectator of the conflagration sees the famous clock in the belfry destroyed, and hears its farewell to the city to which "it has counted a whole century of time, hour by hour," amid the marvellous changes which have occurred during that era. The sight of the ruins causes him to express his melancholy regrets almost in the words of Jeremiah.

The Argentine D. F. Sarmiento in reviewing the poem propounded the question, "Why are there no poets in Chile?" He answered it in a second article when discussing the foundation of a literary society in May, 1842, by a number of young Chileans, mainly pupils of Bello. Sarmiento said that the Chileans lacked poetry, "not through incapacity but on account of the bad tendency of their studies." Herein he referred to Bello's grammatical teaching, for the latter had opposed a proposition of Sarmiento's that orthography should conform to pronunciation, with the statement that young men should study good Castilian models, so that their language might not degenerate as among "another American people into a Spanish-Gallic dialect." Sarmiento met this fling by declaring that "the Argentines had written more verses than the tears they had shed over the sad fate of their country." Moreover, "the influence of grammarians, respect for models, and fear of breaking rules" brought about a lack of spontaneity of ideas.

The young Chileans rallied to the defense of Bello's methods by founding a periodical, *El Semanario Literario*, in which to print their polemics and their literary productions. The most important contributors were Salvador Sanfuentes, Bello's sons Francisco and Carlos, and J. J. Vallejo. The topic of discussion was nominally romanticism. The Argentine V. F. López published a long article about it and Andrés Bello reviewed the romances of the Duque de Rivas. He also printed translations of two poems by Victor Hugo, entitled in Spanish *A Olimpio* and *Las Fantasmas;* the latter is the well-known poem beginning, "Hélas! que j'en ai vu mourir de jeunes filles!" To López' article Sanfuentes replied that romanticism was not well understood in Chile; besides it was going out of fashion in Europe. In its place he urged "faithful pictures of life." In illustration he began the publication of his long poem, *El Campanario.*

In the theater, a translation of Hugo's *Angelo* was produced as an example of the romantic drama. Other translations followed. Then Carlos Bello (1815–54), wrote a piece in two acts, *Los Amores del Poeta* which was welcomed with great applause. A month later Rafael Minvielle (1800–87), put on the boards *Ernesto*, which was praised by Sarmiento as superior to the former. Minvielle also translated *Hernani* and Dumas' *Antony*. Juan Bello (1825–60), likewise made translations of romantic dramas and attempted to rival Sanfuentes in a poetic legend, *Elena y Eduardo*.

Satirical treatment of the controversy was undertaken by José Joaquín Vallejo (1809–58), who poked fun at romanticism by saying that "it was the cheapest thing that had come to Chile from Europe by way of the Río de la Plata." And as original productions under the now famous pen name of "Jotabeche," he wrote sketches of manners and customs in the mining camps of Chile. These vivid pictures of the landscape and the miners, their dances and fights, the vivacious record of their conversations and the satirical account of their superstitions form one of the classics of Chilean literature.

In his story of the literary controversy J. V. Lastarria, in his *Recuerdos Literarios*, is inclined to deny Andrés Bello's leadership, and attributes its origin and bitterness to the efforts of the young men to outshine the Argentines in the drawing rooms of Santiago by the declamation of original compositions in verse, and to the poetical contest of 1842, promoted by the society of which he was president, La Sociedad Literaria.

Whatever its origin the best fruit of the controversy was the establishment of the University of Chile, of which Andrés Bello was installed as rector, September 17th, 1843.

And a month later he brought to a climax his part in the controversy by publishing *La Oración por Todos*. This poem is not a translation but an adaptation of Victor Hugo's *La Prière pour tous;* "strongly Castilian" according to Menéndez y Pelayo, "in which Bello seizes the original thought and develops it in our language in conformity with our lyrical habits; and he accomplishes this in such fashion that *La Oración por Todos* is known by everybody in America and considered by many as Bello's best poem. There is no Spaniard who reads those melancholy and sobbing strophes and again looks at the French text without finding it very inferior."

To the setting of the poem, the landscape bathed in evening twilight, Bello added certain features essentially Spanish, the old tower, the isolated farmhouse and the church. On the moral side he urges a prayer for Spanish types of sinners. And while the French poem is not specific in its invocation for the dead, Bello pleads for "My Lola." Death being an ever present preoccupation of the Spanish mind, Bello widens the scope of the argument for kind thoughts toward the dead in this wise: "I too at no distant day shall be a guest of the dark house and shall invoke the prayer of a pure soul."

After Bello's installation as rector of the University of Chile his poetical production was slight, a few translations, fables and verses for ladies' albums. He was occupied with his professional labors and the preparation of his scientific works which served as text-books. The names of a few suffice to show the wide variety of his learning: *Teoría del Entendimiento*, 1843; *Proyecto del*

Código civil, 1843; *Principios de Derecho internacional,* 1844; *Gramática de la Lengua castellana,* 1847.

As secretary of the University of Chile, was chosen Salvador Sanfuentes (1817–60), in some ways Bello's most distinguished pupil. At the age of sixteen he wrote an imitation in verse of Racine's *Iphigenie,* which Bello printed in the *Araucano.* In 1836 he became secretary to the Chilean legation in Peru, in 1843 general secretary to the University. From 1847 to 1851 he was a member of President Bulnes' cabinet, first as minister of justice and later of state. As a member of the House of Deputies he was considered brilliant, while he was also acknowledged to be an able practitioner of law. In 1853 he resigned his position as secretary of the University, but became its dean in 1856. Appointed a judge of the Supreme Court, 1858, he held this position until his death.

Throughout his political career, his interest in poetry never failed. His enemies could find nothing worse than to call him the author of *El Campanario,* which he wrote at the age of twenty-four, in order to demonstrate so valiantly to the carping Argentines that poets did exist in Chile. His purpose, moreover, was to prove the superiority of real pictures of life over the fancies of romanticism. The poem is written in three cantos. The scene is laid in Santiago about the middle of the eighteenth century. A marquis proud of his nobility has two children, Cosme and Leonor. To this family is introduced by the president of Santiago, Don Antonio de Gonzaga, a young Captain Eulogio to whom he owes his life. But the latter, being of plebeian birth, is not favored by the parents of Leonor. As long as the president lives, Eulogio's

suit for the young lady's hand prospers; but when Don
Antonio suddenly dies, Captain Eulogio is turned away
from the marquis' house. The young man, however,
persuades Leonor to elope with him during the favorable
opportunity presented by Holy Week. Their marriage
is in progress in the chapel of a neighboring town when
her father and his slaves appear and interrupt the ceremony. Eulogio, unwilling to injure the father, does not
defend himself from arrest. Loaded with chains he is
tried for abduction and banished. That night, however,
he escapes from prison. A few days later, a letter containing four letters traced in blood, of which only Leonor
understands the meaning, is brought to her together with
a portrait. She retires to a convent. One moonlight
night the nuns are awakened by an unseasonable ringing
of the bells. Ascending the belfry they find there hanged
the hapless Leonor. The poem contains descriptions of
ancient customs, especially of the royal court of justice,
the celebrations of Holy Week, the nunnery and the taking of the vows by the novice. The episodes possess a
real interest and the whole poem, written in a variety of
meters, has a fresh and animated style.

In 1850 Sanfuentes published as a collection in one
volume, two other legends and his romantic drama, *Juana
de Nápoles*. The legend entitled *El Bandido*, opens with
a scene on a mountain where a negro bandit, Fernando, a
man who had sworn to avenge the wrongs of his race, is
feasting with his followers. With him is María who had
yielded to Fernando to save her father's life after she had
been carried off from her village just as her wedding to
Anselmo was being celebrated. As the feast progresses,

the bandits perceive clouds of smoke arising from the forest, which warns them of the approach of a band of pursuers led by Anselmo. When they come up, the latter fights with Fernando, but is severely wounded and defeated. María, however, persuades Fernando that Anselmo is her brother and so is allowed to nurse him back to health. She confesses to him her disgrace, whereat Anselmo scorns her. That night coming to him, with the statement that she has taken poison, she falls dying at his feet. Anselmo calls Fernando and they fight. Anselmo, however, is again beaten and falls beside María's corpse whose hand he clasps in his last moments. Fernando, kicking their hands apart, leaves them, breaks camp and surrenders to the authorities, who execute him.

Superior to this poem is *Inami ó la Laguna de Ranco*. Alberto has fled from the Chilean city of Valdivia because he has killed a superior in a duel. He escapes his pursuers by taking refuge on an island in the lake of Ranco. Falling in love with Inami, the beautiful daughter of the Indian cacique Colpi, he marries her and a son is born to them. One night Alberto saves from the waters of the lake an old man, Alejo, who proves to be his father, come in search of him. Alejo is angry when he learns that Alberto has married Inami and demands that he leave her and return to Valdivia. The young man refuses, but in his distress at being obliged to choose between his wife and his father, exhibits some coolness to the former. Their suspicions aroused, the Indians kill Alejo. Beside his corpse, Alberto finds a dagger which he recognizes to be Colpi's. The Indian when confronted admits his guilt; in the ensuing fight Alberto kills his father-in-law on the top of a cliff whence he throws the body into the lake. Alberto obtains a canoe in preparation for removing his father's body. As he is about to start, Inami, with her child, appears at the top of the cliff. Beckoning to her husband, she plunges into the water to swim toward the canoe. About to reach it, she strikes against Colpi's body. Then with a cry of horror, she places her child in the canoe, turns back to embrace her father's corpse and sinks with it to her own death.

Sanfuentes admitted his indebtedness to that old epic of Chilean history, Ercilla's *Araucania*. He succeeded fairly well in making his Indians natural and in exhibiting their sentiments of hospitality toward strangers. Especially interesting, however, is his description of the city of Valdivia.

His drama, *Juana de Nápoles*, derived its story from Sismondi. Roberto, king of Naples, had usurped the throne from his nephew, Carlos Huberto, king of Hungary. Roberto determines to bring about a reversion of the throne by arranging a marriage between Andrés, the second son of Carlos, and his own daughter Juana, at the time seven and five years old respectively. Their parents dying when he is eighteen and she sixteen, the young couple are left to adjust their differences and difficulties according to their own notions. Juana, holding that a papal bull had legitimized the usurpation, wishes to inherit her father's dominions while Andrés asserts a superior right. The dramatist complicated their quarrels by introducing a love affair between Juana and a certain Luis de Tarento and thus made more tragic Andrés' death at the hands of conspirators.

The poetic rendering of a legend again occupied Sanfuentes' attention in 1853. He found the material in
Olivares' *Historia Militar*. Huentemagu, an Araucanian
Indian, received as his share of the sack of a nunnery a
beautiful nun. With her he fell so much in love that she
was able to persuade him not only to respect her but also
to restore her to her fellow countrymen; whereupon he
followed her and became a servant at the nunnery in
order to be near the object of his adoration.

Four years later from the same pen came *Ricardo y
Lucía ó la Destrucción de la Imperial*, comprising 17,626
hendecasyllabic verses in octaves. This is a tale of love
between a Spaniard and an Indian maid, thwarted by
the jealousy of a disappointed lover who assists a conspiracy to raid the city of La Imperial. The actors all
perish in the tumult of its destruction. Somewhat different in character is Sanfuentes' last work of which he published four parts before his death. *Teudo ó Memorias de
un solitario* purports to be the diary in verse of the impressions of a solitary monk.

The poetic merit of Sanfuentes' compositions varies
greatly. The later ones become monotonous from ex-
cessive description. Though he lacks at times dramatic
force and psychological truth, he never fails in a feeling
for nature. He has written more verses than any other
Chilean and though the first to sing the beauties of primitive nature in Chile, no other poet in this respect has
equalled Sanfuentes.

The poetic activity in Chile about 1842 was not entirely
devoid of the classical note which sought perfection of
form. Even in *El Semanario* were published poems of

that type by Hermógenes de Irisarri, a Guatemalan, whose father, Antonio José de Irisarri, a very wealthy man, had played an important part in Spanish-American affairs during the revolutionary period. Another poet of classical leanings was Jacinto Chacón, who continued to an advanced age to occupy high positions in Chilean politics. As a leader the classical school may have looked to Felipe Pardo who came to Chile as Peruvian envoy in ₁836. A pupil of the celebrated Sevillan Alberto Lista and an enthusiastic man of letters, he wrote much and even published a periodical, *El Intérprete*, during his sojourn in Chile.

In some respects the most successful writer of occasional verse of classical type during this epoch was Doña Mercedes Marín de Solar (1804–66). Being a bright child she was given an excellent education, contrary to the prevailing notions about female education. She even knew French, which is remarkable for it is on record that in 1821 a priest refused to absolve a young woman because she was studying that language. Doña Mercedes came into public notice by her *Canto a la Muerte de don Diego Portales*, printed by Bello in the *Araucano*, July, 1837. This composition of three hundred and twenty-four lines was the work of a single night, and reflects as a historical document in verse the social conditions of the time. Her numerous pieces concern mainly events in family life bearing such titles as, To my daughter Luisa on the death of her husband; To my daughter Elena on her departure for North America; To my daughter Caroline on going to live in the country. Recollecting in her dying hours that she had written no verses for her youngest daughter Matilda, she composed a sonnet remarkable under the circumstances for containing no hint of death or separation and speaking only of the joy with which the daughter had blessed her mother.

Owing to the character of the race poetry has been more of a forced product in Chile than in some other Spanish-American countries, though versifiers have been numerous. The upper class of this race is composed of Spaniards largely of Basque origin, somber and practical, with an element of Anglo-Saxon merchants and sailors. The lower class differs from that of other South-American republics because their aboriginal ancestors, the Araucanians, were not submissive but warlike and difficult to conquer. Furthermore there are no Africans nor Asiatics. The geography of the land also contributes to homogeneity of race. A narrow strip of coast walled on the east by a range of lofty and almost inaccessible mountains, the sea affords easy communication between its parts. Shipping, mining, and agriculture in the numerous valleys in a climate favorable to labor by white men thus become its natural industries.

The same conditions explain the type of government projected by Diego Portales and adopted in the constitution of 1833. This gave the balance of power to an oligarchy of the landholders represented by senators whose term of office was nine years and a president elected for ten years. In the struggle which preceded the victory of the patrician conservatives, they were called "pelucones" by the liberals who in turn were dubbed "pipiolos." The strong rule of the "pelucones" preserved Chile from the anarchy which held back the progress of the other republics. But the descendants of the "pipiolos" kept alive and developed a liberalism, as the years passed, which found an expression not only in literature but also in armed uprisings.

The constitution of Portales made the church an institution of state because the church stood for order and the defense of property; in return the church supported the temporal power of the oligarchy. Against the union of church and state came the first attack of liberalism, Francisco Bilbao's (1823–65), *Sociabilidad chilena*, a book of great literary and social importance in the history of Chile. It was first printed in the short-lived periodical *El Crepúsculo*, 1844. The journal was suppressed and the author was prosecuted by the ecclesiastical authorities, who accused him of blasphemy, immorality and sedition because Bilbao attributed the extremely wretched condition of the working class in Chile to the domination of the clergy. The ecclesiastical tribunal found Bilbao guilty and sentenced him to pay a fine of fifteen hundred pesos or in default of its payment to serve six months in prison. His friends promptly subscribed the money and sufficient additional funds to allow him to leave the country. In *Sociabilidad chilena* a Chilean writer, Isidoro Errázuriz, sees the outcome of Andrés Bello's philosophical teaching, not in its substance but as a "wild plant" that grew in the intellectual ground prepared by his hand.

Isidoro Errázuriz, by the way, was a clever journalist and a brilliant orator whose political activity extended from 1860 to 1890. As a historian he published an important sketch of the political parties in Chile from 1823 to 1870 as an introduction to his extensive *Historia de la Administración Errázuriz.*

Francisco Bilbao went by way of Buenos Aires to Paris where he made the acquaintance of Michelet and Edgar Quinet. The latter, after reading Bilbao's book congratulated him. Quinet, the philosopher of democracy, was then producing his own works against the influence of catholicism in the modern world. When Bilbao returned to Chile, he established, on the basis of Quinet's ideas, a liberal society with the name of La Sociedad de la Igualdad. To it were attracted many liberal thinkers.

One of the most prominent was Eusebio Lillo (1826–1910). At the age of eighteen he attracted attention by winning a prize for verses on José M. Infante, a popular hero. Three years later he was honored by the adoption of a poem of his as the national anthem of Chile. The older one by De Vera was displaced because its virulent hostility to Spain seemed antiquated. In 1848 he was one of the founders of the *Revista de Santiago,* a somewhat notable periodical for it united as collaborators under the leadership of J. V. Lastarria many important men of letters. To this magazine Lillo's first contribution was a legend, *Loco de Amor,* in two cantos.

Lillo now became interested in politics, supporting the ideas of Francisco Bilbao by editing a journal, *El Amigo del Pueblo.* And as a rallying song for his party he wrote a *Himno de la Igualdad.* Words led to deeds in the liberal insurrection of 1851. Lillo took part in the fighting in the streets of Santiago. After this affair he was banished and took refuge in Peru.

His experiences in that country Lillo incorporated in a

long poem, *Fragmentos de los Recuerdos de un Proscrito*, generally considered his best poem on account of its interesting description of Lima. Lillo's verses give evidence of a delicate feeling for the softer moods of nature. He was fond of flowers and wrote so much about them that he was called the poet of the flowers. In a simple style which found imitators he sang the perfume of the mignonette and the pale and drooping calyx of the flowering rush. Even in the *Himno Nacional* he remembered the flowers of Chile and expressed the hope that the invader might never trample them down.

On reaching middle life Lillo applied his poetic imagination to the problems of speculative business. In Bolivia he embarked on various enterprises by supplying capital to miners. As a result he returned to his native Chile a wealthy man at the age of fifty-two. Once more in politics he was elected alcalde of Santiago. Under President Balmaceda of liberal tendencies he held various high governmental offices. And when the latter committed suicide in 1891, Lillo was the executor of his will.

A poet of a more purely romantic type than Lillo was Guillermo Blest Gana (1829–1904). His poems and sonnets say little of nature but treat intimately of his feelings. The romantic pose of his lines was not justified by the material circumstances of his life. Nevertheless he made Alfred de Musset his model. Not only did he translate the *Nuit de mai* but imitated it in twenty-three compositions which are grouped under the title of *Noches de Luna* in the edition of his *Poesías*, 1854. With the moon he converses about his love, her beauty and her deceitfulness. Being a good reader he became a parlor favorite with the ladies, who delighted to hear him read his verses. His later poems reflect with fascinating delicacy the spirit of Chilean home life.

In 1857, on account of political troubles he had to seek asylum in Europe. On his return he became a professor of literature in the University of Chile; then he entered the diplomatic service of his country. While minister to Ecuador he had an opportunity to enact in real life something as dramatic as any of his poetic fancies. The poetess, Doña Dolores Veintemilla de Galindo, slandered unjustly in her wifely honor by a priest, committed suicide near her child's cradle. At her funeral, unattended by others because it was that of a self-murderer, Guillermo Blest Gana was the only mourner and he attended in full diplomatic dress.

Beside the poems of personal character, Guillermo Blest Gana's literary productions include various poetic legends, *El Bandido, Las dos Mujeres, La Flor de la Soledad;* some tales in prose; and two historical dramas, *Lorenzo García* and *La Conjuración de Almagro.* The magazine, *La Revista del Pacífico,* which he founded offered encouragement to many of the minor poets of the day.

The following year, 1859, was marked by a revival of literary interest in Chile. This crystalized into the establishment of a society, El Círculo de los Amigos de las Letras, which inaugurated a poetic contest destined to bring into notice a number of young men. This society and contest was promoted by José Victorino Lastarria (1817–88), the former president of the Sociedad Literaria in 1842. For his activities of this kind (he was also a prime mover in founding the Academía de Bellas Letras in 1873), and his many journalistic enterprises, he has been called the "father of literary development in Chile." The major part of his writings, such as the somewhat visionary *Lecciones de Política positiva*, were political, but his sketches and tales, partly autobiographical of his political career, collected in the volume *Antaño y Hogaño*, form a classic of Chilean literature. No less valuable for literary history is his *Recuerdos Literarios*.

The general tone of the verses submitted for the contest of 1859 was that of romantic melancholy such as G. Blest Gana had made popular. A protégé of his, Martin José Lira (1833–67), gave it an original turn by drawing his inspiration from the contemplation of nature. His adaptation from Robert Burns, entitled *A una Ave Herida*, in which the bird reproaches the man for killing it, and his translation of Longfellow's *Psalm of Life* are characteristic of Lira's own productions.

The leading figure in poetic literature during the sixties was Guillermo Matta (born 1829). His first work, *Cuentos en verso*, printed in 1853, consisted of two long legends, *Un Cuento endemoniado* and *La Mujer misteriosa*, which smack strongly of his models Espronceda and Byron. They are love stories with digressions and apostrophes on whatever struck his fancy, Greece, Seville, Rome, Byron himself. Their open attack on the conventional religious ideas and prejudices shocked the Chilean public of the day; but his lightness of touch with a happy combination of jest and earnest made the poems attractive.

His literary free-thinking had a logical consequence in his adherence to a political insurrection in 1857, on account of which he was obliged to betake himself to

Europe. In Madrid he made use of the opportunity to print his writings in two volumes. The experiences of travel strengthened his philosophical ideas and on his return to Chile he expounded them with greater conviction. In an address on literature when installed as professor in the University of Chile, 1864, he touched on the marvels of steam railways and the electric telegraph and insisted that the new poetry must take into consideration such changes in the state of the world.

The most copious of poets, his practice in this respect made Matta the leader of a new school which praised the love of science, adoration of justice, and respect for industry. The improvement shown in his own literary style gave evidence of his wide study of the leading French, English and German poets. In fact the German note is his special contribution to Chilean poetry.

Guillermo Matta's brothers, Francisco and Manuel Antonio, were journalistic champions of the same advanced ideas. The latter won for himself an immense reputation in the Chilean congress. Guillermo supported a movement led by certain ladies for the better education of women. He even assisted Doña Rosario Orrego de Uribe to publish a *Revista literaria* for the same purpose.

Guillermo Matta's greatest popularity both at home and abroad was achieved in 1866. At that time Spain had seized the Chinchón islands off the coast of Peru and was at war with that country. At the same time she threatened an attack on Chile. Matta sent forth his verses calling on all America to rouse herself in common defense against the invader and they met a response in many lands.

One of the most stirring poems evoked by this war was written by Doña Rosario Orrego de Uribe (1834–79), *A la República peruana con motivo de la derrota de la Escuadra española en Callao.* The virile tones of this poem and of other patriotic utterances are remarkable. Her verses on mother love, on duty and to persons show the influence of Matta. She began writing for G. Blest Gana's *Revista del Pacífico* and in one of her early poems, *A mi hijo Luis,* made certain prophecies of his future character which proved true when second in command of the famous Chilean warship "Esmeralda." It was a strange coincidence that she died at about the very hour when he was distinguishing himself for valor in battle.

For correctness of expression and classicism of style Domingo Arteaga Alemparte (1835–80) held first place in this decade. His best remembered poems are a pair of sonnets, *El Llanto* and *La Risa,* in which he maintains the paradox "How often to cry is to be happy!" and an ode *Los Andes del Genio.* In the latter the poet admires the Andes mountains as they rear their rugged outlines above the smiling valleys; but there is a more sublime cordillera, the genius of man. Like the rivers from the mountains its influence streams through humanity.

The brothers Domingo and Justo Arteaga Alemparte were constantly associated in journalistic enterprises. They contributed to the literary activity of 1859 by establishing *La Semana.* Several years later they brought out *El Charivari* and *La Linterna del Diablo,* comic and satirical periodicals. These opened a new vein in Chilean journalism, for the serious and sober Chilean character has little liking for Andalusian salt so typical of Peru. Domingo Arteaga Alemparte also won fame as an orator.

In jocose verse, burlesque fables and satire, Manuel Blanco Cuartín (1822–90) specially excelled, and his journalistic work during a long period was graced by his humor. He wrote also two fantastic legends in verse, *Blanca de Lerma* and *Mackandal.*

A companion in light satire was Adolfo Valderrama (born 1834). But his writings were not limited to verse for he wrote amusing prose sketches afterwards collected in a volume entitled *Después de la Tarea.* His serious work was that of a physician and professor of medicine in the University. And he performed a service to the history of Chilean letters by preparing a *Bosquejo de la Poesía chilena,* 1866.

The martial lyrics of Guillermo Matta, to which reference has been made, initiated a fashion of heroic verse which, assisted by historical events, remained in vogue about two decades. In dramatic productions a parallel movement occurred. Matta's friend and admirer, Luis Rodríguez Velasco (b. 1838), the politician Carlos Walker Martínez (1842–1905), leader of the conservative party and diplomat, the talented José Antonio Soffia (1843–86), were the first to write in the heroic style. Then the war which Chile fought with Peru for the possession of the nitrate fields gave fresh impetus to the heroic, and brought into the field Víctor Torres Arce (1847–83), Ambrosio Montt (born 1860), and Carlos Lathrop (born 1853).

In the theater José Antonio Torres Arce (1828–64) produced in 1856 *La Independencia de Chile,* one of the best Chilean historical plays. Since the action concerned mainly the exploits of Manuel Rodríguez, a popular hero of the revolution, the lines were filled with tirades of exalted patriotism. The author wrote other plays and was a successful journalist.

The revolutionary hero, Manuel Rodríguez, was again staged in 1865, shortly after a statue of him had been erected in Santiago. The author's, Carlos Walker Martínez', patriotic tirades were enthusiastically received and especially the finale of his drama *Manuel Rodríguez*, which consisted of an apostrophe to the national flag. During the next six years, Walker Martínez wrote a series of *Romances americanos* based on colonial and revolutionary history. Though composed in rather a prosaic style they have been popular enough to call for a second edition.

On the other hand, Luís Rodríguez Velasco used for the material of his ballads the history of the day and followed closely the events of the Spanish-Peruvian war. Written at his post of observation in Peru the poems gave evidence of keenness of impression. His experiences also supplied him material for a legend in verse in six cantos, *Amor en el Hospital*. In 1869 he wrote a comedy of manners, *Por Amor y por Dinero*, which his contemporaries hailed as the best produced by a Chilean author. Ten years later when the war between Chile and Peru brought the victory of the Chilean warship Esmeralda over the Peruvian ironclad Huascar, Rodríguez Velasco again greeted his countrymen with a pæan of victory.

The daily occurrences of this war were celebrated in verse by Víctor Torres Arce. He was known to Chileans for his sensual bohemian lyrics, some plays and a novel,

Los Amores de un Pije, which scandalized the public of 1872 by its narration of erotic adventures.

But Juan Rafael Allende (1850–1905), wrote with greater talent the same sort of verse chronicle of the war in his *Poesías de " El Pequén,"* filled with patriotism, amusing for their witty sayings, and entertaining by reason of their pictures of camp life. By order of the secretary of war thousands of copies were distributed to the soldiers. At the same time Allende produced his patriotic plays *José Romero* and *La Generala Buendía.* The latter's exploits were being narrated in fiction by the novelist Ramón Pacheco. Allende, during the decade of the eighties, was a fertile writer for the popular stage, depicting many native types. Among his dramatic sketches were many bitter satires of the wealthy classes.

The most gifted Chilean writer during the seventies, whose real poetic feeling and delicacy of expression place him in the front rank of Spanish-American poets, was José Antonio Soffia. Though his verses attracted attention when he was but twenty years of age, his best work was produced after his appointment as ambassador to Colombia in 1874. The cultivated society of Bogotá was very stimulating to his talents. There were written his poetical romance, *Bolívar y San Martín,* generally considered his best poem, and the twelve cantos of the epic *Michimalonco,* awarded a gold medal at a literary contest held by the University of Chile, 1877.

This poem, based on Ercilla and the early historians of Chile, related in a variety of meters the story of Michimalonco, the first Araucanian cacique to rebel against Pedro de Valdivia. The trouble began when three Indian

women murdered a Spaniard, Roque Sánchez. His beloved, Ines de Suárez, led her countrymen to avenge his
death.   But the pleasing parts of the poem are the idyllic
pictures of primitive life, the love of the Indian maid
Guajilda for Michimalonco, her plaintive "yaraví" or
love song, their marriage by Christian rites.

Soffia's journey to Bogotá by way of the river Magdalena supplied him with the theme and the setting for a
pathetic tale in verse, *Las dos Hermanas*, about the
daughters of a fisherman who was drowned in a vain attempt to save another man's life.   In this as in all Soffia's
poems, the description of nature is unexcelled.   In *Aconcagua* he sympathetically pictured the beauties of his
native province.   In *Las dos Urnas* he rendered a tradition about the river Aconcagua and the city San Felipe.
Though love of nature inspired so many of his lines, love
for his wife and love of country, were also springs of his
muse.   His patriotic apostrophes to national heroes delighted his fellow Chileans.

The eloquence of patriotism was a more specialized
form of the grandiloquent verses on abstract themes
which were in fashion about 1880.   Ambrosio Montt y
Montt, for example, who first wrote odes and sonnets to
commemorate the naval victory at Iquique, and the valor
of the Chilean commander Arturo Prat, easily shifted to
compositions in praise of art and the mission of the poet.

This fashion was an echo of the poetic activity in
Buenos Aires in the late seventies.   The later romanticists, following perhaps the example of Victor Hugo,
had a theory that poetry should serve humanity by inspiring it with lofty ideals.   This school found its noblest

exponent in the grandiloquence of the Argentine poet Andrade.   In all Spanish America poets began inditing odes to Humanity, to Science, to Reason.

In Chile, the first prize for the poetic contest of 1877 was awarded Pablo Garriga (b. 1853) for an ode *Al Progreso*, and again in 1878 for *El Poeta*.   He was frequently applauded for his contributions to periodicals, for poems on such abstract topics and especially for an ode, *A la Ciencia.*

Pedro Nolasco Prêndez (b. 1853) openly acknowledged his debt to Andrade.   But he gave a note of originality to his verses by the form in which they were conceived, calling them *Silhuetas* when he praised the heroes of duty.   As Prêndez was quite successful in catching Andrade's lofty tone and wrote mainly after the latter's death, his admirers pretended to see in him a reincarnation of the Argentine bard.

Reactionary against the new philosophies, and a champion of the old religious ideals, arose Francisco A. Concha Castillo (b. 1855).   The virtues of the soul, of self-sacrifice, of faith, the discipline of pain, as celebrated in his *Dolor Generator*, were the sources of inspiration for his graceful and fluid verses.   A fantasy, *Apoteosis*, written in 1878 on the anniversary of the death of Cervantes, attracted wide notice outside of Chile.

Metaphysical poetry gradually disappeared before the style of writing brought into vogue by the Spanish poet Bécquer.   In 1887 a wealthy Chilean, Federico Varela, announced a literary contest to cover a wide variety of topics, in both prose and verse.   One prize was offered for the "best collection of poems of the suggestive or insinuating kind of which the Spanish poet Gustavo Bécquer is the prototype." The jury finally divided the prize between two collections which proved to have been written by Eduardo de la Barra (1839–1900).

He was a veteran writer, for at the age of twenty he had won first prize in the famous literary contest of the Circulo de los Amigos de las Letras, in 1859, by an ode *A la Independencia de America*. Though he contributed verses to periodicals for a while thereafter, he stopped suddenly in order to devote his time to politics, and political writing such as that contained in his investigation entitled *Francisco Bilbao ante la Sacristia*.

The Varela poetic contest again drew his attention to the writing of verses, in which he proved himself superior not only in the Becquerist rima but also in the fable and in a discussion of the theory of Spanish prosody. In 1889 he published his poems in two volumes, to which he gave the descriptive names *Poesía Subjectiva* and *Poesía Objectiva*. Beside the prize-winning verses they contained poems of passion, micro-poemas, and parodies of an early collection of poems by Rubén Darío, *Las Rosas andinas*. The micro-poema was so named by De la Barra from the fact that it told a tragic tale briefly, even in so few lines as a couplet. In the parodies of Rubén Darío to which De la Barra gave the title Rubén Rubí, he showed himself a master of the jocose verse so rare in sober Chile. By this wide diversity of form, De la Barra has proved himself the most clever artificer of verse produced by Chile.

The Becquerist rima was practiced by others than De la Barra, for example, his disciple Leonardo Eliz

(b. 1861), whom he made the legatee of his manuscripts. In 1887 Eliz published an interesting book useful to the student of literature, *Silhuetas líricas y biográficas*. In this he appreciated in sonnets many Chilean poets and added in prose a biographical note about each one.

Of the same age was Narciso Tondreau (born 1861), whose *Penumbras* was published in 1887, through the generosity of friends enthusiastic at the true feeling for nature displayed in his melodious though melancholy verses. The contents of the volume were well characterized in a prefatory poem by Rodríguez Velasco who urged the reader to enter these "shadows" without fear if he possessed a love of flowers, of leafy trees and the air of the woods.

The literary revolution known as the modernista movement and dating from the publication in Valparaiso in 1888 of Rubén Darío's *Azul* soon found recruits among the young Chileans. Pedro Antonio González' volume *Ritmos* and Gustavo Valledor Sánchez' *Versos sencillos* initiated the public into the new style. Francisco Contreras printed in blue ink his *Esmaltines*, dedicated to the Princess Zafirina and won notoriety by *Raúl*, a long narrative poem in verses of twelve syllables, showing the influence of Baudelaire and the exaggerations of the symbolist school. Contreras later went to Paris and continuing to write was thus the only one of the early group to remain to the present day a producer of literature. Antonio Borquez Solar's *Campo lírico* offered flowers of poesy gathered "apart from the beaten path"; his companions esteemed most highly a joyous bacchanal song *Jérez alegre* and reprinted it in their journal *Pluma i Lápiz*.

When the Peruvian José Santos Chocano gave a new

direction to the modernista movement by his American poems he opened a path more congenial to the Chilean mind and conforming to the tradition of Chilean poetry. Consequently Chocano called Diego Dublé Urrutia "the poet of Chile" when he read the latter's volume *Del Mar a la Montaña*, containing verses descriptive of the forests and mines, and the native types of men and women and their customs. In the same spirit Manuel Magallanes Moure in *Matices* painted the splendor of the Chilean landscape. Samuel A. Lillo not only sang the beauties of nature in his *Canciones de Arauco* but also the wild life of the mountains, the Indians, the hunting of the puma and other animals; and in *Chile heróico* he evoked the historic past from the days of Michimalonco to the fight of the " Esmeralda."

The illustrated weekly *Pluma i Lápiz*, founded in December, 1900, is an interesting document for the study of the modernista development in Chile. The young men just mentioned who filled its pages with their prose and verse were determinedly enthusiastic in their love of art. To aid and abet them in their devotion they secured contributions from renowned modernistas of other countries such as Rubén Darío, Guillermo Valencia, and Fabio Fiallo.

Other contributors and younger men were Miguel Luís Rocuant whose *Brumas* showed the influence of the Mexican Gutiérrez Nájera and a pantheistic turn of mind; the even more philosophical Federico González who sang the struggle of the soul for the infinite. Víctor Domingo Silva having lived among the poor in Buenos Aires wrote in a pessimistic strain about the outcasts of society in his volume of verses, *Hacia allá*. But in a long poem, *El Derrotero*, he imitated Chocano. This poem narrates the efforts of a young man to get rich quickly in order to marry a wealthy girl. He attempts to find a mine of which an old Indian had told him the location, but he is lost on the pampa and dies miserably.

A review of verse writing in Chile shows that from the time of Andrés Bello and the introduction of romanticism it has closely followed the currents of European literature without producing more than a very few poets of first rank among its numerous versifiers. Poetry may safely be called a cultivated plant. On the other the genius of the Chilean character reveals itself spontaneously in prose forms of literature, especially historical writing and the kindred novel.

The first novel published by a Chilean was *El Inquisidor Mayor o Historia de unos Amores*, brought out by Manuel Bilbao in Lima, 1852. It depicts society in that city during the eighteenth century. Perhaps the author had in mind his brother Francisco's recent persecution when he described the evil fortunes of a young Frenchman brought before the tribunal of the inquisition and condemned for his opinions. The novel portrays the wealthy and pleasure-loving descendants of the conquistadores disturbed by the first stirrings of the ideas which were to have their outcome in the revolution. The impression produced on the public was so great that the book passed through several editions. This fortune did not fall to the author's later stories *Las dos Hermanas* and *El Pirata del Guaymas*.

Alberto Blest Gana (1830–1922), the next novelist in

point of time, is the greatest of Chilean writers of fiction
and in the opinion of Chileans the greatest of American
novelists. He aspired to be the American Balzac. In a
letter to Vicuña Mackenna, he wrote: "One day reading
Balzac I made an auto de fe in my fireplace condemning
to the flames my youthful rhymes. (He had published a
few narrative poems.) I swore to be a novelist or abandon
the field of literature. The secret of my persistence is that
I write not from a desire for glory but from a necessity
of soul."

His first stories published in 1858 were *Engaños y
Desengaños, El Primer Amor, La Fascinación* and *Juan
de Aria* which immediately attracted attention for the
quality of keen observation which the author displayed.
Moreover, they aroused such general interest that the
University of Chile proposed in 1860 for its annual literary
contest, usually limited to serious historical or critical
topics, "a novel in prose, historical or of manners, the
theme of which should be purely Chilean." The prize was
awarded to Blest Gana's *La Aritmética en el Amor*. The
title is descriptive of the morals of its chief character who
uses any means to attain wealth and power. His selfish
conduct is contrasted with the self-sacrifice of his betrothed whom he abandons. Blest Gana's next novel, *El
Pago de las Deudas*, entered still more deeply into criticism
of contemporary society. And in *Martín Rivas*, published
1862, he produced his masterpiece.

The action of this novel takes place in Santiago about
the year 1850. Martin Rivas is a young man from the
country who is taken into the family of a very rich man,
Damaso Encina, who acquired from Martin's father the

mine which is the source of Encina's wealth. The novel is a satire on the manners of newly rich people and the vices of a lower class who ape the rich. In the Encina family are two children, a son Augustine, and a daughter Leonor. The son has just returned from Paris, wherefore he interlards his conversation with French words and fashions his conduct after a model learned in France. He has a love affair with Adelaide, a daughter of the lower classes. Her vicious and lazy brother, Amador, forces Augustine to marry her by coming with a priest and surprising him at night in her company. Martin saves Augustine from this disgrace by proving that the man who performed the marriage ceremony was not a priest but a disguised friend of Amador. Martin becoming interested in politics takes part in the uprising of 1851. He is arrested and condemned but escapes death because Adelaide's noble-minded sister, Edelmira, consents to marry a police official in order to save Martin's life. Martin and Leonor had been interested in each other from the first moment of their acquaintance but her pride had forbidden her from accepting his attentions. At last before Martin's cleverness and ability her pride yields and they marry.

The scenes and incidents of *Martin Rivas*, in spite of its many pages, are so many and so varied that the story moves rapidly. The types of character, according to the Chilean critics, are true to life: the rich parvenue who feeds her lapdog at table; the matron of lower class who is ambitious to marry her daughter to the scion of wealth; the worthless and dissipated Amador, a "siútico," as the Chileans name the type; the politicians, "real beings," says Barros Arana, "whom we all know."

A different type formed the subject of *El Ideal de un Calavera*, published 1863. Abelardo Manríquez is a modern son of a Spanish conquistador, a seeker after adventure either in love or war, handsome, brave, quarrelsome, ardent. His fate finally leads him into a conspiracy which ends in his execution by a shooting party. Just before the fatal discharge, he voices his ideal with the words: —"Adios, love! only ambition of my soul!"

With this novel closed the first period of Blest Gana's activity. He was sent abroad in the diplomatic service of his country and lived almost continuously in Europe. After thirty years he again essayed the writing of novels. In 1897 he published a historical novel, *Durante la Reconquista*. The title refers to the two years following the disaster of Rancagua, 1814, when the Spanish army had temporarily suppressed the revolution and the forces of San Martín were drilling beyond the Andes for the ultimate victory. The author portrays the many leaders in the guerilla warfare which filled these years and describes the customs and social diversions of the epoch.

In 1905 Blest Gana made a study of a South American family as a type of those who endeavor to use wealth as a means for breaking into aristocratic European society. *Los Trasplantados* is a severe satire of every member of the family Canalejas and their associates from their rage for spending money to their peculiar jargon, half French, half Spanish; from the married daughters' disgust at the grandmother, who clings to her mantilla at church to the exclusion from their society of other Americans except a rich bachelor uncle, whose worn and unfashionable clothes they tolerate, because they hope to inherit his property. The youngest child Mercedes is compelled to marry a Prince Roespinbruck, but she commits suicide on learning that her husband has taken along his mistress on the wedding journey. Even this tragedy fails to move the family from their frivolity.

In 1910 the octogenarian novelist put the scenes of his novel of that year, *El Loco Estero*, again in Chile. As in his first work his latest displays the same keenness of observation and vigor of characterization.

The novels of Blest Gana's early period aroused a desire in Chile, for novel reading. The efforts of the periodicals to satisfy it so stimulated original composition that mention can be made here only of the most important productions. Imitation of Blest Gana resulted in what may be termed his school; but his imitators, led on by the necessity of filling space in the daily paper, often spun out exaggerated and improbable adventures. The custom of selling novels in parts resulted in similar prolixity. While the study of contemporary life was frequently animated by a doctrinaire purpose, the search for sensation turned to notorious crimes or the horrors of the past. The model of the latter seemed to be the Spaniard Fernández y González.

The most readable novelist among Blest Gana's immediate following was Martín Palma (1821–84). A trip to California at the time of the gold fever of 1849 gave him a wider outlook on life. After his return to Chile he edited a paper and wrote many tracts on social questions, which gave him a reputation as a free thinker. In 1869 he published his first novel, *Los Secretos del Pueblo*. The success which greeted it, helped on by the hostility of a few, induced the author to extend the length of the novel to fifty parts, afterwards published as a whole in four volumes. The introduction frankly states:—"We have had in mind the improvement of the people. Our customs are examined attempting to improve them, our vices to correct them, our virtues to enhance them, at the same time tilting full against our prejudices, against our social and political errors, against our bad habits for the sake of exalting the dignity and independence of man."

In spite of the doctrinairism there is little declamation, for the lesson is inculcated by striking pictures of vice and its evils. The plan of the novel resembles that of *Martin Rivas*. The adventures of two wealthy families are contrasted with those of an honest artisan. The wealthy hesitate at no crimes either to increase their riches or to procure their pleasure, while the poor perform the most extraordinary deeds of virtue or courage. The wealthy young libertine Guillermo pursues the sister of the carpenter Enrique López to her ruin; in revenge her father and Enrique get bodily possession of Guillermo and brand him with a red hot iron on the shoulder. The rich Luisa falls in love with the sterling qualities of Enrique, but her family force her to marry Guillermo because he threatens to divulge his knowledge of the skeleton in the family closet. Guillermo finally dies in a drunken orgy when the vapor of the alcohol rising from the spilled brandy explodes, setting fire to the house. Luisa is thus free to marry Enrique.

Palma later brought out a sequel to this story in *La Felicidad del Matrimonio*, 1870. His anti-clerical tendencies were given full play in *Los Misterios del Confesionario*, 1874, of which an English translation was printed in London in three volumes under the title of *Julia Ingrand—A Tale of the Confessional*. These two themes of Palma indicate the direction taken by a small army of novelists engendered by the success of his work.

Of the novels professing a moral purpose *Un Drama Intimo* by Moises Vargas possesses a certain interest by reason of the portrait of its heroine, Eugenia, shamefully deceived by the libertine Alberto. He falls in love with Amelia Reynal and wishes to marry her, but her father learns from Eugenia's own lips the story of Alberto's villainy and repeats it to his daughter. New lovers appear on the scene, Eduardo for Amelia and Ricardo for Eugenia. Eugenia dies and Ricardo kills Alberto in a duel. The other couple marry and live happily. The local color of this novel places it relatively high in its class.

Among the most successful of Palma's rivals was Liborio E. Brieba. The original note of his very voluminous work consisted in the setting of his novels. . . . He selected the early history of the revolutionary period for his dramatic narratives. One of these, *Los Talaveras: novela histórica (1814–17)*, has been several times reprinted. The period is the same as that chosen later by Blest Gana for his *Durante la Reconquista*. Brieba also essayed the fantastic tale as well as the exploitation of crime.

In the latter he was excelled in the next decade by Francisco Ulloa whose *Astucias de Pancho Falcato* has passed through five editions in Chile besides the reprints made of it in Buenos Aires and Barcelona. It is merely one manifestation of the bandit literature common to all Spanish-American countries.

The historical novel found many admirers and producers. Ramón Pacheco began to write in 1875, and brought out several novels before the Peruvian war. That opened a new field of which he took full advantage. The most important of his early work was *El Subterráneo de los Jesuitas*, 1878, in two volumes of more than seven hundred pages each. The scandal implied by the title preserved enough interest in the story to warrant another edition in 1899. Of the novels dealing with the Peruvian war, *La Chilena Martir* exploits an episode which occurred just prior to hostilities while *La Generala Buendia* fills two volumes with her heroic and patriotic adventures.

The masterpiece of Chilean historical fiction is undoubtedly *Pipiolos y Pelucones*, by Daniel Barros Grez (born 1839). This is a carefully planned reproduction in the manner of Walter Scott of the period of the supremacy of Portales and the struggles between the parties whose popular names furnish the title. The characters moreover are well developed and interesting. Barros Grez' next novel, *El Huérfano*, published 1881, though a series of adventures in the style of Don Quixote, extended through six volumes, has been termed a "photograph of the Chilean people in their infancy." While the adoption of the picaresque form allowed the author to penetrate all classes of society and portray all kinds of character, his use of an antiquated language imitating Cervantes has not proved so pleasing. The main action of the novel concerns a young man of obscure birth but of brilliant talents, who, by overcoming a thousand difficulties, achieves a fine social position and finally marries a distinguished lady. Marriage with her had been coveted by an old man, very influential because of his intimacy with Portales. The scoundrel being unable to win Julia by fair means hires some bandits to carry her off. The story of this attempt and its frustration by the astuteness of Julia's father forms one of the most dramatic episodes of the book. Imitation of Cervantes carried Barros Grez still farther. In his last very popular book he strung together a series of adventures in the city of Santiago as the observations of his dog, published 1898, with the title of *Primeras aventuras del maravilloso perro Cuatro Remos en Santiago*. Barros Grez' talents for observation and satire were also applied to the production of sketches for the popular stage and a historical play, *El Tejedor o La Batalla de Maipú*.

The application of naturalistic principles in novel writing, a more exact description of physical details and a more careful psychological analysis was first made in Chile by Vicente Grez (1843–1909). The same ability at characterization which he displayed in *Emilia Reynals*, 1883, and in *La Dote de una Joven*, 1884, was shown in a superior degree in *Marianita*, 1885. This is a tragedy caused by the activity of match-making relatives. Marianita is a simple motherless country girl who lives with her father by the seashore. A handsome young naval officer, Camilo, on a vacation, falls in love with her but his relatives prevent his plans for marriage. Besides, an ambitious neighbor, Doña Carmela, desires that her son Sergio should marry Marianita. After an absence of two years, during which Camilo had both married and been left a widower, and Marianita had been betrothed to Sergio, Camilo returns to the village by the sea. The old love between him and Marianita revives and quickens into passion. After a time tiring of his relations with her, Camilo one night fails to keep an appointment, and when she seeks him out on the beach, searching for a pretext to break with her, he calls attention to her engagement ring. As proof of her attachment to Camilo, she promptly throws Sergio's ring into the sea. But even such devotion does not prevent Camilo from hearkening to his aunt's plans for a marriage between him and a rich heiress. When Camilo leaves the village, Marianita, filled with despair, attempts to drown herself but is saved by a fisherman. Her father in his perplexity at her conduct calls on Sergio for assistance. When Marianita witnesses the young man's real grief on learning her fault, she rushes from his presence crying that she is going in search of her engagement ring. Though Sergio pursues her, he is able to bring back from the waves only her lifeless body.

Grez' next novel, *El Ideal de una Esposa*, 1887, was greeted with enthusiasm in Chile by critics who believed that he had produced a work of art worthy of Zola. Faustina, wife of Enrique and mother of a sickly son, notices a certain neglect on the part of her husband. Moved by suspicion she hunts him down one night when he is spending his time drinking with women of loose character. Thereafter she lives only for her son. Her love for him keeps her from falling into the snare laid for her by a doctor. When the son dies his parents are reconciled beside his dead body.

Vicente Grez was not only a novelist but a literary

worker in many fields. As a journalist he contributed widely to the periodicals of his day. In this line he won fame as an art critic. His volume of Becquerist verses, *Ráfagas*, published in 1882, found favor with many. He essayed also the writing of popular history, and for an animated account of the famous victory of the Chilean warship " Esmeralda " was generally known as the author of *El Combate Homérico*.

A number of minor novelists were contemporary with the foregoing. Valentín Murillo began to write as early as 1863, and continued to produce at intervals for twenty-five years. His most noteworthy novel was *Una Víctima del Honor*, 1871, an attack on the death penalty based on circumstantial evidence. Another novelist who had admirers was Enrique Montt, author of two studies of female character, *Mujer y Angel*, a tale of seduction, and *Laura Duverne*, 1883. Of greater value in realistic description were the tales of Pedro Nolasco Cruz, especially one entitled *Estéban* and his picture of country life, *Flor de Campo*, 1887.

Alejandro Silva de la Fuente promised greater achievement by his *Ventura*, 1885, and *Penas que matan*, 1887. In *Ventura* he followed rather Spanish or English models than French by relying for interest, not so much on a complicated intrigue as on observation of manners and psychological analysis. Ventura is a young man, who comes to Santiago from a small village where he is a leader. Ambitious to rise he enters politics, and forgetful of his village sweetheart, Margarita, he courts a rich heiress for the purpose of using her money to further his plans. He fails utterly in his courtship and his politics. He falls sick and, ashamed to return home, plans to commit suicide. But Margarita and her mother who have been informed of his illness come to Santiago. They take the disillusioned youth back to his country home where he marries Margarita.

In *Penas que matan*, Silva de la Fuente again studied the character of a young man. Fernando in love with Berta is compelled to witness her marriage to an old man. For pique he straightway allies himself with Angela Rosales. When, after their marriage, they pay a ceremonious visit on Berta and her husband, love reawakens, so that presently Fernando stops one day at Berta's house, determined to declare his passion. The consequent excitement brings on a severe attack of his chronic ailment of the heart. As he falls completely unconscious, it is necessary for Berta to call for assistance. After this revelation of his soul to all the world, Fernando at the end of a week's suffering is graciously removed by death.

The influence of President Balmaceda on the constitutional history of Chile also found an echo among the novelists. During a period of ferment, Balmaceda had effected many changes, even conferring on the Congress powers which the old constitution had granted only to the president. When, however, a dispute with the Congress arose he was unwilling to yield the old prerogatives. An uprising began in 1891 which he was unable to suppress. Finding himself thus in a position without a way of escape except by flight or death he chose the latter.

The anticlerical agitation of Balmaceda's time found a supporter in fiction, 1889, in Borja Orihuela Grez' *El Cura Civil*. The scene is laid in a provincial city whose in-

habitants side with the old priest when the new func-
tionary arrives to supplant the priest in his duties of
conducting the register of vital statistics.   The provision
of the law establishing a civil register which especially
aroused the priest's ire was that permitting the official
to perform civil marriage.   Hence arose the nickname of
"cura civil."   One old inhabitant in grim humor even
sent to get "the blessing of the government upon their
union" a pair— of chickens.   The young official, however,
is both wealthy and discreet.   As a result of his conduct
he finally wins the esteem of town and its prettiest girl.

Of different type was an explanation of Balmaceda's
failure published in the form of a novel, 1897, *Los últimos
Proyectos de Eduardo Castro* by René Brickles.   The book
aroused much discussion because the author attributed
the failure to the bad character of the soldiers who supported the president.   Brickles drew a long and amusing
series of caricatures with considerable realistic power.

Balmaceda's constitutional changes threw the governing power into the hands of the plutocrats who had been
increasing greatly in numbers.   In fact, a rapid increase
of wealth in Chile during the last quarter of the century
is an economic fact to be borne in mind.   It appears in
fiction at the end of the last decade of the century.

Emilio Rodríguez Mendoza published in 1899 a short
novel, *Última Esperanza*. The idea of the author was to
show the evils brought into the country by bad French
novels.   The Spanish critic, Juan Valera, in reviewing
the book declared that Rodríguez Mendoza had merely
imitated them, that his story might have taken place
in Paris as well as in Chile.   In *Vida Nueva*, 1902, however,

Rodríguez Mendoza introduced more local color. Then Miguel de Unamuno inquired "why in these new countries do they insist on depicting everything to us so corrupt?" Rodríguez Mendoza replied that he had described a genuine phase of life in Santiago, that "the evils come from the fact that the people have tried to attain European culture at one bound."

Vida Nueva concerns one Pedro who withdraws from club life, its gambling, drinking, and horse racing, and retires to write a few predictions of what he expects will happen to his various acquaintances. He tells them on taking leave that they will all end in poverty or the grave. After an absence of four years, during which he receives no letters or papers, he returns to Santiago. Contrary to his expectations he finds that the sports and high livers are not only alive but have advanced commercially, politically and socially. Pedro's nervous system is so upset that his physician orders him to an asylum for the insane.

Luis Orrego Luco (born 1866), who began his literary labors by writing short stories and sketches of travel, is a novelist of versatile talent. His *Un Idilio Nuevo*, 1900, depicts that class of society in Santiago in which money is the thing of greatest value in life. Before its power, neither love nor duty can stand. His *Memorias de un Voluntario de la Patria Vieja*, 1905, is a historical novel which puts before the reader both the state of society and the important personages of the year of revolution, 1810. His *Casa Grande*, 1908, excited much discussion.

Fiction in the form of the short story was little practiced in Chile, before the twentieth century. A virgin

field lay thus ready for the exploitation of the present
generation.   There have always been of course examples
of a similar kind of literature so closely allied that the
division line is hard to draw, namely, the descriptive, often
jocose, article of manners.   But the distinction between
the descriptive article and the tale should be borne in
mind.

The earliest prose tales written by a Chilean were
those of J. V. Lastarria, collected several years after their
appearance, in a volume entitled *Antaño y Hogaño* because some of the tales were in the nature of historic
legends.   Much later in time came the short stories of
Orihuela Grez and of Orrego Luco, whose longer works
of fiction have been discussed.   Of the younger writers
who have sought to rival Maupassant, several are worthy
of mention.   G. Labarca Hubertson and R. Maluenda
have portrayed Chilean country life and country people
in an artistic manner.   Their men and women are real
beings with whose loves and sufferings the reader is compelled to sympathize.   The characteristic irony of the
Maupassant tale seemed the important thing to F. Santi-
bañez and to A. C. Espejo.   For that reason their stories
of domestic life though entertaining are not so thoroughly
Chilean.   A master of the short story is Baldomero Lillo
whose two collections, *Sub terra* (1904) and *Sub sole* (1907),
interspersed with descriptive articles, reveal many classes
of the Chilean population, farmers, fishermen, the Araucanian Indian, children, miners.

The descriptive sketch which has flourished so widely
in all Spanish-American countries, on account of the
necessities of journalism has on the whole a less jocose

character, less Andalusian salt, and more matter of fact than elsewhere. The Chilean model has been J. J. Vallejo, "Jotabeche," whose sketches are both instructive and amusing.

Forty years later, Daniel Riquelme became his first serious rival in the same line. Just as others were able to extract comic verse from the war with Peru, Riquelme found much material for humoristic sketches of military life.

The palm, however, for humorous description of manners must be awarded to Román Vial (1833–96). Besides, he was the favorite author of comic sketches for the stage, from his first comedy in 1871, *Los Extremos se tocan* to *Gratitud y Amor* in 1881. His *Mujer-Hombre* was awarded a prize in a literary contest.

The legend or historical anecdote is a form of literature made especially popular by the Peruvian, Ricardo Palma. In Chile this form was cultivated by Enrique del Solar (born 1844), son of the poetess, Mercedes Marín del Solar. He frankly abandoned any historical purpose though he borrowed from written or oral tradition the main facts of his narratives wrought out with wealth of detail. For example, *Una Aventura de Ercilla,* an anecdote from the poet's life, gave opportunity to present the character of the warrior bard against the background of colonial days. Enrique del Solar also wrote several novels which won applause at the time of their appearance. *Dos Hermanos* won a prize in a newspaper contest in 1886. He also performed a great service to literature by the editing and publishing of his mother's poems.

Alberto del Solar (born 1860), began his literary career

by a legend *Huincahual* dealing with a love affair between an Araucanian Indian and a white woman, a topic
which allowed the author to present many descriptions
of former days. Alberto del Solar has spent a part of his
life in the diplomatic service of his country. His impressions of South Americans in Paris are rendered in *Rasta-
quoere*, 1890. Of his novels *Contra la Marea*, 1894, and
El Faro, 1902, the latter is the more interesting. That
again treats of the exotic in the sense that the action takes
place on a distant island of the Chilean coast where elemental passions hold sway in the little colony of three
men and the daughter of the keeper of the light.

From the legend to genuine history is but a step, and in
the writing of their history Chileans have excelled. The
striking characteristic of their historical style, the impartial narrative fortified by citation of original documents,
has been attributed to the influence of Andrés Bello. From
the moment of his installation in 1843 as the first rector
of the University of Chile, he superintended the publications of the various faculties which were obligatory upon
their members. It was voted that one member of each
faculty should each year present to the university a study
of some topic in national history.

Of the vast result of such labor only this cursory mention can be made. And it is possible to consider here only
those writers who have been most prominent by reason of
their copiousness. In this respect Benjamín Vicuña
Mackenna (1831–86) holds first place not only in his own
country but in America. The sum of his published work
has been calculated at one hundred and sixty volumes
comprising forty-three thousand four hundred and two

printed pages. Every epoch of Chilean history seems to have been investigated by him, and the results of his researches narrated in an interesting, almost popular style. His favorite form was the biographical account of a leader, a form which allowed full scope and play to the human interest of the narrative.

Of a more strictly scientific form were the labors of the brothers Miguel Luis and Gregorio Víctor Amunátegui. On account of the similarity of their style it is considered impossible to separate the individual work. It is certain, however, that the interests of Miguel Luis, the elder (1828–88), concerned literary topics and literary men. To the brothers Amunátegui the world owes the earliest general discussion of Spanish-American poetry in their *Juicios críticos de algunos Poetas hispano-americanos*, written for the literary contest of the Circulo de los Amigos de las Letras in 1859. For the literary history of Chile the biographies of Andrés Bello, of Sanfuentes and of Camilo Henríquez, and the researches in early efforts in letters contained in the volumes *La Alborada poética en Chile* and *Las primeras Representaciones dramáticas en Chile* by M. L. Amunátegui are indispensable. Miguel Luis Amunátegui also took an important part in politics and rose to be President of the Chamber of Deputies and a candidate, though unsuccessful, for the presidency of Chile.

While the historical researches of other men dealt with separate individuals or periods, that of Diego Barros Arana (1830–1908) formed a comprehensive study of the whole. Whatever he published earlier in life found a summary in his final monumental *Historia general de Chile*. After Bello, Chile's greatest scholar is undoubtedly Barros

Arana. Objection has sometimes been made to his dry impartial style, but no reproach can be cast at the historical accuracy of this last word on Chilean history.

The literary history of Chile owes much to Luis Montt (1848–1909), formerly director of the national library, author of a bibliography of the older historians of Chile, whose private library was purchased by a friend of Harvard University and given to it as a remembrance of the Panamerican scientific congress at Santiago de Chile. Luis Montt's literary labor was diverse in character including a volume of poems, a life of Camilo Henríquez and an edition in forty-eight volumes of the works of D. F. Sarmiento; an edition of Pedro de Oña's poem *El Vasauro* and the memoirs of Vicente Pérez Rosales, entitled *Recuerdos del Pasado*.

The assistance to the historian of such memoirs is considerable. Important and interesting for the period which it covers is *Recuerdos de Treinta Años*, published in 1872 by José Zapiola (1802–85).

Encyclopedic in its thoroughness has been the labor of José Toribio Medina (born 1852) who has investigated the history of printing in every Spanish-American country during the colonial period. Equally authoritative is his *Historia de la Literatura colonial de Chile*.

Concerning the immense amount of historical writing which has been produced in Chile no statement could be more precise or illuminating than that of Jorge Huneeus Gana in his *Cuadro histórico de la Producción intelectual de Chile*. "It is a very interesting circumstance for anybody who tries to investigate the social traits of our people to discover from the very moment of its independent constitution an extraordinary zeal for the patient investigation of our past. Each epoch, each administration, each general, each revolution, has had its special historian. This trait in itself reveals the seriousness of the Chilean character."

CHAPTER VII

In Peru the period immediately following the expulsion of the Spaniards was not propitious for the production of literature. For twenty years incessant quarrels between contending factions, the speedy overthrow of one dictator after another kept the country in a state of anarchy, until a strong man, Ramón Castilla (1797–1867), became president in 1845. He reëstablished order and prosperity, introduced the first telegraph and the first railroad, abolished negro slavery and the personal tribute exacted from the Indians, set up a new constitution, stimulated foreign trade; in short he ruled Peru with an iron hand for her own good. During the fifteen years of his administration literature began to flourish.

The principal figure in this renaissance of letters was one of Castilla's foremost political opponents, Felipe Pardo y Aliaga (1806–68). His activity, however, was largely limited to journalistic satire, but his son Manuel Pardo became Castilla's successor in the direction of Peruvian affairs, being actually President of Peru from 1872 to 1876. Felipe Pardo was sprung from the old Peruvian aristocracy. His mother was a daughter of the Marqués de la Fuente Hermosa, while his father was regent of the royal audiencia of Cuzco. Taken to Spain when Peru passed from Spanish control, he became a pupil of the famous teacher Alberto

Lista and even one of his favorite pupils. In 1828 he returned to Lima. He signalized his arrival by a comedy presenting national manners, *Frutos de la Educación,* in three acts. In this play are revealed the characteristics, gay wit and subtle irony, which mark all his writings. In fact these qualities in varying form, a modification of Andalusian salt, give a peculiar individuality to all Peruvian literature.

Lima being the seat of the Spanish government in America, the residence of the viceroy and the place of resort for persons of wealth, there developed a distinctly urban society with customs, ideas, and manners of its own. Its love of pomp and display found satisfaction in bullfighting, in the theater, and in religious processions on the many feast days. Its necessity for chatter, laughter and gallantry gave rise to parties, picnics, and serenades to the sound of the guitar beneath the balconies. Its love for dancing came from its Andalusian blood; from its more distant Moorish ancestors the custom among the women of covering the face. The ladies of Lima adopted the odd habit of wearing over their heads a black shawl which with one hand they held drawn about the face disclosing only one eye. What havoc that one sparkling eye is said to have caused in the hearts of youth! The girls, capricious and willful before marriage, became tyrannical mothers of large families. In both men and women the soft climate of Lima engendered an easy-going insouciance, a frivolity of mind which took few things seriously and was immensely pleased by the laughter-causing jest at any trifle. For the kind of wit which could set a whole company in an uproar of laughter, as a spark can set going a

pack of firecrackers, they coined the term "chispa."
One successful writer of epigrams entitled his productions
"chispazos." Naturally there developed in such quick-
witted persons a special vocabulary.

When Pardo portrayed this society in his three comedies,
he could not deny free rein to his fun-loving disposition
but he so guided it in accord with his European education
and aristocratic breeding as to censure vulgar or immoral
tendencies. In *Los Frutos de la Educación*, he ridiculed
the father who tries to impose a husband upon his daughter as harshly as he judged the young woman who loses
her sweetheart because she dances with too great abandon the "zamacueca." In *Una Huérfana en Chorrillos*,
produced in 1833, the fop, Don Quintín, who imitates
everything French, even speaking Spanish badly from
affectation, apparently a common type of youth, is not
permitted to carry off the young heiress, because morality
in the form of her two aunts interferes; nor do the manners
of the seaside resort where dancing continues till daylight
escape satire. *Don Leocadio* is another play of manners in
which Pardo thought to chastise by ridicule.

In 1836 Pardo was Peruvian minister in Chile and took
rather an active part in the intellectual life in Santiago,
even to the extent of publishing a periodical, *El Intérprete*. At this time were written some of Pardo's famous
letrillas. These are clever humorous verses without bitterness, composed merely for the sake of jesting on a
variety of homely topics, as his coat, a bathing suit, an
incident in the bull fight or the peculiarities of an individual.

After Pardo's return to Peru he placed his pen at the

service of the conservative party. The cleverest of his efforts appeared in 1859, when President Castilla was promulgating his new constitution. Pardo edited a satiric sheet, *Espejo de mi Tierra* in which he held up to scorn those democratic proposals which grated on his aristocratic nerves. To him the cry "Viva la libertad" was the sublest irony, when liberty meant for the negro and his former master equality before the law. In number three of the *Espejo de mi Tierra*, he published a very amusing parody on the new constitution. Article by article he commented in verse on the various provisions after this fashion. Citizenship: Property is not a requisite condition; still one would advise the citizen to have trousers and a shirt. Property: It is inviolable, except when taken by the soldiers of the dictator. The manner of saying these things in fluent verse adds immensely to the effect. But of course in spite of their evident cleverness, Pardo's political satires could not live beyond the occasion which called them forth. They did, however, set the tone for subsequent writers.

Manuel A. Segura (1805–71) was not Pardo's equal in satiric verses but excelled him in the comedy of manners, both in character drawing and in style. He has twelve comedies to his credit. As he did not begin to write till after his discharge from the army in 1839, his work covers a slightly later period than the comedies of Pardo. But both men described the same world of gayety and frivolity. The girl who meets a lover at the window contrary to her father's command reappears in Segura's *La Moza Mala*. In *Ña Catita* and *Saya y manto* the Peruvian type of Celestina, ready for any sort of errand or intrigue, holds the center of interest. *El Sargento Canuto* entertains the public with his account of the battle of Ayacucho and his preparations to meet the Spaniards if they dare return to Peru. The *Lances de Amancaes*, produced in 1862, stage the occurrences at a picnic attended by half the population of Lima. In these plays Segura proves himself a better observer of native manners than Pardo and unlike him cared nothing about inculcating a moral.

The contemporaries of Pardo and Segura who cultivated lyric poetry were younger men. To them the spirit of European romanticism came across the seas stimulating them to ambitious imitation. But so foreign to Peruvian temperament was the melancholy pose that Ventura García Calderón [1] writes thus: "Read in succession the works of the whole romantic generation in Peru seem like the productions of a single author, so uniform are their common lamentations. Imitating the same masters with servility, they did not always succeed in expressing their melancholy with individuality. And because they confused lyric poetry with eloquence, a frequent confusion with us, they exaggerated their accent. They rivaled each other in disappointment. Each cried louder than the other."

It is, however, not strictly correct to say that no distinctions between the poets exist. For example there arose in Arequipa a whole flight of minor poets with an individuality as different as is the invigorating climate of their mountain city situated eight thousand feet above sea level in sight of lofty volcanic peaks, as different as such a situation from that of Lima. The most important

[1] V. García Calderón, *Del Romanticismo al modernismo*, page 105.

of the Arequipans was Manuel Castillo (1814–70). His first poem was indited to the tomb of the revolutionary hero of his native town, Mariano Melgar. Castillo himself suffered banishment for participation in an uprising. His poems showed a genuine feeling for nature. Especially did the verses *Al Misti* reveal that his soul was filled with the majesty of the mountain that dominates the landscape of Arequipa.

The majesty of nature again was the stimulus that incited Manuel Nicolás Corpancho (1839–63), to his best work. At eighteen he had written a drama *El Poeta cruzado*. In 1853, when returning from Europe through the straits of Magellan the sublimity of the scenery inspired him to compose a poem, *Magallanes* of epic form concerning that navigator. The first canto described the interview of Magellan with Cardinal Cisneros from whom he obtained five ships; the second canto depicted the departure from Seville; the third the death of Magellan, followed by a "corona poética," laudatory lines on the great achievements of the hero. Corpancho also essayed the heroic note in poems on the past of Peru. The Argentine poet Mármol who wrote an introduction for Corpancho's collected poems, *Ensayos Poéticos*, 1854, asked him why he chose to write of the past rather than the future. The question indicates the difference between the outlook of the two countries represented by the two men. Corpancho's praises of Peruvian greatness made him popular. In 1860 he was appointed minister to Mexico. Three years later he met a tragic death in the burning at sea of the steamship "Mexico."

The most genuine in his lyric grief because it accorded

with his natural temperament and circumstances of life was Carlos Augusto Salaverry (1831–90). The impression made on his youthful mind by seeing his father shot as a rebel was never effaced. His melancholy was sincere when his verses linked love and death. The theme of love, particularly in the series of poems *Cartas a un Angel*, he treated with pleasing and unusual delicacy but with emphasis on the sadness of separation from the beloved. Loneliness and yearning for the distant sweetheart has rarely been more poetically expressed than in his poem *Acuérdate de mí*, brought to a climax with the cry from the depths of his soul, "Remember me!"

Clemente Althaus (1835–81) was rather more of a professional littérateur. For that reason he imitated many different styles and passed from romanticism in his early poems to classicism in his later verses. There is also a heroic note in the denunciation of the Spanish fleet which seized the Chinchón islands in 1866, a note inherited perhaps from his father who was a general at the battles of Ayacucho and Junín. There is even a hint of the native Peruvian ironical jest. In his abundance, some six hundred printed pages of verse, there are essays at the poetical legend, as *Justina* and *Carmen y Rafael*.

A more philosophical poet who wrote from his personal experience in life was José Arnaldo Márquez (1830–1904). He tried to put the theory of the cosmos into verse by setting up the atom and force as opponents. His scientific turn of mind led him to become an inventor of a machine to print with a reduced number of types, a sort of forerunner of the linotype. Attempts to interest capital in its perfecting carried him to Buenos Aires and thence to

Paris where he lived in extreme poverty. The pitiful story of his struggles he told in *Meditación*. His poem *A Solas* expresses the resignation of a fatalist to the evil of loneliness inevitably suffered by a poor man.

In Pedro Paz Soldán y Unánue (1839–95), his country possessed a poet whose peculiar excellencies not only placed him without a rival in Peru, but gave him a marked individuality among the foremost in Spanish America. The name "Juan de Arona" with which he signed his poems was derived from that of the family estate situated at some distance from Lima. And the beauty of that region appeared most minutely observed in his poems, so minutely that critics have blamed him for trying to write poetry about the common things of everyday life on the farm. Though his first collection of poems, *Ruinas*, had echoes of the romantic pose suggested by the title, it was full of life and color, love of flowers and birds, whose song he even tried to imitate as in the lines,

> La ronca cuculí cuya garganta
> Rompe con sus arrullos la espesura.

But his temperament was too healthily Peruvian to be long depressed, rather on his blue days (as he says in *Los Días turbios*) he was inclined to rage like a hyena at whatever vexed him and to delight in the misfortunes of others. His state of mind was usually one which expressed itself in jesting at everything and everybody. Most wonderful was the amount of fun which he extracted from an account in facile verse of a journey made by a mixed company from Lima, twenty leagues into the country. The persons in the cavalcade, the places and incidents on the way all furnished him with ample material for burlesque. At greater length he told in mock heroics, *La Pinzonada,* the deeds of Admiral Pinzón. Or he sympathized with the complaints of the wife of a mule driver. If the verses of a poet signing himself "Roterup" struck him as bad, he addressed the unlucky author several *Roterupadas.*

As time brought disappointments to Paz Soldán, the tone of his satire became more and more bitter till in the periodical *El Chispazo,* edited by him, the acme of political irony was reached. As if to relieve his mind by resort to nature, without the gall which for him now pervaded the Peruvian landscape, he busied himself by translations of Virgil's *Georgics* and extracts from Lucretius and Ovid. In estimating Paz Soldán, however, the most intrinsically valuable and interesting of his works will always remain the pictures of native life and Peruvian scenery in the *Cuadros y Episodios peruanos,* published in 1867.

Wherever romanticism flourished as a fashion in verse making, a translator was in demand. Such a place fell to Manuel Adolfo García, whose renderings of Victor Hugo were popular in Peru. Temporarily popular also were some of his own compositions both those of lyric character and those with epic ring as the eloquent invocation *A Bolívar.*

The last of the romanticists was Ricardo Rossel (1841–1909). And he followed the spiritualistic ideal of Lamartine rather than the sensual and pessimistic trend of later French poets. His most notable poem, *Meditación en el Cementerio,* written on a text from Lamartine, expresses the hope that after death the great secret of human destiny will be revealed to him though he will be unable to communicate it to a questioning poet who may come to sit on his tomb. Like other Peruvians, however, Rossel loved the merry laugh and wrote more than one letrilla on a native topic. Historical legends too interested him. One of them in verse, *Hima Sumac*, won a prize in a Chilean contest, 1877.

One of the most widely known Peruvians was Luis Benjamín Cisneros (1837-1904), both because his productive period was long and because he lived much in other countries and contributed to their periodicals. Moreover, the breadth of spirit in the kind of epic verse which he cultivated lifted his poems from the narrow circle of the merely local. As Peruvian consul in Havre for eight years in the sixties, he made the acquaintance of many Spanish Americans, an experience which gave rise in him to a strongly Pan-hispanic feeling. This is voiced in his *Elegía a la Muerte de Alfonso XII*, expressing a certain degree of real grief at the loss suffered by the nation to which the Spanish Americans are bound, both by ties of blood and by a common historical past. While Cisneros' ode *Al Perú* in 1860, was a romantic outburst of grandiloquent patriotism, his fervid prophecy of a glorious future, *Aurora Amor; canto al Siglo XX*, in 1885, was written in almost classic style.

Likewise a wanderer from Peru, Carlos G. Amézaga (?-1906), derived his originality from his mercurial and excitable temperament. In Mexico, the vehemence of the verses of Díaz Miron pleased him so that with like arrogance he threw out the challenge of an active rebel against the injustice of fate. An admirer of heroism

Amézaga celebrated its manifestations among the humble. The most interesting of his poems of this kind is the incomplete *Leyenda del Caucho* which in epic style exalts the hardships of the poor Indian rubber gatherer in the tropical forests. In Buenos Aires, Amézaga won a prize with his meritorious *Mas allá de los Cielos*, in which he voices the belief, despite assailing doubts to the contrary, that humanity will be redeemed by means of science and poetry. Amézaga was the author also of a couple of dramas along the same lines as his verses, but they were not staged and are rather too lyrical for presentation.

Another philosophical poet but one who, finding verse too confining for his thought, adopted the essay in the style of Montaigne was Manuel González Prada (born 1844). At twenty years of age he expressed his pessimism by elegies to solitude, but being influenced by the anticlericalism of the Ecuadorean Montalvo he began to attack religion till he seemed to many good people "an agent of Satan in Peru." His radicalism finally developed into anarchism, a nihilistic tendency to overthrow everything existent. The essays in *Páginas libres* fulminate not only against religion but against such things as grammar and orthography. In contrast to his demand for freedom of style in prose are both the form and thought of his later verses published with the title *Minúsculas*. In such highly artificial forms as the triolet and the rondel he sings in mystic strain a happy humanity redeemed from its present misery. As a professor of literature, González Prada is said to have taught a whole generation to write well.

In Ricardo Palma (1833–1919), Peru may claim the

inventor of a new form in literature, the tradition, to give it the name which the author himself employed. It is nothing more than the historical anecdote, frequently only a bit of scandal, a sensational or unusual crime, a practical joke, just such things as appear in the newspapers every day, but Palma's traditions were gleaned from the historical chronicles of Peru. Though he vouched for their accuracy they were written in such a vein of humor with the striking points so skillfully brought out that his critics accused him of falsifying history without succeeding in producing a novel. None of his imitators ever quite caught the trick of style which made his work popular in all the periodicals of Spanish America for thirty years. The inimitable was probably the dash of Peruvian wit. Besides he ransacked so thoroughly both the oral and written traditions of Peru that he left little in that field for anybody else.

Palma, when scarcely twenty years of age, was banished for participation in a political plot. Accordingly, in Paris he published a volume of verse, *Armonías, libro de un desterrado.* While it contained enough laments in romantic tone to justify the sub-title, the most original poems were certain "cantorcillos" miniatures in verse of his later traditions in prose.

In the first series of traditions, Palma, aiming more at the historian's task, related the acts of the viceroys; but as the number of the series lengthened into nine between 1863 and 1899, any sort of anecdote afforded him material. Consequently he played upon a great diversity of emotion from the thrill of horror to the broad laugh, and introduced members of every class of society from the viceroy to the slave. Being somewhat skeptical himself, he delighted in stories referring to religious superstitions, belief in ghosts or tales dealing with loose living by friars. At the same time he paid willing tribute to heroism, as in the story of Fray Pedro Marieluz, who died rather than reveal the secrets of the confessional even when his political sympathies would have persuaded him to do so.

But to excite laughter was Palma's chief aim. As an example take the tale of the skeptical Andalusian shopkeeper, who did not believe in hell. A fanatic priest wished to buy some provisions of him on credit. The man refused to sell, saying discourteously: "I won't trust you in order to be paid in hell, that is, never." The priest accused the shopkeeper of being a heretic because he did not believe in hell and so worked on the sentiment of the villagers that the shopkeeper had to flee to save his life. The priest incidentally excommunicated him. To lift the decree of excommunication, the shopkeeper betook himself to the archbishop in Lima. The latter imposed as penance marriage with a certain young woman of ill repute, daughter of a famous vixen. After the shopkeeper had been married a short time, he admitted to a friend that the priest was right in affirming the existence of hell "because I have it at home."

The plastic character of Palma's traditions owes much to his constant effort to cull the homely phrase or the picturesque turn of expression from the speech of the people or from old books. He put together some observations of this sort in his *Papeletas lexicográficas*, a continuation of Paz Soldán's *Diccionario de Peruanismos*.

As a result of this careful documentation and Palma's resolve not to inject into the narrative any fancies of his own, the reader of his traditions feels that the vivid picture of colonial times and ideas possesses historic value and is thankful that Palma has wiped from it the dust of ages.

That more than one of Palma's traditions related in a few pages of print might be expanded into a novel has been indicated by Valera. But fiction by a curiosity of fate was cultivated in Peru by women. This may have been due to the influence of a remarkable woman of Argentine birth, Juana Manuela Gorriti de Belzu, whose life story equalled the inventions of fiction.

Born in 1819, at the age of twelve she emigrated with her father when he was banished and lived with an uncle in Bolivia. At the age of fifteen she was married to Manuel Belzu, then a colonel in the Bolivian army, and later one of the most noted if not notorious characters in Bolivian history. Belzu being partly of Indian blood, a "cholo," he wielded great influence with the Indian element so strong in his country. In 1847, when ordered to take his command to the frontier, he started a rebellion. Though unsuccessful he merely suffered temporary deprivation of his position for soon thereafter he was made minister of war. In 1848, pretending to make an inspection of the frontiers, he organized an uprising which put him at the head of the government. As President of Bolivia he ruled despotically for seven years. Driven out then he lived in Europe for ten years, till in 1865 he returned and started a revolution. Momentarily successful he was assassinated in the presidential palace by his beaten rival

Melgarejo who was accepted as president by the troops assembled in the square below.

During Belzu's exile and after his death, his wife, Juana Manuela Gorriti, lived in Lima where she became prominent for she instituted a girls' school and edited a periodical, *El Correo del Perú*. As early as 1845 she had written a considerable tale, *La Quena*, dealing with the history of the Incas and the days of their splendor in Cuzco. She continued to write stories mainly with a historical plot, some of which were based on events in Argentina in the time of Rosas. In Buenos Aires in 1865, a wave of popularity in her favor was inaugurated by the editors of a review who printed and sold by subscription a collection of her stories with the title *Sueños y Realidades*. Since then Juana Gorriti has been lauded in Argentina as one of the literary glories of the country. In Lima where she made her home for so many years her influence was very great. No literary gathering was complete without her presence.

For example, she arranged a magnificent ovation to Clorinda Matto de Turner when she came to Lima in 1877. Clorinda Matto, born 1854, was a well-educated and talented young lady of Cuzco who married an Englishman, Dr. Turner, in 1871. She wrote verses and articles for various papers and attracted special attention by traditions in Ricardo Palma's manner dealing with her native city Cuzco. Palma was present at the reception in Lima and congratulated her. After his remarks and the reading of various poems Juana Gorriti crowned the guest with a wreath of silver filigree and presented her with a gold pen. Two years after this ceremony at the time of the war with

Chile, her popularity among her compatriots enabled her to carry out successfully a public subscription to equip a regiment of soldiers known as the "libres de Cuzco." After her husband's death in 1881, Clorinda Matto devoted her attention entirely to literature.

In her writing as in her conduct love of country was the distinguishing characteristic, both of the traditions of which she published two series and of her famous novel *Aves sin Nido*. The latter for its social importance has been compared to *Uncle Tom's Cabin*. The Peruvian novel written in picturesque style, portrays the wretched condition of the Indian living in subjection to the exactions of the governor, the parish priest and the land holder.

"*Aves sin Nido*," says the Mexican critic F. Sosa,[1] "is a book which the President of Peru and the head of the Peruvian church ought to learn by heart; the first in order to learn in all its enormity the depraved conduct of the civil oppressors of the Indians and the second in order to root out the race of bad priests."

More successful purely as a novelist was Mercedes Cabello de Carbonero. She may truly be called the one Peruvian writer who has produced realistic pictures of Peruvian society. In *Las Consecuencias* she studied the evil of gambling as it develops in Peru. The frequent revolutions originating in some politician's disappointed ambitions are explained in *El Conspirador*, as well as the moral and social degeneration of the individuals concerned. *Blanca Sol*, published in 1889, is the drama of a woman of society borne on to ruin through her desire to shine, her bad education and the evil example of the world about

[1] F. Sosa, *Escritores y Poetas sud-americanos*.

her, a Madame Bovary in a Peruvian environment. This, the most popular of her books, has passed through several editions and been reprinted in many Spanish-American reviews.

In the present generation of writers Peru has given the world one of the dominating figures of the latest phase of Spanish-American literature, José Santos Chocano. Though his works have their roots in Peruvian soil their fruits have been shared by the whole Spanish-American world. They will therefore be considered in connection with the modernista movement.

A few of his leading contemporaries in Peru should be mentioned. Clemente Palma, son of Ricardo Palma, having inherited his father's ironical ability, displayed it in a field of his own selection. His *Cuentos Malévolos* exploit the malice in mankind. Wherever he could find an anecdote of a man who rejoiced in his neighbor's harm or ill luck, he put it in artistic form, whether the individual was a stolid Russian peasant who watched a peasant carter's load of fish being jolted into the river without warning him or whether it was Satan behind the cross sneering at the dying Christ.

Of poets José Gâlvez has most shown the influence of Chocano, but is more original in his erotic sonnets, and poems. A melodic *Conversión de Venus* retells in epic form with a curious mingling of Greek and biblical elements the story of Mary Magdalen. To the erotic and musical practitioners of verse belong also Juan del Carpio and Leonidas N. Yerovi.

The novel, also of the erotic type, has been practiced by Felipe Sassone of Italian parentage and by Enrique A.

Carrillo; and with the same tendencies the realistic drama by Manuel Bedoya.

Speaking now of serious literature José de la Riva Agüero has studied the *Carácter de la Literatura del Peru independiente* as well as the historians of his country. But Francisco García Calderón has won international fame by his essays on contemporaneous historical or philosophical topics in his *Hombres e Ideas de neustro Tiempo* and his *Profesores de Idealismo.* Written in French *Le Pérou contemporain* was crowned by the French Academy; while his *Democraties latines de l'Amerique* is an authoritative work in comprehensive form of the whole history of Latin America. The latter volume makes clear the influence in every country of the local politician, the demagogue, or using the Spanish word, the caudillo, in stirring up the mob to support him as a dictator. The problems which face each country from the character of its population and its geographical position are graphically outlined.

BOLIVIA

In colonial days the mountainous region beyond Lake Titicaca was known as Alto Perú. As the Inca stronghold Cuzco was also situated in Upper Peru some of the most dramatic events in the history of the western continent occurred in this locality. Not to be forgotten is the fact that the famous hill of Potosí, which has yielded more than two billion dollars worth of silver, is now in the Bolivian province of that name. In the town of Potosí, which once held 160,000 inhabitants but now dwindled to small proportions as her mines have been exhausted, were heard the first mutterings of revolution in Peru. And in the province of Potosí almost the last remnant of the Spanish forces in America was rounded up by General Sucre, the victor at the great battle of Ayacucho, and compelled to surrender in March, 1825. An assembly of delegates from Upper Peru declared the independence of the region and gave it the name of Bolivia in honor of the Liberator, Simón Bolívar, whom they named perpetual protector of the republic, and invited to prepare a constitution. Under it General Sucre was elected the first president. He was ousted from the presidency in two years and from that time till 1871 nearly every president was a usurper who ruled by force of arms.

The population of the country contains only about twelve per cent of pure whites. And they, probably on account of the climatic conditions on the high tableland averaging above twelve thousand feet above sea level, have never shown much energy apart from the exploitation of the immense mineral wealth of the country. Consequently the literary production of Bolivia has been slight with neither a noteworthy journalistic current accompanying its succession of dictators nor a capital poet whose work commands attention.

The romantic movement in literature, however, stimulated three contemporaries to poetic effort, Benjamín Lens (1836–78), Nestor Galindo (1830–65), and Daniel Calvo (1832–80). The melancholy tone of Galindo's poems published under the title of *Lágrimas* had its justification in his life, for he suffered proscription more than once and was finally executed by a firing party. Calvo's first volume is described by its title *Melancolías*. His later *Rimas* contains some romantic legends, of which *Ana Dorset* contains interesting descriptions. One of his best lyrical pieces is addressed to Galindo.

Of a younger generation Rosendo Villalobos (born 1860) has been an active writer contributing to the press of Lima where he was a member of the Ateneo. Of his poems of which he put forth several volumes *Tic-tac, a mi reloj*, meditations caused by the ticking of his watch in the silent night, makes good reading.

To the modernista movement Bolivia gave Ricardo Jaimes Freyre who was associated with Rubén Darío. He has lived all his manhood days in Argentina, however, and is now a professor in Tucumán.

CHAPTER VIII

ECUADOR

THE geography of Ecuador has exercised great influence on both its political and literary history. Its two chief cities with their respective provinces are absolutely diverse in character. Quito, the capital, is situated at an altitude of 9,300 feet above sea level; Guayaquil, its seaport, lies amid pestilential swamps at the mouth of a tropical river directly under the equator, one of the most unhealthy spots on earth. Before the opening of the railroad in 1908, the journey between the two cities required several days. As Quito was connected with Bogotá by an old trade route between the ridges of the cordilleras, greater affinity existed naturally between these two high lying cities than between the capital of Ecuador and its seaport.

At the time of the expulsion of the Spaniards there was a movement under the leadership of the poet Olmedo to establish the province of Guayaquil as an independent republic. But Bolívar succeeded in uniting Ecuador, Colombia, and Venezuela into one republic under the name of Nueva Granada. When this ill-assorted union fell apart at the Liberator's death a Venezuelan general, Juan José Flores, became president of Ecuador, and remained in office for fifteen years. It was a partisan victory of this president that Olmedo sang in his last great poem. When Flores fell from power his successor attempted to establish a government along radical lines, but Ecuador was too conservative to permit it. Under the leadership of García Moreno the conservative catholic element won complete control and set up a clerical dictatorship.

Gabriel García Moreno (1821–75) first attracted attention by his journalistic articles and his satirical verse in the style of Juvenal. His epistle in verse to Fabio on the wretched condition of his country assigns as a cause the irreligion of the governing party. A mystic and yet a man of action, García Moreno summed up his whole mental attitude and political policy in the sentence, "I am a Catholic and proud to be one." As leader of the conservative party, he welcomed the Jesuits when they were expelled from Colombia and published a lengthy political tract in two volumes, *Defensa de los Jesuitas*. When he became president in 1861, he established a sort of theocracy of which he was the secular arm, ruling with absolute tyranny. If his enemies in Guayaquil plotted revolution, he appeared so suddenly in the city with an armed force that they were easily crushed. On the other hand, to bad friars he was no less severe. For example, a drunken friar was ridden through Quito on the back of an ass, with his face turned toward the animal's tail. But severity which results in the execution of many creates embittered enemies. Of these, the most persistent and able was Juan Montalvo whose journalistic attacks finally resulted in the assassination of García Moreno, in 1875. García Moreno, both from the point of view of individual intelligence and of the extent of influence on the affairs of his country, was one of the most remarkable of Spanish Americans, and he differed from all in the rigid character of his religious principles.

Juan Montalvo (1833–89), the ardent advocate of tyrannicide, preferred his independence to all else. Though President Veintemilla, successor to García Moreno, tried to buy his silence by political preferment, Montalvo refused to be aught but a critic of the government. Though a Christian who esteemed the *Imitation* the greatest of books, he was actuated by the most intense hatred of friars and the clergy. In literature he developed a style unique in America and instinct with the best qualities of the older Spanish prose. For that reason his *Siete Tratados*, written about 1873, is one of the most widely known Spanish-American books, but as a critic points out he is more admired than read, because his qualities are such as appeal chiefly to literary men.

The *Siete Tratados* are seven essays on the following topics:—nobility, beauty in the human race (women), reply to a pseudo-catholic sophist, genius, Bolívar and Washington, the banquets of the philosophers (i. e., food), and El Buscapie (the prologue to an unpublished book, *Chapters forgotten by Cervantes*). Written in the manner of Montaigne (Montalvo said he was moved to write by "that pruritic egoism which made the old Gascon celebrated") these rambling discourses full of subtle irony and illustrative anecdote prove interesting reading on account of the brilliant ideas and amusing turns of thought on familiar matters. The author never neglects an opportunity for a thrust at a friar or a bit of religious superstition. To North Americans, his comparison between Washington and Bolívar might be instructive. He finds them both greater than Napoleon, because their work still prospers whereas his has been destroyed.

After 1882, Montalvo lived continuously in Paris. He attempted to found a quarterly, *El Espectador*, a name borrowed from Addison's famous periodical, in which he would discourse on current events in the style of his *Tratados;* but lack of financial success soon terminated its issue. He probably spent much of his time on the *Capítulos que se olvidaron .a Cervantes*, published posthumously in Besançon.

So successful was he in copying both the style and spirit of Cervantes that the book must be adjudged one of the very best of the numerous imitations of *Don Quixote*. One seems to be listening again to the sage discussions of the doleful knight and his squire, though there is plenty of Montalvo's own personality in such passages as the following. Don Quixote is examining the treasures of a village church. "The first thing which offered itself to his eyes were some large paintings which represented the principal miracles of the patron of the village. 'This happened in the Bay of Biscay,' said the priest, indicating a shipwreck. 'All the passengers were saved except those who were drowned.' 'Weren't they all saved then?' inquired Don Quixote. 'Not a third of them, sir.' 'And those who perished, where are they?' again inquired Don Quixote. 'Wherever God may have put them. On the canvas are only those of the miracle.'"

The dying hour of Montalvo is worthy of narration for the phase it reveals of his strange personality. Having caught a severe cold he suffered an attack of pleurisy, which the doctors found necessary to relieve by a surgical operation. He refused the administration of ether, because "on no occasion in my life have I lost the consciousness of my acts." Though he bore the operation stoically, it failed to save his life. An hour before death he had himself dressed in his best clothes and seated in an easy chair, saying,—"Whenever we are going to perform a solemn act, or when we expect to meet a person of consequence, we dress in our best. As no act is more important than quitting life for death, we ought to receive her decently." (The feminine gender of the Spanish words for life and death, allowing one to speak of death as "her," gives the point to the sentiment.) Montalvo at the same time had given a silver coin to an attendant to buy flowers to adorn his apartment. The price of flowers being high in Paris in January, the man returned with nothing more than four pinks, which exhaled their fragrance as Montalvo's spirit passed away.

Another native of Ecuador who attained a wide reputation outside of his own country was the poet Numa Pompilio Llona (1832–1907). Born in Guayaquil, he was educated in Colombia and in Lima where from 1853 for nearly ten years he was a professor of literature at the college of San Carlos. He then spent several years in Europe. On his return he lived chiefly in Ecuador with periods of absence in the diplomatic service of his country. While he wrote many sonnets and some patriotic pieces, his most popular work consisted of long poems with philosophical content, such as were the fashion in Spanish America in the sixties; for example, *Los Caballeros del Apocalipsis*, inspired by a painting which he had seen in Paris, *Noche de Dolor en las Montañas*, religious thoughts experienced among the Apennines, and most famous of all, *La Odisea del Alma*, written in 1864, so admired by the Argentine poet R. Obligado that he wrote a poem to record his feelings on reading it.

This poem, *La Odisea del Alma*, addressed to his mother, is a philosophical discourse on life. It begins by a reference to the idyll of childhood, its response to the wonders and beauties of nature, his boyish plans for an education in the classics. Filled with patriotic pride, strong for the struggle, armed with theories and maxims, the youth aspires to intellectual triumphs. When he meets reality the first effect on his illusions is indifference, but as he continues to mingle with human society, his ideals break on the reefs. The poem concludes by comparing life with the combats in the Roman Coliseum in which the gladiators "fell with haughty expression and in a posture artistic and gallant."

Of minor poets in Ecuador an anthology shows a decent number. Of these the poetess Dolores Veintemilla de Galindo waged an unequal battle for better consideration for women in Ecuador. Accused unjustly by a priest she committed suicide, and the only mourner at this funeral of a suicide was the Chilean poet Guillermo Blest Gana, then minister to Ecuador, who attended in full diplomatic dress.

Other writers of verse were Honorato Vásquez, Julio Zaldumbide (1833), and Luis Cordero (1830–1912). Cordero's lines struck a patriotic note with something of the tone of the Argentine poet Andrade to whom he dedicated his best poem, *Aplausos y Quejas*. Zaldumbide was a lover of Byron's poems and translated *Lara*. Though the philosophic strain predominated in *La Eternidad de la Vida* and the *Canto a la Musica*, his *Soledad del Campo* revealed true feeling for the beauties of nature.

Juan León Mera (1832–99), was the literary man of most universal talent yet produced by Ecuador, poet, scholar, antiquarian, novelist, excellent in all. His first volume of verse, published in 1858, showed both acquaintance with and love for the Indian traditions and lore of his country. The short romances and poems of this volume, of which should be mentioned an ode to the sun from the top of Panecillo, a small mountain on which the aborigenes had a temple, were followed in 1861 by the long legend *La Virgen del Sol*.

This pleasant poetic tale in verse is one of the most interesting of the many which Spanish Americans have written concerning the life of the Indians. The reader's sympathy is awakened and held by the dramatic course of the adventures of the lovers, while the introduction of verses in imitation of the native serenades or "yaravíes" adds a strange exotic element. The story is laid in the time of the conquest of Ecuador. It introduces the legend of Uiracocha, an Inca, who had prophesied that the country would fall into the hands of conquerors when the volcano Cotopaxi should be in eruption. The maiden Cisa, one of the virgins dedicated to worship of the sun, elopes with Amaru. They live in a cabin in the woods but their idyll is rudely disturbed by an eruption of the volcano, which they believe is a sign of the wrath of the deity at their sin. They flee but are captured by a band of Indians who were searching for them. They are bound to stakes and about to be executed when a Spanish army surprise the Indians. When the Spaniards learn why the young man and maid are bound, the friar Marcos Niza baptizes and marries them.

Mera next occupied himself with various literary and scientific investigations on topics mainly connected with Ecuador. He wrote a history of its literature, *Ojeada histórico-crítica sobre la Poesía ecuatoriana*, prepared an edition of the poems of the celebrated Mexican nun Sor Juana Ines de la Cruz, and some years later elucidated some obscure points in the life of Olmedo, whose letters he edited. In 1879 he published a prose novel, *Cumandá o un drama entre salvajes*.

Cumandá is a beautiful young woman living with an Indian family. A Spaniard, Carlos de Orozco, falls in love with her but she is married to an old Indian chief. The latter dies on the night of the wedding. When his tribesmen plan to sacrifice her to his departed spirit, she escapes through the woods to the Spanish mission. However, to save Carlos, who had been taken prisoner, and to avoid making the mission the object of a threatened attack by the Indians, she voluntarily gives herself up to the savages, who thereupon sacrifice her. Carlos and Father Domingo set out to rescue Cumandá but succeed only in finding her charred body. Father Domingo discovers that the girl was his own daughter whom he supposed killed in babyhood when his farm had been sacked by savages.

The Spanish critic Valera was much pleased by this novel, to which he gave such high praise as the following: "Neither Cooper nor Chateaubriand have better depicted the life of the woods nor have felt and described more poetically exuberant nature still free from the power of civilized man."

Other writers of prose fiction were Francisco Campos with his historical and fantastic legends and Carlos R. Tobar. The latter's *Timoleón Coloma* in the form of an autobiography gave interesting sketches of life in Quito. Other sketches he printed in volumes entitled *Brochadas* and *Más Brochades*.

In the field of verse Emilio Gallegos Naranjo not only complied a *Parnaso ecuatoriano* but published volumes of his own compositions, 1888. Dolores Sucre wrote a patriotic ode to her ancestor General Sucre, 1896. Among the young men who have written in modernista manner Emilio Gallegos del Campo has won the greatest praise from critics outside of Ecuador.

An intellectual leader of the present day in Ecuador is Alejandro Andrade Coello, a student of literature and founder in 1913, of *La Revista nacional* in Quito.

CHAPTER IX

COLOMBIA

In studying Colombian literature, certain geographical and historical facts about the country must be borne in mind. Colombia occupies the northwest corner of South America adjoining the isthmus of Panama. The first settlements were made on the isthmus and at Santa Marta and Cartagena on the coast of the Caribbean sea. The climate here is excessively hot and unhealthy. Three ranges of mountains forming part of the Andes come down to the ocean. Between the ranges flow great rivers, the most important of which are the Magdalena and the Cauca. Their sources lie amid lofty mountain peaks whose elevation above sea level frequently exceeds fifteen thousand feet.

The first expedition to the interior set out from Santa Marta in 1536, under the command of Gonzalo Jiménez de Quesada. Following the Magdalena he arrived at the site of the present city of Bogotá, situated in a wide plain at an elevation of eight thousand five hundred feet. The soil of the "sabana" of Bogotá, comprising an area of two thousand square miles, is very fertile. Though directly under the equator the region enjoys a mild and agreeable climate. On account of its general resemblance to the situation of the vega of Granada, Quesada gave the country the name of New Granada. Being rich in minerals, it attracted a fairly numerous immigration from Spain.

To reach Bogotá required in the old days a journey of at least three weeks, and even to-day when a portion of the distance may be traversed in a steamboat on the Magdalena and by rail around some of its rapids, not less than seven days are necessary for the trip. As a consequence of their geographical isolation, the people have retained many characteristics of their ancestors, with less change than is the case in other Spanish-American communities. The educated class having then distinction of ancestry as well as inherited wealth, it is natural that their literature should have aristocratic traits. Several of the poets who deserve individual mention, even in so brief an account as the present, have held the office of president of the republic.

As the term of this office during a large part of the nineteenth century was only two years, and there have been no less than thirty-seven revolutions in Colombia, many men have had an opportunity for a brief period of enjoying the honor. The great revolution against Spanish dominion was successful when Bolívar, in 1819, defeated the royal soldiers at Boyacá. But the republic which the Liberator formed from the countries now known as Venezuela, Colombia, and Ecuador and named Colombia lasted only till his death. The three parted company in 1831, and New Granada reassumed her colonial name. The political changes of 1861 guaranteed great freedom of individual action to the various sections of the country, which was symbolized by the name United States of Colombia. Such turmoil resulted from the federal form of government that in 1886 a new constitution setting up the unitarian type of republic was adopted; and the former states became departments as in the French Republic. The latest important episode in Colombian history was the separation of Panama, in 1903, and its establishment as an independent republic.

Among the young men of prominence in the Republic of New Granada, was José Eusebio Caro (1817-53), who with his friend and fellow poet, José Joaquín Órtiz (1814-92), founded the first purely literary journal, *La Estrella Nacional,* in 1836. Caro was also editor of the political journal *El Granadino.* His share in political life was considerable as he was not only a member of Congress, but also held various cabinet offices. An incident that occurred in 1844, when he occupied a position in the office of the Secretary of the Interior, illustrates the character of the man. Julio Arboleda accused Caro in open congress of designs on the constitution. Caro replied that Arboleda being a slave holder, it was not fitting of him that he should think anybody an enemy of liberty. Arboleda retorted that Caro was a parasite of the government, whereat the latter instantly resigned his position, though he needed it to support his family.

Character in fact is the distinguishing note of Caro's poems. He is the Puritan of South American literature. The severity and sternness of his temperament seems to have been inherited from his grandfather or imbibed from his teachings. His own father, an officer in the Spanish army, threw in his lot with the colonials on account of his marriage to José's mother, but the grandfather, a judge in the Spanish court, refused to take part in the re-

bellion.   Being unable to leave Colombia on account of
a chronic ailment, he suffered much persecution.   With
him the boy José lived during the absence of his father in
Europe on a mission for the young republic.   From his
grandfather, a learned man, the boy received also much
of his early education and the first inspiration to verse
writing.

His poems are an echo of his life experiences, a sort of
diary of his moral emotions.   He records his feelings at
his father's death in *El Huérfano sobre el Cadáver*.   While
the poems to "Delina" are not so very different from the
kind of poetry that men ordinarily write to the women
they subsequently marry, those inspired by his marriage
and the events of his married life possess a strange originality of conception.   His *Bendición Nupcial* treats the
subject of marriage from a point of view that ought to
delight the present day advocates of eugenics.   But even
they might balk at the poet's procedure in *A su Primogénito*, written before the child's birth.   Accused by his
contemporaries of obscenity in this poem, he replied that
he would give his son the pen with which he blessed him
before birth.   Upon the occasion of the baptism of his
second son, Caro wrote *El Bautismo*, a defense of Christianity.   No less vehement was he in political verse, especially on topics dealing with liberty.

In this regard he was ready to stand by his opinions, a
fact which led to the one great event of his life and perhaps ultimately to his death.   He dared to defend in
print and before the government, a man whom he believed was being unjustly treated.   The result, however,
was a sentence of imprisonment against Caro.   But his

friends succeeded in getting him out of the country, and he lived in banishment for three years in New York. When politics at home allowed his return, he set out in fine spirits and health, but on arriving at Santa Marta he was seized by a fever and died the sudden death of the tropics.

The lyrical quality of Caro's poetry is considerable. At the same time his poems are filled with ideas, so that they resemble to some extent brilliant declamatory orations. He was accustomed to use unusual meters and rhyme schemes. A fair notion of his workmanship and his worth as a poet may be obtained by the following translation of the lines, *En Boca del Último Inca*, rendered in approximately the meter of the original with the same scheme of rhymes.

> To-day arriving on Pichincha's slope,
> The deadly cannon of the whites I flee,
> Like the sun a wanderer, like the sun aflame,
> Like the sun free.
>
> O Sun, my Father, hearken! Manco's throne
> Lies in the dust; Thy altar's sanctity
> Profaned; exalting thee alone I pray,
> Alone but free.
>
> O Sun, my Father, hearken! A slave before
> The nations of the world I'll not agree
> To bear the mark. To slay myself I come,
> To die though free.
>
> To-day Thou wilt perceive me, when afar
> Thou dost begin to sink into the sea,
> Singing Thy hymns on the volcano's top,
> Singing and free.

To-morrow though, alas! when once again
Thy crown throughout the east will shining be,
Its golden splendor on my tomb will fall,
My tomb though free.

Upon my tomb the condor will descend
From heaven, the condor, bird of liberty,
And building there its nest, will hatch its young,
Unknown and free.[1]

To his friend and co-editor, J. J. Órtiz, the poet
Caro owes the publication of his collected poems. Órtiz
is himself reckoned among Colombia's great poets, but
his inspiration had its sources more directly in the romantic school, and he lived a much longer life. On the
other hand, Caro's congressional opponent, Julio Arboleda,
was exactly his contemporary, as they were both born
in the spring of the same year. Arboleda must be accounted, however, the greater poet.

Julio Arboleda (1817–1862) was descended from one of
the earliest settlers in the bishopric of Popayán, a district
on the headwaters of the Cauca near the border of Ecuador
on the old trade route between Bogotá and Quito. His
father, Rafael Arboleda, was a trusted friend of Bolívar
and ruined his health on a mission for the Liberator. In
1830, taking with him his son Julio, he went to Europe in
search of relief. The father died within a year, but the
son remained for eight years till he received the degree of
Bachelor of Arts from the University of London. On his
return to Popayán he plunged with all the ardor of youth
into politics. Though he was one of the richest proprietors
of the locality, he enlisted in the national guard then form-

[1] Version of Alfred Coester.

ing to put down a serious revolution against the government at Bogotá.

His personality was attractive. Throughout the country he became known as "Don Julio." His bravery won for him steady advancement in military rank so that at the end of the war, 1842, he went home as a colonel. Then he married and devoted his time to his estate and to letters. His neighbors interrupted this manner of life by sending him to the Congress, where he was conspicuous for his oratory.

As a member of the opposition he published an important pamphlet against the Jesuits, but when in 1849 his party won the upper hand and electing José H. López president, proceeded to expel the order, Arboleda was unwilling to follow all his measures. He withdrew to his native town and began the publication of a satirical journal, *El Misóforo*, against the democratic and socialistic liberal party. For this he was thrown into prison. From its walls he sent forth his two most noted political poems, *Estoy en la cárcel*, and *Al Congreso granadino*. In the former he lashed with bitter invective "López el Tirano" and his judge, Miguel Valencia, who was recklessly condemning to death even women. In the latter poem he urged the Congress to stand firm in "the defense of the people" and "restore to the Republic her ancient majesty."

Having been set free from prison by reason of money paid by his brother, Arboleda joined the revolution that was beginning in the province on the frontier of Ecuador. Badly beaten he and his companions made their way through Ecuador to Lima. At this time his property was sacked and the papers in his house destroyed. Among them was the manuscript of the long poem which is Arboleda's chief claim to fame as a poet, the epic history of Gonzalo de Oyón. After residing in Peru till the beginning of 1853, he set out for New York, bidding farewell to "gaya Lima" in a lyric outburst that contrasted his melancholy state as a proscribed person with the dwellers in an earthly Eden. This gem begins:—

> Me voy de las playas alegres, süaves,
> Do el Rimac corriendo tranquilo murmulla;
> Do el céfiro alienta, la tórtola arrulla,
> Do nunca ha apagado sus rayos el sol.

The next year with a change in the government Arboleda returned to Bogotá as a senator. It was not long before civil war again prevailed. Arboleda held this time a high position in the army of the constitutionalists operating against the dictator Melo. Success crowned their arms. As President of Congress Arboleda inducted into office the new President Mallarino. In 1856 Ospina of the conservative party was elected President, but the caudillo Mosquera instantly started a revolt. At this period Arboleda was in Europe for the purpose of educating his children. When affairs were going badly with Ospina he called upon Arboleda to assist. The latter felt that duty claimed him and leaving Paris he reached Colombia in the autumn of 1860. He took command at Santa Marta where he was promptly besieged. After a month he was obliged to evacuate. He transferred his troops and munitions of war by sea to Panama, thence he organized an expedition along the Cauca river to march upon Popayán. In this region the popularity of "Don Julio" brought hundreds of the country people to his standard. As the government of Ospina had legally come to an end, his enthusiastic followers elected Arboleda President, but the ratification by the Congress required by the constitution was impossible, because Mosquera had taken Bogotá by assault and the members had fled. As general in chief of the constitutional forces Arboleda held his own against the dictator for upwards of a year. In one of his battles he defeated and took prisoner the President of Ecuador, García Moreno, who had taken a part in the struggle near the border. But his lieutenants were less successful and his soldiers opposed to expeditions that would take them far from home. The end came on November 12, 1862, when he was killed by an assassin who lay in wait for him by the wayside.

Something is added to the comprehension of Arboleda's character by the perusal of extracts from a letter to an English friend about the time of his resistance to the government of López. "Fortune has of late smiled upon me most graciously. My business has not only gone on very well in general, but my lands have such a great quantity of excellent quinine that for many years I shall be able to export two thousand sacks annually. I have a contract for three thousand which I am sure to deliver within these twelve months. The export will cost me very little because I have more than five hundred idle mules, which by the exercise of taking my bales to port will gain in vigor and value. . . . The quinine on my lands seems inexhaustible. In twenty years I shall have cut the last trees and then the first will have grown again."

It is apparent that such a man was moved to take part

in politics not through hope of personal gain but from the highest motives. The analogy between himself and the hero of his great poem, *Gonzalo de Oyón*, gives it an added interest.

Though the author spent the leisure moments of ten years upon the poem, it was left unfinished. The manuscript of a large part was destroyed by the soldiers who sacked his house. Rewritten, another large section was lost during the transport of some of Arboleda's effects. As a result of its fragmentary state and the conditions under which it was produced the whole lacks unity of conception both of character and action.

The foundation is a legend which Arboleda found in the local history of his native Popayán. Fleeing from the fate' of those involved in the rebellion of Gonzalo Pizarro there came to New Granada one Álvaro de Oyón. Having gathered a band of malcontents to the number of seventy-five, they planned to seize the city of Popayán, thence to march on Quito and Lima. The assault took place in 1552 but with disastrous results to the conspirators. Álvaro was killed.

The poet gave to Álvaro a brother, Gonzalo, who is a foil to his schemes as well as a contrast to his character. The latter is represented as coming to Popayán with the conquistadores. His kind heart leads him to intercede for the cacique Pubén about to be killed by the Spaniards so that he saves the Indian's life. Now Fernando, the son of the Adelantado, Sebastian de Benalcázar, has cast eyes upon the cacique's daughter, Pubenza, and forces her to marry him in order to save her father's life during Gonzalo's absence. A few years later Álvaro de Oyón in rebellion against the authorities after getting auxiliaries among the savage tribes, marches on Popayán. Gonzalo, supposedly dead, appears at the fight and decides it in favor of the royal cause. Fernando in jealousy declares Gonzalo an outlaw and sets a price on his head, but Pubenza warns him in time for him to take refuge among the Indians. Once more Álvaro de Oyón attacks the city and again Gonzalo sallies forth in its defense. In the night the brothers engage in single combat, but recognizing each other they fall into discussion about their respective behaviour. A truce follows. During this the unhappy lovers Gonzalo and Pubenza have an interview at which they are surprised by Fernando, who in mad jealous rage kills his children. In the form of a specter he presents himself again to Gonzalo and Pubenza but disappears then forever.

The fragments break off here. Report has it that Arboleda intended to have Álvaro desist from his rebellious plans at the solicitation of his mother. Of this there are some evidences in the poem.

The style and language of the poem is purely Castilian with only a slight admixture of native words in certain familiar scenes. The narration shows the author's acquaintance with both the Italian poets and Byron and like the Spanish romanticists he preferred to write in a variety of meters.

In regard to the application of the poem to affairs in Colombia, the words of Miguel A. Caro [1] are illuminating. "Putting aside the improbability of the conversation between Gonzalo and Álvaro, it is of the highest interest because it has natural application to the perpetual struggle

[1] Introduction to *Poesías de Julio Arboleda*, New York, 1884.

which in our Spanish America is sustained by the broad genuine patriotism which respects tradition and loves national unity against those bastard ambitions which proclaim liberty but demolish whatever exists. The language which Arboleda put in the mouth of Álvaro is historically exact. It is the same as that of all those rebels and political dogmatists of colonial times. In their turn are symbolized in Gonzalo all the champions and martyrs of political and religious faith in our country and among them most of all Julio Arboleda."

Whatever may have been the sources of Arboleda's inspiration, the romantic spirit that moved other Colombian poets entered the country by way of Caracas, according to Rafael Pombo.[1] From there came not only the works of Zorrilla and Espronceda but also the literary journals containing the poems of Abigail Lozano and J. A. Maitín. Their most important effect was the awakening of an interest in the beauties of nature, that wonderful scenery of Colombia, its great rivers, its magnificent cascades, its stupendous mountains, and its strange and varied flora. The falls of Tequendama especially became the topic of literary exercise.

This fall though with less volume of water drops four times the distance of Niagara, about four hundred and eighty feet. In descending the water strikes a ledge of rock and rebounds, then drops in several streams. Much of it is turned to vapor which ascends and when gilded by the sunlight the iridescence may be seen in Bogotá five leagues away.

Among the earliest poems of Gregorio Gutiérrez Gon-

[1] Introduction to *Poesías de Gutiérrez González.*

zález (1826–72) is one written at the age of twenty with the title *Al Salto del Tequendama*. That it was not conceived wholly in the romantic mood is shown by a quotation from Andrés Bello which serves as a sort of sub-title, referring to the river Magdalena and this fall. The great master's influence becomes again apparent in Gutiérrez González' longest and most famous poem *Sobre el Cultivo del Maíz en Antioquia*, 1866. Written in quatrains it depicted in a lively and poetic style scenes of agricultural labor in the author's native province; and was accompanied by a glossary of terms peculiar to that country. The poem opens with a description of the clearing of a piece of land by a gang of thirty laborers. The poet, more attentive to the landscape than they, sees many things which he describes to the reader; and in the four sections of the poem takes him through the various tasks required before the final storing of the grain.

The poet belonged, however, wholly to the romantic type. Sent away from home to school in Bogotá he began writing verses at the age of eighteen. He was gifted with extraordinary ability in improvising, with which he used to amuse his schoolmates. To this fact is due perhaps the peculiar quality of his lines that made him the popular poet of Colombia, and his pen name "Antioco" a household word. Even illiterate persons knew his poems by heart.

In his life too he was a true romantic. When not quite twenty he fell so violently in love at first sight with a young lady that when she passed near him he became so faint that he had to be supported by his companions. He consulted a physician on the disorders of his heart and this worthy told him to go home and prepare to die. He went home but not before he chided in verse the beauty whose "barbarous scorn had opened for him the last dwelling," and though for her he descended to the sepulcher, he would never receive "even one tear from her divine eyes."

The mournful tone did not long predominate. Soon thereafter he married the Julia who then appeared in his lines as the source of the joy which filled his life. After ten years of matrimony in reply to the question of a friend why he no longer sang, he wrote those verses on his happiness comparing himself to the dove that in the noonday heat attends silent but happy on his beloved in the nest; happiness, moreover, resembles the morning-glory that blooms in the shade but withers in the sunlight.

In his material fortunes he was not so happy. Though he was born wealthy, he became involved in the civil wars of 1860 and 62, and his property was swept away. After the restoration of peace he was not successful in his business enterprises. Besides he had eight children to support. His discouragement was expressed all too plaintively in the verses addressed to various friends and to his wife during his last years. The evident sincerity of these poems confirms one in the opinion that Gutiérrez González' wide popularity is due to the predominance of that quality in his work. Therein lies its firm appeal.

Less popular were the poems of J. J. Órtiz, and much less numerous though he lived to be nearly seventy-eight years old. To his romanticism he joined a certain classical finish for which reason Menéndez y Pelayo reckoned one of his poems, *Los Colonos* "one of the finest jewels of

American poetry;—descriptive and lyrical at the same
time." In this gem the poet represents himself on his
horse galloping to the distant city. His imagination
carries him back to the time of the conquistadores who
first planted the cross on that spot to the amazement
of the aborigines. Then he invites the Muse to listen
to the resounding blows of the pioneers' axes as they clear
the forest and build their homes; to watch the bull breaking
the black soil to receive the grain brought from beyond
the seas; to observe the other domestic animals; to consider the Spanish woman who brought with her as a re-
minder of her homeland the seeds of the flowers whose
beauty and fragrance now delight the senses; to admire,
when the bell calls to prayer, the holy ardor of Christ's
disciples who have penetrated the most distant parts of
the new world.

But, though the great Spanish critic may have admired
Órtiz' descriptive verses, his countrymen preferred those
with the Tyrtæan note. It is related that one evening he
nearly started a riot by the recitation of his stirring lines.
The special object of his admiration was Bolívar. In his
boyhood he had seen the great man and had been a childish
witness of the armies that fought the battle of Boyacá
in his native province. To that battle he dedicated an
ode which for patriotic inspiration will bear comparison
with Olmedo's verses. When at seventy years of age
Órtiz was one of the few living contemporaries of that
victory, he wrote his greatest ode *Colombia y España* in
which he compares Columbus and Bolívar. If the one
discovered a world the other freed it from the yoke of
tyranny. The memory of the champion of liberty gives

consolation to the poet in the midst of the civil discords in which he lives.

Órtiz' influence as a man, apart from his poems, was considerable. He opened a school in 1852 that became a center for the cherishing of literature and culture. Four years later he successfully promoted the establishment of a literary society, El Liceo Granadino. He also took part in the protest against the expulsion of the Jesuits, that event which stirred Colombian society to its very depths in 1863. A pamphlet of his on this topic was sold in the unprecedented quantity of four thousand copies in Bogotá. Throughout his long life as a journalist and educator, his own writings and the editing of those of others, such as the poems of J. E. Caro and the revolutionary Vargas Tejada and the compilation of school textbooks in literature kept his name ever before the public.

The year 1854 may be taken to fix the period of greatest literary activity in Colombia. Poetry did not alone claim attention in this decade, but there were representations of original dramas and an important development in the publication of literary journals. The latter opened a field for the production of novels and tales.

Of dramas the authors most worthy of mention were the brothers Felipe and Santiago Pérez, José Caicedo Rojas, and José M. Samper. Their writings, however, were not limited to the theater but appeared in both prose and verse in periodicals or daily papers. Felipe Pérez being interested in the early history of South America dramatized the story of Gonzalo Pizarro in five acts, and retold as tales the story of both Pizarros and that of

Atahualpa. Santiago Pérez, who later became president of the republic in 1874, turned to European history for the matter of his historical dramas *Jacobo Molay* and *El Castillo de Berkley* and his legend *Leonor*. Spanish history on the other hand was the inspiration of *Miguel Cervantes* and *Celos, amor y ambición* by J. Caicedo Rojas and of his historical romance *Don Álvaro*. Caicedo Rojas also published a volume of descriptive articles of manners, *Apuntes de Ranchería*, which met with some success.

José Maria Samper (1828–98) devoted his attention more to his native country. He is perhaps Colombia's most prolific writer in many lines of literary endeavor. Seven of his dramatical pieces were produced in Bogotá in the years 1856 and 57. Of these the most successful was *Un Alcalde a la antigua y Dos Primos a la moderna*, a comedy of national manners. In 1858 Samper went to Europe in a diplomatic capacity where he remained five years, returning to Colombia after a visit in Lima. Many years later he put into a novel, *Los Claveles de Julia*, his memories of that capital. After his return to Bogotá he wrote a novel about every four years, beginning with *Martín Flórez*, 1866. The dramatic element and the dialogue is the strongest part of his tales as the description of places and persons is prolix. To the study of Colombian history Samper performed a real service by publishing a series of sketches of notable compatriots. Toward the end of his life he made quite a sensation by publicly renouncing his views as a freethinker and embracing Catholicism. The book which he made out of his profession, *Historia de una Alma*, is packed with interesting personal and social reminiscences. Samper's journalistic work was perhaps the most extensive of his contemporaries. At one time he carried on a periodical with the sole assistance of his talented wife, Doña Soledad Acosta.

To her we owe an interesting account of the methods employed by the contributors to the *Mosaico*, the most important literary journal of the golden decade of the fifties. Beside her husband and Caicedo Rojas, they were José Joaquín Borda (1835-78), to whose constant activity in promoting literary magazines Colombia remains in debt; Ricardo Carrasquilla (1827–87), schoolmaster and poet; Eugenio Díaz (1804–61), writer of realistic tales; and J. M. Vergara y Vergara (1831–72), lover of letters. She makes the very illuminating remark, "We edited the *Mosaico* to amuse ourselves without considering the public." But the magazine to which she contributed this article, *El Papel Periódico Ilustrado*, beginning publication in 1881, did take the public very much into consideration because it was the first illustrated periodical on an elaborate scale, printed in Colombia.

In regard to José María Vergara y Vergara it has been said that, "whoever makes a formal study of Colombian letters will find his name somehow connected with most of the publications of his epoch and will see his enthusiasm for stimulating and sustaining the literary aspirations of friends and strangers." [1] Of his own writings the most important is his *Historia de la Literatura en Nueva Granada desde la conquista hasta la independencia, 1538–1820,* published in 1867. As a compiler of poems he rendered a service in *La Lira granadina, coleccion de poesías nacion-*

[1] I. Laverde Amaya, *Apuntes sobre Bibliografía colombiana.*

ales. His own verses, though he wrote with great ease and was famous as an improviser, were slight. Little more can be said of the tale, *Olivos y Aceitunas, Todos son unos.*

But he discovered the talent of Eugenio Díaz, the most realistic of Colombian novelists and writers of articles on manners. Born in 1804, he was over forty years of age before he began to write. Having been a small farmer he brought to his work an intimate knowledge of the types that he depicted. His longest tale, a real masterpiece of characterization, was *Manuela.* The heroine is the keeper of a small provision store through which pass all the interesting individuals of the town and where their affairs are thoroughly discussed.

Vergara, on his trip to Europe, made numerous friends and brought back to Bogotá authorization for himself, José María Marroquín, and Miguel Antonio Caro to form an Academy allied to the Spanish Academy. Marroquín was a popular schoolmaster, author of works on Castilian spelling, and a poet whose verses were favorites on account of their humor. M. A. Caro (1843-1909), though but twenty-seven years of age at the time, was noted for his learning. He was the oldest son of J. E. Caro to whose famous poem blessing his firstborn before birth we have already alluded. The father, had he lived, would not have been disappointed in the son for he became Colombia's most learned man and president of the republic. His greatest service to Colombian letters was the preparation of an edition of Arboleda's poems which included the inedited epic *Gonzalo de Oyón.* Miguel A. Caro's own poems were somewhat coldly classical in form and idea.   Nevertheless two of them are well known and liked, *La Vuelta a la Patria* and *A la Estatua del Libertador*.   The latter is a presentation of the moral character of Bolívar, accomplished in part by incorporating in the poem certain historical sayings of the Liberator, such as:—"Who knows whether I have ploughed on the sea and built on the wind," and, "Perhaps the curses of a hundred generations will fall on me, unfortunate author of so many ills!"   These sublime doubts, says the poet, have been expressed by the sculptor who wrought the great statue of the Liberator in the main square of Bogotá.

The *Vuelta a la Patria* expresses in sweetly melancholy fashion the idea that the sight of his old home does not satisfy the longings of the pilgrim because his true home lies beyond the term of this life.   The Spanish critic Valera thinks that, "Everything in this composition, in which there are more sentiments and ideas than words, make it a perfect model of sentimental poetry in any language." [1]

Reference has been made to Ricardo Carrasquilla.   He was a well-beloved schoolmaster who delighted his pupils by jocose verses on homely topics.   His lines on *Las Fiestas en Bogotá* are called "a real photograph of what our popular festivals are."   But more important for his contemporaries were such tracts on the religious question as *Sofismas anti-católicos vistos con microscopio.*

The mention of writings of this character would seem to lie outside our limits, but in studying the history of Colombia whether literary or political, it is impossible to ignore the religious question.   The liberal party that

[1] J. Valera, *Cartas americanas.*

came into power in 1849 were dominated by the theories of French freethinkers. Though their action in expelling the Jesuits was resented and they fell from power, they were successful in 1861 in setting up a new constitution which enabled them to disestablish the Church, disfranchise the clergy, and confiscate the property of the convents. It is natural then that such profound changes emanating from radical principles should have echoes in literature which is not in itself controversial. Hence arises the significance of the great amount of religious verse.

As a controversialist for the conservatives nobody was more active than the Manuel María Madiedo (1817–00), whose writings include whole volumes on social science, logic and law. A very learned man and acquainted with the whole range of European philosophy, he devoted his intelligence to the defense of the Christian religion. Many of the poems in his volume of collected verse published in 1859 preach the mission of Christ. As a poet, however, Madiedo is more generally known for his lines descriptive of the great river Magdalena, "a picture taken from nature, where primitive man rules, free and strong, but struggling with natural forces terribly powerful, beautiful, and rebellious." With equal enthusiasm Madiedo also depicted his native city Cartagena and the ocean before her walls. A series of poems with strongly patriotic note on Bolívar, Sucre, Ayacucho, and America likewise came from his pen. Dramas he wrote in his youth, and at the age of nineteen had a tragedy, entitled *Lucrecia o Roma libre*, produced in Bogotá. To the end of his long life he contributed to the press of Colombia.

Contrasted with Madiedo may be Rafael Nuñez (1825–94), a man of action and yet a poet. For twenty years he dominated the political situation in Colombia, being at times both president and dictator. As a young man he was the secretary of General Mosquera, the leader of the liberal party and dictator in 1861. From this period dates Nuñez' poem with the title ¿Que sais-je?, one of the most skeptical bits of verse ever written. Everywhere the poet finds the good and the bad so inextricably mingled that he cannot separate them. Every object in the world has its good and its evil side. Sometimes innocence and candor are malignity, prudence is daring, impiety piety. In another skeptical poem Nuñez compares himself with the Dead Sea; his illusions and pleasures are the cities which God destroyed.

From this attitude of mind Nuñez traveled very far before his death. Sent to England as Colombian consul in Liverpool, he absorbed many English ideas regarding the functions of government. In 1878 he became President of the Senate and two years later President of Colombia. He adapted his English ideas to the conditions of his country. His ideal seemed to be an oligarchy as set forth in his book *La Reforma política en Colombia*. His model was Moses if we can trust his poem on the Hebrew law-giver. At any rate, he brought about many needed reforms in Colombia laid waste by anarchy. To combat it, he protected the clergy, restored them to the rights of which his own liberal party had deprived them and ordered religion to be taught in the schools for the purpose of inculcating respect for authority. The civil power was strengthened by his new constitution of 1885, for the term of office for the president was increased to six years. With vice presidents of his own creation, he then held the position till his death.

While Nuñez' philosophical verses reveal him as a skeptic, the poems of Diego Fallon (1834–1905), present the ancient faith in accord with modern geological knowledge. There is something of the Celtic imagination, due undoubtedly to his parentage, in the originality of his conceptions. Perhaps also his English education had its influence just as his expert attainments as a musician are revealed in the rhythmical beauty of his lines. At once the most striking and original of his poems is *Las Rocas de Suesca*. The poet finds himself among these gigantic rocks overhearing the confidences of Miocene and Pliocene till their chatter is interrupted by Siluria the elder. She at his request relates her own creation. Another poem, *A la Luna*, depicts the beauty of the tropical moonlight on the slope of the Andes. The silence leads him to think of God, to feel that his soul is merely a prisoner of the flesh, while the moon reminds him of its divine mission. Fallon's skill in difficult and intricate meter is displayed in *La Palma del Desierto*, in which he philosophizes about the barren desert and the strange power of the palm tree to withstand the heat of the sun and the tree's service to man. While the quantity of Fallon's verses is not great, their quality places him in the front rank of Colombian poets.

And the main body of Colombian poets with an individual note is fairly numerous. Joaquín Pablo Posada (1825–80), for example, had an astounding facility in handling language, though his compositions were limited to jocose or satirical matter. Even on his deathbed he dictated as gay a parting letter in verse to a friend as any that he had ever written when begging for a little loan of money to tide him over a hard place. A poet who knew how to hit the popular taste was José María Pinzón Rico. His erotic tendencies appear in the poem usually given in anthologies *El Despertar de Adán* though the intention of the verses is praise of God. A very prolific versifier was César Conto (1836–91). His original pieces are not so valuable as his translations from German and English. Of the latter the most praiseworthy is perhaps Long-fellow's *Psalm of Life*. For religious intensity and force the lines of Mario Valenzuela, a member of the Society of Jesus, should be mentioned. An attractive poem, *Tu triunfaste*, describes the appearance of a beautiful woman riding on horseback, and again at a dancing party; on neither occasion, however, did she make an impression on the writer's heart: but when he saw her as a sister of charity ministering to the sick, he quite succumbed.

A leader of this flight of poets, surpassing them, both in versatility and in technical skill, was Rafael Pombo (1833–1912). He began his literary career at the age of twenty by a mystification of the public in giving out a series of verses entitled *Mi Amor* signed "Edda," which led readers to believe that they were perusing the erotic confessions of a lovesick damsel. In 1854 he was sent to New York as secretary of the Colombian legation where he remained five years. He so successfully mastered the English language that poems of his in English were published by Bryant in the *New York Evening Post*. Of his sojourn his poems have many recollections. *Las Norte-*

americanas en Broadway reveals the young man beneath the portico of the Saint Nicolas Hotel admiring the throng of passing beauties. Though he pays his compliments to the various Spanish-American types, he is bewitched by the brilliance of the New Yorkers' eyes and the crimson of their cheeks. But "woe to him who sees the fascinating army!" Their hearts, like the swirling water of Niagara, are cruel, insatiable and cold. On his sensitive soul the sudden death of a young girl, Elvira Tracy, with whom he had been at church, made such an impression that his poem on her last words, "The mass is over; come, come, let us go home!" possesses unusual intensity of feeling. For that reason it is a classic expression of the uncertainty of human life.

Of totally different character are *Cuentos pintados* and *Cuentos morales*, many of which are said to be known by heart by children. After his return to Colombia, Pombo was interested for several years in popular education and in the publication of an educational journal. Of a popular type also are a series of quatrains written to be sung to the music of the national air, *El Bambuco*.

About this song, J. M. Samper has written the following: "Nothing more national and patriotic than this melody which has for authors all Colombians: it vibrates as the echo of millions of accents, it laments with all lamentations, it laughs with all the laughter of the country. It is the evocation of our moonlit nights and our days of happiness. It is the companion that animates our weddings, that enlivens our sentimental ceremonies. It is the soul of our people turned into melody."

Pombo's maturer lines belong to the elegiac type, and

are written with great depth of feeling. A rather long poem, *Angelina*, after relating the death of a young girl of fifteen with emphasis on the grief of her mother and little brother, passes to reflections on love and grief. In them the poet finds symbolized the struggle between our higher and lower natures. In "love and grief, there is Christ, there is God." When Pombo revisited the United States and again stood before the falls of Niagara, he was stirred to write some verses in "contemplation." The greatness of God is the main thought with which the sight inspires him. When he seeks for the terror felt by the Cuban poet Heredia, he finds it not; for the very worst that Nature can do to human kind, to serve for a tomb, is in reality a good. On the contrary, man is the monster who disturbs this earthly paradise. As for the falling waters, though they send forth a hymn of strength and life, his soul has no enthusiasm left to sing them because life is a sarcasm.

Poets of a younger generation than Pombo, such as Antonio Gómez Restrepo (b. 1869), Diego Uribe (b. 1867), Joaquín González Camargo (b. 1865), naturally show the influence of contemporary literature. To the latter J. Valera paid the unusual compliment of saying that his becquerista verses pleased him even better than those of Becquer or Heine.

No account of Colombian literature would be complete without mention of a few of the many female poets and writers who have graced their country. Their prominence is partly due to the fact that in the population of Colombia women greatly outnumber men, in some towns, according to a recent census, in the proportion of three men to four women, as a result of the numerous civil wars which have ravaged the republic. The Christian resignation required of women in such a state of affairs is clearly reflected in their verses.

For the religious tone of her poems expressed in fluent language Doña Silveria Espinosa de Rendon (?–1886), was one of the first to attract attention. Though she essayed with some success the patriotic lyric, the majority of her verses celebrate the glories of the Cross, the virtues of Mary and the joys of friendship.

In descriptive poetry too, so far as it deals with the famous falls of the Tequendama, a woman, in Valera's opinion, has excelled her numerous competitors both native and foreign. Therefore, Doña Agripina Montes del Valle should be acclaimed the "Muse of the Tequendama." The superiority of her lines arises not alone from the wealth of color and the minuteness of the description but from the fact that at the background of the picture the reader sees the poetess herself. "The depression which possesses her spirit in the presence of such a grand scene makes one form a better conception of its magnificence." Doña Agripina gathered poetic laurels also outside of Colombia, for she won a gold medal for a poem offered in a Chilean competition in 1872.

The theme of love treated with deep emotion and sincerity fills the verses of Doña Mercedes Álvarez de Flórez (b. 1859). They render the story of her courtship and marriage to Leonidas Flórez (1859–87), himself a poet. As they were poor, their parents opposed their union. After their marriage, she has given a poetic record of her moods. Matrimony has chains, yes; but they are golden,

let her kiss them. At times she is jealous of her husband
for she knows he lies awake at night, with thoughts which
are not of her but of his ambition. Seek not riches, she
urges him, let her whisperings suffice at night. When he
fell sick at the age of twenty-four, her heart cries out that
they are too young to separate. He should struggle
against death by drawing strength from her kisses. To
God she prays not to "snatch from my heaven this bright
star which thine does not need! Listen. In his delirium,
he says that he loves me so much, that he does not wish
to die!"

Of Doña Soledad Acosta de Samper (1831–1913), wife
of J. M. Samper, mention has already been made. Her
literary interests covered many fields though her specialty
was the historical or biographical article, for which she
inherited a natural aptitude from her father, the historian
Joaquín Acosta. Her most original effort was the publication of a periodical for women, *La Mujer*, which appeared from 1878 to 1881.

In the matter of novels it has fallen to the fortune of
Colombia to send forth the most widely read work of
fiction of any written by a Spanish American, one of the
very few which have been translated into French and
English, the idyllic romance, *María* by Jorge Isaacs.
Perhaps its popularity proves it to be the representative
Spanish-American novel. At any rate it presents an un-
matched picture of home life in Colombia. Its characters
are true to life. Its landscapes exist in the valley of the
Cauca where its author was born.

The plot is simple. Efraín, a boy of twenty, returns
home after an absence of several years. He finds that

María, his father's ward and the playmate of his childhood, is now in the first beauty of young womanhood at fifteen. They fall in love. The father, not wholly opposed to the match, wishes the boy to delay marriage, first, that he may study medicine in Europe, and second, because María has shown symptoms of epilepsy, a disease of which her mother died. Efraín yields to his father's desires and prepares to leave for Europe. Before his departure, however, María and he are betrothed. After he is gone, María's malady becomes worse and she imagines that only his return will save her life. Efraín is sent for, but when he reaches home María is dead.

The interest lies in the incidents by which the characters of the leading personages are revealed and in the details of home life in the mountains of Colombia. What intensity of passion is displayed over trifles! Efraín, for example, had brought home some mountain lilies as a present to María, but when he notices that she has neglected to observe her custom of placing fresh flowers in his room during his absence, he petulantly throws his intended gift out of the window. María, finding the flowers, understands and makes amends by wearing one of the lilies to the evening meal. It is not surprising then, that the same Efraín should urge his horse at the risk of his own life into a stream swollen with tropical rain, as he rides three leagues through the night to get a physician to attend María.

Strange details of real life constantly entertain and charm the reader. Though Efraín's father is the proprietor of a vast estate, he is not unwilling to attend the

wedding of a negro slave and dance with the bride. When
Efraín visits the home of a certain white tenant, he is
honored by being provided with the only knife and fork
in the house, and again at his morning ablutions by the
zealous production from its precious box of the family's
one treasured towel. A striking episode is a jaguar hunt,
in which Efraín's English cartridges and unerring aim
save the life of the mountaineer Braulio. This man is
something of a wag, for when a young visitor from the
city makes fun of his dogs, Braulio takes revenge in an
original manner. He sees to it that there are no bullets
in the smarty's gun and then drives a fine buck by his
stand in the hunt. The callow youth is mortified to miss
so easy a shot before his friends. In Efraín's home, the
details of the daily routine in which appear his father, his
mother, his sister Emma, and María form an exquisite
idyllic picture. To relate them all would, in the words
of Vergara in his preface to the first edition of 1867,
"necessitate writing another *María*."

The author of this romance, Jorge Isaacs (1837–95) was
the son of an English Jew domiciled in Cali in the valley
of the Cauca. It was in this region that the civil war of
1862 raged with special intensity. In consequence of it
his property gone and left an orphan, the young man
emigrated to Bogotá. In 1865 he published a volume of
verses which received more attention after the appearance
of *María*, 1867. The success of the novel was immediate.
His reward was an appointment to a diplomatic post in
Chile where his fame as a literary man assisted in preparing for him a warm welcome. In time political changes
at home brought about his retirement. Again in Bogotá

he was not successful in business, and the latter years of his life were passed in great want.

Later novels in Colombia follow the example of Isaacs in his nationalistic tendency, though few deserve mention. *Frutos de mi Tierra*, published 1896 by Tomás Carrasquilla, is a fair sample of the type consisting of a series of sketches of manners strung together on a thin plot.

Of greater literary value is *Pax* by Lorenzo Marroquín which recently created a storm of indignation because certain politicians believed they had been caricatured. At any rate the author has pilloried the plague of politics which besets Colombia. The personages and the incidents of the novel give the reader an unusual insight into the character of a perplexing country.

Of scholars Colombia has produced several of whom she may well be proud. The most important historian is José Manuel Restrepo (1782–1863) whose *Historia de la Revolución de la República de Colombia*, originally published in 1827 and enlarged in 1858, is the fascinating narrative of a participant and eyewitness.

J. M. Torres Caicedo deserves the praise and thanks of everybody interested in Spanish-American literature. His *Ensayos biográficos y de Crítica literaria* in three volumes, 1863 and 1868, was the first attempt to treat the whole field and is still invaluable.

The name of Rufino José Cuervo (1844–1911) is familiar to many otherwise ignorant of Colombian writers, on account of his services to the grammatical and lexicographic studies of the Spanish language given to the world in his notes to Bello's *Grammar* and in his *Apuntaciones críticas sobre el Lenguaje bogotano*. The latter is the basis of all the many studies which have, since its publication, been made of the changes undergone by Castilian in America. The study of the language was a cult with Cuervo who lived for long years in Paris a bookish recluse. His house was a shrine to be visited by Spanish Americans pretending to a love of letters.

To the modernista movement of recent years Colombia had the honor of contributing José Asunción Silva (1860–96). Though contemporary to its inception, Silva's inventions and experiments in rhythm were eagerly taken up by others who made them widely known. At the same time the music of his lines, their originality of conception, their intimate reflection of an artist's personality have made his poems worthy to rank with the best productions of the modernista school. Through them Silva has done his part in sustaining the reputation which Colombia has long enjoyed for the high quality of the poetry written by her sons.

CHAPTER X

LITERATURE in Venezuela reflects the progress of its people toward a higher state of culture. During the colonial period perhaps the most backward of the Spanish colonies, it suffered acutely from the Spanish policy of maintaining the creoles in ignorance. An evidence of this is the fact that there was no printing press in the colony until one was brought there by the revolutionist Francisco Miranda in 1806 as an auxiliary weapon against the Spaniards. Among Miranda's two hundred foreign volunteers were two typesetters who printed on October 24, 1806, the first number of *La Gaceta de Caracas*. This was the first of the many periodicals that have since offered their welcoming pages to Venezuelan writers.

The influence of the press must not be overlooked in a study of their literary production. Without a public to encourage an author by the purchase of his books, the only channel for the dissemination of his ideas was the periodical. Though the early journals were almost wholly political, the literary section soon became important. In time periodicals devoted mainly to letters were published.

In point of time the earliest Venezuelan to achieve fame as an author was Andrés Bello, who wrote his first poems before leaving the country on his political mission to England. As he never returned to the land of his birth but produced his most influential work in Chile, he may best be considered as an adopted son of that land. Bello's Venezuelan poems were either translations or imitations of Virgil and Horace.

They were written during the period of his social intercourse with the brothers Luis and Franciso Javier Ustáriz, who maintained in their house a sort of literary society. The literary exercises of their coterie, of Miguel José Sanz and José Luis Ramos, written in the most frigid classical manner, were slight and have been forgotten.

After Bello the Venezuelan of widest reputation in letters is Rafael María Baralt (1810–60). His youth and his family connections having thrown him in the way of learning much about the history of his country, he was inspired to write his *Historia Antigua y Moderna de Venezuela*. In order to print this work he went to Paris in 1841 and two years later took up his residence definitely in Madrid. He became one of the literary lights of the capital, was elected a member of the Spanish Academy, and appointed director of the government printing office and editor of the official gazette. In addition to his other labors he rendered a real service to the lexicography of the Spanish language by compiling a *Diccionario de Galicismos*, 1855.

As a poet Baralt followed closely the classical tradition. His desire to combat the extravagances of the romantic school led him often into the archaic and the obscure. His sonnets and odes were written on such topics as *La Anunciación, A España, Adiós a la Patria, A Colón*.

The ode to Columbus is a masterpiece. The poet addresses the great mariner as if trying to warn him against his contemplated journey to the West. "Dost not see that ocean, man, and sky oppose?" The results of the venture will be a new world filled with such marvels as the river Amazon, the Andes, the condor, the wealth of the Incas. The King of Portugal lost his opportunity, but Isabella turned her jewels into empires. As a reward for the navigator King Ferdinand's crown would scarcely be sufficient. What he will receive beside the palm of triumph is nothing but vile chains. His real reward will be the grateful esteem of the new world. The artistic workmanship of this ode merits a permanent place in Spanish literature for Baralt.

Of the same age was Fermín Toro (1807–65). He was a politician from boyhood, gifted with notable ability as an orator. At the age of twenty-five he went to London as secretary to the legation of Venezuela. After his return, though employed by the government in various capacities, he took an active interest in furthering the cause of education. In 1846 he was sent to Europe as minister plenipotentiary in Great Britain, France and Spain. From the latter he obtained a ratification of the treaty confirming the independence of Venezuela. The following year there occurred a revolution which retired him to private life for ten years. Then he was again sent to negotiate treaties with Spain and Italy.

Actively participating in the life of his time, Toro's literary work has two diverse aspects. To his friends of the classical school he offered the *Silva a la Zona torrida* and the conceits of Anacreontics like *La Ninfa del Anauco*. For the romanticists he pointed out a new field, the aborigines of Venezuela, whose fate at the cruel hands of the Spanish conquerors he lamented in a series of fragmentary elegies entitled *Hecatonfonía*. In the romantic manner also he wrote the tales, *La Viuda de Corinto*, and *los Martires*. The latter is a story of the un-Christian charity with which an unfortunate woman in London may be treated by a class of society that prides itself on being the most cultured in the world.

The romantic movement of European literature had its followers in Venezuela, where it may be considered in full swing at the time of the arrival in that country as Spanish minister of José Heriberto García de Quevedo (1819–71). Coming with the prestige of being the collaborator of the Spanish poet Zorrilla as well as the author of poems, plays and novels of his own invention, he was warmly received in Caracas and claimed by the Venezuelans as a native son. As a matter of fact he was six years old when he was taken by his tory father to the island of Puerto Rico and later to Spain where he was educated and continued to live. His sojourn in Venezuela lasted but a few months, so, whatever his influence in promoting the Zorrillan legend, the story of his literary labors belongs more properly to Castilian literature.

On the other hand, José Antonio Maitín (1804–74) and Abigail Lozano (1823–66) were the standard bearers of romanticism in their land and both were widely read throughout Spanish America. The former sought his inspiration in the luxuriance of the nature about him; while the latter was more popular among his countrymen because he wrote heroic verses full of lyric movement and enthusiasm for the national heroes. But Lozano is well-nigh forgotten now, whereas the personality of "the poet of the Choroní," as Maitín was called, still lives in his verses redolent of the damp American forest.

The exact date of Maitín's birth is uncertain, but he was old enough to remember his family's flight to Cuba from the revolution in 1812. He returned to Venezuela, however, and from 1824 to 1826 was an attaché of the legation in London, where he must have come into contact with Andrés Bello and Fernández Madrid. His verses certainly show first-hand acquaintance with the English romantic poets. Like the Lake Poets, he preferred to spend his life in the country on his estate in the vale of the river Choroní. There amid the perfume of the tropical flowers we may lie with him in the shade listening to the song of strange birds or watch the changing colors of the sunset. We may fish with him or read Lamartine at will. At night we may breathe the odors that distill through the brilliant moonlight. From such natural objects, Maitín, like a true romanticist, pretended to seek consolation from the deceit of men. His wife's death gave an opportunity to add sincerity of feeling to the romantic pose. In a *Canto fúnebre* the usual classical expressions receive a domestic touch when the poet refers to the disarranged chairs of his home, the dust that lies thick on the furniture, and the lady's sewing with the needle still in the unfinished work.

Maitín's narrative poems also have their admirers. *El Máscara* relates the story of a thief who gains admission to the home of a wealthy widow by courting her daughter. One night, instead of leaving the house, he hides in a corridor until the lady retires. Then entering her bedroom he demands her jewels as the price of her life. The wily widow, however, succeeds in trapping the intruder and securing his arrest before he leaves the house. Another tale in verse, *El Sereno*, introduces the reader to an individual who has become a policeman in order to occupy his mind and assuage his grief at the loss of a bride taken from him on his wedding night. The policeman invites a chance stranger to see the sights of the town with him. They see a lover lamenting the scorn of a lady who has jilted him. They converse with an old beggar beneath the window of the hard-hearted master who had turned him out when incapacitated by old age. They address an insane woman who had lost her reason when abandoned by a faithless lover. She recognizes the policeman's companion as her perfidious seducer. The latter offers his dagger to the policeman requesting him to put an end to his existence. Since the woman was the bride of his sorrow, the policeman is rendered nearly frantic by the stranger's act admitting his identity. But he restrains his impulse to comply with the request to slay. Instead he pardons the sinner and prays Heaven to do likewise.

Such are the rather bizarre legends of Maitín. His political poems, overloaded with metaphor and hyperbole, were not very successful either. On the other hand the lyrics are still readable of the poet who sang,

A las orillas del río Choroní.

His younger contemporary, Abigail Lozano, the virile poet with the feminine name, owed his really great popularity to his patriotic verses. His lines to the national hero, Bolívar, were admired even in Spain. For a short time his talents were used by the editor of a political journal, *El Venezolano*, but Lozano soon withdrew his services and established a literary magazine, *El Album*. About 1846 he collected his verses in a volume entitled *Horas de Martirio*. The romantic pose assumed in these compositions, mainly on the theme of love, is well indicated by the title. They are wordy and extravagant but attractive on account of a certain novelty of metaphor and a splendid coloring. In 1864 he published a second volume, *Otras Horas de Martirio*. These poems were written during a more active participation in politics, for he joined the opponents of Monagas and after their success held some political offices.

Another important member of the group of Venezuelan romantic poets was José Antonio Calcaño (1827–97), of whom his compatriots were fond of saying that he belonged to a family of nightingales. He, however, was the poet, while his brother Eduardo was primarily an orator and Julio a critic and novelist. The saying arose undoubtedly from the conspicuous fluidity of his lines and the ease with which he essayed various styles in imitation of Leopardi, Lamartine, Hugo, Byron and Zorrilla. His *Silva a la Academia española* was written in the strictest classical style. On the other hand, the major part of his poems are filled with romantic regrets and bitterness of heart. *A Orillas del Tamaira* offers a series of pictures taken from the memories of his childhood accompanied with repining at their inevitable loss. Thus the poet runs the gamut of the romantic emotions; homesickness in *La Saboyana*, the disillusion of the world in *Amor e Inocen-*

cia, the torturing doubts of a jealous lover in *El Ciprés*, the desire for rest from his sorrows in *La Muerte*. The attraction of many of his poems lies in the delicacy with which he evokes images of the Venezuelan landscape. In this regard should be mentioned *La Maga y el Genio de las Selvas*, *La Flor del Tabaco*, and especially *La Hoja* to which the saying about the nightingale might well apply, to judge by the following lines. The poet describes the place where he received the first kiss of a childhood love.

> Nos saludaron mirtos y palmas;
> su frente al sauce doblar miré;
> a augurar dichas a nuestras almas
> cantó en las ceibas el Dios-te-dé.
>
> Hízonos toldo, fresco y sombrío,
> con sus ramajes el cafetal;
> epitalamio nos hizo el río:
> cantó las nupcias un cardinal.

The lyrical quality of these lines will appeal even to those who must be told that the ceiba is a giant tree, one of the most conspicuous in the Venezuelan landscape, while the cardinal is famous for the brilliance of its plumage and the Dios-te-dé owes its onomato-poetic name to its song.

The poetic possibilities of the country were being taught at this time by Juan Vicente González (1808–66) both by precept and practice. He was not a versifier but a voluminous writer on the history of his native country. Possessed of a remarkable intellect fertile in ideas, his influence on his contemporaries was considerable. Beside his *Manual de Historia universal*, his most important book from a national point of view was his *Mesenianas*, a series of prose elegies written in a florid oratorical and romantic style on men who had died for their country. To González is attributed by Picón Febres the initiative of a truly national literature through his propaganda in favor of nationalizing it.

The interesting personality of the man is well illustrated by the following anecdote. A large fat man, he was ridiculed for his weak feminine voice, though at the same time he was feared for his sharp tongue. Once in a public café he was approached by a certain general concerning whom he had written that the general had set fire to many towns and was the horror of the country. Facing González, the man demanded with threatening bluster:— "Why did you say that about me?" González rose from his seat, "And you, who are you?" "General Fulano," replied the soldier. "Ah," replied González flourishing his enormous cane, "I said it because it was the truth."

Local color without special effort to obtain it abounds in the poems of José Ramón Yepes (1822–81). He was the son of an old family in Maracaibo. Showing a fondness for the sea, he entered the Venezuelan navy where he rapidly rose in rank because he showed great bravery in the factional fights in which the marine took part about 1850. It seems strange that a seadog should write verses, but the man had a truly poetic faculty, and was dubbed by his acquaintances the "Swan of the Lake." To him the wind, the clouds, the color of the sea and sky mean more than to the ordinary sailor. In *Las Nubes* he gave a record of the fancies with which their varying shapes inspired him, entirely pictorial and descriptive, and the only words of the poem which are subjective are the closing lines, "I bless you, apparitions of Heaven." His fancy again ran riot in *Las Orillas del Lago* when he saw a child knock at the gate of the palace of the fairies. His experiences as a sailor he utilized in a marine ballad, *Santa Rosa de Lima*, relating a legend that she once appeared to some storm-tossed sailors who invoked her assistance and by casting roses on the troubled waters, rescued them. In *La Golondrina* after describing the swallow's flight he compared it to his own thoughts. To poems of a philosophical turn he was fond of giving the title *Niebla*. The prettiest of these is one written to comfort a mother whose little girl had just died. The poet represented the child contemplating a cloud and expressing a wish to be one; when the mother comes, the child's wish had been fulfilled. In the homelike character of his subjects Yepes resembles Longfellow just as his attitude toward nature and the lyric swing of his lines reminds the reader of Shelley.

Yepes also tried his hand at description of aboriginal life in a poem *Los Hijos de Parayauta* and in two prose romances, *Anaida* and *Iguaraya*, in which Yepes appears to have taken Chateaubriand for a model. The most successful parts are the descriptions of tropical scenery.

Though Yepes was more artistic in his criollo verse, Domingo Ramón Hernández (1829–93) surpassed him in popularity with their fellow countrymen. His sentimental melancholy voiced Venezuelan feelings in such beautiful poems as his *Canto de la Golondrina*. It depicts the swallow returning after a long absence to find that the nesting place which had been its cradle has been destroyed.

Though it found another fine nest and enjoyed life greatly
it never met with the repose and contentment of its birthplace. Hernández was a poet essentially romantic in
sentiment unexcelled in true tenderness by any Venezuelan. The sorrows in which his verses abounded plainly
sprang from the spectacle of human misery.

The power of eloquent speech is nowhere greater than
among Spanish Americans. The rhythmic flow of their
vocalic language excites in them an æsthetic emotion
incomprehensible to people of other races. To this psychological peculiarity has been ascribed the frequency of
revolutions in some of the countries, especially Colombia.
Would the facts of the following anecdote be possible in
England or the United States? It is related of Cecilio
Acosta (1831–81) that one day after he had delivered a
speech in praise of the fine arts before the Academía de
las Bellas Artes in Caracas, he was accompanied home by
a crowd composed not only of enthusiastic students and
ordinary persons but also of members of the society, the
clergy and government officials. One of the latter, not a
personal friend either, addressed Acosta's mother in these
terms:—"Señora, accept my most sincere congratulations
because your son has just uttered the most eloquent
discourse that I have ever heard."

Acosta was an orator and learned lawyer, a clever
journalist and a poet. His poems are not numerous, but
he shows in the two best, *La Casita blanca*, and *La Gota
de Rocío*, the same qualities that distinguished his prose.
He was expert at developing an idea by repetition, in
throwing about a common object the most brilliant background of verbal images. His manner was distinctly

original. The significance of it is not merely in the power of persuasion which he exercised over his audiences but also in the influence which his writings have had on younger men, orators, journalists and poets.

Another famous orator was Eduardo Calcaño called by an admirer "the prince of the artists of speech." When Venezuelan minister to Spain his oratory was greatly praised by the press. Though author of some verses, such as his *Balada indiana,* he did not write so well as his brother José Antonio.

Everybody familiar with classical Spanish plays knows the part played by the Andalusian gracioso. The ready quip and satirical comment were his stock in trade. In modern literature he is represented by the journalist that grinds out his daily article more or less funny according to circumstances. Of this type of humor Venezuelan literature can show as many successful examples as any other in Spanish America. Daniel Mendoza (1823–67) chose for the mouthpiece of his satire the "llanero" or cowboy from beyond the Orinoco who comes to Caracas and is amazed at the foolish expenditure of money by all classes in the capital. Nothing escapes his observation, neither the fashionable ladies nor the dandies, least of all the politicians. As a sample of his wit, take the following:

"I was saying, continued the doctor, that in that edifice are made our laws.—Caramba, Doctor, for such a little thing such an immense building!"

Of these "costumbristas" a considerable list of names might be given. The value of what they have written is apparent to anybody in whose hands their articles have fallen, for in them the Venezuelan people live and think. If you wish to know how the buyer and seller plan to outwit each other with the advantage on the side of the seller, read Francisco de Sales Pérez who flourished about 1880, in the collected volume of his collected articles *Ratos Perdidos*. For amusing portraits of persons in the public eye, read Nicanor Bolet Peraza. Though these descriptions of manners are mainly in prose, examples in verse are not lacking. For that sort of writing, Aristophanic bitterness has been ascribed to J. M. Nuñez de Cáceres.

Pedro José Hernández wrote his humorous sketches of manners in verse in the form of fables, of epistles to persons and of jocose sonnets. For example, one of the latter begins by describing a tumbledown cabin suggestive of the vanity of human affairs; but not in this lies the occupant's sadness but in the fact that he owes a month's rent. Or coming along the street one beautiful Easter morning, everything contributed to his joy, even the finding of a coin at his feet. On picking it up, alas! it proved to be false.

Nicanor Bolet Peraza (1838–1906) became widely known through the fortunes of his political career. An opponent of Guzmán Blanco he was obliged to live by means of journalistic work in the United States. As he was able to speak English his trenchant wit was in demand at banquets and other public occasions, so that for a time he was to North Americans a representative Spanish American. He used to urge his fellow countrymen to strive for the blessings of peace and industry, such as were enjoyed by the people of the United States. Besides his numerous journalistic articles both amusing and serious in character he wrote a play *Luchas del Honor* which was enthusiastically received in Caracas.

Antonio Guzmán Blanco (1830–99), though he ruled Venezuela as a tyrant directly or through puppets for about twenty-five years, was a great civilizing force. He was able by rigorous measures to put an end to a long-standing anarchy in the country. He reëstablished Venezuelan finances by the successful contraction of a loan in London and by rigid economies in the internal administration of the country. In the matter of education he wished for "a school in every street." Though his vanity made him somewhat ridiculous by reason of the many statues of himself which he erected, from 1872 on he brought a large measure of material prosperity to Venezuela. Under his régime literature flourished. During the seventies it was somewhat artificial in character, but with the introduction of liberal studies at the University of Caracas, and the teaching of the theory of evolution fostered by Guzmán Blanco, the younger generation was able to comprehend and adapt the new tendencies in literature of which Zola and the naturalistic school were sponsors.

In 1869 was established in Caracas the Academía de Ciencias sociales y de Bellas Letras which, to celebrate its foundation, offered a prize for an ode on *La Libertad del Viejo Mundo*. The title shows the trend which romanticism had taken under the leadership of Victor Hugo himself. He developed and practiced the theory that literature should place itself at the social service of mankind. Accordingly odes on abstract topics became the fashion. The first prize in the contest of the Academía was awarded

to Heraclio de la Guardia (1829–1907).   Later he was presented with a gold medal by the University of Caracas for
an ode to science.   The totality of Guardia's verses is
large, but their tone is not so frigid as their titles would
indicate.   Like every Venezuelan poet he could sing the
beauties of tropical nature.

Another winner of academic poetry was Francisco
Guaycaypuro Pardo (1829–82) whose odes, *La Gloria del
Libertador*, *El Poder de la Idea* and *El Porvenir de América*
carried off prizes in the years 1872, '75 and '77.   But
Pardo, though not equalling the originality of Yepes, had
something of the poetic feeling which distinguished the
latter, "the swan of the lake."   This is apparent in the
descriptions of nature in *Las Indianas*.   With greater
unity of substance, these poems would compare favorably
with Longfellow's *Hiawatha*, by which they seem to be
inspired.

Academic poetry tended to an epic accent and glorifica-
tion of America.   In Venezuela, this was furthered by the
centenary of Bolívar, celebrated in 1883 with great pomp
by Guzmán Blanco, "the Regenerator," as he styled himself; in contrast with the Liberator.   To this epic tendency
were due many poems such as *La Colombiada* and *La
Boliviada* by Felipe Tejera, though not all were so ambitious in scope.   The tendency to philosophize which marks
academic poetry took an original turn toward the end of
the decade of the seventies, through imitation of the
German poet Heine and his Spanish adapter Becquer.
Becquerista verse was immensely popular throughout
Spanish America.   In Venezuela it was made known by
Juan Antonio Pérez Bonalde (1846–92).

In 1877 appeared his first volume entitled *Estrofas*. These were mainly translations of Heine's poems. Besides them, Pérez Bonalde translated Poe's *Raven* in a masterly manner. But he was not merely a translator, for in original work Pérez Bonalde must be reckoned among Venezuela's greatest poets. He excelled in verse expressing purely human sentiments. His *Vuelta a la Patria* contained sublime words on a topic which appeals to the hearts of all Spanish Americans. In *Flor*, dedicated to his daughter Flor, snatched from him by death, he rebelled against the cruel fate of sudden death, which threatens all humanity. Pérez Bonalde's fame is however mainly grounded on his *Poema del Niagara* written in 1880.

In the opening lines the poet challenged comparison with the "Poet of Niagara," the Cuban Heredia. We can do no better than to accept in this matter the judgment of the Cuban orator, José Martí, who contributed to the second edition of the poem a preface beginning: "This man who comes with me is a grandee, though not of Spain, and he comes with his hat on: he is Juan Antonio Pérez Bonalde, who has written the Poem on Niagara. And if you ask me more about him, curious passer-by, I will tell thee that he measured his strength with a giant, and did not come away hurt, but with his lyre on his shoulder and with something like an aureole of triumph on his brow. Do not ask more, for it is sufficient proof of greatness to have dared measure one's strength with giants; because the merit is not in the outcome of the attack, although this man returned in good condition from the struggle, but in the courage to attack."

In the poem, after describing the smoothly flowing river

above the falls, the poet arrives at the rush of waters upon
the rocks, the foam, the rain of diamonds, the rising vapors.
He demands to know where is the deity of the falls. He
entreats Virgil to lead him, because it is the poet's business
to be a leader and conquer time and death. As the Man-
tuan makes no reply, the poet urges himself forward to
solve the mystery. He propounds three questions to
which Echo gives answers. "Terrible genius of the torrent,
whither goes mortal man?" And Echo responds, "To the
tomb." "Is the tomb the end? what remains?" "Nothing." "Then why the struggle? will man ever know the
secret of Being?" "Never." Farewell, cries the poet,
your secret is the same as the thinker's; rebellion, doubt,
the agony of the heart in tears. As the poet emerges from
behind the falls he shouts Hosanna! at the beauty of the
light, and turning again to the rushing waters, he says you
are like man on an enormous scale, as ignorant as he. You
issue pure and beautiful, but like the child fall into sin.
You have your crown of iris, man has the iris of love and
hope. In winter all is frozen about you but the torrent,
just so man has poetry, his constant aspirations, the ideal.
Some day you will disappear in a grand cataclysm. I too
with my lyre will pass away.

The immediate disciple in this sort of verse was Miguel
Sánchez Pesquera (born 1851). In his early poems he
sang passionate love, but attracted by Heine's lieder, he
wrote excellent verses of the type which draw a moral by
means of dramatic anecdote or dramatic setting. *La
Tumba del Marino* begins:—He is dead! They say on the
ship speeding to distant Spain. Into the water with him,
exclaims indifferently the captain. And the poet envies

the ship wishing he might throw his dead heart into the waters. *El último Pensamiento de Weber* is a poetic interpretation of a musical composition much admired by Venezuelans. "Virgins, listen," the poet cries, and they hearken to a rhapsody on the transitoriness of human life.

The theory of poetics which makes beauty the supreme object of art, while the personality of the artist is subordinated to the point of disappearance, sometimes called the Parnassian school, as exemplified in Leconte de L'Isle and the French poet, J. M. Heredia, had its followers in Venezuela toward the end of the nineteenth century. Jacinto Gutiérrez Coll and Manuel Fombona Palacio were perhaps its two closest adherents. But the spirit of individuality is too keenly felt by Spanish Americans to be long subordinated. Moreover, the modernista movement soon changed the direction of the poetic current. Men like Gonzalo Picón Febres, Andrés Mata, and Gabriel Múñoz, who began to write in the Parnassian style became modernistas.

Manuel Fombona Palacio (1857–1903), achieved a reputation for correctness of diction. By temperament, he was a classic as is evident in his odes *A Andalucía* and *A la Muerte de Alfonso XII*, which are read for their excellence of form. A later poem with its Latin title *Hannibal ante portas* is purely Parnassian, as it depicts the alarm of the citizens of Rome at the news of Hannibal's latest triumphs.

Gabriel E. Muñoz strove to give his poems an Attic intonation and published them under the title *Helénicas*. One of them, *El Himno de las Bacantes*, won widespread popularity in Spanish America.

Andrés Mata with similar intent named his productions *Pentélicas*, suggestive of the cold beauty of a classic marble. But some of them were written under the spell of the Mexican fire-eater, Díaz Mirón. Consequently Mata sings his struggles and personal triumphs with manly vigor. Nor is there anything cold about the little poem *Del Pasado*, in which he relates the memory of a youthful kiss bestowed on a barefoot maiden beside a spring.

Manuel Pimentel Coronel (1863–1907) wrote copious verses which were intended to impart a thought, as well as to be works of art. *Los Paladines* is a good example of his method. After describing the defeat of a lion by an eagle whose nest on a cliff the beast tried to rob, he urges poets to remember that victory awaits them in their struggles with titanic forces. The narrative element in his poems makes them interesting reading.

Literature in Venezuela always returns to nature for its inspiration. As a describer of Venezuelan landscape Víctor Racamonde was eminently Venezuelan. Even more a follower of Yepes in this regard was Samuel Darío Maldonado. In *Non serviam*, he openly proclaimed himself a Venezuelan rebel in the matter of following rules of art. And in lines of capricious length he relates in *La Gloria* his pursuit through a Venezuelan landscape of the nymph glory. *En el Río Zulia* and *Al Pastel* are other charming pictures of natural beauty. His rebellion against classicism led him to use native words and phrases at will.

Another poet to cultivate the criollo in his verses was Francisco Lazo Martí, who combined therewith a certain philosophical symbolism. His *Silva criolla* is a beautiful description of landscape and manners in the Orinoco basin.

The first attempts at fiction in Venezuela were produced under the influence of the romantic school. The orator and poet, Fermín Toro, imitated the manner of Victor Hugo in *Los Martires* and *La Viuda de Corinto*.

Julio Calcaño (b. 1840), of the famous family of that name, published in 1868 the attractive *Blanca de Torrestella*, which has deservedly seen its third edition. As it treats of the period of the renaissance in Italy it may still be read with interest like any other historical novel. In other tales Julio Calcaño made his native country the background of the story and could write such vivid description as this portrait of Padre Larrea, parish priest and colonel of revolutionary forces:—"Tall and vigorous, his sturdy neck revealed energy and determination in every movement. To see him on his mule, a palm leaf hat on his head, his soutane thrust into his trousers which in their turn were thrust into campaign boots, a sabre dangling from his belt which also held two double barrelled pistols, was the same thing as seeing the Devil with a medal of Christ at his neck. When the ecclesiastical authorities suspended him from his sacred duties, he did not complain but exclaimed,—'They will erect triumphal arches for us yet and make me archdeacon or bishop when we win.'"

Julio Calcaño was an active figure in the world of letters for many years, to which he performed an important service by a valuable treatise on the peculiarities of Venezuelan speech, *El Castellano en Venezuela*.

Other writers of romantic fiction were José María Manrique, whose moralizing tales of impossible men and women were enjoyed by his readers; and Eduardo Blanco, an exponent of the fantastic and miraculous. His *Zárate*, published in 1882, the story of a Venezuelan bandit, was transitional to the realism coming into vogue.

About 1880 the younger generation in Venezuela began reading Zola. At the same time the professors in the University of Caracas, supported by President Guzmán Blanco, were teaching the elements of the Darwinian theory. Very soon the conflict of the new scientific ideas with the old order was reflected in fiction, while a heated controversy raged about Zola and the naturalistic school.

Among the first students of Zola was Tomás Michelena whose realistic tale *Debora*, 1884, argued the social necessity of divorce. Other tales were more psychological in character, as *La Hebrea*, which attempts to disclose the result of the marriage of Sara with Raúl, a freethinker.

The psychological story in the manner of Bourget was practiced by José Gil Fortoul. His autobiographical *Julián* was followed by *¿Idilio?* This latter concerns Enrique, a precocious youth, who has heard his professor say that the sun is fixed in space while the earth swings about it; but he remembers that the parish priest in relating the story of Joshua had said that the patriarch stopped the sun three hours in its course. The doubt in which this conflict of statement plunged the lad of fifteen made him "beat the earth, pluck handfuls of grass, perspire, gesticulate." Enrique is in love with Isabel, who is struck by lightning and he rebels against God, but instead of being morally ruined, he is filled with fresh energy to pursue his studies. A third story, *Pasiones*, attempts to reveal the mental attitude of the young men, during the last years of Guzmán Blanco's rule. Gil Fortoul had himself been imprisoned for his utterances on public

questions. He has since become a learned man, whose
Historia constitucional de Venezuela is an authority on the
subject and places the author among the leading men of
his country. This history was written with great care and
deliberation. Begun when Gil Fortoul was in the diplomatic service of Venezuela, a pension from the government enabled him to complete and publish it. In the
opinion of a competent critic, R. Blanco Fombona, "it
is the most complete, most attractive, and most worth
reading of any general history of Venezuela."

The sensuality of Zola is reflected in the tales of exotic
manners by Pedro César Dominici, and in the novels of
Venezuelan life by Rafael Cabrera Malo and Arévalo
González. But the manners depicted in these imitations
of French fiction are not racy to the soil of Venezuela like
those described by other novelists. Somehow in Venezuela
though a movement in literature may come from outside,
it very soon adapts itself to the genius of the country.

Thus in 1890 written according to naturalistic methods,
so true to Venezuelan life and dialect that it is difficult
for anybody not a Venezuelan to understand, was published *Peonía*, by Manuel Romero García. The author
announced as his purpose "to photograph a social condition," namely, family life in the rural parts of Venezuela
during Guzmán Blanco's régime. The chief character,
Carlos, who tells the story, has just graduated from the
university as a doctor of law. Therefore he is invited
from the city to visit an uncle on his plantation in order
to assist him in settling a boundary dispute. The young
man finds there a dreadful state of affairs. His uncle is a
brutal tyrant who not only maltreats his servants and

employees but even beats his wife and children with a rawhide whip. The oldest daughter has a love intrigue with a man beneath her social position who eventually sets fire to the house and shoots her father. The various incidents of the story introduce many customs of the country. The bad moral conditions depicted are ascribed by Romero García to two facts, one that the laws of Venezuela do not admit of divorce, and the other the persistence of the old Roman tradition in the household that the father's word is law. "We have in the home," he says, "an odious dictatorship, a school in which slaves are trained for political dictatorships."

Peonía launched the nationalistic or "criollo" movement in fiction. It was helped by the establishment in Caracas about the same time of *El Cojo ilustrado*, a review whose pages were open to the publication of creole stories. The honor of being the first to write short stories in this new form of art is attributed to Luis Urbaneja Achelpohl. Others who have published collections are Rafael Bolívar and Rufino Blanco Fombona.

As some of the latter's tales were translated into French they have had a wide circulation. Blanco Fombona began his literary career by writing verses. Political conditions compelled him to leave Venezuela, but he was later Venezuelan consul in Amsterdam. When fortune brought him to Paris he published sketches of travel in *Más allá de los Horizontes* and a volume of verses, *Pequeña ópera lírica*, 1904. In Paris he was a personal associate of Rubén Darío. As a modernista poet, Blanco Fombona must be reckoned as the foremost representative of Venezuela in the modernista movement; while his tales and

his criollo novel *El Hombre de Hierro* give him a high place
as a writer of fiction.

This novel is a bitter satire on social conditions in Venezuela written from the fullness of personal knowledge.
Blanco Fombona was appointed by Cipriano Castro,
governor of the territory of Amazonas, which in his own
words "is as wild as in the days of the conquistadores
and its population has the reputation of assassinating
governors." Having defended himself against an armed
attack, he was criminally accused and put in prison. There
in 1905 he wrote *El Hombre de Hierro*. The title is the
nickname given to Crispín Luz for his extraordinary application to business and fidelity to his employer. The latter
is portrayed as the type of the unscrupulous foreigner
exploiting the commerce of Venezuela. Crispín, however, wins but little reward from him and after Crispín's
death, his widow's lament consists merely of the exclama-
tion, "Poor Crispín, always so busy!" Social life in Venezuela, the smart and sarcastic conversation of certain
types, the priests, the pious women, the general idleness,
even the earthquakes and the revolutions are brilliantly
satirized. The revolutions are shown to be often the product of some man's personal vanity like that of Joaquín Luz
who appears on the family estate at the head of a band
of men whom he has persuaded to follow him. His gaudy
uniform contrasts with their ragged clothes while the
absurdity of his pretensions is revealed in the harangue
which he makes them. "Redeemers! Let us depart
for war. Our cause demands it. Our country needs it.
Let us abandon our homes. Let us sacrifice our lives to
overthrow tyranny and restore law and justice. Weapons

the enemy has. Take them away from him. Hurrah for the revolution." The harm which such action as Joaquín's brings on his family is depicted in the arrival of the government troops a few moments after the departure of the "redeemers." The soldiers shoot a harmless countryman, the cook's son, the only man left on the estate, as he tries to escape them by running away. Then they set fire to the farm buildings, shake the ripening berries from the coffee trees, carry off the chickens, the kitchen utensils and "whatever else came to hand."

When President Castro fell from power, Blanco Fombona was again imprisoned by the new President Juan Vicente Gómez. He brought from the prison a volume of verses published in 1911 as *Cantos de la Prisión y del Destierro*, of which he said, "Every strophe is a monument to existence, life lived, a human cry of a man who has suffered." In these poems he retaliated on his jailers. In one of them he depicted Juan Vicente Gómez in a frenzy in a forest appealing in turn to the trees, the wind, the moss, the monkeys, and the hamadryads. Their only answer is "Juan Vicente Gómez, Traidor!"

Blanco Fombona has remained away from Venezuela of recent years. In Paris he has busied himself with various literary enterprises. His critical articles about Spanish-American men of letters in the *Revista de América* and other periodicals have been valuable and interesting. His most ambitious work has been an annotated edition of Bolívar's correspondence for which students will always owe the author a debt of gratitude.

The most ardent advocate in Venezuela of the criollo in literature is Gonzalo Picón Febres (b. 1860), who has ably practiced his own preaching. His first writings were contained in two volumes of poems, *Caléndulas* and *Claveles encarnados y amarillos*, titles suggestive of the Parnassian verses they exhibit. But one long poem, *La Batalla de las Queseras*, celebrates the victory of General Paez over the Spaniards. After writing some tales, *Fidelia, Ya es Hora, Flor*, with Venezuelan setting but inclining to imitation of Zola's methods, and a novel *Nieve y Lodo*, a picture of corrupt living among society people, Picón Febres published in 1899 *El Sargento Felipe*.

This is a criollo novel of the purest type, unexcelled in form and substance. Its reading is recommended to anybody who desires a knowledge of Venezuelan life. Whatever details language cannot make clear are pictured in the many photogravures of persons and landscapes.

The story relates the fortunes of Felipe, an industrious small farmer snatched from his home to serve in the army of Guzmán Blanco against the rebel Salazar. During Felipe's absence his daughter Encarnación is seduced by the wealthy young Don Jacinto Sandoval. The jealous and rejected suitor Matías sets fire to the house where the couple are in expectation of trapping and destroying his rival. News of these misfortunes is brought to Felipe when he is convalescing from his wounds in a hospital. Though weak and barely able to drag himself along, Felipe sets out for home. On arriving he finds his buildings destroyed and learns that his wife is dead. After praying at her grave in the village cemetery, he seeks out Don Jacinto Sandoval and shoots him; then terminates his own life by throwing himself from a cliff.

The novel abounds in realistic pictures of Venezuelan life. The reader is introduced to the "pulpería" or country store and the men who resort there for drink and conversation. For him are minutely drawn the details of Felipe's home and simple daily existence before the tragedy. His daughter Encarnación appears in all her finery ready for the ball. Felipe with the tyranny of a Venezuelan father forbids her to dance with anybody but Matías; with equal stubbornness she replies to his threats, "Beat me if you wish but I will not dance with Matías." The party is attended by young men from the city who attempt to lord it over the country swains till they retaliate by starting a fight which in turn is broken up by the cry that the recruiting officers are coming. In the army Felipe's sturdy reliability raises him to the rank of sergeant, trusted by his superior officer, General Cipriano Castro. He is interestingly sketched as "lazily swinging in his hammock but observant of details, quick to act but sparing of words, ready of purse and pistol."

As a scholar Gonzalo Picón Febres, doctor of science and letters, has demonstrated in his *Literatura venezolana en el Siglo XIX* that the best and most enduring productions of Venezuelan literature from Andrés Bello's *Agricultura de la Zona torrida* down to the present day have their roots deep in the soil of Venezuela. This history, indicative of an immense amount of labor on the part of its author, is the first attempt at a comprehensive account in its chosen field; and is rendered more valuable by the portraits of nearly every writer mentioned.

Another study by Picón Febres of the criollo is his *Libro Raro*, 1912. Though a book on the peculiarities of Venezuelan speech completing and rectifying Julio Calcaño's *El Castellano en Venezuela*, Picón Febres clarified his explanations of most of the terms discussed by anecdotes of persons. The result is a book on philology so readable as almost to belong to the domain of folklore.

The criollo novel easily lends itself to satire. A notable instance is *Todo un Pueblo*, renamed *Villabrava* in the Paris edition from the nickname bestowed on Caracas by the author, Miguel Eduardo Pardo. The tone of this picture of its customs is indicated by the author's preface. "I abandoned literature for politics. I happened to be elected a member of Congress and I was stoned in the streets. So I packed my valise and departed. When I arrived in Spain my friends did not know me for I was thin and white—green sometimes. In Paris Gómez Carrillo advised me to eat rare meat, but Bonafoux told me what I needed was human flesh dripping blood."

Bitter satire of Caracas and hatred of Cæsarism in American politics also fills *Idolos Rotos* by Manuel Díaz Rodríguez. It is the story of Alberto Soria, a sculptor, who returns from his studies in Paris to practice his art in Venezuela. His ideals and ambitions come into harsh conflict with the realities of life and the people about him, just as the fruits of his labor, his statues in the school of fine arts are smashed when the building is turned into a barracks by the military authorities.

Symbolical interpretation of a social condition or the solution of a psychological problem characterize Díaz Rodríguez' other works of fiction. In *Sangre Patricia* he studies Tulio Arcos, scion of a family long prominent in public affairs and descended from a conquistador.

Tulio Arcos inherits only the family pride and uneasy temperament. He is a timid neurotic, afraid in the dark, dreaming of great things and poetry. While living in Paris he is married by proxy to a young lady who unfortunately dies on the steamer on her way from Venezuela and is buried at sea. He resolves to return to America. On reaching the waters of the tropics he imagines that his bride is a siren calling to him, so he leaps overboard to join her.

Díaz Rodríguez is an artist and writes the most graceful prose. As a critic he continues in Venezuela the tradition established by Luis López Méndez, César Zumeta and Pedro Emilio Coll for excellent æsthetic judgment. Díaz Rodríguez' discussions of certain ideals of art and other theoretical questions collected in the volumes *Confidencias de Psiquis* and *Camino de Perfección* have won unlimited praise from Spanish-American readers who delight in that form of literature. They place him with J. E. Rodó of Uruguay as an intellectual leader of the modernista movement.

CHAPTER XI

MEXICO

Mexican literature presents great variety of form, not only an abundance of lyric and narrative verse but also numerous dramas, prose tales and novels. This literary activity during the nineteenth century is partly due to the inheritance of culture which stood on a high plane in Mexico during the colonial period. The numerous theaters built at that time even in small towns provided an opportunity for the productions of local dramatists. To them the storied past of Mexico afforded a wide field when the stimulus of the romantic movement turned minds in that direction. The history of the Aztecs, of the conquistadores and of the heroes of the struggle for independence furnished themes for all branches of literature. On the other hand, the classical tradition maintained itself in a steady outpouring of religious verse both in poetical renderings of scripture and in forms intended to combat anticlericalism.

The character of the population has exerted as much influence on Mexican literature as on Mexican politics. The educated and ruling class of whites live marooned and greatly outnumbered among a rude and depraved population of Indians. The latter are the laborers. Among them individuals sometimes rise above the common level. In politics there has been constant turmoil in the effort to adjust the clashes between the interests of the property owners and the laboring classes. Literature naturally has reflected the supremacy of the one or the other party.

After the separation from Spain the drama was a form of literature much cultivated in Mexico. The Cuban poet, J. M. Heredia, won his way into public notice by his adaptations of French plays full of tirades against tyrants. A native-born Mexican, Manuel Eduardo de Gorostiza (1789–1851), who had achieved notable successes in Spain by his comedies, recast some of them for the Mexican public and made translations and adaptations of such plays as Lessing's *Emilia Galotti*. But his literary career belongs rather to the history of Spanish literature than to Mexican. In his own country he played an important part as a politician and diplomat. Gorostiza's comedies based on observation of Spanish manners were not so well suited to please a Mexican public as the great romantic dramas in the style of García Gutiérrez.

When the first editions of the works of the Spanish romantic poets and dramatists reached the book store of Mariano Galván in Mexico City and fell into the hands of his young clerk and nephew, Ignacio Rodríguez Galván (1816–42), the seed of romanticism had crossed the seas and fallen where it would flourish. In 1838 was produced the first drama of the modern type written in Mexico, Rodríguez Galván's *Muñoz, Visitador de Mexico*. The scene is laid in the early colonial days during the reign of Philip II. The visitador, portrayed as a tyrant, woos Celestina, wife of Sotelo. The latter in revenge incites a rebellion the failure of which results in Sotelo's execution. At the sight of his corpse Celestina dies.

To a periodical and an annual review which his uncle published at this time Rodríguez Galván contributed several short tales and various legends in verse. The tales are mainly tragic. *La Hija del Oidor*, for example, narrates the sad story of a young girl, saved from drowning by a criminal who ruins her and persuades her to elope with him. Surprised in the attempt he kills her. The legends in verse though tragic have greater artistic value. In one of them, *Mora*, a Mexican insurgent by that name loves Angela, the daughter of a loyalist who prefers for a son-in-law Pinto. Angela is married to Pinto during Mora's absence. When the latter returns Angela explains to him how she was compelled to marry Pinto; but, since she prefers to remain faithful to her husband, she begs Mora to depart. The sudden appearance on the scene leads to a duel in which Mora is killed. Angela dies of grief.

In *La Visión de Moctezuma* Rodríguez Galván related a legend of the period preceding the conquest of Mexico. The taxgatherers of the Aztec monarch demand the tribute of a poor old woman, Nolixtli. Unable to pay, she and her daughter Teyolia are cruelly ill treated. But Moctezuma, coming on the scene, falls in love with Teyolia whom he orders placed in his royal barge. As it is being rowed across the lake, Nolixtli attempts to swim in pursuit but is drowned. Her specter appears to the tyrant and prophesies the arrival of the Spaniards who will terminate the oppression of the people by the Aztec rulers.

The same machinery of a vision was utilized in what may be considered Rodríguez Galván's masterpiece, *La Profecía de Guatemoc*. The political note which the poet sounded in some of his lyrics here became dominant. This poem opens with a description of the wood of Chapultepec where the poet is wandering. The locality reminds him of Guatemoc, the unfortunate last emperor of the Aztecs, whom Cortes tortured by applying fire to the bare soles of his feet. "Come," the poet cries aloud; "hear me!" The Aztec monarch replies by appearing amid terrifying phenomena. Displaying his charred feet with imprecations on the cruelty of the Europeans, Guatemoc reveals the future invasions of Mexico which will force their descendants to repay with blood the crimes of their fathers. The poet then awakes choking in a river of blood.

Rodríguez Galván's legends in verse and occasional lyrics brought him into public notice. The production of another drama, *El Privado del Virrey*, of the same type as his earlier one served to clinch his reputation. Having long desired to travel, he managed by means of his literary popularity to obtain appointment in the diplomatic service to South America. He set out for his post, but on the way was overtaken in Havana by a fatal sickness. When one considers that he was then but twenty-six years old, it will not be surprising that his dramas are somewhat crude in form and suffer from the defects common to the romantic school. Nevertheless they pointed to the ideal of a drama essentially Mexican, drawing its inspiration from the traditions of national history and customs.

This ideal was not followed by his contemporary, Fernando Calderón y Beltrán (1809–45). In fact, the latter began writing plays even earlier in his native town of Zacatecas. Here he produced in 1826 *Reynaldo y Elina,* the best of many early pieces. By profession he was a lawyer. Thus being involved in politics, he joined the rebels of his state against Santa Anna and was wounded in the battle of Guadalupe in 1836. Banished from his native place for complicity in the revolt, his property gone, he came to Mexico. Here he wrote and produced his most important dramas, *El Torneo* and *Ana Bolena* and a comedy, *A Ninguna de las tres.* The latter was an imitation, perhaps even a parody on Breton de los Herreros' *Marcela o a cual de las tres;* but the scene of Calderón's comedy is laid in Mexico, and gives a picture of three silly maids who fail to please a fussy suitor. His dramas, on the other hand, followed rather the manner of García Gutíerrez and continued to please the Mexican public after Rodríguez Galván's were out of date. Though Ana Bolena treated a topic so foreign to Mexico as the famous amour of Henry VIII of England, yet it contained certain commonplaces which the public liked to hear.

Calderón was also the author of a few good lyrics and some narrative verse. Of the former, the most original is *La Rosa marchita* in which he compared the present state of his fortunes to the withered rose. Popular, however, was *El Soldado de Libertad,* an imitation in form of Espronceda's pirate song; and *El Sueño del Tirano,* which pictures the nightmare of a tyrant steeped in crimes. Of the narrative poems, *Adela* relates the sad mischance of a young man arrested as he was on the way to marry a lady of that name, and shot as an insurgent. There was an echo of his own misfortunes in *La Vuelta del Desterrado.* An old man returned to the site of his former home to find

nothing recognizable but a tree; embracing it he expired
from grief. Though Calderón's verses place him among
Mexico's best poets, the popularity and number of his
plays give him even greater fame as a dramatist.

Contemporaneous with the romanticists were certain
poets who belonged to the conservative and clerical party
in politics. The revolution which resulted in the separation of Mexico from Spain originated with the property
holding classes,[1] so that the constitution adopted in 1824
gave great power to them and to the church as the bul-
wark of the state. Attacks more or less successful were
made by the liberals on this system during the decades
of the thirties and forties. The loss of Texas and the
war with the United States enormously weakened the
hold of the conservative party. In literature the party
at this time was represented by Manuel Carpio, J. J.
Pesado and others who strove by religious verse to contribute their little to uphold the established order.

Manuel Carpio (1791–1860) was a physician and teacher
of science, of a kindly and religious disposition who wrote
himself into his verses though these are mainly biblical
stories retold. The most sustained and famous is the *La
Cena de Baltasar*, but he also versified the stories of the
witch of Endor, the destruction of Sodom, the Annuncia-
tion. Even a sonnet on Adam and Eve is a mere statement of fact. Carpio's suave manner made these agreeable reading. Originally published in periodicals, the
poems were collected by his friend Pesado.

José Joaquín Pesado (1801–61) was a leader politically
as well as in a literary way of the conservatives, and held

[1] See Chapter III.

various cabinet offices. A rich man, he devoted much of his time to purely literary pursuits. His many-sided activities are testified to by the facts that in 1838 he was a member of President Bustamente's cabinet, and in 1839 he published the first edition of his poems, which were received with great acclaim by his party. His frigid mannerisms make them hard to admire to-day. His verse renderings of portions of the Bible lack the feeling which Carpio could put into his lines. Pesado's imitations of classical lyrics, even those with sensual titles, and his so-called pictures of Mexican life are couched in such general terms that they leave no definite impression. His longest poem of religious character concerns the city of Jerusalem. The poet apostrophizes the city, expresses his regret at not having seen it, refers to its misfortunes under the Mohammedans and the crusaders, describes it as it will appear after the day of judgment, and hymning the risen dead, depicts the celestial Jerusalem. The best of the ideas in this poem were borrowed from Italian poets, with whose works Pesado was acquainted.

His most enduring work and one for which Mexico must remain indebted to Pesado is entitled *Las Aztecas*. These are translations of the poems of the Aztec monarch Netzahualcoyotl, who flourished before the coming of the Spaniards. Pesado commissioned a native Indian to translate them and then he put them into Castilian verse. Though the suspicion may be true that Pesado injected some of his own Christian ideas into these poems, for the most part commonplaces on death and the transitoriness of earthly affairs, yet they reveal a grave and peculiar individuality not completely obscured by Pesado's version.

About 1855, the political skies loomed dark for the conservatives. The religious orders were being threatened in some of their cherished prerogatives by measures proposed by the liberals. To combat them Pesado founded *La Cruz*, a journal which both for its intrinsic worth as well as for its significance must be considered in Mexican literary history. Its publication was continued till the clerical party went down to absolute defeat before the promulgation of the reform constitution of 1857.

A Catholic poet whose verses graced the pages of *La Cruz* was Alejandro Arango y Escandón (1821–83). His work is sufficiently characterized by the titles of his best odes, *Invocación a la Bondad divina* and *En la inmaculada Concepción de Nuestra Señora*.

In *La Cruz* appeared the first work of a younger member of the conservative party, José María Roa Bárcena (1827–1908). He was later a supporter of the French intervention and an office holder under Maximilian. His originality consisted in a utilization of Mexican history for poetic narratives. In this respect he was a follower of Rodríguez Galván. But Roa Bárcena conceived the idea of putting his pieces together in chronological order as in the volumes *Ensayo de una Historia anecdota de Mexico* and *Leyendas mexicanas*.

The best ideas of the latter are given in the author's introduction. "My legend *Xochitl* gives an idea of the destruction of the Toltec monarchy which preceded the others established in Anahuac. After noting the traditions relative to the emigration, wanderings, arrival, enslavement, and emancipation of the Aztecs and the foundation of Mexico, I trace some of their domestic customs in the

Casamiento de Netzahualcoyotl and proceed to describe in *La Princesa Papantzin* the prophecies concerning the coming of the Europeans and the symptoms of the great change brought about by the Spanish conquest."

Roa Bárcena busied himself in literary production during a long life. His last volume of verses was published in 1895. The legendary history led him to a serious study of history on the one hand, while the historical anecdote incited him to the composition of original tales on the other as well as translations of Hoffmann, Dickens and Byron. Of his rendering of Byron's tales Menéndez y Pelayo says:—"Seldom has Byron been so well interpreted in Castilian and perhaps never." The same critic said of his historical legends in verse:—"I consider them the best of their kind. . . . The *Princesa Papantzin* has a certain prophetic grandeur."

On the purely historical side Mexico is indebted to Roa Bárcena for an excellent account of the war with the United States which he entitled *Recuerdos de la Invasión norte-americana.* The student of literature will be interested in his biographies of Pesado, Gorostiza and others. Narrative verse like his Mexican legends dealing with episodes in Mexican history has bulked large enough to form almost a special branch of Mexican literature.

Belonging to this ballad type of verse is the work of an earlier poet, José de Jesús Díaz (1809–46). As his poems long remained uncollected they were soon forgotten and had no influence on other writers. But they possessed a peculiar excellence, due to his personal knowledge of geographical conditions. Being a soldier in the army operating near Vera Cruz and the state of Jalapa, he could place the popular traditions in their correct setting amid the rich vegetation of that region when narrating episodes of the first uprisings against the Spanish. The best of these legends are *La Cruz de Madera* and *El Puente del Diablo*. Somewhat more historical are *La Órden* relating the capture of Oaxaca by Morelos and *El Fusilamiento de Morelos*.

Díaz' work was not without influence at least on his son, Juan Díaz Covarrubias (1837–59). At the early age of twenty he published a volume of poems, *Páginas del Corazón*, written in the manner of the Spanish poet Zorrilla then living in Mexico. But Díaz Covarrubias' place in Mexican letters is founded on his historical novel *Gil Gómez el Insurgente*. His other essays in fiction are insignificant.

The protagonist of this novel was one of those remarkable persons unknown to their contemporaries, but famous to posterity. Gil Gómez, according to the author, was present or associated with the chief occurrences in Mexico between 1810 and 1812. In the intervals between battles he managed to carry on an exciting love affair, so that his adventures offer the reader an interesting picture of the period.

Díaz Covarrubias had scarcely completed his novel before events allowed him to imitate his hero. In 1857 the liberal party proposed in the Mexican congress a new constitution to supersede that of 1824. The bitter opposition to it by the conservatives led to an armed struggle. The liberals, though beaten at first, reorganized under Benito Juárez. When the latter was planning an attack on

Mexico City in 1859, Díaz Covarrubias joined one of the numerous small groups which were gathering in various parts of the country. His band, however, was surprised by the soldiers of General Márquez before it was fairly organized, and Díaz Covarrubias was one of sixteen executed.

A poet more fortunate than he was Juan Valle (1838–64) because he lived to see his party triumphant, and even to enjoy a small pension from his friends in power. As he had been blind from the age of three, it is remarkable that he could take so active a part among fighting men. At any rate his fiery patriotic verse roused them to enthusiasm. To those who know his misfortune, the many lines in his poems alluding to his blindness have a truly pathetic ring. Especially touching is a poem with the refrain, "I suffer so much."

The political events of the decade of the sixties were reflected in literature, both by the presentation of the stirring events of the period, and in the persons and doctrines of the writers. Mexicans term this epoch, beginning with the legislative proposal for a new constitution in 1857, "la reforma." The reforms consisted in a liberalization of the laws, respecting the freedom of the press and of speech and the secularization of church lands. By such means it was hoped to undermine the political power of the clergy. The elements favoring these changes in the constitution gradually grouped themselves under the leadership of Benito Juárez (1806–72). His pure Indian blood is indicative of the character of the revolution. After years of fighting Juárez succeeded in 1861 in obtaining complete control of the government, and in bring-

ing about the confiscation of much of the land held by the
clerical corporations.

In handling the business of state, however, Juárez
played into the hands of the conservative and clerical
party, who were intriguing for European intervention by
making the disastrous mistake of repudiating the foreign
debt of Mexico. To enforce its payment English, Spanish
and French troops were landed at Vera Cruz. A body of
French soldiers advancing into the interior were routed
in a smart fight with the Mexicans under General Zaragoza
on May 5th, 1862, an event which was long celebrated as a
national holiday, "el cinco de mayo." The government
of Louis Napoleon retaliated by sending a more formidable
force under Marshal Bazaine and by inducing Maximilian
of Austria to accept the throne as Emperor of Mexico.
Juárez and his guerillas were obliged to retreat to the
northern mountains. In 1867, however, the French army
was withdrawn leaving Maximilian to his fate, for without
the French the Mexican imperialists were speedily defeated by Juárez. Maximilian was taken prisoner and
shot at a locality known as the Cerro de las Campanas.
Juárez was elected president in August, 1867, and again in
1871.

The year 1868 witnessed an important revival of letters
in Mexico. Newspapers were established, literary societies formed and literary evenings held when poems, prose,
articles and addresses were read to enthusiastic listeners.
Beside Juárez other men of Indian blood came into prominence, notably Ignacio Ramírez (1818–79) and Ignacio
Manuel Altamirano (1834–93). Just as their political
activities were directed against the land holdings of the

clergy, their literary and philosophical doctrines were inclined to extreme liberalism. Ignacio Ramírez, by his savage articles signed "El Nigromante," won for himself a reputation as a Mexican Voltaire for he openly professed atheism in discussions concerning the existence of God. He introduced the study of modern psychology into Mexico. The constructive side of his criticism of life, a sort of stoic philosophy, he set forth in verses written with care and classical finish.

With Guillermo Prieto and Altamirano he edited the important liberal journal *El Correo de México*. Guillermo Prieto (1818–97) deserves praise for his narrative poems of episodes in Mexican history. Altamirano became one of the most important Mexican men of letters.

Born a full-blooded Indian, Altamirano went to school for the first time at the age of fourteen, ignorant even of the Spanish language. As his father had just been appointed alcalde of the village, the schoolmaster took a little more than ordinary interest in the lad in whom he discovered unusual intelligence. The schoolmaster encouraged him to attend the Institute of Toluca, open according to law to free attendance by young Indians. Again his studiousness and capacity captivated his teachers who assisted him to go to Mexico City to study at the Colegio de San Juan Letrán. Like other students he participated in the excitement of the politics of the day and enlisted in the army of Juárez. Under the orders of Porfirio Díaz at the attack on La Puebla he distinguished himself for bravery. In 1861, elected a member of congress at the age of twenty-seven, his first important speech was delivered against a law of general amnesty which his fiery and bloodthirsty eloquence succeeded in defeating. After the expulsion of the French he received from the public treasury by the order of President Juárez the repayment of a considerable sum of money which he had expended during the war. With this money he established the *Correo de México.*

From that time Altamirano was a prominent figure in Mexican literature, editing various periodicals and founding or encouraging literary societies. He also conducted classes as a professor of law, of history and of literature. His published remains consist of poems, addresses and tales. His semi-historical novel, *Clemencia La Navidad en la Montaña,* giving interesting pictures of Mexican life while relating the exemplary conduct of its hero, a Christian priest, has reached a fifth edition. Of the many governmental positions held by Altamirano the most important was that of consul general at Barcelona, to which he was appointed in 1889.

Altamirano's early verses belong to the erotic type. Later in life when he collected his fugitive pieces in a volume he combined four of them into a connected whole with an explanation in prose that he had attempted an imitation of Theocritus, in describing the different periods of the day in his native province of Acapulco, while the human beings who figure in the poems appear merely for the purpose of giving animation and relief to nature. Perhaps a scientific interest may have prevailed in his mind when he wrote *La Flor del Alba* and *La Salida del Sol* since he calls the many trees, plants and birds by their Indian names, but in *Los Naranjos* the orange trees in blossom like the rest of nature suggest love to the young

man who invites his beloved to "leave her bath" and
"come quickly," and in *Las Amápolas*, descriptive of the
midday heat, the lover begs the beauty "to have pity,"
but "with languid glance she replies with a smile—y
nada más." There is a torrid directness about these
idyliic pictures which is characteristically Mexican. Another poem, *Las Abejas*, contains the advice to a lovelorn
swain to observe the bees, how they seek out humble
flowers; like them turning away from the proud false
beauty, he should seek the honey of love among the
simple flowers. Altamirano's later verses were more
purely descriptive, and in his journalistic work he was
rather a stern censor of morals.

But his contemporary, Manuel María Flores (1840–85),
wrote erotic poetry of the most straightforward type.
Resembling the least ideal of Alfred de Musset's work,
he delights in the physical effects of love. Kisses abound
in his lines; he dreams that at midnight his beloved knocked
at his door; "perhaps at the terrible contact of thy lips
my heart would break." He published his poems under
the apt title of *Pasionarias*. Of this collection the best
is *Bajo las Palmas;* and the worst from a certain point of
view, *La Orgia*, which seems to have been written after
an attack of delirium tremens. Later poems as *Hojas
Secas* reveal weariness of sensual excitement; and certain
it is that after living a freethinker he died a Catholic.
His vigorous ode, *A la Patria en el 5 de mayo de 1862*,
shows what he might have accomplished in political verse.
Flores is said to be the most widely read of Mexican poets.

Of the same age José Rosas Moreno (1838–83) preferred
the grave and reflective kind of poetry. He came into

notice through an elegy on the death of Juan Valle. As a
journalist he was connected with various papers and also
essayed the drama. But his special originality consisted
in verses on domestic topics and his fables. The American
poet, Bryant, thus translated one which pleased him.

The Elm and the Vine

"Uphold my feeble branches
By thy strong arms, I pray."
Thus to the Elm her neighbor
The Vine was heard to say.
"Else, lying low and helpless,
A wretched lot is mine,
Crawled o'er by every reptile,
And browsed by hungry kine."
The Elm was moved to pity.
Then spoke the generous tree:
"My hapless friend, come hither,
And find support in me."
The kindly Elm, receiving
The grateful Vine's embrace,
Became, with that adornment,
The garden's pride and grace;
Became the chosen covert
In which the wild-birds sing;
Became the love of shepherds,
And glory of the spring.
Oh, beautiful example
For youthful minds to heed!
The good we do to others
Shall never miss its meed.
The love of those whose sorrows
We lighten shall be ours;
And o'er the path we walk in
That love shall scatter flowers.

The skepticism which Altamirano and Ignacio Ramírez set forth in their prose and verse was furthered by the teaching at the University of Mexico. The clash between science and religion due to the spread of the theory of evolution was presented by a student of medicine, Manuel Acuña (1849–73), in a daring poem which made him famous by the sensation it excited. In *Ante un Cadáver* he discussed the problem of existence. According to the poem science finds that everything finishes in the tomb. Immortality resides only in matter. The body given back to earth may ascend again to life as wheat or flowers; "for the being that dies is another being that comes into existence: matter, immortal as glory, never dies."

The enthusiasm aroused by Acuña's poems resulted in the founding of a literary society to encourage the writing of verse. It was named after the Aztec poet-king Netzahualcoyotl and elected for its president Altamirano. To the versifiers of the society, among whom should be mentioned Agustín F. Cuenca (1850–84), every poem became the resolution of a social problem.

Acuña won a triumph also with a play, which kept the stage for some time, entitled *El Pasado*. It dealt with an artist who married a girl who had been ruined by a rich villain. After years of residence in Paris, they return to Mexico where the artist attempts to introduce his wife into polite society. She is pursued by her former lover assisted by an equally villainous friend. In spite of the husband's efforts these men so drive the woman to despair that she leaves her home and commits suicide in order to spare her husband further disgrace and annoyance.

Acuña's own death by suicide at the early age of twenty-four seemed to give the right to those who were shocked by his bold skepticism. But his last poem explains the act as due to disappointment in love. The poem relates the marriage of a young girl to another man than the one she loves. After years have elapsed she comes one day upon a tomb. The poet explains to her curious questioning, "You know the dead; you know the executioner."

While the mental attitude of a certain part of the Mexicans was exhibited in the verses of Acuña and his friends, the populace found their spokesman in Antonio Plaza (1833–82). His was the bitter voice of the mob that hates and curses. His skeptical sarcastic diatribes won him a temporary popularity which may have solaced him for the loss of a foot injured by a cannon ball in 1861. From different angles Acuña and Plaza epitomize the ideas and emotions of their epoch.

Another type of verse writing which assumed large proportions during the seventies was the production of ballads dealing with various periods of revolutionary history. The most assiduous producer of them was Guillermo Prieto. Several newspapers vigorously encouraged writing ballads so that some are found among the poems of nearly every writer. In 1910, as part of the festivities of the centenary of the Mexican revolution, the editors of the series of books known as the *Biblioteca de Autores Mexicanos* collected the best of the historical ballads and printed them in chronological order in two volumes with the title of *Romancero de la Guerra de Independencia.*

Literary interest in Mexican warfare did not, however, confine itself to ballads but also extensively cultivated fiction. The novel as a variety of literature has flourished in Mexico throughout the nineteenth century and whenever its theme at all concerns contemporary life it offers many realistic details. It will be remembered that both Rodríguéz Galván and Pesado practiced the short story, but the example of Fernández Lizardi in his *Periquillo Sarniento* had no followers before 1845. In that year appeared Manuel Payno's *El Fistol del Diablo*. The author was a man of some education and literary talent which he had strengthened by travel and acquaintance with European literatures. He attempted a study of Mexican types, customs and language very similar to those described in the *Periquillo;* and his book met with a popularity almost as great.

Justo Sierra (1814–61) wrote a novel in the form of letters, *Un Año en el Hospital de San Lázaro* for the first literary journal published in Yucatán in 1841. Sierra desired to establish a special literature of Yucatán and with this end in view wrote a historical novel *La Hija del Judío* based on an incident from the early annals of his province. Don Alonso de la Cerda, justicia mayor of Yucatán in 1666, having no children, adopted María, the daughter of a woman who died in his house. When the girl became of marriageable age, it is the duty of a priest who has hitherto kept the secret to reveal the fact that María is the child of a Jew. Her adoptive father and her betrothed lover are, however, unmoved in their love for her. Justo Sierra was a successful and learned lawyer At the period known as the reform he was chosen by the government to draw up a code of the civil law of Mexico, a labor which he accomplished at the ruination of his health.

His son by the same name, Justo Sierra (1848–1912) was a diligent and prolific man of letters, a poet and a critic as well as a successful lawyer. In journalism he introduced the light and gracefully satiric French style of writing, which pleased his readers. For a long time he was a prominent figure among lovers of good literature in Mexico. He was the author of various tales, poems and books of travel.

The influence of the French Romantic novelists, particularly of the type of Alphonse Karr and Eugene Sue, made itself felt about the middle of the century. In imitation of the former was written *Guerra de Treinta Años* by Fernando Orozco y Berra. The story depicts a soul once eager for love and enjoyment, but now filled with disillusion. It is the personal history of the author who died soon after its publication. His friends pointed out a certain beautiful young lady as the original of the scornful and fickle Serafina so that to her house began a veritable pilgrimage of the romantically inclined.

The sentimental tale was also cultivated by Florencio del Castillo who gave to his heroines the most complete beauty of person and character, angels of sweetness, whose passionate love ends not in marriage but in suffering or grief. But the tales have the considerable merit of presenting accurate pictures of life among the lower and middle classes of Mexican society.

As a study of social conditions should also be mentioned *Ironías de la Vida* by Pantaleón Tovar (1828–76) who gave a certain realistic touch to his novel by introducing the argot of the lower classes. Tovar was also a prolific versifier on familiar topics.

The historical novel can show many notable examples in Mexican literature though they seldom can be rightly called more than embellished history. After the success of *Gil Gómez el Insurgente* whose unfortunate author, Juan Díaz Covarrubias, was so cruelly executed, a series of similar novels dealing generally with contemporary events appeared. The story of the French invasion which terminated in 1867 by the execution of the Emperor Maximilian was given to the reading public by Juan Antonio Mateos in a so-called novel whose title, *El Cerro de las Campanas*, bore the same name as the locality where the Emperor was shot. Its publication was an event in Mexican literary annals on account of the extremely large number of copies sold. The author being an eye-witness of much that he described, competent critics are inclined to the opinion that his book gives as accurate an idea of what really happened as can possibly be gleaned from the badly mutilated and falsified official records. Moreover, to the Mexican people *El Cerro de las Campanas* is the source of their knowledge of the French invasion. Mateos wrote other novels and even some plays without meeting with the same success.

The French period was also depicted by General Vicente Riva Palacio (1832–96) in *Calvario y Tabor*. He had seen the heroism of the common soldiers under his command in the central part of the republic as, hungry and naked, with prices on their heads, they maintained a stubborn war against the invader, relying for support on captured spoils even at the very gates of the capital. He did not hesitate to describe so horrible a thing as the poisoning of a whole division of soldiers. On the other hand, interesting descriptions of various localities on the southern coast and the hot land of Michoacan afford agreeable reading. The author was personally so popular that the book met with considerable success so that he was encouraged to try his hand on a novel drawn from the archives of the Mexican inquisition, entitled *Monja y Casada, virgen y mártir*. Riva Palacio was an important personage in the journalism of his day and known favorably as a poet.

A more fertile novelist was Manuel Sánchez Mármol (1839–1912), a journalist who served with the Republican forces at the time of the French intervention. He early performed a service to Mexican letters by rescuing from oblivion the verses of his fellow natives of Yucatán, especially those of Quintana Roo and Alpuche which he published in 1861 under the title of *Poetas Yucatecos y Tabasqueños*. The titles of some of his novels are *El Misionero de la Cruz, Pocahontas*, a political satire, *Juanita Sousa*, the story of an unfortunate love affair, and *Antón Pérez*. The last named portrays the troublous times as the author witnessed them in the province of Tabasco. Antón was the typical bright Indian boy who has attracted the attention of the village priest. The latter's influence, however, fails to obtain for him the coveted scholarship in the seminary at Mérida, so he is obliged to remain as an ordinary poor laborer helping to support his relatives. When the French come, he enters the local guards who on account of his intelligence make him a lieutenant. As a boy at school he had been annoyed by the childish admiration of a girl of wealthy parents, Rosalba del Riego. Now that they are both grown, he falls in love with her but she rejects his attentions. An aunt of hers, Doña Socorro Castrejón, however, conceives a passion for the handsome young soldier. By her he is induced to desert to the imperialist cause. In a battle that follows Antón is mortally wounded. Then the author drives home to the reader's mind the lesson of the man who has turned traitor to his country through the influence of a foolish love. Antón, helpless from his wounds, is finally despatched and his body eaten by vultures. "Whoever has read it," says the critic Francisco Sosa, "will never forget how Antón Pérez died."

A thoroughgoing reconstruction of the period of the French intervention was attempted by Alfonso M. Maldonado (b. 1849) in his novel *Nobles y Plebeyos*, written, according to the preface to his children, that they might form an exact idea of the years from 1862 to 1867 from the relation of his personal experiences. Writing years after the events the author lays claim to an impartiality of judgment acquired by long experience as a judge. Maldonado wrote many shorter tales and historical legends.

Some of these belong to that considerable body of Mexican literature which lies on the borderland between fiction and history. The tales of Manuel Domínguez and Rivera y Río, for example, are fiction, while those of Hilarion Frías y Soto and Luís González Obregón are mainly popular history.

Of serious historical students there have been a great number in Mexico. Carlos M. Bustamente and Lucas Alamán treated the history of Mexico with a large degree of partisanship, but Joaquín García Icazbalceta (1825–94) was painstaking and accurate in his exhaustive erudition concerning the period of Spanish control. Alfredo Chavero delved deep into the history and antiquities of the aboriginal races.

In the matter of biography the student owes a debt to Francisco Sosa (b. 1848) who has also written much literary criticism of importance. For literary history the only work is the unsatisfactory and defective *Historia crítica de la Literatura en México* by Francisco Pimentel. Victoriano Agüeros (1854–1911), during the golden period of the early Díaz régime, attempted to acquaint Spanish readers with Mexican authors by writing articles for foreign periodicals. Later he performed a great service by printing popular editions of the best Mexican writers in the series entitled *Biblioteca de Autores Mexicanos*.

The death of Juárez in 1872 was followed by a period of political uncertainty and turmoil terminated four years later by the elevation of Porfirio Díaz (1830–1915) to the presidency. His pacification of the country gave opportunity to a fresh growth of literary effort, especially in the theater. Like the other literature of this decade the drama dealt mainly with Mexican history. The most successful and popular dramatist, who for his work was dubbed "the restorer of the theater," was José Peón y Contreras (1843–1909).

A native of Yucatán he came to Mexico to study medicine, but in his leisure moments tried his hand at narrative verse and the prose tale as well as the drama. The complicated and tragic plots of his plays are laid during the colonial period. The personages speak the language of exalted passions and are much alike. In fact the author wrote too much and too swiftly for anything else to be the case. However, the public was charmed by the love-lorn maids and romantic gallants whose tragic stories were presented to its attention. The titles of the dramas are attractive: *La Hija del Rey*, produced in 1876, *Hasta el Cielo, Luchas de Honra y de Amor*, also of 1876; *El Sacrificio de la Vida, Por el Joyel del Sombrero*, 1878; and many others some of which have never been staged.

The last named is a fair example of them all. Doña Mencia loves Don Juan de Benavides but is beloved by Iñigo, the son of a squire who died defending the honor of her father. The young men are about to depart from New Spain for the war in Flanders, Iñigo because his love is not reciprocated, Benavides because he has learned an impediment preventing his marriage to Doña Mencia. Iñigo discovers the identity of his more fortunate rival by recognizing the "jewel of his hat." Doña Mencia's father, after Benavides had taken his farewell, finds out that a man has entered his daughter's apartment by means of the balcony. Jealous of her honor and his own he reproves her and decides to kill both her and himself. At that moment Iñigo who has overheard the angry words enters from an adjoining room and begs to be slain as the guilty person. The old man reproaches him bitterly, but refuses to comply on account of the lad's father. "Go, both of you, the altar awaits you." Doña Mencia makes no objection, partly because the young man has saved her from disgrace, partly because she thinks Benavides has left her forever. After the wedding ceremony while Doña Mencia still wears her wedding gown, Benavides reappears, having obtained a dispensation from the Pope, and demands Doña Mencia's hand from her father. A glance, however, reveals to him the true state of affairs. It is now Iñigo's turn to depart. On taking leave of his wife he begs her to cherish her honor. Benavides seeks a rendezvous with the young woman which she, after a struggle between duty and love, refuses. Again Benavides climbs over the balcony into her room. Iñigo had seen him and pursuing him engages him in a duel. The father also enters and kills Iñigo before he recognizes his antagonist. As Iñigo lies dead his nobility of conduct appears in sharp contrast with the behavior of Benavides. The latter is ignominiously kicked out of the house.

As a narrative poet, Peón y Contreras preferred the same types as appear in his dramas. His earliest romances related episodes and traditions from the history of the Aztec people and portrayed their heroes and customs. In his *Romances Dramáticos* (1880) the poems are original in form, with few details, rapid movement and clear-cut characters. Their themes are love and jealousy, virtue and its struggle against vice, tempests of the soul arising from outraged honor. *Doña Brenda*, for example, kills her husband through mistaken jealousy. *Sancho Bermúdez de Astorga* kills his wife in the garden of their house with her lover and then goes calmly to bed. *Gil* spends his time away from home. His wife begs him not go tonight because this will be her last one on earth. He replies mockingly that he has heard that story before. On his way to the evening's pleasure he sees a bridal party leaving the church. Reminded thus of his own marriage vows he hurries home only to discover his wife's dead body. About to kill himself in remorse, his attention is attracted

by the wail of the infant in the cradle. For its sake he
resolves to live. Not less dramatic are the poems about
Columbus and the incidents of his career in *Trovas Colom-
binas*, 1881. Somewhat longer, but similar to his earlier
ballads, are his *Pequeños Dramas*, 1887.

The "restoration" of the theater by Peón y Contreras
brought about public interest in the dramas of Alfredo
Chavero (1841–1906). He was a student and professor
of history whose researches in Mexican antiquities and
history are embodied in several volumes. The romantic
character of the pre-Spanish period he endeavored to present in dramatic form. *Quetzalcoatl*, produced March 24,
1878, enacts the legendary story of that monarch. He
is a king from the East who has substituted the cross
for the worship of the aboriginal deities. After a series of
misadventures in which he is worsted by his neighbors,
he appears to his people as they are assembled to elect
a king in his stead. To them he prophesies the coming
of the Spaniards beneath the banner of the cross. Another
drama, *Xochitl*, is laid at the time of Cortés' invasion.
Gonzalo Alaminos, the conquistador's youthful attendant,
is brought a wounded prisoner to the Aztec temple where
the maiden Xochitl is serving. As she nurses him back
to health ardent love springs up between them. When
the city is captured by Cortés, the lovers are separated.
Xochitl is sent as a present to Marina's sister. Now
Marina, being the mistress of Cortés, sends for her sister
to come to Mexico. On the journey thither, the sister
dies, but her attendants, fearful for their lives, resolve
to substitute Xochitl. The deception succeeds. Taken
into Cortés' household, that amorous warrior falls in love

with her and decides to rid himself of the querulous Marina by sending her away. He orders Gonzalo to accompany her. But the youth had already arranged an elopement with Xochitl. She, however, fails to keep the appointment on account of a riot in the city. In this disturbance Gonzalo is killed. In her distress Xochitl relates her story to Marina and reveals even to Cortés the love that had existed between herself and Gonzalo. Marina hands the unhappy girl a dagger with which she stabs herself. Dying she discloses her identity as the last survivor of the royal house, sister of Cuauhtemoc. Cortés in his grief over Gonzalo and Xochitl persists in his determination to send away Marina.

Verse writing in the early eighties is represented by Juan de Dios Peza (1852–1910). Apparently he strove to be a sort of Mexican Longfellow. Very prolific, all sorts of exercises in verse on all manner of topics appear in his volumes, published from 1874 to the *Cantos del Hogar*, 1890. Continuing the school of Rosas Moreno his most successful poems belong to the domestic and didactic type. Perhaps of this sort nothing in Mexican verse or even in the Spanish language equals his lines that deal with children, for example, the description in *Fusiles y Muñecas* of the poet's children, Juan and Margot, playing, the boy with his gun of tin and the girl with her doll. But Peza wrote so much that was prosaic and trivial that his reputation as a poet was injured thereby. Peza went to Spain as secretary of the Mexican legation in 1878 and there published several articles on Mexican poets that aroused an interest in them among the Spaniards.

Landscape poetry has always been practiced by Mexicans. The classic type was revived by .Joaquín Arcadio Pagaza (b. 1839) whose greatest service to literature despite his numerous sonnets was a Castilian version of Landívar's great Latin poem written in the eighteenth century descriptive of the natural beauties of Guatemala.

Original verse of a similar kind was written by Manuel José Othón (1858–1906), who must be ranked among Mexico's best poets for his real appreciation of nature's moods. Like Pagaza he chose for his favorite form of expression sonnets which he arranged in sequences. One of these, *Noche rústica de Walpurgis* (*Sinfonía Drámatica*), depicts the experiences of a poet invited to leave the singing of arms and listen to the "things of the night." A sonnet is devoted to each experience. He sees the moonlight play on the foliage of an old and enormous tree as on a harp. In the distance, the nightingale sings, the river discourses garrulous and the stars reveal their respect for man. The cricket and the night birds lead to the cemetery. Witches and ghosts appear. Finally the cock crows, the matin bell rings, and a gunshot resounds, suggestive either of an execution or a hunter's escape from a wild beast. A dog alert for his master's safety barks. The morning light floods the earth and men pass to their daily avocations.

There is in this sonnet sequence a certain gloominess of imagination characteristic of Mexican verse. The point has been well expressed by the well-known critic from Santo Domingo, Pedro Henríquez Urena, who writes:— "Just as the landscape of the high Mexican plateau, accentuated by the rarity of the air, rendered barren by the dryness and the cold, under a pale blue sky, is covered with gray and yellowish tones, so Mexican poetry seems to take its tonality from them. A moderation and a melancholy sentiment suggestive of twilight and autumn agree with that perpetual autumn of the heights very different from the ever fertile spring of the tropics."

The most autumnal poet of all was Manuel Gutiérrez Nájera (1859–95), who is the incarnation of gentle melancholy. Admiration of him is so great among the younger Mexicans that they say Gutiérrez Nájera is the only real poet born in Mexico since Sor Juana. Perhaps they mean that he voiced in a preëminent degree the mental qualities derived by the educated Mexicans from their race and environment. His verses, often suggesting more ideas than they expressed verbally, possessed a rare musical quality. And that marriage of music and words was his special contribution as a precursor of the modernista movement of Spanish-American literature.[1]

In his earliest poems, written before 1880, Gutiérrez Nájera followed the Catholic tradition of Pesado and Carpio. For this reason the Catholic element of Mexican society suffering severe defeat at the hands of the triumphant liberalism of such writers as Ignacio Ramírez and Altamirano backed by the Juárez administration hoped to find a champion in Gutiérrez Nájera. In this expectation they were disappointed in spite of the intensely religious feelings of his typical poems *Non omnis moriar* and *Pax animæ*. His attitude toward death is beautifully expressed in his elegiac poem *Para entonces*.

In this poem he utters the wish to die at the decline

[1] See page 452.

cf day on the high sea; where in his last moments he will hear only the prayer of the waves; to die when the sun casts its last ruddy glow on the green waters; to be like the sun, something luminous which is extinguished; to die young, when life still attracts "though we know she deceives us."

In the technique of his verse Gutiérrez Nájera endeavored to amalgamate the French spirit and the Spanish form and thus produce a type of poetry which should be the flower of romanticism. His success was such that in the words of his panegyrist, Justo Sierra, "the singers of all Spanish America awoke in his nest and flew from it.."

In the grace and elegance of the poet spoke the individuality of the man. For his modest reserve he was nicknamed by his friends "El Duque Job." His innate good taste never permitted him to carry the sensualistic tendency of his verse to the point of vulgarity, as, for example, in his playful *La Duquesa Job*, in which he sings the physical perfections of his wife.

The same grace and good taste marked his journalistic work in prose. In this he was a forerunner of the modernista prose for he abandoned the heavy Spanish period for the lighter French style. And his clear logic and vehemence as a prose writer stand in sharp contrast with the vague sentimentality of the poet.

In 1894 Gutiérrez Nájera in company with Carlos Díaz Dufóo founded *La Revista Azul*. Without reference to Rubén Darío's book *Azul*, from which, however, extracts were printed from time to time in this weekly review, the editor, "El Duque Job," explained its title thus: "Why blue? Because in the blue, there is sunlight; because in the blue, there are clouds; and because in the blue, hopes fly in flocks. Blue is not merely a color, it is a mystery." Later to defend the purely artistic purpose of the magazines from the critics who assailed his adherence to French models, he wrote, "Whoever would cultivate art must get his supplies from France where art lives a more intense life than elsewhere." The review concerned itself only with works of literary art in prose and verse. News items were rigidly excluded. Even the death of Gutiérrez Nájera himself received scant attention.

Frequent contributors were Luis G. Urbina (b. 1867), José Juan Tablada (b. 1871) and Rafael de Zayas Enríquez; but the names of nearly every writer interested in the modernista movement appear in its pages, even that of the Andalusian poet Salvador Rueda, through whom the spirit of the new poetry passed into Spain.

Another Mexican poet whose manner was widely imitated outside of his own country was Salvador Díaz Mirón (b. 1855). His originality lay in the fiery eloquence of his verses and their spirit of revolt. He came from the hot region of Vera Cruz, which may explain in part his torrid pugnacity and sensuality. Moreover, he cultivated the quatrain as a form of verse expression, till he put on it a personal stamp. Later he developed certain theories of prosody in which others have not followed him, so that his more recent poems exhibit a second mannerism peculiar to Díaz Mirón.[1]

The landscape school of poetry so ably represented by Othón has had many followers in Mexico, for example,

[1] See page 452.

Luis G. Urbina and Rafael López. Urbina's excellent verse is exhibited in his *Poema del Lago* and *El Poema del Mariel*. The latter was inspired by the marine scenery and fisher folk of Cuba where the poet sought refuge during the recent upheaval in Mexico. Both poems are sonnet sequences, pictures of landscapes and life with the thoughts suggested by them in the mind of the poet.

To the modernista movement Mexico not only contributed Gutiérrez Nájera, Díaz Mirón, Urbina but also Enrique González Martínez (b. 1871), Alfonso Reyes, and especially Amado Nervo (b. 1870).[1] Writers of verse have at all times been so numerous in Mexico that space forbids mention of all.

The naturalistic doctrine of novel writing found in Mexico ready imitators upon a promising field. Among the first of these was José López Portillo y Rojas (b. 1850), for a short time minister for foreign affairs under General Huerta, 1914. His father being a wealthy and eminent lawyer, the son enjoyed the advantages of a good education and wide travel in Europe and the Orient of which he has left a record in *Impresiones de Viaje*. Knowledge of his own country he has set forth in his novels. In *La Parcela* he offered a study of the morbid affection for land displayed by the native proprietors. Don Pedro Ruiz, a rich Indian, has an only son, Gonzalo, twenty-three years of age who is engaged to marry Ramona, the only daughter of Don Miguel Díaz. The latter is envious of Don Pedro's wealth, so at the suggestion of a shyster lawyer he seizes a lot of land adjoining his own property. When the matter is carried into court,

[1] See page 469.

the boundary line is determined by means of bribing the
judge in Don Miguel's favor. In a higher court, however,
the same means resecures the property for Don Pedro.
Don Miguel then attempts to injure his wealthy neighbor
by various mean and underhand methods such as assassinating his tenants and breaking a dam that impounds
water for driving the latter's mills. During all these
quarrels of the parents, the lovers are naturally having
a hard time, but at last a sudden reconciliation permits
their marriage and an end of the story.

The devious ways by which men rise in Mexican politics,
the eagerness for disorder and revolution prevailing
among the lower classes in Mexico, the peculiarities of
Mexican journalism are all set forth in a four-volume novel
by Emilio Rabasa (b. 1856). Each volume is really
complete in itself but the four relate the fortunes of Juan
Quiñones, in love with the niece of Don Mateo, all natives of an obscure village. Don Mateo, however, is
carried upward on fortune's wheel while Juan comes
trailing after. In spite of the uncle's increasing ambitions for his niece, Juan finally wins her. The author,
Emilio Rabasa, represented Mexico at the A B C conference at Niagara in 1914.

A popular writer who followed the changes in taste
was Rafael Delgado (1853–1914). His first literary efforts
were plays written and produced during the great dramatic
revival of the late seventies. *La Caja de Dulces* is a drama
in three acts, which made his friends so enthusiastic
that they presented him with a crown of silver and a gold
pen. The following year, 1879, he produced a translation
of Feuillet's *Une Case de Conscience*. Living in his native

province of Vera Cruz, he became a very active member of a literary society, la Sociedad Sánchez Oropesa, which met monthly under the leadership of Silvestre Moreno Cora, then rector of the college of Orizaba. Delgado's stories and sketches were printed in the newspapers of Vera Cruz and have been collected in book form. They are written in a manner that suggests Daudet's but deal realistically with the types of humanity in his province, as "el Caballerango" and "la Gata," by which local terms the stable boy and the maid servant are known. The stories contain realistic views of the hard and degraded existence led by the lower classes. Historical traditions also form part of his sketches written at this time.

In novel writing Delgado began by an imitation of Jorge Isaacs' romantic idyll *María*. Delgado's love idyll *Angelina* appears to be a chapter from the author's personal experience. Its hero, Rodolfo, is dependent on two aged aunts who have sent him away to school. When he returns to their house to undertake his duty of supporting them, he finds that they have taken under their protection at the solicitation of the parish priest an orphan girl, Angelina. The young people fall in love with each other. After some months of innocent and idyllic intercourse they are separated because the priest recalls Angelina to his own house while Rodolfo goes to service on the estate of a rich proprietor by the name of Fernández. This man has a beautiful daughter, Gabriela, possessed of extraordinary talent in piano playing. Rodolfo falls in love with her, though at the same time he retains his affection for Angelina. Her correspondence with him is a careful study of feminine passion. At last, she learns

Rodolfo's attentions to Gabriela. Then Angelina resolves to become a sister of charity and writes the recreant lover a very beautiful letter of renunciation. Gabriela, however, has paid little or no attention to Rodolfo and finally banishes him absolutely from her presence. Rodolfo seeks solace in work.

Delgado's later novels followed more closely the ideas of the naturalistic school. *Los Parientes Ricos* is a satire on the customs of the middle class, while *Calandria* is a picture of lower-class manners. In the latter Carmen is the natural daughter of a man of the world, Eduardo Ortiz de Guerra who attempts to repair his fault by money. She is thus brought up to a love of luxury beyond her station in life and consequently falls an easy victim to the seductions of the rich Alberto Rojas though she is being honorably courted by an honest young carpenter Gabriel. Their last interview in the garden is very touchingly described and is excelled in tragic pathos only by the scene in which Gabriel is at work building her coffin after her amour with Alberto has brought Carmen to her death. This novel is praised by the professor Moreno Cora for its "admirable exactness" in the portrayal of contemporary manners, and he asserts that he has known many men like the sinning and grief-stricken father, Eduardo Ortiz.

The field of politics and social strife is claimed by an interesting novel, *Pacotillas*, written by Porfirio Parra (b. 1855), who is also the author of a long ode on mathematics somewhat in the style of Acuña, his friend and fellow student of medicine. The novel ostensibly follows the fortunes of four young men friends. One of them, el Chango, rises by toadyism in politics and marries great wealth. Pacotillas is a sort of modern picaro who drinks hard and lives with Amalia without marrying her, sometimes in comfortable circumstances and sometimes in great poverty. By antagonizing the government in articles which he published in the papers, he is thrown into prison where he finally dies. Like his prototype, el Periquillo Sarniento, he takes the reader through various classes of Mexican society.

In some respects the best writer and the closest adherent to the French naturalistic was Federico Gamboa (b. 1864). From early youth Gamboa lived abroad and was connected with the Mexican diplomatic service in many capitals including Washington. His literary work began by adapting French vaudevilles and he has written several original plays of not much consequence. As a novelist, however, he has been fairly prolific and successful. A volume of sketches, *Esbozos contemporáneos*, brought him a nomination as corresponding member to the Royal Spanish Academy. The first novel to bring him into international notice was published during his sojourn in Buenos Aires in 1892, *Apariencias*, which may be briefly described as a Mexican variation of the universal theme of adultery.

The scene of this novel is laid in a small village during the French occupation under Maximilian. A realistic picture of the farcical court proceedings in which judges and defenders speak different languages without interpreters opens the story. A youth, Pedro, is successfully defended upon the charge of being a spy though his father is condemned and executed. The reader's sympathy is thus thoroughly aroused and made ready to share the

intense patriotism of the pages descriptive of the retreat
of the French army from a town occupied only by women,
children and old men. Pedro's defender, the lawyer
Don Luis, a man some fifty years of age, is so greatly
touched by the lad's orphan helplessness that he takes
him to his home in the city of Mexico and adopts him.
The lawyer's sister, Magdalena, falls in love with the boy.
In the meantime the susceptible lawyer also falls in love
with the young daughter of a client and marries her.
The wife Elena and Pedro thus brought into intimacy
succumb to a guilty attraction to each other. The lad
is thus false to his benefactor and adoptive father and to
his first love, Magdalena. The amour progresses rather
openly until the couple are surprised by the outraged
husband, who instead of following the time-honored custom of killing the guilty ones condemns them to live.
The course of this affair is related with psychological
minuteness in the manner of Bourget just as the military
scenes imitate the intensity of Zola. Realistic also are
certain pictures of Mexican life such as the wedding break-
fast in a public café and the description of Mexico City
at night when the public places are full of joyous revellers.

The title of "dissector of souls" conferred on Gamboa
by his critics was confirmed by *Suprema Ley*, published
in 1896. The soul in this case belongs to Julio Ortegal,
a poor law clerk, whose wife, Carmen, is the hard working
mother of six children. Julio, to his destruction, comes into
contact with Clothilde, a siren, who has been thrown into
jail on suspicion of murdering her lover who had in reality
committed suicide. Julio is infatuated to the extent that
when Clothilde is acquitted he abandons his wife and

children to follow her.   Though a consumptive he works
overtime to pay for her extravagances.   Finally, however,
she casts him off.   Julio broken in spirit and body returns
to his family in time to die.

Gamboa's ability to write was brought sharply to the
attention of the North American public when he was
secretary for foreign affairs for provisional President
Huerta.   The unassailable logic of his masterly replies
to the first notes of our Department of State demanding
Huerta's resignation elicited widespread admiration.

CHAPTER XII

CUBA

To say that Cuban literature is wholly a literature of revolution would be an exaggeration. But in verses sufficiently innocent in appearance to escape the censor's pencil often lurked a thought that was evident to the patriot. If the word "libertad" occurring in a drama was deleted by the censor who substituted "lealtad," nobody was deceived; for a patriot liberty presupposes loyalty. Again the lover's melancholy on account of his sweetheart's illness might be a thin disguise for the poet's lament over Cuba prostrate beneath the oppressor's heel.

Verse undoubtedly was written with a purely artistic intent. In fact the bulk of verse produced in Cuba was so great that its very quantity has been explained as due to the political disability of the people.

Prose on the other hand was generally a weapon in the fight for separation from Spain. Though some of it was journalistic and some oratorical, the censor's eye was too keen to allow every dry-as-dust title prefixed to a passionate protest against some act of the authorities to pass unchallenged. Consequently there sprang up and flourished a form of literature, essentially Cuban in its fullest development, the political tract. It could be circulated secretly and even printed in a foreign country and smuggled into Cuba.

The first revolutionary, in whose lines Cubans sought and always found inspiration was also the greatest of Cuban poets, José María Heredia. As his work and early banishment occurred during the period of revolution in the rest of Spanish America, he has been considered elsewhere. While his fame was widespread beyond the seas, the same upheaval which caused his expulsion from Cuba brought about that also of a man, Félix Varela y Morales (1788–1853), whose reputation and influence remained peculiarly and locally Cuban. His importance to the cause of separatism lay, not in the emotional appeal of poetry but in the persuasive power of abstract reasoning.

To Felix Varela the Cubans pay the tribute of saying that he taught them to think. He is the first of a notable line of teachers who shaped Cuban mentality. An intellectually brilliant young priest, professor of Latin, philosophy and science at the University of Havana, Varela began his innovations by giving instruction in the vernacular. In 1820 the famous society, Los Amigos del País, founded in Havana in 1793 and still in active existence, resolved to establish a professorship of public law and this chair was won in public competition by Varela. Soon thereafter he was elected a deputy to the Cortes of Cádiz dispersed by Fernando VII in 1823 for its liberal tendencies. Though Varela was one of the proscribed deputies marked for arrest, he succeeded in reaching Gibraltar and from there New York. He took up his residence in Philadelphia and began to issue a periodical, *El Habanero*, eagerly read in Cuba. Though this journal was short-lived, in others he continued to exert an influence on the affairs of the island till the day of his death. He died and was buried in St. Augustine, Florida, where his tomb became a shrine of pilgrimage for patriotic Cubans. After their independence was won, in gratitude for his work they removed his bones to Cuba.

Varela in his philosophical teaching urged less attention to abstractions and more to the study of things. He proclaimed the right of human reason to investigate for itself. He preached against fanaticism and for tolerance in religious thought, especially against that abuse of religion which made it an aid to political despotism.

When only Cuba of all the vast extent of Spanish possessions in America was left to Spain, the island began to enjoy great prosperity on account of the relaxation in the rigor of the laws concerning trade. Moreover, an immigration of loyalists from the rest of Spanish America swelled the number of the population. Assisted by this naturally loyalist disposition of the people the wiser and freer colonial policy of the Spanish government made all but a few irreconcilables incline favorably toward Spain. Dwellers in Cuba felt themselves Spaniards rather than Cubans. Even the outbursts of Heredia against the hanging of the Spanish rebel leader Rafael del Riego were delivered more as the protests of a Spaniard than of a Cuban in spite of their possible local application. Moreover, the stimulus to literary endeavor came from Spanish affairs.

In 1830 when the childless Fernando VII married María Cristina, the Spanish poet Quintana addressed the royal pair an ode which was nothing more or less than a hymn to liberty. To Cubans his words seemed an augury of a new epoch. Cuban poets imitated even the form of the verses. The society, Amigos del País, was moved to establish a literary section, of which Domingo del Monte, who was later to be a sort of Cuban Maecenas, was made secretary. When the little heiress known to history as Isabel II was born, the society held a poetic contest which, being the first of the kind in Cuba, aroused great enthusiasm among the youth.

The first prize was awarded to José Antonio Echeverría (1815–84), then a lad of sixteen. Shortly thereafter he became an editor of a literary journal, *El Plantel*, in which appeared several of the important literary productions of this period. Though Echeverría wrote other poems and some prose tales, notably *Antonelli*, he became more prominent in later life for his active participation in separatist politics.

María Cristina as queen regent awakened great expectations. In 1834 she appointed as her prime minister the poet Francisco Martínez de la Rosa (1789–1852), who had just produced his masterpiece, the romantic drama, *La Conjuración de Venecia*. Again in Cuba there was rejoicing among the poets for they thought the queen regent and her minister would favor a more liberal policy in the government of Cuba. The best of the Cuban verses were gathered in a volume with the title of *Aureola Poética* and sent to Martínez de la Rosa. The sponsor for this volume was Ignacio Valdés Machuca (1800–51) more praiseworthy as a patron of letters than as a poet. Still his little volume of youthful effusions, *Ocios poéticos*, published in 1819, makes a date in Cuban literature. In material ways also Valdés Machuca assisted striving poets. The most notable instance was that of the negro poet,

José Francisco Manzano, a slave. He succeeded in raising a subscription of five hundred dollars with which he bought the man's freedom. This occurrence seemed so sensational to J. R. Madden, an English judge in the mixed court in Havana, that he published an English translation of several of Manzano's poems.

In the liberal constitution granted to Spain by María Cristina in 1834, Cuba expected to have her part. But the degree of freedom allowed her was by vote of the Cortes denied and the Cuban deputies were excluded. Moreover, the despotic Miguel Tacón was appointed Governor of Cuba and given absolute powers of repression. To the conduct of his office from 1834 to 1839 may be ascribed a rapid growth of separatist sentiment in Cuba.

Coincident with Tacón's administration was the first flourishing period of Cuban literature due to a literary circle which formed about the person of Domingo del Monte (1804–54). He was wealthy and allied to aristocratic families in Spain. Del Monte's letters to his brother-in-law, José Luis Alfonso, form an excellent picture and chronicle of events in Havana during the governorship of Tacón. Before the latter's arrival Del Monte's patronage of Cuban letters was purely literary, but when the tyrannous acts of the governor excited his disgust, it assumed a political aspect.

Poetry was Del Monte's passion though he himself wrote but indifferent verses. It was Del Monte who called the attention of the great Spanish critic Alberto Lista to Heredia's poems by sending him a copy of them with a request for an opinion. It was to Del Monte that Heredia dedicated "in testimony of unalterable affection" the second part of his poems as arranged in the edition of Toluca. While in the United States Del Monte had printed at Philadelphia, 1828, a collection of the poems of the Spanish heroic poet Gallego. And on taking up his residence in Havana, Del Monte's house became a center for poetic endeavor.

One of the first poets to receive his encouragement was Ramón Vélez y Herrera (1808–86), who published a little volume of poems in 1833 which attracted attention because it was the first book of poetry printed in Cuba since the *Ocios Poéticos* of Valdés Machuca, in 1819. Vélez y Herrera worked according to an idea which Del Monte suggested in the phrase "cubanizar la poesía." This meant the development of the rude art of the "guajiros," the white country people of Cuba, who, descended from the peasants of Andalusia and Estremadura, preserved the custom at social gatherings of improvising verses on local events. Accordingly Vélez depicted the life of the guajiros, their horse races, cock fights, boating contests, dances, and love affairs. In 1840 he combined a handful of similar poems into a connected narrative, *Elvira de Oquendo o los Amores de una guajira.* This luckless maiden in love with Juan receives his attentions against the wishes of her parents. Juan persuades Elvira to elope. Pursued by her father's retainers, Juan is forced into a fight in which he kills several of them, but he is taken prisoner, tried and executed for murder. Elvira wandering about alone is finally found, but when taken into her father's presence she falls dead. The reader, however, does not feel very poignant grief at the sorrows of the unfortunate pair, because he is being constantly enter-tained by digressions concerning the customs of the country. In 1856 Vélez y Herrera published a new collection of similar poems in his *Romances Cubanos*, but the public was tired of poetic cock fights.

Utilization of popular poetry was also practiced during the thirties, quite independently of Del Monte's influence, by Francisco Poveda y Armenteros, an almost illiterate peon living in the eastern end of the island. In spite of his gift for song, his verses being scattered among various newspapers which had published them over the pen name of "El Trovador Cubano," he would probably have remained in oblivion, had not some enthusiastic young lovers of poetry discovered him when an old man, and to relieve his poverty brought about the production, in 1879, of a sort of drama of his, *El Peón de Bayamo*.

The most popular poet developed in Del Monte's circle was José Jacinto Milanés (1814–63). Though he began to publish verses at the age of twenty-three, his period of literary production was terminated in seven years in 1843 by his becoming insane. He put Del Monte's literary theories into practice by giving his poems a setting amid the tropical beauty of the Cuban landscape. Thus he taught later poets the value of local color. At the same time he believed in making poetry the handmaid of morality. In this respect, especially in his choice of topics, he seems to modern critics to have exceeded the limits of good taste. A third characteristic of his lines was his sentimental melancholy. His most famous poems illustrate these peculiarities.

La Madrugada offers to the poet the beauty of the dawn, but since he has seen a certain beautiful woman, who, however, scorns his advances, he has no eyes for nature because the sight of two doves, two stars, two waves, or two clouds reminds him of his "continual solitude." In *La Fuga de la Tórtola*, the poet laments the flight of his turtle dove and though he approves her passionate longing for liberty, he feels he will die unless she returns. *El Beso* presents the poet sitting beside a beautiful young girl "at night in a cool garden"; the situation inspires him with a desire to kiss her; he goes so far as to seize her hand but is deterred from his intention by the thought that, although his own kiss is pure, another man's kiss might prove her ruination. "I went away in peace, a tear of sweetness bathed my face." *El Expósito*, originally printed in the little periodical, *El Plantel*, made a sensation. A critic objected to the poem on the ground that not all illegitimate children grew up depraved and vicious. Milanés stoutly defended both the logic and the morality of his teaching that an abandoned and illegitimate child could scarcely avoid being a criminal. In *El Mirón Cubano* the author appears as a sort of doctor of morality who offers his advice to those who bring their troubles to him. This poem in dialogue form is a series of observations and criticisms of Milanés' fellow townsmen in the city of Matanzas.

These moral, or philosophical, poems as their author termed them abound in touches descriptive of Cuban life undoubtedly true of the epoch in which they were written. It was even possible for contemporary readers to name the individuals who served as models. The local color and the real musical quality of the lines has made Milanés' poems popular among his countrymen. In the words of Zenea:—"They glide along like the still water."

Milanés also wrote a drama, *El Conde Alarcos*, which aroused enthusiasm among his friends. This is a romantic drama in the manner of the Spaniard García Gutiérrez. The Conde Alarcos, a prisoner of war of the King of France, is allowed, through the influence of the Princess Blanche in love with the count, to revisit his country after pledging his word of honor that he will return. During his visit he is married to a Spanish lady. When, however, the Princess Blanche learns this fact, she is unwilling to give up the count, though he has proved so faithless to the favors she had bestowed on him in his captivity. She persuades her father, the king, to procure the assassination of the innocent wife in order that she may herself marry the count.

Under Del Monte's influence, Milanés wrote a few verses with political significance, but Del Monte's own political writings were in prose. He is perhaps the initiator of the political tract, that form of literature so flourishing in the peculiar circumstances of Cuban life. His most important effort was *La Isla de Cuba tal cual está*. Written in 1836 to refute a pamphlet by a Spaniard, F. Guerra Bethencourt, who praised the condition of the island, Del Monte's tract was an honest protest against the harsh methods of the colonial governor, Miguel Tacón.

It was followed the next year by the famous *Paralelo entre la isla de Cuba y algunas colonias inglesas*, by José Antonio Saco (1797–1879). The main argument of this tract was that a union with Great Britain or the United States would be an advantage to Cuba. The governor

Tacón reported these pamphlets to the government of Spain as the work of "pernicious men."

José Antonio Saco, suffering banishment by order of Tacón, became in a literary way one of the foremost champions of the cause of Cuban independence. In early life he was a brilliant scholar, one of the chief opponents of Felix Varela in the contest for the professorship of public law, and Varela's successor in that chair when the latter went to Spain as Cuban member of the Cortes. In the United States he was Varela's partner in literary enterprises. In 1832, Saco being in Havana, they edited the celebrated *Revista bimestre Cubana*. Regarding the literary merit of this review, George Ticknor, the historian of Spanish letters, wrote to Del Monte under date of April 24th, 1834:—"I have been struck ever since I first began to read the *Revista bimestre Cubana* with the amount of literary talent and accomplishment in your island. Nothing to be compared with it, has, so far as I am informed, ever been exhibited in any of the Spanish colonies and even in some respects, nothing like it is to be seen in Spain. A review of such spirit, variety and power has never been even attempted at Madrid."

The government at Madrid had authorized the establishment in Havana of an Academía de Literatura; but to General Tacón such a society seemed a gathering of malcontents and he forbade it. At the same time he ordered Saco to leave the island. The immediate cause for his expulsion was his attack on African slavery, the source of many evils in Cuba. From his first writings against the slave trade grew a book, *Historia de la Esclavitud*, to which he devoted his leisure for thirty years before its complete publication. Saco returned to Cuba only in 1861, and then merely for a short visit. But he kept in touch with the affairs of the island. When the political situation became acute about 1850, he wrote some of his most famous tracts, and again in 1865 when reforms by Spain seemed imminent he came into public notice. Even after his death extracts from his book on slavery served in the literary fight preparing the successful revolution of 1895. Thus Saco's life and writings correspond to a long epoch in Cuban history.

Before passing on, however, a word must be said about Del Monte's influence on prose literature other than political. "Without doubt Domingo del Monte y Aponte was one of the persons to whom Cuban letters must be most grateful."[1] By example Del Monte tried to demonstrate the literary value of fiction, but in this department he was surpassed by two young men in his circle, Anselmo Suárez y Romero (1818–78) and Cirilo Villaverde (1812–94). Both wrote with the inspiring idea of realistically depicting Cuban life.

Suárez y Romero as the painter of Cuban customs is one of the foremost Cuban writers of prose. By Del Monte's advice he chose to write articles on manners in which he should touch on evils that ought to be corrected. What Milanés was doing in verse Suárez continued in prose. His *Colección de Artículos*, published in 1857, aroused such enthusiasm for its excellent diction that it

[1] D. Figarola Caneda in *Cuba Contemporanea*, Vol. V, 433. To Señor Figarola Caneda, the distinguished librarian of the Cuban national library, Cuban letters are indebted for many literary studies, such as is *Bibliografía de R. Merchán*.

was adopted in the Colegio de San Salvador as a text for lessons in reading. The evil which Suárez mainly attacked was negro slavery. In 1838 appeared his first tale *Francisco*, the dramatic story of a pair of lovers, negro slaves, who for frivolous reasons are forbidden to marry. This act of their wealthy mistress results in much misfortune. When the young woman passes into the possession of the owner's son, Francisco hangs himself. The local color of the whole tale and especially the portrait of the old stage driver was greatly praised by the poet Milanés.

The same theme of African slavery is the basis of Cirilo Villaverde's story *Cecilia Valdés*. On account of its length and its purpose of depicting the whole of Cuban society from the Captain General down to the humble negro it well deserves the name of the first Cuban novel. Cecilia is a beautiful mulattress the daughter of an ignorant and vulgar Spaniard enriched by the slave trade. His legitimate son, Leonardo, ignorant of the blood tie which unites him to Cecilia falls in love with her, successfully baffling his father's efforts to keep them apart. A mulatto, Pimienta, is also in love with Cecilia, who, proud of Leonardo's wooing, scornfully rejects the humble suitor. A day arrives when Leonardo marries a young lady of his own class. Cecilia, mad with jealousy, incites Pimienta to attack the couple on their way to church for the wedding ceremony. Pimienta stabs Leonardo.

This novel, left unfinished by its author in 1839, was completed forty years later. It has been called a photograph of Havana in the thirties, because it minutely relates real events, giving the names of the persons con-

cerned. The Captain General is not spared but appears
in the act of granting an audience at a cockfight to which
sport he is much attached. The guajiro bravo and assassin and the negro Tondá employed by the governor
for underhand enterprises are also types of the period.
The rich slave trader Gamboa who buys a title of nobility
and his spendthrift and worthless son spoiled by an in-
dulgent mother are drawn from life.

The negro problem soon after the period described in
this story, took on extreme significance in Cuban politics.
Connected with this problem was the personal fate of
one of Cuba's leading poets who though a mulatto was
received at Del Monte's tertulias. His execution on suspicion of being a leader in a negro uprising has lent an
additional interest to his poems.

Gabriel de la Concepción Valdés (1809-44), commonly known by his pen name "Plácido" was the son
of a Spanish dancing girl and a mulatto hair dresser.
Following the condition of his mother he was free but
therefore compelled to earn his living. He learned the
trade of making tortoise shell combs. Somebody taught
him to read and his acquaintances loaned him books. A
volume of Martínez de la Rosa's poems incited him to
attempt the composition of verse, whereby he discovered
that he possessed a real gift of song. A druggist, Francisco Plácido Puentes, supplied him with writing materials and an opportunity to write in his store. In return
he selected "Plácido" as a pen name. Some say, however,
that the name was derived from Madame de Genlis'
novel *Plácido y Blanca*. He was introduced into the
circle of Valdés Machuca by Vélez y Herrera. Thus he

became one of the poets who composed the *Aureola Poética* in honor of Martínez de la Rosa. Plácido's contribution, *La Siempreviva*, was considered the best poem in the garland. At any rate the minister wrote a personal letter of thanks to his poor mulatto admirer.

Plácido's earlier poems and perhaps the majority of those in the volume of his collected verses are occasional in character, birthday congratulations, condolences and the like. According to some, he was all too ready to purchase crumbs of favor by reciting at evening parties such verses as he had written for the occasion. Milanés probably referred to him as *El Poeta envilecido* in the lines reproaching an unnamed poet for degrading his art by singing at the magnate's feast "without shame or sense, and disputing a bone with the mastiff." But there is rich grain among the chaff of Plácido's work.

Among the purely lyrical pieces are some letrillas with such fragrant titles as *La Flor del Café*, *La Flor de la Piña*, *La Flor de la Caña*. These alone have carried Plácido's name over Spanish America. They are not descriptive but are little pictures of native life and love making, in which the words of the title serve as a refrain.

Among Plácido's compositions with a historical theme is a remarkable romance, *Xicontencal*, remarkable because the author has quite caught the spirit and movement of the old Spanish ballads. Xicontencal, a young Tlascalan chief who has just triumphed over the warriors of Montezuma, is being carried in a litter through his native city. His eye happens to rest on some Aztec prisoners bound to stakes in preparation for their burning alive. Leaping down, the young chief frees the prisoners, bidding them

return to Mexico with the message that his victories will
not be stained by such cruelties as their monarch prac-
tices, but he is ready to fight him even at the odds of one
to three hundred.

To a talented man in the social position of Gabriel de
la Concepción Valdés, whose very name, according to the
custom of the foundling asylum which had sheltered his
infancy, commemorated the charity of the good bishop
who established the asylum, life must at times have seemed
very bitter. An expression of such feelings can at least
be read into some of his poems. In the beautiful lines on
La Palma y la Malva, the insignificant mallow nestling
in the grass of a lofty hill is full of pride at her position
and speaks with condescension to the palm tree on the
plain below. With head erect the palm replies:—"Do
you consider yourself the greater merely because you
were born in a high place? The place where you happen
to be is great, not you."

His feelings about liberty, expressed with all the ardor
of African blood, are revealed in a sonnet on the death
of the tyrant Gessler. It pictures Tell standing exultant
over the quivering corpse of the tyrant and holding his
bow as a symbol of liberty. More explicit are the poet's
words in verses to the Mexican general, Adolfo de la Flor,
which he is to read on reaching Mexican soil. "Go, yes,
go to the shores where liberty is; and on arriving at the
beach, draw forth my verses, bend your knee and touch
them three times to the earth. Since my ill fortune and
the seas prevent my enjoying the divine essence, may
my songs enjoy it. And when you learn of my death,
send dust moistened with your tears in a litter to some

faithful friend and that shall be the most precious flower with which you can adorn my tomb."

As the author of such verses and a prominent member of the African race it was natural that Plácido should fall under the suspicion of the authorities when, in 1844, they scented a negro uprising. Moreover, he was denounced as the author of certain patriotic lines circulating in manuscript. With ten others he was thrown into prison. After a sort of trial he was condemned to die. He had stoutly defended his innocence of any complicity in sinister plotting and expected eventually to be released. When however the sentence of death was announced to him he replied:—"I shall die singing like the Cuban nightingale." On the way to the place of execution he did recite verses of his own composition. After his death there were put into circulation three fine poems whose excellence combined with the tragic circumstance of his end did more to confer on him the name of real poet than all the remainder of his work.

The shortest is a sonnet, *Despedida a mi Madre*, in which he bids his mother not to grieve, for his lyre utters its last sound to her memory while the mantle of religion covers him. In the *Adiós a mi Lira* he expressed in noble words the consolation which the cultivation of poetry had been to him. His lyre, he declared, will not remain in the dust of a vile prison; he begs God to accept it. He has dreamed of a world of pure glory and justice which men do not understand but angels have seen, that world which he hopes to see within a few hours and then he will praise God that he has departed from this mansion of crimes. The final stanza runs thus: "Farewell, my lyre, commended to God. Farewell! I bless thee! My calm spirit inspired by thee scorns the cruelty of hostile fate. Men will see thee consecrated to-day. God and my last farewell remain with thee, for between God and the tomb one tells no lies. Farewell! I am going to die—I am innocent."

Somewhat shorter, the *Plegaria a Diós* is the most famous of all by reason of its lofty sentiment and artistic form. It was said that Plácido recited this prayer on the way to execution. It has been translated into English.

O God of love unbounded! Lord supreme!
In overwhelming grief to thee I fly.
Rending this veil of hateful calumny,
Oh let thine arm of might my fame redeem!
Wipe thou this foul disgrace from off my brow,
With which the world hath sought to stamp it now.

Thou King of Kings, my fathers' God and mine,
Thou only art my sure and strong defence.
The polar snows, the tropic fires intense,
The shaded sea, the air, the light are thine:
The life of leaves, the water's changeful tide,
All things are thine, and by thy will abide.

Thou art all power; all life from thee goes forth,
And fails or flows obedient to thy breath;
Without thee all is naught; in endless death
All nature sinks forlorn and nothing worth.
Yet even the Void obeys thee; and from naught
By thy dread word the living man was wrought.

Merciful God! How should I thee deceive?
Let thy eternal wisdom search my soul!
Bowed down to earth by falsehood's base control,

Her stainless wings not now the air may cleave.
Send forth thine hosts of truth and set her free!
Stay thou, O Lord, the oppressor's victory!

Forbid it, Lord, by that most free outpouring
Of thine own most precious blood for every brother
Of our lost race, and by thy Holy Mother,
So full of grief, so loving, so adoring,
Who clothed in sorrow followed thee afar,
Weeping thy death like a declining star.

But if this lot thy love ordains to me,
To yield to foes most cruel and unjust,
To die and leave my poor and senseless dust
The scoff and sport of their weak enmity,
Speak Thou, and then Thy purposes fulfill;
Lord of my life, work Thou Thy perfect will.

The three posthumous poems on which Plácido's reputation as a great poet mainly depends, have given rise to
a controversy concerning their authenticity.   Manuel
Sanguily, recently Cuban secretary of state and in early
life an active partisan of Cuban independence, contends
that the poems are apocryphal, basing his belief on the
following arguments.   The poems circulated in manuscript for some time after Plácido's execution.   An eye-
witness to his death testified that the words which the
poet recited on the way to the place of execution were
not those of the *Plegaria*, but of his sonnet, *La Fatalidad*.
Moreover, during the months of his incarceration Plácido
firmly expected to be released, so that certain expressions
in these poems do not ring true.   The *Despedida a mi
madre* implies that she had lost track of her son, whereas,

it is known that mother and son maintained their rela.
tions. Finally there is no tradition respecting the manner
by which the poems were transmitted from the prison.

Sanguily has not, however, revealed the name of the
man who he believes is their author; but he has promised
to do so when his book about Plácido is ready. Sanguily
first advanced his theory in his revolutionary journal
Hojas literarias, in 1893, at a time when a sensational discussion of the famous poet's last hours would direct
attention quite as much to the part played in them by
the Spaniards, and to the political question in general
as it would to the question of fact in literary history.

Plácido's death marks the end of an epoch in Cuban
letters. Succeeding poets with the exception of Ramón
de Palma belong to a younger generation. Ramón de
Palma y Romay (1812–60), though he was a member of
Del Monte's tertulia and joint editor with Echevarría of
El Plantel, followed in his later poems the new fashions.
In using poetry to inculcate morality, Palma showed himself a disciple of Milanés. In the flight of a gull, for example, he could find grandiose thoughts to describe the
journey of the poet through the desert of selfish human
society. That poem of his early period most praised by
his friends was an ode on an epidemic of cholera which
in 1833 ravaged the city of Havana. Against this background he sketched the power of God. The same theme
also served him for a prose tale full of realistic details.
This was not the only tale which he produced, however,
for by profession Palma was a schoolmaster who wrote
continually for the papers both in prose and verse. He
even essayed the drama, and it is said that he was the

first Cuban to have a play staged. In 1837 was produced *La Prueba o la Vuelta del Cruzado*. Ten years later he had the pleasure of listening to an Italian opera troupe in an operetta for which he wrote the libretto. *Una Escena del Descubrimiento de América por Colón*. Of the poems which he wrote in his later period when the whisperings of liberty were beginning to stir in Cuba, the most important was a very excellent translation of Manzoni's famous ode on the death of Napoleon, *Il Cinque Maggio*. On account of his literary activity Palma fell under suspicion of complicity in the troubles of 1852, and suffered imprisonment for a short time.

These troubles were the outcome of the activity of a party which believed that a solution for Cuba's ills lay in the annexation of the island by the United States. The ferocity with which the captain general Leopoldo O'Donnell suppressed the supposed negro insurrection of 1844, spared neither whites nor blacks. Prominent Cubans of all classes fell under suspicion. Even Del Monte, at whose tertulias the negro poets Plácido and Manzano had been welcome was accused. Fortunately at this time he was in Europe where influential friends were able to save him from disgrace. But the stern measures of the government only fanned the flames of discontent.

José Antonio Saco from his safe retreat in the United States sent many tracts to Cuba. He had modified somewhat his earlier views and demanded, in case Spain refused to grant reforms, absolute independence for Cuba. In his *Ideas sobre la incorporación de Cuba en los Estados Unidos*, 1848, he opposed the annexationists on the ground that immigration from the United States would bring about a gradual disappearance of Cuban nationality. His *Situación de Cuba y su remedio*, 1851, showed the necessity of granting to Cuba an ample degree of liberty; in default of which Spain would lose the island. He set forth these alternatives in the eloquent *O España concede a Cuba derechos políticos o Cuba se pierde para España*. This essay is now the classic example of Cuban political literature.

The annexationist party found it an easy matter· to arouse popular enthusiasm in their favor throughout the United States. Besides, Southern politicians believed that the annexation of Cuba would provide more slave territory. In the island, Narciso López, a native of Venezuela, who had been a general in Spain in the Carlist war, was fired by the ambition of becoming the liberator of Cuba. For that purpose he came to the United States and organized two filibustering expeditions. The first failed through the interference of the government of the United States. Despite its activities López found little difficulty in securing in several cities parties of adventurers. It is noteworthy that they enrolled under a flag with three blue and two white stripes, at the top of which was a red field bearing a single white star, the present emblem of free Cuba. López' second expedition sailed from New Orleans, August 3d, 1851. On reaching the Cuban coast, his steamer ran aground about sixteen miles from Havana. Though López and the main body of filibusters succeeded in gaining the mountains, an American colonel Crittenden and fifty others in charge of the equipment were captured by Spanish soldiers, taken to

Havana and shot in the public square. López himself somewhat later suffered a like fate.

Political agitation in the United States for the purchase of Cuba from Spain nevertheless continued. Bills were introduced into Congress appropriating money for that purpose though without success. Spain's attitude was well expressed by a Spanish minister who frankly told Americans who broached the subject that he believed it to be the feeling of his country that sooner than see the island transferred to any power they would prefer seeing it sunk in the ocean. In 1854 James Buchanan, then minister to Great Britain, met the American ministers to France and Spain, and together they formulated and issued a remarkable document known as the "Ostend Manifesto" in which they declared that "from the peculiarity of its geographical position Cuba is as necessary to the North American republic as any of its present members." Buchanan when president continually urged in his annual messages the purchase of the island. And in the presidential campaign of 1860, one slogan of the Democrats was "Cuba must be ours."

In Cuba, however, there was little enthusiasm at the idea of annexation, a fact which is sometimes given as the cause of López' complete failure. The contribution to Cuban psychology made by Saco's writings in propagating the ideal of a Cuban state is the most that came of the agitation of these years. For a decade the young men wrote verses with a minimum of political significance. And during the fifties there was a second flourishing period of Cuban poetry.

The year 1853 witnessed the publication of an attractive collection of poems by four writers, in a volume entitled *Cuatro Laúdes*, by name Ramón Zambrana, J. G. Roldán, R. M. de Mendive and Felipe López de Briñas. The first was a man of great culture and taste, a physician by profession, and a professor of the natural sciences who wrote much on his professional studies. As a poet Dr. Ramón Zambrana (1817–83), acknowledged Del Monte as his "master in literature" during his student days. To Del Monte he dedicated a volume of his poems which he says "are stamped by Del Monte's approval" having been read and criticised by the latter shortly before his death. The poems belong to the metaphysical type and deal with abstractions, the mystery of existence, light and harmony, or the creation. If he dwells on the beauties of nature it is for the purpose of drawing an allegory as in the tender lines of *La Azucena y el Agua*. The water addressing the lily laments that the most beautiful flower on her course should be surrounded by brambles. The sympathetic personality of the man is here revealed. His popularity due to his character was somewhat enhanced by his romantic marriage to the poetess, Doña Luisa Pérez (born 1837), and her agreeable qualities. Their acquaintance began through the reading of her first little volume of verses, which she published at the age of nineteen. After correspondence with her, for she lived at the eastern end of Cuba, he paid a visit which resulted in their marriage, 1858.

The freshness of her poems, redolent of the fields and the country, must have delighted him. His own poems have nothing so fragrant as *El Lirio*. The poetess feigns to have discovered a lily beside a stream running through a valley paved with green, whither she betakes herself daily to attend the treasure. Perhaps his own little allegory on the lily may have been suggested by her lines and refer to her personally.

José Gonzalo Roldán (1822–56) essayed unsuccessfully the elevated style. In a softer mood, however, he wrote a most charming little poem, *El Aguacero;* charming for its tender delicacy of suggestion in rendering the situation and the setting. The poet explains to a trembling country girl that the storm which frightens her is only a passing shower; he invites her to keep her clothing dry by coming under shelter and tries to calm her agitation by calling her attention to the phenomena accompanying the rain and to the sweet odors from the vegetation.

Nature in various moods as reflected in the sentimental spirit of the poet furnished the matter for the other two contributors to *Cuatro Laúdes*. In florid language, Felipe López de Briñas (1822–77) sought to render the music of the woods in *La Música del Bosque* or the sentiments inspired by the dawn, *El Amanecer*. His best piece, *Canto sáfico*, was addressed to his wife whom he calls in the opening line "Chaste dove." He bids her awake because the morning calls him to his daily task and pray for him. At work he is cheered by thinking of her. If men should refuse him assistance he would take her into the beautiful woods where they would live apart from men on the bounties of Providence.

Of more sustained inspiration was Rafael María de Mendive (1821–86). Yet the verdict of a Cuban critic, "Mendive's lyre has but one string," has long been considered a just characterization of his sentimental and melancholy poetry. His first volume of verse appeared in 1847 with the title *Pasionarias.* Its contents so pleased our poet Longfellow that he sent an inscribed copy of his own poems to the Cuban bard. Shortly after, Mendive went to Europe by way of the United States and during his four years there he made the acquaintance of prominent men in France, Spain and Italy. He returned to Cuba possessed of a love of letters and eager to be of service to his native island. Thus he not only published the collection of poems, *Cuatro Laúdes,* but in 1853 with Quintiliano García founded a fortnightly, *Revista de la Habana.* This magazine was ambitious in its scope and became the medium of publication for a group of young writers. In respect to its importance and his influence a Cuban has said, "After Del Monte, Mendive is the man who has done most to prevent the dying out of enthusiasm for art among us."

His enthusiasm for poetic art led Mendive to make many metrical translations. His rendering of Byron's song beginning,

> I saw thee weep—the big bright tear
> Came o'er that eye of blue;
> And then methought it did appear
> A violet dropping dew,

has long been a favorite with Cuban lovers. His versions of Tom Moore's *Irish Melodies* earned for him the sobriquet of the Cuban Moore. He also arranged for the stage *Gulnara,* an operatic version of Byron's *Corsair.* Original dramatic efforts of his which he made for his mother-in-law's theater have been forgotten.

In this theater occurred an incident which led to Mendive's banishment from Cuba. When the revolution of 1868 broke out Mendive was the principal of a school for boys in Havana. In January of the following year there was a popular demonstration of an unusual sort in protest against a tyrannical proclamation of a Spanish general. The performance of a certain comedy in the theater Villanueva was attended by groups of women with their hair flowing loose and attired in garments of white and blue bespangled with stars, thus suggesting the Cuban revolutionary colors. Rioting and bloodshed resulted. Mendive was arrested by the authorities as the instigatoɪ of this picturesque protest and deported to Spain for four years' imprisonment. There, however, literary acquaintances succeeded in procuring his release. He recrossed the Atlantic and settled in New York where he lived in great poverty till permitted by the general amnesty at the close of the revolution to return to Cuba.

During these years he made use, however, of his poetic gifts to encourage the revolution. When his son had departed on the ill-fated filibustering steamer "Virginius," he wrote those lines with the refrain,

> Has hecho bien, hijo mío,
> has hecho muy bien en ir
> a donde el honor te llama
> por la patria a combatir.[1]

lines in which like a father who has cheerfully given his own son for the cause, he strove to stimulate to patriotic action other Cubans living at ease in New York. An even

[1] Thou hast done well, my son, thou hast done very well to go where honor calls thee to fight for thy country.

seVerer flagellation of unpatriotic Cubans was his poem
Los Dormidos, "these slaves of pleasure who patiently
endure the whip on their shoulders and fetters on their
feet." If they will not bestir themselves, "let them sleep
on till the avenging bolt of celestial anger surprises them."

Mendive's work as a poet, however, is more essentially
that of a lover of nature in whom its beauties inspire a
train of moral or melancholy suggestions. The favorite
A un Arroyo is of this sort. Another favorite poem, *La
Gota de Rocío*, exemplifies the delicacy of his fancy. How
beautiful, the poet exclaims, is a drop of dew; whether it
be on the feather of a bird or on the petal of a flower,
whether on any of the trees of the forest or gliding among
the roses. Perhaps it is an angel's tear. After his death
the mysterious light of a drop of dew will illumine his name
on his tombstone. Some thirsty bird will view it with
rapture, a poet's tear shining on the marble. Mendive's
tenderness is exhibited in his *Sonrisa de la Virgen*, of
which there exists this metrical translation ascribed to
Longfellow:

> Purer than the early breeze,
> Or the faint perfume of flowers,
> Maiden! through thine angel hours
>   Pass the thoughts of love;
> Purer than the tender light
> On the morning's gentle face,
> On thy lips of maiden grace
>   Plays thy virgin smile!
>
> Like a bird's thy rapture is,
> Angel eyes thine eyes enlighten,
> On thy gracious forehead brighten
>   Flashes from above;

Flower-like thy breathings are,
Free thy dreams from sinful strife,
And the sunlight of thy life
    Is thy virgin smile!

Loose thou never, gentle child,
Thy spring garland from thy brow,
Through life's flowery fields, as now,
    Wander careless still;
Sweetly sing and gaily run,
Drinking in the morning air,
Free and happy everywhere,
    With thy virgin smile!

Love and pleasure are but pains,
Bitter grief and miseries,
Withered leaves, which every breeze
    Tosses at its will;
Live thou purely with thy joy,
With thy wonder and thy peace,
Blessing life, till life shall cease,
    With thy virgin smile!

A new type of poetry was introduced into Cuba by
José Fornaris (1829–1890) and became so popular that
books of verse sold by thousands in Cuba. Bethinking
himself of the aborigines of his native island, he sang:—

The memory of the sunburnt maids,
With slender forms and soft black een,
Who dwelt by murmuring cascades
Beneath an arch of leafy green:
Of stories of other witching days,
Caught by surprise at the Caonao,
Beside Bayamo as it plays,
Or in the pure waters of Arimao.

Fornaris' *Cantos de Siboney* are a series of legends partly traditional but in large measure imaginary. Some are conversations between lovers, as the one entitled *Eliana y Guanarí* in which the maiden is reluctant to leave her home but at last yields to her lover's persuasions to live in the beautiful valley of Yumurí. The *Cacique de Ornofay* is revealed to us disputing with Columbus. The discoverer invites him to see the splendors of Spain and the Spanish court, but the Indian chief refuses to believe that anything more beautiful in this world than his woodland home exists. At last the European concurs in that opinion. The legend of the *Laguna de Ana Luisa* explains the origin of a pool thus named. An Indian maid with the Christian name Ana Luisa prefers a member of the Siboney tribe to a Carib. The latter does not observe with as much pleasure as the reader of the poem their wooing among the flowers but steals treacherously upon them. With an arrow he slays his rival; then seizes the bride. But the river rising in wild indignation, overwhelms the criminal and buries in its waters the bodies of all three. The pool so formed still remains. On its banks by night the ghost of Ana Luisa bewails her fate. These poems are written with the utmost ease and simplicity of style. The author seemed to be able to turn out an illimitable quantity.

His contemporaries held diverse opinions about their value. Dr. Zambrana was enthusiastic over the "new genre, because it leaves the beaten path." On the other hand, the poet's enemies pointed out that his local color did not agree with history; that he made no effort to depict manners and customs; that his Indians made love and were jealous in the conventional style; that, apart from the Indian canoes or piraguas and numerous names of places and persons, his verses differed little from anybody else's. Moreover, in the actual ethical composition of the Cuban people, the Indian element was entirely lacking. The many names ending in two vowels were a topic for sport. Probably the worst that can be truthfully said is that the extreme facility which he possessed in composing verses enticed him to write too many.

He should not be blamed for the excesses of his imitators, however, the most notable of whom, Juan Cristóbal Nápoles Fajardo (born 1829), "El Cuculambe" enjoyed considerable reputation at the eastern end of Cuba. His volume *Rumores del Hormigo*, 1857, piles up the Indian names in the descriptions of their love affairs. But he was more successful in giving literary form to the popular poetry and songs of the people among whom he lived, in both essential qualities of local color and truth. He excelled his master Fornaris as a painter of customs and the beauties of nature.

Miguel Teurbe de Tolón (1820–58), without being an imitator of Fornaris, was at least stimulated by his example to bring out in 1856 a little volume entitled *Romances Cubanos* in which he strove to live up to his doctrine that the "Cuban ballad was the true road to emancipation for our literature." Unfortunately he had very little popular history to work on, so that his ballads contain little that is realistic beyond the cockfights of the countrymen and their incorrect language. His bandits are not very attractive. On the other hand, some poems of personal inspiration are pleasing, because he wrote from experience. He lived an exile from Cuba for many years as secretary of the Cuban revolutionary junta in New York. He wrote for newspapers in both Spanish and English, so that versions of his poems exist in both languages. He even prepared a textbook for the study of Spanish. The notes of inspiration in his poems are love for his mother, for Emilia and for his distant native land, whose political freedom he ardently desired.

Among the poems of permanent value which were first printed in the *Revista de la Habana* should be mentioned *La Caída de Misolonghi* by Joaquín Lorenzo Luaces (1826–67). This begins with the clarion call,

> Revenge, oh Greeks! Misolonghi in ruins
> To Ibrahim fell with all her brave;
> Let the Moslem find within her walls
> The Greek a corpse but never a slave!

The quatrain is repeated after each octave in which the poet urges patriots to hasten to battle with the tyrants and to shed their blood for their wives and their homes. What is the life of a Greek? Slow death and infamous slavery in which he licks the chain that binds him. Such language, since it was applied to faraway Greeks, was permitted by the Spanish censor to appear in print; but as Rafael Merchán remarks, the poem "has never been Greek to the Cubans."

Luaces, having studied Greek, took for his model the Pindaric ode. Moreover, he was willing to polish his diction till he made a good imitation. For that reason perhaps, he lacks the spontaneity of either Heredia or Plácido but everybody is willing with Menéndez y Pelayo to concede him the third place in the Cuban Parnassus. In his symbolism, in his care for form, in his wealth of imagery, as in the exquisite sonnet *La Salida del Cafetal*, he is par excellence an artist.

Beside the odes in which he concealed his love of liberty, under foreign names, he wrote one to Cyrus Field, 1859, upon completion of the laying of the transatlantic cable. The language and the sentiments are as noble as his subject. Field is placed among the great heroes of mankind. While Alexander and Cæsar won their laurels by bloodshed, Field has achieved his glory by uniting peoples of different race. If Columbus overcame space and opened America, if Fulton with his steamboat has hastened the flight of time, Field has dominated both space and time. Mankind should honor him to the utmost and his fame should be perpetuated forever.

In imitation of Milanés' moral poems, Luaces wrote several, the best of which is *La Vida*. But they do not contribute so much to his reputation as his dramas wherein perhaps he also followed the older poet's example. Taken from his favorite Greek history, he wrote *Aristodemo*. More in the romantic style is *El Mendigo Rojo*, the dramatization of an incident in the legend of the Scotch king James IV. The legend held that the king was not killed at Flodden Field but, disguised as a beggar and assisted by his bastard son John, he wandered about his kingdom. The situation is very similar to that in Zorrilla's drama, *Traidor, inconfeso y mártir*. Another play, *Arturo de Osberg*, as well as a long poem in three cantos of epic character on Cuba is said to have been left among Luaces' papers. His fame however is quite secure without these.

In the year 1860 there occurred an event which stirred

the Cuban literary world to its depths. Cuba's most
renowned daughter, "La Avellaneda," after twenty years
of literary triumphs abroad, returned for a brief sojourn.
Doña Gertrudis Gómez de Avellaneda, in the words of
Enrique Piñeyro, "is considered (nemine discrepante) as
the foremost of all women who have written verses in the
Castilian language." Her career, however, belongs wholly
to the literary history of Spain and, except for the enthusiasm and pride which it inspired, had little influence
in the island. But her admirers gave her on this occasion
a royal welcome. Her play, *La Hija de las Flores*, the
scene of which is laid in the Antilles, was produced in the
theater. The Liceo Habanero voted her a civic crown and
appointed to put it on her head their resident poetess, Doña
Luisa Pérez de Zambrana.

Doña Gertrudis Gómez de Avellaneda (1814–73) left
her Cuban home in Camagüey at the age of twenty-two
in order to accompany to Spain her mother who had
married a colonel in the Spanish army. In 1839 she published in Cádiz her first volume of verses. Arriving in
Madrid in 1840 where her poems had already made her
known she soon became an important figure in literary
circles. Though she continued to write verses which displayed a union of the classic tradition with the best features
of the Byronic romanticism, she made her mark on the
Spanish theater with a succession of dramas of great merit.
More numerous were her prose tales, some of which were
long enough to be classed as novels. The first of these in
point of time, *Sab*, having for its chief character a mulatto
slave contained a protest against slavery. Of her poems
a few had Cuban inspiration, *La Estrella de Occidente*, a

sonnet expressing her farewell to Cuba, *A la muerte de Heredia*, an elegy, and other lines which showed that her heart always beat with love for the country of her birth.

In as great degree as she met success in literary endeavor was she unfortunate in love.   The first man with whom, to judge from her published correspondence she fell in love, but did not marry, proved cold and indifferent, perhaps overwhelmed by her superior intelligence.   Her first husband lived less than a year after their marriage.   Her second husband was attacked by a political enemy and stabbed.   And it was for the purpose of seeking an improvement in his health that they came to Havana in 1860.   But as he died after a few months, she returned to Spain. For her troubles she sought consolation in religion.   Consequently the tone of her poems is eminently religious in spite of the passionate robustness of her lines on historical topics.   Her dramatic masterpiece, *Baltasar*, embodying the well-known biblical incident of the writing on the wall at Belshazzar's feast, and her less effective tragedy *Saul*, show the same tendencies.

Poetical activity during the early sixties was fostered by Nicolás Azcárate (1828–94).   Like Del Monte he aspired to be the patron of Cuban literature by inviting poets to read their compositions at evening parties in his home.   And he published some of their effusions in an elegant volume, *Noches literarias en casa de Nicolás Azcárate*.   Moreover, he assisted needy poets financially. To Mendive he gave the principalship of a secondary school which Azcárate founded at his own expense.   In Saturnino Martínez, a youthful poet, Azcárate thought he had discovered a genius; but in spite of the magnate's assistance Martínez never became more than a weak disciple of Fornaris. At a later date when Azcárate's own fortune had considerably dwindled he still had sufficient influence to launch a subscription amounting finally to $22,000 for the widow and children of Dr. Zambrana.

Azcárate's fortune was derived from a very successful practice as an influential lawyer famed for his oratorical ability. In politics he was a reformer rather than a separatist. In 1865 discontent in Cuba becoming very great, the Spanish minister for the colonies, Antonio Cánovas del Castillo, agreed to listen to a request for reforms. On this mission Azcárate went to Spain as a member of the "Junta de Información" of which the veteran J. A. Saco was also a member. Little came of these efforts though Azcárate even founded at his own expense a newspaper, *La Voz del Siglo*, to awaken public opinion in favor of reforms in the conduct of Cuban affairs. In Cuba discontent continued to rise like the tide till it broke against the bar of official indifference and became open rebellion. Azcárate, however, maintained his attitude as a reformer so that on his return to Havana he was unable to regain either his popularity or his legal practice. His fortune of over a hundred thousand dollars having been spent it was necessary for him in his last years to earn his living as a government clerk.

One of the forces which prepared the revolutionary outbreak in Cuba was undoubtedly the type of education which the future leaders were receiving in their youth at the Colegio de El Salvador. This school was opened and maintained by a farsighted sagacious man to whom education was a passion, José de la Luz y Caballero (1800-

62). Opened in 1848 for boys over twelve years of age, the school became immensely popular among the Cubans but not with the Spanish authorities who asserted that the director "was preparing the boys for conspiracy and the scaffold." Later they termed Luz "the patriarch of the Cuban revolution." But his pupils insisted that "Don Pepe," as they affectionately called their principal, never discoursed on politics. His influence had its strength in weekly lessons on morals which he gave the boys. He preached to them the virtue of manly energy, of firm resistance to every form of oppression and injustice, of self-sacrifice on the altar of duty. The Spaniards were probably right in seeing in this teaching a symbolism not unlike that which characterized the poems of Luaces when he sang the patriotism of Greeks and Poles. At any rate the leaders in the demand for independence testify to the value of the training they received. And regarding Luz y Caballero the Cubans declare that, "with Felix Varela he created in philosophy a local tradition which is one of the constituent elements of Cuban psychology."

José de la Luz did not live to see the outbreak of the great struggle which lasted for ten years. The signal for the revolt, since known as "el grito de Yara," was given at Yara in the eastern end of the island by a wealthy planter, Carlos Manuel de Céspedes (1819–74), on October 10th, 1868. His demands were for a recognition by Spain of equal rights for creoles and peninsulars, the abolition of slavery with compensation for owners and the grant of universal suffrage. Long before the end of the war Céspedes was killed. In 1878 hostilities were terminated by a grant of general amnesty and a promise of a large measure of reforms in an agreement called the "pacto de Zanjón."

The poet of this revolution, one of the foremost Cuban lyrists, was Juan Clemente Zenea (1832–71). Not only did he supply the symbolic poem suggesting the condition of Cuba but for his active participation in affairs he was unjustly executed. The pathetic verses written during his imprisonment and published after his death became a monument to his memory.

Zenea was born in Bayamo, the son of a native Cuban officer in the Spanish army, and Celestina Fornaris, older sister of the poet who sang the aboriginal Siboneyes. He was educated in that hotbed of conspiracy, the school directed by José de la Luz. At seventeen he began to write for the newspapers of Havana under the pen name of "Adolfo de la Azucena." At twenty he emigrated in haste because he was implicated in the publication of a revolutionary journal which the authorities saw fit to suppress. After arriving in New York he continued to write seditious articles. The impetuous youth sent one of these with his personal compliments to the Captain General of Cuba, "thus insulting in the person of this authority the whole Spanish nation," according to the words of the decree of the council of war in Havana which on December 6th, 1853, condemned Zenea to death. Such a decree had probably for its real purpose the discouragement of the Cuban revolutionary junta then active in the United States. Two years later under the terms of the amnesty proclaimed by the new governor of Cuba, Zenea returned to Havana. Here he began to support himself by private teaching of French and English and by occasional journalistic work in prose and verse.

In 1860 he put forth a modest collection of his poems in a volume with the title, *Cantos de la Tarde*. The opening poem, *Fidelia*, immediately sprang into such popularity that the name became almost a sobriquet of the author. Curiosity as to whether the incidents constituted a real love story or an allegory lent it additional interest. A legend sprang up in Havana that "Fidelia" was a personification of Cuba. But there exists in Zenea's prose writings a passage that seems to contradict such an idea, at least in so far as it was his conscious purpose to write an allegory. The poem served, however, as a symbolic and pathetic picture of Cuba to those patriots who chose to regard it in that light.

Very tenderly, in a manner reminiscent of De Musset, the poem opens with a relation of the vow which the poet and Fidelia made to love each other forever. Circumstances separated them and he departed to foreign lands. Returning after ten years he found Fidelia a corpse. From the first hint of disaster which the refrain,

> Yo estoy triste y tú estás muerta!

introduces into the first love scene, the pathetic note swells to a finale of despairing melancholy.

The other poems in the *Cantos de la Tarde* are written with the same elegiac tone though not with the same perfection of form. As Rafael Merchán says, "they are the echo as much of his own heart as of the distress of the period."

In 1865 Zenea again went to New York to engage in

a business enterprise. That failing, he departed for Mexico where he wrote for the daily papers. Hearing in 1868 of the outbreak of the insurrection under Céspedes the ardent patriot hastened to New York to join the literary forces of the newly proclaimed Republic of Cuba and became an editor of *La Revolución*. In 1870 the Spanish minister was induced to make secret overtures to President Céspedes who was then successfully maintaining his forces against the attacks of the Spanish soldiers. Zenea against the advice of his friends volunteered to be the bearer of the message because he placed confidence in a safe-conduct given him by the Spanish minister in Washington. He landed safely, visited Céspedes, and had returned to the coast when he was surprised by a Spanish patrol. Had it not been for the safe-conduct, the messages and a sum of money in gold in his possession, he would have been immediately executed. However, he was sent to Havana where he was placed in the fortress la Cabaña. When news of his confinement reached Madrid an order to release him was telegraphed to the Captain General, Conde de Valmaseda. That official, alleging incriminating circumstances, paid no heed to the order. Moreover, he protracted the investigations for eight months until a crisis in the Spanish ministry occurred. Then a hastily conducted court-martial condemned Zenea to death. He was executed August 25, 1871. This barbarous deed of Valmaseda's cost Spain twenty-five thousand dollars in indemnity to Zenea's widow.

In the edition of Zenea's poems which his boyhood friend, Enrique Piñeyro, brought out in New York, the editor grouped four compositions under the heading *En*

Días de Esclavitud. He considered them to offer an adequate idea of the man, the poet, and the patriot. The
first part reveals Zenea's feelings upon leaving Havana,
in 1865, where conditions made life unbearable. The
second part, composed of earlier poems with the title
Nocturno resembles in its pessimistic note his model De
Musset. Then comes the beautiful hymn to the ocean
which vies with, if it does not surpass, Heredia's. Zenea
emphasizes the long period of time in which no ship sailed
over the surface of the ocean and then demands why it
did not pour forth its anger and drag into its depths the
first Spanish caravels. The final section, written during
the voyage to New York, terminates with a vision of a
free Cuba when "a victorious people salutes the flag with
the single star."

After Zenea's execution there were published in Madrid
the poems which he wrote in prison. Composed to while
away the tedium of existence they form a remarkable
human document, a record of trifling events as they
affected a sensitive mind. The title of the first poem,
El 15 de enero en mi prisión, refers to the anniversary of
his marriage, formerly such a happy day but now, just
as the storm overtakes the mariner sailing smoothly along,
so disaster has come upon him and his family. The place
of his confinement was open on one side to the sky so that
one day he was able to see a swallow as it flitted back and
forth. To the swallow then he committed a message to
his wife and daughter with the wish that he too might fly
northward.

His thoughts recurred so often to his daughter Piedad,
that not only did he inscribe her name in several places

on the walls of his cell but he mentioned her in a majority of these dozen poems. One day he recollects the story books which she used to read. Another day he promises that, if anybody will have pity on his poor orphan child, he will come from his tomb and thank him. Again he explains to his wife why he did not say good-bye to the child when he left home; so he requests her to tell the little girl that he had gone away thus for the sake of not seeing her cry, but later he would embrace her in heaven.

His wife Zenea addresses more directly in poems which concern the happiness of former days. One evening a ray of moonlight straggled into his cell. He remembers wandering with his adored and listening with her on many similar nights to the song of the nightingale without a presentiment of such dreadful change. Another evening echoes of a woman's voice singing in the apartments of the prison commander floated to his ears. He knows that song. "Do you remember," he asks his wife, "how once at the piano you told me in the same words the mysteries of the soul?" Finally he bids his wife meet him in heaven. "Do not forget me!" he cries; and he warns her that if she fails to pray God for his soul, his ghost will return to beseech her not to forget him but to remember him night and day.

The ablest journalistic champion of the revolution of 1868 was Rafael Merchán (1844–1905). From an article of his with the caption *Laboremus* was derived the name "laborante" commonly applied, at first by the Spaniards, to the Cuban revolutionaries. In Cuba a "comité laborante" directed the affairs of the revolution. In the United States a "sociedad de laborantes cubanos" was organized in many cities.   Periodicals entitled *El Laborante* came into existence in Cuba and Santo Domingo.   And a defense of the insurrectionists in the form of a novel was published in 1872 with the title *Escenas de la Revolución de Cuba: Los Laborantes* by "H. Goodman."   Its author who thus concealed his name is unknown.

Merchán, under sentence of death by the Spanish authorities, found refuge in New York where he edited the journal *La Revolución* in 1871.   In the same year he put forth an important pamphlet on the situation, *La Honra de España en Cuba.*   Three years later he was invited to go to Colombia, his father's birthplace, to act as secretary of a railroad company.   In Bogotá he continued to live for many years and became a prominent figure there in the world of letters.   His critical articles on literature, his prose version of Longfellow's *Evangeline,* and his poems of a metaphysical character made his name widely known. Nor did he forget his beloved Cuba, for he strove constantly with his pen to influence in her favor the public opinion of the rest of Spanish America.

In 1890 when the Cuban question was again becoming acute even the leading Spanish review, *España Moderna,* opened its pages to Merchán's articles.   His point of view that "we make war because we desire to be independent, not because we hate Spaniards" seemed at least reasonable to open-minded men in Spain.   When the revolution came in 1895, Merchán wrote several pamphlets in justification of the Cuban cause which were translated and published in London and New York for the purpose of influencing public opinion.

When independence was won the Cuban Republic remembered Merchán's services by sending him as her ambassador to France and Spain in 1902. Unfortunately his health, undermined by hard work, was unequal to the strain and he had to come home to die after a short period. Cuba provided his widow with a pension.

Another literary champion of the revolution was Enrique Piñeyro (1839-1911). In his school days he was a favorite pupil of Luz y Caballero who had such faith in his ability that he left him money by will to enable him to pursue his studies in Europe. And it has been said that for his complete assimilation of the spirit of that educator Piñeyro has a right to be considered as the typical pupil, the glory of his school.

Piñeyro's reputation in the future will rest on his many excellent essays in literary history, but as a revolutionary his activity consisted in the practice of delivering lectures to groups of Cuban refugees. To the *Revista cubana* he contributed articles combining literary history with biography from which the reader could derive by the inspiration of example fresh determination and patriotic resolve.

His most important work of this sort was a biographical account of José Morales Lemus (1808-70). This man established, 1863, in Havana a newspaper, *El Siglo*, which espoused the cause of reforms in Cuba. A reform party very soon sprung up to which the Spanish government paid enough heed to call a conference with representative Cubans, since known as the "junta de información." Morales Lemus, Azcárate and the venerable Saco were elected among others as members of the junta to speak for the island. As nothing came of these efforts Morales

Lemus returned to Cuba greatly disappointed. Instead of reforms the Spanish government levied a new and heavy income tax which increased the discontent. The conspiracies and uprisings in Spain itself possibly acted by suggestion in 1868 to start the flame in Cuba. Morales Lemus left the island to take up his residence in New York and Washington. When the Cuban insurrectionists established a provisional government, their president, Céspedes, appointed Morales Lemus envoy plenipotentiary to the new American administration of General Grant. American public opinion was so favorably inclined toward Cuban aspirations for independence that the House of Representatives passed a resolution recognizing the Cuban rebels as belligerents. In the summer of 1869 President Grant appointed Daniel E. Sickles a special commissioner to Spain to propose a plan, which Morales Lemus had had a part in formulating, to the effect that Spain should grant Cuba independence in return for a large indemnity to be paid by Cuba under the guarantee of the United States. The Spanish government, however, was able to protract the diplomatic maneuvers until the matter fell through. Moreover, Morales Lemus' special friend in Grant's cabinet, General Rawlins, Secretary of War, died in September. Hamilton Fish, Secretary of State, was afraid of possible hostilities with Spain and paid no further attention to the Cuban envoy, and in June of the following year Morales Lemus died.

The spiritual aid of such biographies as this appears to have been great. And the short biography was Piñeyro's specialty. In putting before the Cubans the lives of their heroic fellow countrymen and of other persons who fought

Spain like San Martín and Bolívar, he performed an important service to the cause of Cuban independence. During his later years he lived mainly in Paris and wrote on topics connected with literary history, such as his excellent *Romanticismo en España.* Whatever Piñeyro has written is worth reading, not only for the scholarly care for truth and fullness of detail which he displays, but also for the sobriety, terseness and interest of his style.

The ten years' war having been brought to an end by the pact of Zanjón and a general amnesty declared by the Captain General Arsenio Martínez Campos, peace prevailed in Cuba. The literary production of the next few years may be followed in the *Revista de Cuba*, established by José Antonio Cortina in 1877 with the avowed intention of "keeping free from party quarrels and aspiring to reflect in its pages the intellectual movement of this island." Though Cortina was a patriot who had suffered imprisonment in 1869 for printing an address by Antonio Bachiller y Morales, he rightly concluded that the time was a period for recuperation. In his review consequently appeared nothing which reflected on Spanish rule. As Cortina was a man of literary good taste the influence which he exercised on the contributors who met at evening for the reading and discussion of prospective articles and poems was pronounced.

The poetry at this time, as generally in the Spanish-speaking world, was influenced by the Germanistic spirit. In Cuba the brothers Antonio Sellén (1840–88) and Francisco Sellén (1838–1907) wrote a multitude of verses both original and translations. Francisco Sellén had been sent by the Spanish authorities to Spain as a prisoner for taking part in the insurrection. He escaped from prison, however, and found refuge for a while in Germany. When he returned to America he brought with him translations of German poets which he published as *Ecos del Rin*. Later he made metrical translations of such diverse works as Goethe's *Faust*, Heine's *Intermezzo lírico* and Byron's *Giaour*, of which the last two appeared in the *Revista Cubana*. His numerous original poems evinced a love of tropic nature with a strain of pessimism toward life which rang true in certain patriotic lines. His greatest effort was *Hatuey*, a dramatic poem vying with Fornaris' *Cantos de Siboney* in depicting aboriginal life. For a time Francisco Sellén's copiousness made him the leading Cuban poet, but his popularity soon suffered eclipse.

The special form of poem known by the German name of "lied," which had been introduced into Spanish literature through imitation of Heine and Gustavo Becquer, appealed to Cuban poets and was successfully practiced by a group of young men composed of Estéban Borrero Echeverría, José Varela, Aurelio Mityans, Diego Vicente Tejera, and Enrique J. Varona. They took full advantage of the fact that the anecdotal character of the lied lent itself to the presentation of stirring tales from revolutionary history.

Aurelio Mityans (1863–89) as a measure of precaution concealed his identity by signing his pictures of pitiable sufferings from Spanish outrages "El Camagueyano." As a student of Cuban literature he had in preparation at the time of his premature death a book which his friends published in spite of its fragmentary condition as *Estudio sobre el movimiento científico y literario de Cuba*, 1890.

Diego Vicente Tejera (1848–1903) excelled in rendering the tropical Cuban landscape flooded with sunlight, suggestive of the noonday siesta in the shade of a rustic hut. His best descriptive pieces, *En la Hamaca* and *El Despertar de Cuba*, were written as memories of home during his campaigning in Venezuela with the party in rebellion against Guzmán Blanco. His love lyrics in imitation of Heine to the collection of which he gave the name *Un Ramo de Violetas*, were printed in 1878. His original "lieder," narratives in rhyme, were intended to inspire sympathy for those Cubans who fought against Spanish authority. He translated the verses of a Hungarian poet with the title of *Cuentos Madgiares* because the conditions of the Hungarian rebels described in them applied to Cuba. In other poems, *La Muerte de Plácido*, *Al Ideal de la Independencia de Cuba*, *La Estrella solitaria*, the patriotic appeal was more direct, and reached a climax in *Esperando*, 1890. In this poem beginning "Yacen allí . . ." the dead who have already given their lives for Cuban independence are represented as lying impatient in their graves, impatient to hear the echoes of a new struggle and the triumphant cheers of a people who have won their freedom.

At the time of the revolution of 1895 Tejera was active among the Cuban refugees in the United States trying to organize a socialist party. The failure of this effort cut him off from the group of men who led the revolution and the reward which its success brought to men like his former associate Enrique José Varona (b. 1849) vice-president of the Cuban Republic, 1912–16.

Enrique José Varona's most important poems were printed 1879 in a volume whose title, *Paisajes cubanos*, is descriptive of the nature of the contents. The poems range in character from the poetic narration of episodes in the ten years' war to symbolistic lines on Cuba. *Dos Voces en la Sombra*, for example, is a dialogue between the poet and the soul of Cuba. *Bajo la Capa del Cielo* and *El Tango* are filled with patriotic and nationalistic inspiration. After 1880 verse writing occupied but little of his attention. On the other hand, the name of Enrique José Varona has been associated during his time with almost every intellectual movement in Cuba.

First of all as a teacher of philosophy, interpreting the system of Herbert Spencer to the Cuban people, he continued the intellectual tradition of Varela and Luz. Like them he made use of his philosophical teaching to inculcate in his pupils a desire for freedom. When after the death of J. A. Cortina he became the editor of the review to which he had so often contributed he found ample opportunity for his peculiar form of separatist propaganda.

Varona signalized his assumption of the editorship of the review, 1885, by changing its name to *Revista Cubana*. The first number announced that it would "be merely the continuation of the *Revista de Cuba*. To present a picture as faithful as possible of the state of our culture, offering a neutral field to all opinions in order to keep alive Cuban sentiment against the discouragements of the present moment, is the first of its objects." The emphasis was laid more and more on the part of this program referring to the keeping alive of Cuban sentiment.

Varona's method of fostering nationalistic sentiment is well illustrated by an oration which he delivered and reprinted in the review, on such an unsuggestive topic as

El Poeta anónimo de la Polonia. To his audience the description of Poland was a picture of suffering Cuba. With similar purpose he printed a remarkable article, *El Bandolerismo en Cuba*, attempting to prove that crime scarcely existed among the native population of Cuba but was confined to persons of Spanish birth. In 1891 he published a volume entitled *Artículos y Discursos* which for the character of its contents was almost the program of a revolutionary party. Each article treated some idea connected with the political or economic situation in Cuba. Four years later broke out the final and successful Cuban revolution which solved these problems in the manner hinted by Varona, namely, by independence.

Before the actual outbreak the *Revista Cubana* was obliged to suspend publication. Its utterances became bolder and bolder so that finally one number was seized and suppressed by the authorities. Varona found it advisable to seek refuge in New York. There he became an invaluable member of the literary cohorts fighting for Cuban independence by his editing of the journal *La Patria*, by his addresses to Cuban refugees, and by revolutionary tracts. One of the latter translated into English, *Cuba against Spain*, was widely circulated. It was a terrible arraignment supported by facts and figures of the frauds and thefts committed by the Spanish bureaucracy in the administration of insular affairs. In addition he showed that the system of voting introduced as a supposed reform after the pact of Zanjón was such a farce that only Spaniards or known Spanish sympathizers were allowed to vote.

After the Spaniards withdrew from Cuba, Varona was

appointed Secretary of Public Instruction during the first North American intervention. Then followed a period in which he took no part in politics. This was marked by the publication of books on philosophy made up of lectures previously delivered and of a collection of essays on literature, *Desde mi Belvedere*. At the time of the second North American intervention he became a leader of the conservative party and in 1912 was elected Vice-president of the Republic of Cuba, a fitting honor for one who had devoted so much of his youthful energies to its establishment.

During Varona's editorship of the *Revista Cubana*, many writers assisted him in carrying out his policies. One of the oldest men enlisted was Antonio Bachiller y Morales (1812–89). He was one of those natural scholars whose learning increases with their years, and who retain their mental vigor to the end. Due to the universality of his studies his published essays embrace almost every field. He even began his career with a few verses like the other students who came under Del Monte's influence. As a professor in the university, however, his intellectual interests led him away from poetry. His most important work will always be considered the *Apuntes para la Historia de las Letras en Cuba*, which is quite as much a history of education in Cuba as of the production of literature. During the ten years' war he was obliged for his journalistic activity to emigrate to New York. His most valuable work there was an edition of Heredia's poems.

It was by articles on Heredia, on Plácido, on Cuban literature in general, with special emphasis on features antagonistic to Spanish rule, that the *Revista Cubana* maintained its policy of cherishing a nationalistic Cuban sentiment. As time went on its articles became more directly political in character, such as a discussion of the aspirations of the Cuban liberal party by F. A. Conte, a history of the filibustering expedition of Narciso López with all its revolutionary implications by the Conde de Pozos Dulces, the chapters from Saco's *Historia de la Esclavitud* which dealt with the iniquities of the slave trade in Cuba. Enrique Piñeyro contributed a sketch of the history of the United States during the struggles over the slavery question and the campaign resulting in the election of Abraham Lincoln. The review of books such as the biographies of Felix Varela and of José de la Luz by José Ignacio Rodríguez offered another opportunity for the preaching of the Cuban ideal.

Books began to reinforce the revolutionary propaganda. Almost epoch-making was *A pie y descalzo*, 1890, by Ramón Roa, the record of a journey which the author had made through the regions devastated by the military operations of the Spaniards during the early years of the ten years' war. As the author had been a lieutenant colonel and adjutant secretary to Generals Ignacio Agramonte and Máximo Gómez he could unfold tales of destitution and distress well calculated to harrow up the soul of his readers. With the same object was written *Episodios de la Revolución cubana*, by Manuel de la Cruz (1861–96), and his *Cromitos Cubanos*, short sketches of prominent fellow countrymen. He contributed articles also to the *Revista Cubana*. Likewise Ramón Meza wrote articles on literature and published books. These were novels picturing social conditions, *Mi Tío el Empleado* and *D. Aniceto el Tendero*. To Meza we are indebted for a sympathetic account of Julián del Casal.

Of all the contributors to the *Revista Cubana* the editor's right hand man was Manuel Sanguily, most vigorous and active. Finally, to throw off all restraint he established just before the outbreak of the revolution of 1895, a journal with the innocuous title, *Hojas Literarias*, which during its year of existence had some of its numbers suppressed, surely not merely for discourses on literature. One of his first contributions to the *Revista Cubana* was *Los Oradores de Cuba*. The discussion of each man's oratorical ability was a peg on which to hang the account of his services for Cuba. If he wrote of Heredia's poetry, he exalted the revolutionary ideal. From Sanguily's first appearance there was scarcely a number of the review without something from his pen.

But all these brave words would have been fruitless without somebody to incite men to action. This man was José Martí to whose efforts more than to any other single individual Cuban independence was due. To this object from the age of sixteen he devoted with a fervor rarely equaled in any cause, both his life and a gift of speech seldom given to mortals. Whatever other title may be conferred on him there is one uniquely his, the "Apostle" of Cuban independence.

José Martí (1853–95), was the son of an officer of artillery in the Spanish army. He attended the school of which the poet Mendive was the principal. From him it is likely that Martí absorbed some of his revolutionary ideas, just as the spectacle of his beloved teacher in prison embittered his spirit. Martí and another pupil used daily to escort Mendive's wife to the prison on her visits to her husband before his deportation. Martí himself was arrested as a conspirator at the age of sixteen and deported to Spain, but he was permitted to study law during his five years' sojourn. In 1873 he went to Mexico where he married. In 1878, he returned to Cuba ostensibly to practice law but in reality to engage in conspiracy which developed into the brief period of hostilities known as the "guerra chiquita." Martí was arrested and again deported to Spain. He escaped, however, to France, from where by way of New York he went to Venezuela, but by 1881 he was back in New York. For the next eight years he earned his living by work at various Spanish-American consulates, by articles for *La Nación* of Buenos Aires and criticisms on art for the *New York Sun*. He even published two little volumes of poems, one, *Ismaelillo*, the out-pourings of a father's heart in joy over his son, the other, *Versos Sencillos*, a collection of love lyrics. In 1889 at a banquet of Spanish Americans he made a speech which he terminated with this peroration: "Those who have a country, let them honor it; those who have not, let them conquer one."

The press report of this speech was such that the Spanish government protested to the Argentine Republic against Martí's employment at her consulship. From that hour Martí was free to devote his whole time to the propaganda against Spain. He became the "Apostle" preaching Cuban independence to Cubans, wherever he could find an audience. He went to Florida to work among the colonies of refugees in the cigar factories of Key West and Tampa. Everywhere among the working-

men he received an enthusiastic welcome, and at his suggestion the organization of revolutionary clubs went on
apace.   In 1892 Martí definitely launched the "Partido
Revolucionario Cubano" with a program expressed in
writing so that its purposes could be positively known and
open to discussion.   Among the more well-to-do Cubans
Martí had to overcome much opposition, which was
summed up in the sarcasm, "Más machetes!   Pobre
Cuba!"

But the enrollment of volunteers and the collections
of money and arms continued to increase.   It was necessary to find military leaders.   He sought out the veteran
generals Cebreco, Maceo, and Máximo Gómez and secured the promise of their support.   Martí's description
of his visit to the latter's home in Santo Domingo where
he was comfortably living with his family on an estate
in the country is one of the finest things from his pen.
Finally on February 24, 1895, the cry of revolution was
raised in the province of Santiago.   In April, Martí and
Máximo Gómez landed in Cuba.   A month later Martí,
who was now considered the president of the new Cuban
republic, set out to leave the island.   With a small escort
he was surprised by a detachment of Spanish soldiers,
and fell mortally wounded at the first discharge.   This
occurred at a locality known as Boca de Dos Rios, on
May 19th, 1895.   The work for which Martí had given
his life resulted in the emancipation of Cuba from Spanish
rule.

Martí's literary work has been published in several
volumes by his friend, Gonzalo de Quesada.   It consists
mainly of speeches and articles written for various papers.

Its value lies in the remarkable qualities of his style. He possessed the secret of contrast with the expert journalist's ability to select details with dramatic value and the artist's eye for color and harmony. If one wishes to know, for example, what the streets and parades in New York were like at the time of the formal acceptance of Bartholdi's statue of liberty, he should read Martí's account sent to *La Nación* of Buenos Aires. It would lose little in translation, for its vivid picturesqueness is based on fact. On the other hand, the fluent rhythm of his speeches can hardly be rendered in translation. At times he speaks in metaphors which are difficult to follow on account of their depth of thought. Rarely, however, does he fall into the merely flowery eloquence which is so characteristic of many Spanish Americans. His tremendous earnestness and dignity are always apparent. In these respects the introductory paragraph of his preface to Pérez Bonalde's poem on Niagara [1] is a characteristic gem from Martí's tongue.

The man's wonderful talent has nowhere been more vividly described than in this statement by Diego V. Tejera: "He who has never heard Martí in a moment of confidential intimacy does not realize the full power of the fascination of which human speech is capable."

Of the two movements which have affected the literatures of all countries at the end of the nineteenth century, the modernista development in poetry and the vogue of the naturalistic novel Cuba took but small share on account of the absorption of her sons in political interests. However, it must not be forgotten that in Julian del Casal

[1] See page 320.

(1863–93) she had the honor of giving to the world one of the most important precursors of modernista verse. His adaptation of certain exotic forms to the genius of the Spanish language are clearly evident to the students of the movement. Had Casal lived longer he might have shared with Rubén Darío the latter's fame, for the admiration of the two poets for each other's work and their reciprocal influence is evident.

In the naturalistic novel Jesús Castellanos (1879–1912) was just beginning to show the possibilities of Cuban life when his career was cut short by death. In *La Tierra adentro* he depicted in a series of short stories and sketches Cuban rural life. But he reached artistic perfection in a tale published separately from that collection, *La Manigua sentimental*. The title was taken from the Cuban name given to the rough woodland country in eastern and central Cuba where the last revolution was mainly fought. Critics agree that his observations of life in that region at that epoch are most exact. At the time of his death Castellanos was rapidly becoming the literary leader of Cuba. His critical articles on literature were eagerly read. In 1912 with the Dominican Max Henríquez Ureña he organized La Sociedad de Conferencias which since then has continued to work for the furtherance of Cuban literature by means of public lectures.

Since the winning of political independence Cuba's material prosperity has grown by leaps and bounds. There can be no doubt that in the future Cuba will maintain her literary fame. At present the periodicals published in the island equal if they do not surpass in literary qualities those of any other nation. Take, for example, the beautifully illustrated *Figaro*, long conducted by the poet Manuel S. Pichardo; *Cuba y America*, whose purpose is "the regeneration of Cuban culture," and whose editor, Salvador Salazar, is an enthusiastic student of literature; or the scholarly monthly *Cuba Contemporánea*, directed by Carlos de Velasco, which is doing an unsurpassed service for the study of Cuban literature. The famous organ of the ancient society, Los Amigos del Pais, entitled *La Revista bimestre cubana*, has also been revived.

The centenaries of certain beloved poets, La Avellaneda and Milanés, have recently given opportunity to foster the love of literature. The prize for the poem in celebration of La Avellaneda's birth was awarded in 1914 to Doña Dulce María Borrero de Luján who for some years has been Cuba's reigning poetess.

Her name appeared in an anthology, *Arpas cubanas*, published in 1904, which in a certain degree fixes a date for the regeneration of Cuban verse after the war for independence. The poems it contained were those of living poets whose names were too numerous to mention here. The collection contained also two sonnets by a poet, Enrique Hernández Miyares (1859–1914), whose life covered the period of transition from colonial to free Cuba. His first work appeared in the *Revista cubana* and he was an intimate friend of Julián del Casal.

The two sonnets *A un Machete* and *La más Fermosa* typify the old and the new Cuba. The first, written in 1892 when the revolutionary agitation was becoming acute, presents the poet coming by chance upon a rusty machete, which though it had spilled Spanish blood in an attempt at redemption, was now lying forgetful of patriotism, idle and a coward.   The other sonnet, *La más Fermosa,* published in 1903, has been called the most beautiful sonnet written in Cuba.   Certainly it voices the spirit of determination so characteristic of Cuban patriots as well as the idealization of the Cuban attitude toward the future.

> Keep on, O knight! With lance uplifted ride,
> To punish every wrong by righteous deed;
> For constancy at last shall gain its meed,
> And justice ever with the law abide.
> Mambrino's broken helmet don with pride,
> Advance undaunted on thy glorious steed,
> To Sancho Panza's cautions pay no heed,
> In destiny and thy right arm confide.
> At Fortune's coy reserve display no fear;
> For should the Cavalier of the White Moon
> With arms 'gainst thine in combat dare appear,
> Although by adverse fate thou art o'erthrown,
> Of Dulcinea even in death's hour swear
> That she will always be the only fair.[1]

[1] Version of Alfred Coester.

CHAPTER XIII

SANTO DOMINGO is the Spanish-speaking republic situated in the southern half of the island of which the negro republic of Haiti, where French is spoken, is the northern half. Mountain ranges in the interior form a natural barrier between the two. The whole island was named by Columbus Isla Hispaniola or Spanish Island. The aboriginal name Quisqueya supplies a poetical appellation to a region whose unhappy history is rich in material for poetry.

Columbus considered this island the chief discovery of his first voyage, for there he found gold in abundance. As the natives were of a friendly disposition he selected it as the site of the first Spanish settlement in the New World. But the record of the colony forms a sad page in history. And to the present day fate has evilly treated the dwellers in this island so blessed by nature.

In 1795 the possession of the whole island passed to the French. In consequence an emigration of the Spanish families set in which materially increased when the blacks in Haiti after 1801 were ravaging the land with arson and murder. By 1821 the Haytians were in complete control.

Then began a hard struggle by the Spanish whites to avoid annihilation. They found a leader in Juan Pablo Duarte (1813–73). Educated in Spain he trained the people to resist negro domination and to cling to their Spanish tongue. For this purpose he imported and distributed Spanish books. No less important was their training in arms, for by 1844 the Spanish element succeeded in freeing themselves and in setting up the Dominican Republic.

The University of Santo Domingo, founded in 1558, had during the colonial period been instrumental in maintaining in the colony a higher degree of culture than that which existed in the other Antilles. Students from them resorted to Santo Domingo. Consequently when the emigration occurred it carried to Puerto Rico, Cuba and Venezuela elements which assisted in raising the intellectual tone in those countries. The great Cuban poet, Heredia, and the patron of Cuban letters, Domingo del Monte, were children of families from the unhappy isle. The same is true of Narciso Foxá and his brother Francisco J. Foxá, one of the first dramatic poets of Cuba. Francisco Muñoz del Monte (1800–68), cousin of Domingo del Monte, contributed verses to the literary movement of the thirties in Cuba which are worthy of being remembered, especially his elegy *A la Muerte de Heredia* and his interesting evocation of the hot season, *El Verano en la Habana*.

The intellectual leader of the republic established in 1844 was Felix María del Monte (1819–99). His national hymn remains as an echo of the bitter struggle against the Haytians. Other poems of his likewise were inspired by personal experience or by the course of events as his *Arpa del Proscrito*, dedicated to Nicolás Ureña de Mendoza (1822–75). The latter in the manner of the Cuban Vélez y Herrera composed verses in description of the life of the guajiros of his native island. Of the same age Felix Mota (1822–61), shot by the Spaniards among other patriots who opposed their reoccupation of Santo Domingo, wrote poems suggestive of Milanés.

The period of peace after 1844 was too troubled for extensive literary production. In 1861 Dominican leaders then in power thought to find protection from the Haytians by asking Spain for re-annexation as a colony. Spain sent a few regiments of soldiers to maintain her authority, but in 1866 she practically abandoned the island by withdrawing the soldiers. The Dominican Republic was re-established, but not until 1873 did political conditions allow settled order and progress.

Among those who returned to the island after the departure of the Spaniards was Javier Angulo Guridi (1816–84), a former colonel in the patriot army. During his exile he had engaged in journalism in various countries, notably in Venezuela, where he appears to have been strongly influenced by the group of poets finding inspiration in Indian life. Though he had the distinction of being the first Dominican poet to see his verses collected in a volume, *Ensayos poéticos*, in 1843, his best poems and prose tales treat Indian legends, as his *Iguaniona* which he also arranged as a drama, in 1867.

Tales of Indian life and the relations of the natives with the first settlers became the popular subjects of literary art during the decade of the seventies. But interest in literature was made possible by a remarkable movement for education and culture in which the poetess Doña Salomé Ureña (1850–97), daughter of Nicolás Ureña de Mendoza was a prominent figure. She began publishing poems in praise of the ideals of peace and progress. A society, Los Amigos del País, was founded to promote the interests of the country along such lines, and in 1878 the society presented to the poetess a gold medal and published an edition of her poems. In 1880 she married Francisco Henríquez y Carvajal (b. 1859). The same year there came to Santo Domingo one of the remarkable thinkers of Spanish America, Eugenio M. Hostos, who as principal of the Escuela Normal introduced into the island a knowledge of modern pedagogical methods. Writing his own texts for his classes, he performed for Santo Domingo much the same service as Andrés Bello for Chile. Doña Salomé Ureña de Henríquez aided the movement by founding the first school for young ladies, which she directed for many years. From this time her poems were echoes of her home life in which vibrated the strong feelings of wife and mother.

In the volume of her poems printed in 1878, the legend *Anacaona*, on an Indian topic, showed her interest in the popular trend in literature. Her one rival in the field of poetry, José Joaquín Pérez (1845–1900), vies with the Uruguayan Zorrilla de San Martín for the primacy of excellence in Spanish-American literary evocation of native life. His first poem of this type, *Quisqueyana*, bears the date of his return to Santo Domingo, 1874, after years of exile in Venezuela. Of the same year was the beautiful *Vuelta al Hogar*, an intense cry of joy at being again in his native land. In 1877 he published the volume entitled *Fantasías Indígenas* to which Pérez mainly owes his fame. These were short narrative poems, perpetuating the memory of the aborigines of Santo Domingo, the best of which were *El Voto de Anacaona* and *Guarionex*. *El Junco verde* relates the impression which was produced on Columbus and his crew by the sight of a green reed, the first sign of land. At the same time Pérez was deeply interested in the movement for better educational facilities in the island and voiced it in his poem *Himno al Progreso del País* written in the style of Doña Salomé. Later when the modernista manner was attracting the young men of Spanish America, Pérez showed his versatility by adopting it in *Americanas*, a series of poems called forth by his sympathy for the Cubans during the rebellion of 1895.

In prose the interest in Dominican life and history produced *Baní o Engracia y Antoñita*, a story full of intense local color by Francisco Gregorio Billini (1844–98), and the historical tales of Cesár Nicolás Penson (1855–1902), entitled *Cosas añejas*. Of similar inspiration was the long historical novel *Enriquillo* by Manuel de Jesús Galván (1834–1911), published in 1882, but written a few years before. In both the style and the interest of the subject-matter *Enriquillo* is one of the very best historical novels that have been written by a Spanish American. It depicts the early colonial period in Hispaniola at the termination of the administration of the governor Ovando, and the beginning of that of Diego Colón, the Admiral's son. The arrival of Diego Colón with his bride, María de Toledo, in 1509 forms an interesting episode. The friar Bartolomé de las Casas, the famous champion of human rights for the oppressed natives, also appears in its pages. Their grievances and last rebellion under the young cacique whose Christian name was Enriquillo compose much of the narrative and make it the foremost work of Spanish-American literary art in prose which deals with the life of the American savages.

Of the generation of men who took active part in the upbuilding of culture in Santo Domingo should be mentioned Federico Henríquez y Carvajal (b. 1848), now chief justice of the supreme court. Though as a journalist in early life he wrote verses and even dramas, of which one, *La Hija del Hebreo*, was produced on the stage, he distinguished himself as a professor in the normal school established by Hostos and in other educational institutions. In Cuba, he is gratefully remembered for the assistance which he rendered the patriots of the revolutions of 1868 and 1895. After the close of the ten years' war, Máximo Gómez and other Cuban leaders found refuge in Santo Domingo. And during his propaganda in favor of a fresh attempt at independence, José Martí received hearty assistance there. Among Martí's writings there is no more glowing page than that which describes his visit to Máximo Gómez in Santo Domingo in 1893, and his welcome by various Dominicans. From there also with their assistance Martí and Gómez set out for Cuba to raise the cry at Baira that precipitated Cuba's final and successful revolution. Martí's letter to Federico Henríquez y Carvajal, dated Montecristy, March, 1895, on the eve of his departure, has been called his "political testament."

Of the fruits of the educational movement in Santo Domingo, the literary activity of her sons and daughters since the beginning of the new century give ample testimony. Of the older generation Emilio Prud'homme is distinguished for his national anthem adopted in 1897. In prose, Federico García Godoy has long been a leading literary critic, while his historical novels *Rufinito*, *Alma Dominicana*, and the recent *Guanuma*, 1915, give realistic pictures of the Dominican struggles for independence. The author's purpose in his writings has been to awaken a strong feeling of nationality. Guanuma, the name of the locality where the soldiers camped, is in the words of the author, "a synthetic name which sums up the second part of the campaign which put an end to the annexation by the withdrawal of the Spanish troops from Dominican territory once more independent through the tenacity and heroism of her sons."

Of a younger generation were the poets Gaston F. Deligne (1861–1913), Rafael A. Deligne (1863–1902), and Arturo Pellerano Castro (b. 1865), whose elegant verses deserve to be more widely known. As a writer of prose Americo Lugo (b. 1871) has attracted attention by his articles on sociological and critical topics and fantastic tales, some of which have been collected in the volume entitled *A Punto largo*.

To the modernista movement, Santo Domingo contributed Fabio Fiallo (b. 1865), who has made himself widely known in Spanish America for his tales in both prose and verse. Tulio M. Cestero (b. 1877) was at first one of the most extravagant modernistas, but his writings now found in *La Revista de América* and other reviews show a considerable modification of his early style. Manuel F. Cestero has also produced excellent work as a journalist and writer of tales.

The educational work so diligently fostered by Doña

Salomé Ureña de Henríquez has done marvels for culture in Santo Domingo. Through her sons, Pedro Henríquez Ureña (b. 1884), and Max Henríquez Ureña (b. 1885), she has enriched the intellectual life of Spanish America. The scene of Max Henríquez Ureña's activity has been Cuba where in company with Jesús Castellanos he founded the Sociedad de Conferencias. His lectures before that society and his many articles on literary topics have greatly furthered the knowledge of literary history. His recent volume of poems, *Anforas*, testifies to his inherited ability in writing pleasing and musical verses.

Pedro Henríquez Ureña's sphere has been even wider. His tragic poem in classical style, *El Nacimiento de Dionisos*, evoked great praise from the Uruguayan critic Rodó. His studies in Greek literature led him to make a Spanish translation of some of Walter Pater's essays, published as *Estudios griegos*. As professor of literature in the University of Mexico, he wrote many useful and interesting articles. The most brilliant of these was a lecture in which he set forth his discovery that the great Spanish dramatist, Juan Ruíz de Alarcón, was brought up in Mexico where his works show he first learned the elements of dramatic art. Other essays have appeared in the volume *Horas de Estudio*. For the history of Dominican literature he has done greater service than anyone both in his essays and the historical sketch preceding the *Antología dominicana* and in his study *Romances en América*, in which he collected the traditional Spanish romances still sung or recited by the people in Santo Domingo.

PUERTO RICO

The small island of Puerto Rico owing to its freedom from political disturbances shows a different type of literary production from that of other more agitated communities. In colonial times it had the distinction of sharing with Mexico the fame of Bernardo de Balbuena. While bishop of Puerto Rico he composed his heroic poem *Bernardo*. When he died, he bequeathed to the church his books and papers, which unfortunately were destroyed in the raid by the Hollanders in 1625.

In the nineteenth century the first literary fruitage was due to the influence of the activity in the circle of Domingo del Monte. He personally encouraged several poets who came in contact with him in Cuba. In 1843 was printed in the form of a gift-book for ladies, the *Aguinaldo Puerto-Riqueño*, a collection of poems by natives of the island. A second and more famous collection of similar character was the *Cancionero de Borinquen*, 1846, which thus made use of the poetic aboriginal name of the island.

In this book the best poem and one which has lived in popular memory is entitled *Insomnio* by Santiago Vidarte (1828–48). Beginning with a barcarole it sings the tropical beauty of Puerto Rico as seen at dawn from the sea.

A contributor to both collections was Alejandrina Benítez (1819– ?). For years she was a frequent contributor to the periodicals of verses with a virile tone like her lines *A Cuba* and *El Cable submarino*. She made a romantic marriage with the poet Arce Gautier, and their son, José Gautier Benítez (1848–80), became one of the best poets who have written in Puerto Rico.

The interest in country people and their customs popularized in Cuba by Del Monte, Vélez Herrera and other poets had its echo in the prose sketches of Manuel A. Alonso (1823–?), which he published under the title of *El Gíbaro*, the name given to the white country people of Puerto Rico. These valuable contributions to folk lore were written from his intimate knowledge of the peasants and their peculiar dialect, a mixture of popular Andalusian, old Castilian, and various aboriginal words.

A native of Puerto Rico connected with the Cuban group about Milanés who sought to put poetry out to social service was Narciso de Foxá. His poems were partly descriptive, partly allegorical. His most ambitious effort was a *Canto épico sobre el Descubrimiento de América.*

Alejandro Tapia (1827–82), who as a youth likewise found encouragement from Domingo del Monte, was the most prolific writer yet produced by Puerto Rico. Beginning with researches into the history of the island, he passed to the writing of historical dramas and novels and finally composed a pseudo-epic poem of great length. Living in Havana in 1862 he printed a volume, *El Bardo de Guamaní,* containing his first productions, various lyrics, a prose tale, *La Antigua Sirena,* and the dramas, *Bernardo de Palissy* and *Roberto d'Evreux.* The latter in representing Queen Elizabeth of England contains a notable monologue by her before she signs the death warrant of Mary Stuart. After the publication of this volume Tapia returned to Puerto Rico. There he wrote and staged several dramas, *Camoens,* 1868, *Vasco Nuñez de Balboa,* 1873, and others.

Tapia then turned his attention to narrative, producing

Cofresí in 1876, a tale dealing with the legendary history of Puerto Rico; and *Póstumo el Transmigrado*, the imaginary story of a man whose soul transmigrated into the body of his enemy. Later Tapia wrote in the same vein *Póstumo Envirgenado*, which related the adventures of a man in the body of a woman. The spiritualistic leanings which led Tapia to interest himself in this sort of tale induced him to spend energy for sixteen years in composing *La Sataniada* in thirty cantos.

The extravagant prolixity of this poem, a curious compound of science and religion, attempts an explanation of the universe according to the fundamental notion that this world is hell, ruled by Satan. Poets are apostles to lead the human race to a superior development here and hereafter. The author expected his poem would take rank as the fourth epic of universal literature after the Iliad, the Divina Comedia, and Faust.

Of more real value than his literary work perhaps was Tapia's influence on his compatriots for he showed them the way to better education and better literary tastes. He died suddenly at a public meeting when explaining a plan for the education of poor children.

Certain journalists and publicists have greatly contributed by their writings to determining the intellectual movement in Puerto Rico. Román Baldorioty de Castro (1822– ?), was the most popular of his countrymen on account of his efforts to obtain better political conditions from the Spaniards. As a deputy for Puerto Rico in the Spanish Cortes Constituyentes of 1869, he strove for the abolition of slavery and attracted considerable attention by his able speeches. In 1874, political reaction compelled him to emigrate to Santo Domingo where he taught at the University. At the moment Santo Domingo was enjoying a renaissance of culture, and was glad to welcome him as well as his compatriot, E. M. Hostos. When Baldorioty was permitted to return home, he spent his time expounding in the papers his liberal views urging political autonomy for Puerto Rico and become president of a society working for that end.

Manuel Corchado (1840–84) was another publicist who strove for improvements in conditions in his native island. To further the efforts for the abolition of slavery, he wrote a *Biografía de Lincoln*. He was famous as an orator and put his talents at the service of his compatriots as a deputy to the Spanish Cortes. He wrote poems also, chiefly of the civic type.

Eugenio María de Hostos (1839–1903), belongs not only to Puerto Rico but to Santo Domingo and Chile, which countries profited by his remarkable intellect. But the course of his life was determined by his patriotic love of his country. He was established in Spain as a young lawyer in 1868, when the stand which he took in arguing with the government for reforms in Puerto Rico resulted in his banishment. He went first to the United States where he worked with the Cuban revolutionary junta. The ideal which he consistently urged all his life was the political union of all the Antilles. Leaving the United States he traveled over Spanish America. In 1880 he was invited to Santo Domingo, where he performed the most important labor of his career in organizing along modern lines the schools of that land. After nine years of labor he was expelled by the reactionary dictator

Heureaux. Chile then offered him a professorship in her national university. As professor of international law he composed a textbook on the subject which is held in high esteem throughout Latin America. In 1898 he tried to organize a league of patriots against the domination of the United States in Puerto Rico and to carry out his scheme for a union of the Antilles.

Poets who flourished in Puerto Rico before the modernista movement were Gautier Benítez, Francisco Alvarez, a becquerista adherent, and D. F. J. Amy who translated many poems by North Americans. The poetess, Doña Lola Rodríguez de Tió, whose first volume, *Mis Cantares*, was published in 1876, achieved her greatest successes in Cuba where for many years she was a favorite at literary gatherings. In the words of a Cuban, "Her poetry is herself, nobility, sentiment, uprightness, love of home, friendship." She still contributes occasionally to the periodicals.

Manuel Fernández Juncos (born 1846) took upon himself the task of preserving the literary history of Puerto Rico. Beside writing articles on its customs he prepared a valuable anthology of its writers.

CENTRAL AMERICA

During the colonial period Central America, now divided into the five republics, Guatemala, Honduras, El Salvador, Nicaragua and Costa Rica, was politically organized, together with the adjoining Mexican state of Chiapas, into the captaincy general of Guatemala. When Mexico won its independence of Spain the whole territory temporarily became a part of that country, but in 1823 the five provinces established themselves as the Republic of the United States of Central America. But after fifteen years of union internal dissensions broke up the confederation into its component parts which despite various attempts at reunion have remained independent republics.

Of the total population approximating five million about two-fifths dwell in Guatemala, one-fifth in the densely inhabited and mountainous El Salvador. The majority of the people are of mixed Spanish and Indian blood, for the native races have been well absorbed. Nevertheless, regions exist where the Indians remain the same primitive savages as their ancestors were at the time of the first Spanish conquests of Cortés and Pedro de Alvarado. In Costa Rica, visited by Columbus on his third voyage and subjugated by Pedrarias de Avila from Panama in 1513, the population of three hundred and fifty thousand contains a much larger percentage of unmixed Spanish blood than that of the other states.

Apart from the numerous revolutions and almost incessant fighting in these republics, the most discussed incident in their recent history was the attempt by the North American filibuster, William Walker, to carve out new slave territory to be added to our southern states. Temporarily successful in Nicaragua in 1856, he was captured and shot during an expedition in 1860 into Honduras.

During the colonial period there was produced in the monastic establishments of Guatemala a considerable bulk of writing mainly in Latin. In that language was written by Rafael Landívar (1731–93), a member of a religious order in Guatemala, a poem *Rusticatio mexicana* which critics have universally praised for its high literary merit. Having for its topic the beauties and wonders of America it belongs to that Virgilian type of descriptive poetry so common to American literature. The poem has attracted many translators, and especially to be praised is the Spanish version of the Mexican Joaquín Arcadio Pagaza.

Natives of Central America who have attained literary fame achieved it often out of their own country where the opportunity for development was too restricted. The most notable instance is that of the leader of the modernista movement throughout America, Rubén Darío, who was born in Nicaragua, and exercised his poetical gifts in Buenos Aires. Yet the Central American aboriginal strain in his blood so evident in his portrait tinges also his writings.

A native of Guatemala whose life was likewise chiefly spent away from his native land was Antonio José de Irisarri (1786–1868). Inheriting immense wealth from his father, he was obliged to go to Peru for the purpose of looking after his property. Moreover, he had relatives there and in Chile among the wealthiest and most influential families. Espousing the cause of the revolution, he held prominent offices in both the military and civil establishments. Obliged by the success of the Spanish arms in 1814 to leave Chile he went to Europe by way of Buenos Aires. When Chile won her independence in 1818 Irisarri was appointed as her diplomatic representative in Paris and London in which capacity he remained till 1825. His principal achievement was the obtaining for Chile of a loan on more favorable terms than those usually

granted to the American republics. From Europe he returned to Guatemala in time to take part in one of the
internal quarrels of the new republic. Though general
of an army he was captured and remained a prisoner for
nine months till he was allowed to escape and betake himself again to Chile. Again he occupied various public
offices. In 1837 he was appointed Chilean minister in
Lima. A year later he removed to Ecuador and lived there
till 1845. Thence by way of Colombia, Venezuela, Cura-
çao, Jamaica, Cuba he came to New York, arriving in
1849. In 1855 he was made the diplomatic representative
of Guatemala in the United States.

Wherever Irisarri resided his pen was diligently employed and his means permitted him to found periodicals
for the publication of its products. One of these periodicals most worthy of mention is *El Censor americano*,
printed in 1820 in London. To it Andrés Bello contributed
and possibly took therefrom the idea of the reviews which
he himself edited. The character of Irisarri's writings was
as diverse as the requirements of his numerous journals.
Many of his political polemics were also printed in pamphlet form. His productions in verse he collected in the
volume entitled *Poesías satíricas y burlescas*, while his
articles on grammar and philology of which he was excessively fond he republished in *Cuestiones filógicas*.

To another native of Guatemala, José de Batres y
Montúfar (1809–44), the Spanish critic Menéndez y Pelayo
accords the highest praise. He ranks him with the best
poets of America, though the Guatemalan's principal work,
Tradiciones de Guatemala, consisting of three merry tales
in verse, belongs to a minor genre. The title is somewhat

misleading because the stories are three bits of scandal which might be localized anywhere. But they are related without offensive details, gracefully, and with merry humor. Moreover, they abound in local color when the author describes the procession on St. Cecelia's day or caricatures the old hidalgo, Pascual del Pescón. The author pretended merely to translate in royal octaves the tales of the Italian poet Casti but his work is original. He imitated Byron to the extent of making, like his Don Juan, skeptical and misanthropic digressions from the narrative. Altogether Batres y Montúfar, according to the Spanish critic, is the "most finished model of jocose narrative."

The romantic movement awakened echoes in Central America. By his *Tardes de Abril* the Guatemalan Juan Diéguez (1813–66) became a most popular poet and his brilliant evocations of nature are known to all his countrymen. His *Oda a la Independencia* fills their special need for an expression of patriotism, while *La Garza*, written in exile, voices feelings experienced by many fellow countrymen.

The most prolific writer in Guatemala was José Milla (1822–82), "Salome Gil," who long held the position of editor of the *Gaceta Oficial*. He busied himself with the study of history and not only wrote a *Historia de Guatemala* but gave forth the results of his studies in many historical novels. One of the earliest, *Don Bonifacio*, written in verse, novelizes an episode which occurred in 1731. His prose novels contain realistic pictures of life in Guatemala.

During the years from 1854 to 1860 a Spaniard, Francisco Velarde, directed a school in Guatemala which exercised a considerable influence on the young men who attended it. Velarde was a romantic poet whose *Melodías románticas,* and *Cánticos del Nuevo Mundo* belong to the school of Zorrilla. The author being personally known these poems have been much imitated in America. Through him the Indian legend became popular.

In the republic of El Salvador there have lived several poets worthy of mention. Juan José Bernal wrote in a mystic vein with a feeling for nature. Juan José Cañas (1826–00) possessed a sentimental and patriotic note. At the time of the gold fever in California he visited the mines there but without material success. Later he fought against the filibustering expedition of William Walker. Then he was sent on a diplomatic mission to Chile. All these experiences were recorded in his poems. Fond of the ocean his best poems recall his voyages, especially the patriotic lines *A. J. M. Dow, capitán del vapor Guatemala* and the sentimental *Se va el vapor,* long a favorite song in Costa Rica.

Isaac Ruiz Araujo (1850–81) and Francisco E. Galindo (1850–00) compete with each other for the place of premier poet of Salvador. Their themes were love, natural scenery and patriotism. The latter also wrote a play in three acts, *Dos Flores,* with a patriotic plot.

Joaquín Aragón (b. 1863) was a diligent versifier of national legends some of which were lengthy. *Milta,* for example, was the story of an Indian maid by that name who fell in love with a young officer in the first Spanish army that came to Cuscatlán (such was the native name for the country) under the leadership of Pedro de Alvarado. The young man for love of her refuses to obey the orders of his superiors. Soon thereafter the woman was ordered by the cacique of her village to kill the Spaniard. As the command was said to be from God, she obeyed but promptly killed herself. When the Spanish soldiers, coming to arrest the deserter, found that he has been murdered, they slaughtered the whole village.

The semi-official anthologies of the Central American states make a brave showing of poets in the matter of number, but a reading of their productions does not impress one with great merit. In Costa Rica the becquerista manner, had a considerable following. Emilio Pacheco, Carlos Gagini, and Rafael Machado were the most prolific. When the modernista movement attracted attention there arose in that state a poet, Aquileo J. Echeverría, who deserves wider recognition for his criollo romances.

To Nicaragua abundance of literary honor has been conferred by having been the birthplace of Rubén Darío. Also born in Nicaragua was Santiago Argüello whose verses in the modernista manner have attracted favorable attention in other countries where he has lived.

CHAPTER XIV

THE MODERNISTA MOVEMENT

The year 1888 may be adopted to make a date for the most recent movement in Spanish-American literature. In that year Rubén Darío (1867–1916), published in Valparaiso a volume of prose and verse entitled *Azul,* instantly received with acclaim by the young men. The peculiar qualities of these poems were not wholly Darío's invention though their excellency of execution displayed the high quality of his poetic gifts. From Mexico, from Cuba, from Colombia, from every country where men were writing the Spanish language, this talented poet absorbed tendencies and methods and welded them into a product of his own. In Buenos Aires, a group of ardent admirers became imitators of the new style. To provide an outlet for their productions they founded a periodical, an example which was followed by young men in other countries who proclaimed themselves adherents of the new school.

The modernista idea consisted in an adaptation to the Spanish language of the form and substance of the French Parnassian, decadent and symbolist schools of verse. Beginning with translation and imitation the Spanish Americans progressed till the content of the poems was largely derived from American sources. In poetic forms and meters they effected a revolution whose influence spread to Spain itself. The poets consciously sought to widen the horizon of poetic endeavor by rejecting the tyranny of ancient rules of prosody. Their cult of beauty led them to evocations of ancient Greece and their love of elegance to the Versailles of the eighteenth century. In reaction against the excesses of the naturalistic school, they believed that art had a mission as a creator of beauty to cover, as it were with a veil, the brutality of human life. In rebellion against the narrowing influences of regionalism they hoped to find a common basis for their literary art in the theory that their civilization was European. The later poets have rejected this theory and built on a universal Americanism which finds its bond of union in a common language and a similar racial origin.

That a type of literature so artificial in its leading characteristics should meet with such wide acceptance proves that it corresponded to the needs and desires of Spanish Americans. Their various countries were passing through a feverish stage of material development which to men of artistic temperament offered little that was stimulating. For that reason they looked abroad. Momentarily the Teutonic spirit as revealed to them in Becquer's poems and the translations from Heine made by Pérez Bonalde and the Cubans Antonio and Francisco Sellén made a strong appeal. But the love of the exotic, so strong in all modernista poets, was better satisfied by the work of the French poets. Verlaine was the favorite, but there was scarcely one of them who has not had his followers.

Though Rubén Darío was the master, his precursors

in America were not without influence on his work. Foremost in point of time was the Mexican Gutiérrez Nájera who strove to adapt to the Spanish language some of the musical qualities of the French. To his efforts may be traced the modernista demand that speech should be endowed with the emotional power of music. Keenly sensitive to music he gave a poetical interpretation to a favorite composition in his poem *La Serenata de Schubert*, of which he says "so would my soul speak if it could." His masterpiece in imparting to words the suggestive quality of music was his last poem, *A la Corregidora*, written for recitation at the laying of the cornerstone of a monument to a lady. The poet bids the attentive ear listen to the opening of the buds in the spring, to the murmuring waters and the singing of the birds; the whole earth is hymning the psalm of life to the lady and offering incense at her altar. The novelty is not in the ideas, but in the method whereby the poet succeeds in conveying them as much by the sheer flow of verbal sound as by the meaning of his words.

Another poet, also a Mexican, to whom Rubén Darío owed something was Salvador Díaz Mirón. The latter put a personal stamp not only on the energetic handling of his personal or social themes, but also on a certain meter, the hendecasyllabic quatrain. This meter, though not widely used in Spain, was popular in Spanish America for religious and love poetry. Díaz Mirón adapted it to heroic themes, in which form it was widely imitated and became associated with his name. Rubén Darío in *Azul* paid him the compliment of a sonnet which gave a just characterization of Díaz Mirón's verses as follows:

Your quatrain is a four yoked chariot drawn by wild eagles who love the tempests and the oceans. Heavy brands and stone clubs are the proper weapons for your hands. Your mind has craters and ejects lavas. Your rude strophes, never slaves, travel over the mountains and plains of art like a herd of American buffaloes. What sounds from your lyre sounds far, as when Boreas speaks or the thunder. Son of the new world, let humanity hear the pomp of your lyric hymns which triumphantly salute liberty.

It is a tribute to Darío's versatility that he could draw inspiration from this fire-eater when his own habit of mind, loving elegance and beauty, was so different. It was easy on the other hand for him to find suggestions in the work of a Cuban poet, Julian del Casal, who was living in a world of his own creation, a bit of Japan set down in Havana.

Julián del Casal (1863–93), completely imbued with the spirit of French poetry, not only composed his verses in the same manner but arranged his daily life in keeping with its suggestions. For a poetic canon he adopted the epistle which accompanies the second volume of Jean Moreas' *Les Cantilènes*. His living-room he furnished in Japanese style so minutely, that he even kept joss sticks scented with sandal wood burning before an image of Buddha. This love of Oriental elegance appears in his poems, notably *Kakemono* in which he describes to the last detail of color and outline the toilet of a geisha, the make-up of her face, the arrangement of her hair and the embroidery of her silken clothing. Parisian elegance had no less a fascination for his mind. As, however, he had never been in Paris, that world was equally an imaginary one, as exotic as the ancient Greek world whose

beauty he loved. The pessimism of Baudelaire and Ban-
ville likewise appealed to his nature. They scarcely surpassed Casal in his expressions of discontent at the universe, or of horror at early death which in point of fact
he did meet.

The sonnet practiced with such perfection by Leconte
de l'Isle and J. M. de Heredia was Casal's favorite form
of verse. Like them he drew vivid pictures whose carefully chosen details leave a strong impression on the
reader's mind. His portraits of individuals, Prometheus,
Salome, Helen of Troy are unique. The sonnet on the
latter, for example, is a gem of great beauty. The first
quatrain refers to the heaps of the slain, the second draws
attention to the smoking ruins of Ilion, the tercets reveal
Helen "wrapped in a vestment of opaline gauze spangled
with gold" as "she gazes indifferent at the murky horizon,
toying with a lily in her rosy fingers." With equal skill
Casal depicted persons of the actual world about him in
Havana; the barefoot friar begging for alms whose mind
is distracted between the call to mass from the convent
bell and the braying of his ass; the maja, clad in a gaily
embroidered Manila shawl, whose little slippers, as she
dances, dart back and forth beneath her skirt of black
lace and green satin "like timid doves in the foliage."

Though Casal lived in an artificial world of his own
creation he took an interest in the troubled politics which
was agitating Havana and his friends who were writing
like himself for *La Habana Elegante*. He wrote not only a
few poems on certain abhorred acts of the government but
also contributed prose sketches on Havana society. One
of the latter containing piquant references to the governor

and his family brought the police to the office of the periodical. Among his essays in prose should be mentioned a study of Joris Karl Huysmans whose work Casal greatly admired. Some of his articles in prose were collected in the volume entitled *Bustos y Rimas*, published in 1893. His earlier poems were printed in *Hojas al Viento*, 1890, and *Nieve*, 1891.

The dates of these collections would show that Casal was merely contemporary with Rubén Darío, but as Casal's poems began to appear in periodicals in the middle eighties there can be no doubt that Darío was conversant with them. And if Casal was not an actual precursor of Darío it is certain that the latter's verses in *Prosas Profanas* show in a more marked degree than in his *Azul* that love of the exotic, that delight in color and that sensual joy in the refinements of elegance which Casal displayed from the first. Moreover, Darío passed several weeks in Havana in intimate acquaintance with Casal. They wrote poems in collaboration from which it is impossible for the critic to separate their respective compositions. And in *Páginas de Vida* Casal, without mentioning Darío's name, described the visitation of a poet who strove to move him from his pessimism.

Another contemporary whose metrical experiments taught Darío something was the Colombian José Asunción Silva (1860–96), truly a poet of the first rank. Silva's verses possess the charm of strong personal feeling set forth sincerely in musical language. Though pessimistic in tone there is no pose about them and at times the joy of living shines through the gloom of disillusion. If ever a man has been harassed by bad fortune it was Silva. Of aristocratic lineage he was born handsome and wealthy. But he suffered one blow of fortune after another. His family inheritance was swept away by a revolution in Colombia. His father dying it devolved on the son not only to support the family but to attempt to recover some part of the lost property. In this he was unsuccessful. The manuscript of a literary work of which he had high hopes was lost at sea during transmission to France for publication. His verses, his chief solace in evil days, were not printed in collected form till after his death. Finally a beautiful sister of whom he was very fond was claimed by death. So he could think of no relief for his ills but the taking of his own life by a pistol shot.

The obsession of death and the pessimistic attitude of one whose joy in living is almost childlike are the striking characteristics of Silva's mentality. Childhood memories frequently recur to him. In the musical poem *Crepúsculo* he retells the fairy stories which delighted his babyhood days and crowd into his mind as he listens to the grandmother singing a child to sleep.

The most widely known of Silva's poems are *Los Nocturnos*, consisting of the brief relation of four love scenes with a tragic note. Metrically these display Silva's originality in the handling of long and short lines in an attempt to adjust the rhythm of the verse to the inward rhythm of the thought. One of his methods was the repetition of words or lines assisted by the mode of printing. He sought, for example, to evoke the shadows of the lovers in the moonlight thus:

> Y tu sombra
> fina y languida

y mi sombra,
por los rayos de la luna proyectadas,
sobre las arenas tristes
de la senda se juntaban,
y eran una,
y eran una,
y eran una sola sombra larga,
y eran una sola sombra larga,
y eran una sola sombra larga.

One of Silva's finest poems is *Ante la Estatua*, referring to the famous statue of Bolívar in the public square of Bogotá. Its pessimistic purpose of pointing out the pettiness of mankind is again characteristic. The poet's attention is drawn to the bronze figure because he sees two boys playing in front of the statue. As he meditates he hears a voice speak of the hero in a depreciative manner. Tales of colonial times occur to the poet's memory, and the form of the Liberator rises before his eyes, who discourses at length on the hours of bitterness falling to his lot in his last years at the hands of the peoples for whom he had labored.

Silva's metrical mannerisms when imitated by others degenerated. He was as inimitable as Edgar Allen Poe whom Silva greatly admired, and whose rendering of the sound of bells he tried to rival in Spanish in *El Día de Difuntos*. In fact Poe was a favorite not only with Silva but with other modernista poets. The references to Poe in their works, as well as to Walt Whitman are numerous. With the latter in fact they seem to feel a certain affinity. Rubén Darío often calls on the name of Walt Whitman as the one singer of the New World who tried to be truly American.

It is a tribute to Rubén Darío's talent that he could gather ideas from so many diverse sources and make them into his own by means of his marvelous ability for writing verses. He was like a bee that could make honey from many flowers. His life too was that of the wanderer. Born in Nicaragua, he emigrated to the west coast of South America and thence to Buenos Aires. While in Chile he made his first great literary success by the publication of *Azul*. This book was partly in prose and partly in verse. It is a mark of Darío's unusual ability that an account of his career must consider both his prose and his verse.

The prose compositions of *Azul* were impressionistic pieces, almost poems in prose. Though most have the form of tales or fairy stories, their scenes being laid in Greece or some other land of the author's imagination, some are mere torrents of imagery. Nearly all teach the compelling force of the desire for the ideal, whether for the poet the ideal is a nymph in the wood, *La Ninfa*, or for the gnome the ruby, *El Rubí*, symbol of the reproductive power of mother earth. Blue is the color of the ideal, like the veil of Queen Mab, *El Velo de la Reina Mab*, who comes in her car made of a single pearl to the four lean unshaven men in the garret, the sculptor, the painter, the musician, and the poet. Complaining bitterly of their luck, their lamentations are turned to laughter after she has wrapped them in her veil through which they glimpse life with a rosy tint.

The most important poems in *Azul* were those which voiced the feelings excited in the poet's mind by the four seasons of the year. Spring of course suggests love; but so do the others. Summer love is symbolized in the mating of Bengal tigers. That day, however, the tigress was killed in the hunt by the Prince of Wales; wherefore the tiger mourning in his lair dreamed of revenge, of sinking his claws in the tender bosoms of children and maidens. Love in the Autumn is tinged with the melancholy of the season of dying things; nevertheless a friendly fairy whispers secrets to the poet, what the birds are singing, what the girls are dreaming. As for Winter, its snows may drive men from the city streets to sit by the fire of crackling logs, but what better music to accompany caresses and kisses?

The peculiarities and excellencies of *Azul* were pointed out by Don Juan Valera in his famous criticism printed in his *Cartas americanas*. The Spanish critic was impressed by the Gallic quality of Darío's style, especially of his prose. As his language was excellent Castilian, Valera termed Darío's Gallicism mental rather than verbal. Azul was a pure work of art with the stamp of originality. Though it showed that its author was saturated with the most extreme type of French literature, he imitated no one writer. His adoration of nature was pantheistic. And though at times there was an exuberance of sensual love, as in the poems on the seasons of the year, there was something religious about that love. Though applauding the perfection of his "mental Gallicism," Valera wished that there occupied a larger place in Darío's art the teachings of Spanish literature. As for the title of the book, or more especially the motto from Victor Hugo, "L'art, c'est l'azur!" it seemed to the critic merely an empty phrase. Why is art blue rather than green, red, or yellow?

Between *Azul,* published in 1888, and Darío's next

volume of poems, *Prosas Profanas,* 1896, he took vast strides along the road of mental Gallicism. While there is no evidence of his following Valera's advice regarding the study of Spanish literature, he was certainly well read in the classics and in the poets of the fourteenth and fifteenth centuries. He even wrote poems in imitation of the archaic and introduced archaic words into his vocabulary. Moreover, he undoubtedly welcomed any suggestion that came to him from the work of his contemporaries. In addition those eight years were full of experience. In Buenos Aires, an enthusiastic group of young men formed a coterie of modernista poets. In 1892 he was in Europe. In Madrid, where he represented Nicaragua at the quadricentennial celebration of the discovery of America, he made the acquaintance of the Andalusian poet, Salvador Rueda. For the latter's *En Tropel* Darío wrote some verses by way of prologue with the title *Pórtico.* To these verses are commonly ascribed the entrance into Spanish literature of the modernista influence. In Paris he made the personal acquaintance of many French poets as well as a rather critical study of the works of the decadent and symbolist schools. The articles which he contributed to periodicals on these men were collected in *Los Raros.* Taken together they express Darío's own literary ideal, art is the rare, the strange, the unusual, so well embodied in the title for the volume of verses which he wrote during these years, " Profane Prose."

But to please this poet's sensibilities the strange and rare must be conjoined with the elegant and the sumptuous. His artistic creed may be art for art's sake, with little concern for conventional morality, but he has no liking for the ugly and vulgar. He is no follower of Baudelaire. Rather his exquisite senses demand clean beauty, fine lace, shining jewels, sweet odors, brilliant flowers, the refinements of classic Greece or of eighteenth-century French society. The lady of his dreams is some-times typified by Leda, more often she is a marquise of the old régime.

From the point of view of versification, *Prosas Profanas* contains all manner of experiments aiming at a greater metrical freedom as well as new poetic forms. It was the poems of this volume that gave models to other mod-ernistas. A single example of the many good pieces in it is the favorite *Sinfonía en gris mayor*. The novelty of this poem, the emphasis given to one color was probably suggested by Gautier's *Symphonie en blanc majeur*, but Darío seems to have applied also Rimbaud's conception of vocalic tone color. The vowel of the word "gris" (gray), the only assonance used throughout the poem, may be employed even in the English rendering for the same purpose.

> The sea as in a silvered glass
> Reflects a sky as gray as zinc;
> Afar some birds in bands, like stains,
> Into the polished surface sink.
>
> The sun, a disk opaque and round,
> Slow climbs the zenith, old and sick,
> The seawind rests within the shade,
> Its pillow a cloud-bank gray and thick.
>
> The waves heaving with leaden beat
> Beneath the wharf their moan begin;

A sailor sitting on a coil of rope,
Puffing his pipe, is rapt in thought
Of fog-clad home and distant kin.

A wandering wolf the old seadog;
Brazilian suns have tanned his skin;
Typhoons in China, fierce and wild,
Have seen him drink his flask of gin.

His nose so red has long been known
To salt sea spray, which knows them still,
His curly hair, his biceps huge,
His canvas cap, his blouse of drill.

Through smoke upcurling from his pipe
His foggy land the old marine
Can glimpse, from where one sultry day
Shook out her sails his barkentine.

In tropic siesta he falls asleep,
While gray on all its mark imprints.
The sky to the horizon shows
A draftsman's scale of grayish tints.

The tropic siesta: the locust old
Essays her guitar hoarse and thin;
The cricket plays in monotone
On the single string of her violin.[1]

The preëminent quality of the verses in *Prosas Profanas* was grace; in his next volume of collected poems, *Cantos de Vida y Esperanza*, 1905, it was force. Many of these poems had been called forth by public events. The Spanish-American world at the turn of the century had

---

[1] Version of Alfred Coester.

been stirred to the depths of its soul, first by the revolution in Cuba, and second by the Spanish-American war. Though sympathizing with Cuba the Spanish Americans felt the call of the race against the great northern republic. In their Tyrtæan outcries Rubén Darío followed rather than led.

He was essentially a poet of personal expression. Writing some verses as an introduction to the *Cantos de Vida y Esperanza*, he made with engaging frankness a confession of his past and a criticism of his literary career which leaves only the details to be supplied by the biographer. He referred to the ideas of his youth, his sensuality, his love of beauty, the bitterness of disillusion, his longing for sincerity in art; at last he feels that "the caravan sets out for Bethlehem." It cannot be said, however, in spite of certain poems on repentance, that Rubén Darío seriously renounced his Epicureanism or became devout as did Verlaine and other French poets of his acquaintance.

Metrically the new experiment in *Cantos de Vida y Esperanza* was an attempt at the classic hexameter, the meter which he selected as most worthy for his political themes. In *La Salutación al Optimista*, beginning with the line,

> Ínclitas razas ubérrimas, sangre de Hispania fecunda,

he not only set a new model for patriotic utterances in verse, but he extended a greeting to Spanish Americans urging them to lay aside their quarrels and look to the future when the ancient Latin stock should rule a new continent. The enemy most to be feared seemed the "colossus of the north" which for the moment was typified

in President Roosevelt.   Accordingly in an ode *A Roosevelt*, Darío thus abjured the bogey of Anglo-Saxon domination.

'Tis only with the Bible or Walt Whitman's verse,
That you, the mighty hunter, are reached by other men.
You're primitive and modern, you're simple and complex,
A veritable Nimrod with aught of Washington.
You are the United States;
You are the future foe
Of free America that keeps its Indian blood,
That prays to Jesus Christ, and speaks in Spanish still.
You are a fine example of a strong and haughty race;
You're learned and you're clever; to Tolstoy you're opposed;
And whether taming horses or slaying savage beasts,
You seem an Alexander and Nebuchadnezzar too.
As madmen to-day are wont to say,
You're a great professor of energy.
You seem to be persuaded
That life is but combustion,
That progress is eruption,
And where you send the bullet
You bring the future.
                        No!
The United States are rich; they're powerful and great;
They join the cult of Mammon to that of Hercules,
And when they stir and roar, the very Andes shake. . . .

But our America, which since the ancient times
Has had its native poets; which lives on fire and light,
On perfumes and on love; our vast America,
The land of Montezuma, the Inca's mighty realm,
Of Christopher Columbus the fair America,
America the Spanish, the Roman Catholic,
O men of Saxon eyes and fierce barbaric soul,
This land still lives and dreams, and loves and stirs!

Take care!
The daughter of the Sun, the Spanish land doth live!
And from the Spanish lion a thousand whelps have sprung!
'Tis need, O Roosevelt, that you be God himself . . .
Before you hold us fast in your grasping iron claws.

And though you count on all, one thing is lacking,—God![1]

This popular and interesting expression of the common Spanish-American conception of the United States was largely repudiated by Darío in a subsequent poem *Salutación al Aguila*, written to welcome the North American delegates to the Pan-American Congress held in Brazil in 1906. In this poem he prays for the secret of the northern republic's political and material success and reminds the Eagle that the Condor exists with his brother in the lofty heights. Together they may achieve marvels. Rather than write such sentiments as these a Venezuelan critic said he would have cut off his hand.

The volume in which this poem was printed, *El Canto errante*, 1907, contained verses of many periods grouped to bring out the idea suggested by the title that the poet's mission is to travel over the universe seeking beauty everywhere and express it in beautiful language, for the soul of all things is Beauty. This pantheistic notion is a leading characteristic of some of Darío's followers.

The modernista school in so far as it was influenced by Rubén Darío, started with imitation of *Azul* and the verses collected in *Prosas Profanas*. The establishment of the *Revista Latina* by his coterie in Buenos Aires was the signal for ambitious young men in other centers of

[1] Version of E. C. Hills.

Latin culture in America to found such periodicals as
La Revista Azul in Mexico, *Cosmópolis* in Caracas, and
Pluma i Lápiz in Santiago de Chile. These periodicals
were short lived but stimulated the establishment of *El
Cojo Ilustrado* of Caracas and the *Revista Moderna* of
Mexico, both of which for more than a decade at the turn
of the century were the leading literary journals of Latin
America. In them might be read the best literature that
was being produced. No poet, however, developed the
versatility of Rubén Darío though in Buenos Aires there
were several writers with distinct personalities working
along original lines.

Of these Leopoldo Díaz, born 1862, selected the sonnet
as his favorite mode of expression and was really a Parnassian in the manner of the French poet, J. M. de Heredia.
The sonnets reveal a sensuous love of beauty under the
guise of Hellenism, which is not derived, however, from
a study of ancient Greece, but from Parisian poets. Following the trend of his contemporary Americans, Díaz
wrote one volume of sonnets devoted to the early Spaniards
in America, *Los Conquistadores*. In all his work Díaz'
special merit is his clever handling of the Spanish language.
In regard to it the French critic, Remy de Gourmont, in a
preface to a French translation of *Las Sombras de Hellas*,
coined the term "neo-español."

He said: "The Spanish language lives again free and
rejuvenated in the old Castilian colonies which have
become proud republics. This new literature owes little
to Spain beside the language; its ideas are European. Its
intellectual capital is Paris. . . . In the purest 'new-
Spanish' Díaz sings of Greek beauty. This language

more supple than the rude classic Castilian is also more clear; the phrase constructed in the French manner pursues a course more logical, more according to the natural course of thought."

Such ideas raised a storm of protest from Spaniards, while Spanish Americans were not quite content to agree to all the implications. Their efforts to enrich their vocabulary were by no means limited to Gallicisms, for they studied the Spanish classics and revived many old terms as well as adopted such Americanisms as appeared necessary in description of local conditions.

CHAPTER XV

NOT long after Rubén Darío arrived in the city of Buenos Aires, he formed a close friendship with Ricardo Jaimes Freyre, a Bolivian, with whom, according to Darío's own words, he discussed "French symbolism, D'Annunzio, English pre-Raphaelites and other novelties of the day, without forgetting the ancestral Hitas and Berceos." The result of Jaimes Freyre's interest in the new poetry was a volume of poems to which he gave the title, *Castalia bárbara* (1897), because their background was Scandinavian mythology. The dark and desolate region where Lok dwelt and the forest where the black eagle and the crows of Odin listened to the moan of icy winds afforded the poet another type of the exotic than Darío's ancient Greece or eighteenth century France. Jaimes Freyre used new metrical forms, derived in part from a personal theory of Spanish versification. Of this he published a complete discussion in his *Leyes de la versificación castellana*, 1912. Later in life Jaimes Freyre cultivated the more serious muse of history and published investigations in the history of northern Argentina and southern Bolivia. For many years he was professor of history in the Colegio nacional de Tucumán. In 1923 he came to the United States as minister from Bolivia.

Another of Darío's friends was Leopoldo Lugones (b. 1874). He came from a small village in the Argentine province of Cordoba to Buenos Aires, at the age of twenty, bringing with him the plan for a long philosophical poem in the style of Victor Hugo, *Las montañas del oro*, which he completed and published in 1897. Lugones accepted many of Darío's artistic theories but wrote his modernistic poems, full of symbolism and exaggerated metaphors, in a style unmistakably his own. They appeared first in periodicals, later in the volume, *Los crepúsculos del jardín*, 1905. A second volume of verse, *El lunario sentimental*, 1909, has a highly ironical prefatory poem showing the rejection of the more symbolistic phase of modernism. The centenary year, 1910, and the prizes offered by Argentine periodicals for suitable poems stimulated Lugones to the production of his *Odas seculares*, some six thousand lines, in which he tried to characterize the features of country life, the growing plants, the harvests, the grazing cattle and the farmers. While his pictures of people were realistic, his landscapes were rendered in a more modernistic spirit, especially in that mood which the Spanish modernista poets, Juan Ramón Jiménez and Antonio Machado, had developed. To them every landscape had a mystic meaning which it was the poet's task to express. Lugones in endowing inanimate objects with a soul was partially successful, but he undertook too big a job when he tried to apply his method to all Argentina.

Lugones tried his hand too, at artistic prose, with eminent success, rivalling even Rodó. He chose for his material historical topics, *El imperio jesuítico* and *La guerra gaucha;* for the centenary of Sarmiento in 1911, he wrote a *Historia de Sarmiento*. The story of the Jesuit missions in Paraguay, with their headquarters at the University in the Argentine city of Cordoba, was a fit subject for an artist; somewhat less so, the incidents of the civil wars of the time of Rosas when the gauchos possessed the land.

It was not in Buenos Aires among Darío's immediate circle that modernistic ideas of art received their greatest development but in Montevideo, on the other side of the Río de la Plata.   There José Enrique Rodó (1872–1917) was editing a literary journal, *La revista nacional de literatura y ciencias sociales*, which welcomed the new doctrine. Rodó wrote an essay on Darío, published as a preface to the second edition of *Prosas profanas*, 1899, and now indispensable to every student of the poet.   He declared himself a "modernista; I belong with all my soul to the great reaction, which gives character and meaning to the evolution of thought at the end of the century."   Rodó founded on the modernistic cult of beauty a philosophy of ethics. His special contribution to modernista literature was the essay written with great care as to style and form.   The most famous is *Ariel*, 1900.

This is in the nature of an exhortation by a teacher who is bidding his pupils farewell.   He urges them to maintain a sanctuary of the spirit, unsullied by utilitarianism. They should lead an active life with beauty as their guide, rather than passion or desire for material gain, because from the love of beauty spring man's highest instincts. Justice and duty are forms of beauty while love is an instinctive longing for beauty.   Man's greatest privilege is to develop his personality, but in doing so he must beware of imitating others, especially of imitating the crowd.   The crowd is incapable of a rational life under the guidance of beauty.   In his collective capacity, as a member of a commonwealth, the Latin American must take care not to be led astray by imitation of utilitarian North America.

Rodó expressed his ideas on all sorts of ethical topics in *Motivos de Proteo*, 1909. By this book he placed his name among the great moralists of the world. It was Darío who first said of him, "He is the Latin Emerson." But his ideas are expressed in rather too fragmentary a fashion to stand a close comparison. On the other hand his essays on the Ecuadorean Montalvo and on Bolívar, both republished in *El Mirador de Próspero*, are carefully finished discourses. For Montalvo, Rodó had a feeling of kinship, because he cultivated the art of writing "with the fervor, the perseverance, respect and care of a religion." For Bolívar, Rodó had special admiration, as the author of the idea that Spanish America should be a "magna patria," a super-country, which Spanish Americans should hold in as great esteem and love with as much fervor as the particular land of their birth. Rodó was a most ardent advocate of a united Latin America. Curiously enough this is the idea with greatest vitality that was fostered by the modernista poets and writers.

The preciosity of language which was present in Darío's poems and abounded in the early verses of Lugones was practiced especially by a compatriot of Rodó, Julio Herrera y Reissig (1875–1910). In the garret of his father's house, from which he could look out on the harbor of Montevideo, he established a retreat, "La torre de los panoramas," where he could compose in peace his singular verses. Just how eccentric they could be may be seen in the translation of a few lines from a sonnet "*Sad morning.*" "Lilac worries disturbed the illusion of the morning. A

Sibylline trembling at times epilepsied the window, when suddenly there rolled into the darkness of my eyes, a foolish myth. Good-bye, good-bye, I shouted; and toward heaven ascended the gray sarcasm of her glove together with the red of my jealousy."

For his later poems Herrera found true inspiration in country scenes. Like other modernista poets in the first decade of the century, he sought the soul of the landscape and found it. The only jarring note is given by the names of his maidens, Alicia and Cloris, instead of Concha and Pepa. But it may be that in the realistic touches of Herrera's poetry, Lugones found the suggestion for his own. When Herrera died, the Uruguayan government accorded him an honor never before shown a poet in that country. It bestowed a yearly pension of six hundred dollars on his widow and bought two thousand dollars' worth of his books, for free distribution in other countries.

Herrera's verses have found a great many admirers. Their preciosity and obscurity have caused them to be compared with those of Góngora. In fact the modernista movement seems to have restored the founder of culteranismo to favor. Darío openly praised him and was proud to be called a new Góngora.

Americanism, or appeal to the solidarity of race, had no attraction for Herrera. If Rodó was its prophet, its high priest was José Santos Chocano, born in Perú in 1875. At the age of nineteen Chocano found himself in prison for participation in a revolutionary movement. He vented his wrath in *Iras santas*, verses written in the pugnacious style of Díaz Mirón and printed for emphasis

in red ink. More significant of his future were the poems
En la aldea, descriptive of country life and produced about
the same time. Five years later when his long patriotic
poem *La epopeya del morro* was given a prize by the Ateneo
of Lima, Chocano had definitely found the path which
was to lead him to celebrity as "the poet of America."
His prize poem narrates the famous incident which
occurred in the war of the Pacific when a body of Peruvian
soldiers, surrounded by a superior number of Chileans on
a mountain near Arica, threw themselves into the sea
rather than surrender. In 1906 was published in Spain,
his volume *Alma América (poemas indo-españoles)* with a
dedication to His Majesty Don Alfonso XIII.

In this tribute to the king, Chocano makes his purpose
very clear. "I wish to give you America in my song;
because the language of Cervantes can make you more the
master of our fertile Eden than the ships of Columbus."
His muse he says at times is "Indian, at times Castilian."
The double character of his poems he frequently stresses,
as in the sonnet *Blasón:* "I am the singer of America,
aboriginal and wild; my lyre has a soul, my song an ideal.
When I feel myself an Inca, I render homage to the Sun,
which gives me the scepter of royal power. When I feel
my Spanish blood, I evoke colonial days."

The volume contained prefatory words by Menéndez
y Pelayo, and by Unamuno, both enthusiastic in praise.
The former said, "Your brilliant and inspired poems will
be a new bond between Spain and America." The latter,
amplifying the poet's idea and quoting his lines, wrote,
"Yes, the language, which is the blood of the spirit, is the
foundation of our spiritual country. America is Greater

Spain; it is part of our great spiritual country constituted by our language."

The variety of topics which Chocano treated in *Alma América* was very considerable, the conquistadores, their horses, the mines of Potosí, the colonial cities, plants, animals, birds, reptiles, rivers and mountains. In a poem on the Panama canal *La Epopeya del Pacífico (a la manera yanki)* he pays his respects to the United States. Though North American energy may open the canal, the Latin race will profit by it most; yet the Latin American should "distrust the man with blue eyes," even though he may depend on the forest, the swamp and the fever to protect him. Chocano's most successful and attractive poems are those in which, in Parnassian manner, he paints a picture. Take for example *Los volcanes*.

> Every volcano rears its outlined height,
> As if, upon a sudden o'er the sky,
> Two unseen hands suspended from on high
> The corner of a veil before our sight.
> The mountain's crest is white, and purely white;
> With hot desire its heart seethes burningly.
> Strange contrast is the ice to fire so nigh,
> Like a stern soul above a passion's might.
> Volcanoes are grim stoneheaps, dark and bare;
> But at their feet the blooming vales we see
> Like carpets, many hued, with spangled bowers;
> And there, amid those fields of colors fair,
> Outlined against the blue, they seem to be
> Baskets o'erturned that pour abroad their flowers.[1]

As a modernista poet, one to whom the form of the verse was all important, Chocano was only a poor imita-

[1] Version of Alice Stone Blackwell.

tor.   He wrote too rapidly and did not think in symbols
and metaphors.   In contrast with him was the Colombian
Guillermo Valencia, born in the high Andean city of
Popayán, 1873.   Valencia's published poems are few in
number but each is as polished and complete as labor could
effect.   In his opinion, a perfect poet was one who would
"sacrifice a world to polish a verse."   His ideals of art
were those of the Parnassians, but in versification, his
model was José Asunción Silva, his fellow countryman.
Valencia perfected the fourteen-syllable Alexandrine.   He
selected this verse for one of his finest poems, *Leyendo
a Silva*, considering it, arranged in rhymed couplets in
Silva's manner, most appropriate for his purpose.   The
poem, full of rare words, suggestive of the most refined
elegance, with many allusions to Silva's lines, is a fine
poetic characterization of that poet's art.

   The constant theme of Valencia's poems is the fate of
artists, especially poets, in a hostile or indifferent world.
Those "conquistadores of the Ideal," the musician, the
painter, the sculptor and the poet, are a "luckless tribe of
wretches" like the miners who for a meager wage bring forth
from the earth with great toil diamonds, emeralds and
rubies (*Anarkos*).   Or again the white storks (*Cigüeñas
blancas*) are "the faithful symbol of the artists' mad
dreams," as they wing their way to a more propitious
clime.

   Valencia's method is to begin with a realistic setting
that will suggest the desired atmosphere.   He sees the
"timid band of white storks softly fold their wings and
settle on the abandoned tower in the dying twilight."
In *Leyendo a Silva* the lady who holds in her slender fingers

the "thin long book of poems, delightful and bitter" is dressed "in brocade of uncertain color" and reclines on "a divan of red velvet." In *Los camellos* "two languid camels measure with great strides a Nubian desert." Driven by "a black maiden in the gloom of the dying day," they seemed like "a procession of Melancholy," as they seek to quench their thirst at a well. Like such camels are artists, though their thirst is the thirst for the infinite.

A fine poem and a real work of art is the one which Valencia indites to his native city, *A Popayán*, but the reader needs a commentary to understand the many allusions. Valencia is the poets' poet. Other people, less versed in the symbolist vocabulary, need a dictionary when reading his lines. Another poem, *Alma mater* (*a Popayán*), is more comprehensible. With these compositions Valencia has rescued from oblivion the cradle of many famous Colombians.

In Colombia, Valencia's influence is chiefly to be found in Alfredo Gómez Jaime (b. 1878), a poet who combined the traditional religious tone of Colombian verse with the new versification. His best known poem is *El hermano Lobo*, an excellent narrative of the story of Saint Francis and the wolf, which sought the saint's protection from pursuing hunters. But at this epoch in Colombia, the romantic attitude still had such a strong hold on readers of poetry, that the really favorite poets of the day were Ricardo Nieto (b. 1878) and Julio Flórez (1865–1923).

Outside of Colombia, Valencia's volume, *Ritos*, published in London in 1898, was a companion to Darío's *Prosas*

profanas. The modernista magazines liberally reproduced both Valencia's original poems and his translations
from D'Annunzio, Eugenio de Castro and various French
poets. In Chile, his influence appears to have been considerable. Poets were numerous in Santiago about 1900.
The most popular was Pedro Antonio González (1863–
1903), a thorough Bohemian and late romantic. Diego
Dublé Urrutia, the Colombian Isiais Gamboa, Antonio
Bórquez Solar, Manuel Magallanes Moure and Pedro
Prado were all members of the group. The last two maintained the modernista tradition for many years. Pedro
Prado's specialty became an artistic and imaginative
prose, which is best read in the prose romance *Alsino* or
in his *Leyenda de la Reina Rapa Nui*.

The popularity of American topics after the publication
of Chocano's *Alma América* led Rubén Darío himself to
versify American legends, yet his manner of doing so is
rather that of the Argentine Rafael Obligado, whose
literary tertulias Darío used to frequent in Buenos Aires.
Momotombo and *Tutecotzimi* are poems that transport
the reader to the savage beauties of the Nicaraguan
landscape and primitive history. In 1908, Darío was
appointed minister plenipotentiary from Nicaragua to
Spain, an honor of which he was prouder than of his fame
as a poet. In 1910, for the Argentine centenary he wrote
his *Canto a la Argentina*, his longest poem. From the
point of view of versification, it is vulnerable to criticism.
As a poetic synthesis of Argentina, it is unsurpassed. The
winter of 1908 Darío spent on the island of Mallorca for
the purpose of restoring his health, undermined by dissipation. There are a few poems from this period, but

thereafter most of his work was journalistic, including a valuable autobiography and three essays about the production of his three chief books, *Azul*, *Prosas profanas*, and *Cantos de vida y esperanza*. With the outbreak of the great war he fell into specially hard straits. In 1915, a fellow countryman persuaded him to attempt a lecture tour in the United States. His first lecture was a fiasco. He lived for a brief time in sickness and poverty in New York. Finally a patron of all things Hispanic in that city provided him with a passage ticket to Nicaragua, where he died soon after his arrival on February 6, 1916. He was accorded a national funeral, carried out somewhat on the lines suggested by his famous poem *Responso a Verlaine*. Since his death his fame has grown enormously in Spain.

Among Rubén Darío's Spanish American friends and fellow poets in Paris was one whom his gayer companions dubbed "the monk of poetry, the Mexican Amado Nervo (1870–1919). After Darío, Nervo is the greatest poet produced by the modernista movement. He was not a brilliant artist in words, like his friend, but in depth of thought far excelled him. His greatest poems, however, were not produced till after the modernista movement had run its course. His modernista poems are often most frivolous. In his later work he was following the tradition both of his own earlier work and of his native Mexico.

Born in the Pacific coast city of Tepic, he was attracted toward studying for the priesthood, but he took only minor orders. Of his spiritual experiences at the seminary there may be a hint in his prose tales *El Bachiller*, *Pascual Aguilera* and *El Donador de almas* with which he began his quest for literary fortune, when he first went to Mexico City in 1895. Here he made the acquaintance of Gutiérrez Nájera and contributed to the *Revista azul*. During his lifetime, Nervo published several volumes of prose, bits of journalistic work which he thought worth preserving. Though many of these articles are stories in one sense of the word, they are often mere anecdotes, told most artistically and concern abnormal cases of psychology, the inevitable and unexpected occurrence of death or poetic meditations on the mysterious presence of the unknown in our daily lives.

These volumes might be called the notebooks of a poet. An idea that is developed at length in the prose pages will frequently be found in synthetic form in his verses. In Switzerland, for example, his imagination was touched by a tragic story of a romantic lover who met death in attempting to scale an inaccessible crag in search of edelweiss, "flor enigmática," to give to his sweetheart. In his verses, the perplexing and mysterious flower becomes a symbol of innocence and virtue. His prose style, characterized by an element of poetic mystery, is always charming.

His earliest important volume of verse, *Místicas*, paid tribute to the famous religious mystics. One poem in it, *A Kempis*, was long a favorite of his for public recitation. When he went to Europe for the first time he took with him for publication a series of poems on nature topics, of which *La Hermana Agua* has remained popular with readers of Nervo's poetry. It treats the mystery behind all the forms and transformations of water, the running streams on the earth and beneath it, vapor, clouds, rain, snow, dew, ice and frost.   In Paris he became an intimate friend of Rubén Darío.   Together they journeyed to Italy to attend and report Pope Leo's jubilee.   In 1902 Nervo published *El Exodo y las flores del camino*, his first poems in the modernista manner, reflections of his travel experiences, with stress on the exotic.   Returning to Mexico, he obtained the post of secretary in the Mexican embassy in Madrid.   In that city he distinguished himself by an *Epitalamio* celebrating Alfonso XIII's marriage in 1906. He pays the king homage, saying, "King thou art still, in a certain measure, of America as formerly, as long as the divine language of Cervantes sweetens the lips and sings in the songs of eighteen republics and fifty million beings."

Nervo remained in Madrid till after the close of the great war.   He became interested in Buddhism, and his verses show a pantheistic tone abounding in Oriental symbolism.   In December 1916 he published *Elevación*, a book of short poems.   Many of them are personal excuses to the "ineffable" for his presumption in having inquired so often the "why of existence."   Others express noble sentiments inspired by Christianity and Buddhism. In a later volume, *El Estanque de los lotus*, 1918, the symbolism and thought is wholly Buddhistic.   The volume *Elevación* has a singular unity despite its diversity of topics, due in part, perhaps, to the poet's method of expressing in the opening lines of a poem, either by a sententious phrase or a bit of symbolism, the thought which he amplifies in the whole.   In the verses, for example, beginning, "The chestnut tree does not know that it is called chestnut, but in the autumn yields its noble fruit of autumnal perfume," Nervo exalts the worth of carrying out one's destiny without ostentation. Concerning the virtue of forgiveness, he writes, "If a thorn wound me, I draw aside from the thorn, I do not hate it. . . . Rancor, of what use is rancor? It staunches no wounds, corrects no evil. My rosetree scarcely has time to yield flowers and wastes no sap giving sharp pricks. If my enemy passes near my rosetree, he will carry away roses of the subtlest essence. If he should note on them any splashes of bright red, it will be from the blood which his illwill of yesterday shed, when he struck me in anger and which my rosetree returns, changed into a flower of peace." Considering solely the content, *Elevación* is the greatest book produced by the modernista movement.

The change that was taking place in the point of view of the poets, leaving behind the more sensuous elements, had been observed by another Mexican, Enrique González Martínez (b. 1871). In his volume, *Los senderos ocultos*, 1911, a memorable sonnet advises that it is time "to wring the neck of the swan with deceitful plumage, which displays his grace without perceiving the soul of things. Consider the wise owl whose eye interprets the mysterious book of nocturnal silence." The poet voiced a general feeling. In Uruguay, Carlos Reyles gave the title "Death of the swan," to a prose essay, in which he urged Latin Americans to adopt a strenuous life in pursuit of realities.

The continuers of the modernista poetry have been women. Several have attained to prominence, and, though natives of different countries, their work has the unity of sex. Like the romantic poets of a hundred years ago, their main themes are themselves and their vague longings. But the remarkable thing is, that it should be representatives of the cloistered women of Latin America who have, from among the women of earth, been the ones who have most candidly voiced the suppressed feelings of sex.

The first to do this was Delmira Agustini (1890–1915), of mixed Italian and German parentage, born in Montevideo.   When but sixteen, she published her first volume of verses, *El libro blanco*, followed by *Cantos de la mañana*, 1910, and *Los cálices vacíos*, 1913.   The last had a preface by Rubén Darío in which he said, "It is the first time in the Castilian language that a woman's soul appears in the pride of innocence and love, unless it be Saint Theresa in her divine exaltation."   Though Delmira expressed the sexuality of women in daring symbolism, she put nothing sensual into her verses.   She was simply outspoken, not only for herself but for all women.   In her *Plegaria a Eros*, she prayed, "Eros, have you never felt pity for the statues ?   Pity for lives that are never mellowed by your fair winds. . . .   Pity for the hands gloved in ice, that never grasp the delightful fruits of the flesh nor the fantastic flowers of the soul."   In *Visión* she addressed an imaginary lover, "Silent you stood by my side.   You bent over me, like the great weeping willow of melancholy, beside the deep lakes of silence."   Other details of the vision would have delighted Freud.   The emotions that Delmira expressed were not joyous; they were vague, tragically intense, as of one in pursuit of an unrealizable dream, and in consequence her verses are praised for their note of sincerity.

Delmira's first disciple was Alfonsina Storni, schoolmistress in Buenos Aires.   Alfonsina (the women quite romantically refer to themselves and to each other by their given names) was brought when a child to Argentina by her parents from Italian Switzerland, where she was born in 1892. At thirteen she was a member of a theatrical troupe, but she preferred the school to the stage. She attended a normal school in Coronda. Her first book of verses, *La inquietud del rosal,* appeared in 1916. The rosetree yields sweet roses unnoticed. In *Dulce daño,* 1918, she says, "I made moaning, weeping, dreaming, alas poor me!" The sweet harm was caused by a bee. "A bee has stung me; a white lily I was; and then flew off after the dahlias." The love affairs and their details in these poems and in *Irremediablemente,* 1919, and in *Languidez,* 1920, smack of reality rather than dreams. In *Ocre,* 1925, the poetess professes much wisdom in the ways of men, but her bitterness and pessimism are expressed with greater art and skill in rhetoric and symbolism. She is just Alfonsina who knows how to say things cleverly.

Another poetess with continental reputation is Juana de Ibarbourou, who lives in Montevideo. She was a happily married woman with one son when she offered to the public a volume of verse, *Las lenguas de diamante,* 1919. The diamond tongues speak with joyous accent, like the woman who comes to her lover, exclaiming, "Take me now when it still is early and I bring fresh dahlias in my hand. Take me now when my flesh is fragrant, my eyes clear and my skin of rose; now, when my light foot is shod with springtime."

Juanita delights in odors and the pagan suggestion of the sunny fields. "I drink the clean, clear water of the brook, eating the juicy flesh of the strawberry, or search-

ing for the fragrant clusters of the raspberry.   My body is
filled with the hot aroma of ripe grain.   My hair, flung to the
wind, scatters an odor of sunlight, of hay, of sage, of mint
and barley flowers.   I am free, healthy, gay, youthful and
brown, as if I were the goddess of wheat and oats."

She belongs wholly to her lover.   "I grew for thee, fell
me.   I flowered for thee, pluck me.   I flowed for thee,
drink me."

Like every pagan, she fears death; but thinks she can
frighten the monster away.   "Charon, I shall be a scandal
in your boat.   While the other shades pray, groan or
weep, I shall go like a lark singing across the river.   I
shall bring to your bark my wild perfume."

If she should die, she begs, "Lover! If I die, do not take
me to the cemetery; bury me near the laughing divine
chatter of some bird retreat, close to top of the ground.
Already I feel the struggle of my flesh to return.   Scatter
seed above me, to take root in my bones.   By the living
path of the roots, I shall come up and look at you in the
purple lilies."

Juana de Ibarbourou's poems were received with great
enthusiasm by the public.   In a later volume, *Raiz
salvaje*, she published some charming prose sketches, filled
with her characteristic fancies; but since then she has
lived more devoted to her family than to literature.   One
critic said of her, "She is a young nymph of the Cytherean
woodland in all the innocence of her nubile instincts."

Another poetess who has achieved the widest celebrity
is a Chilean, "Gabriela Mistral," born Lucila Godoy in
1889.   From the age of sixteen she was a teacher in a
girl's school in a country village.   Personal suffering made

her a poet. The verses which she contributed to a periodical in Santiago possessed such a heart-wringing quality that the public demanded to know more of Gabriela Mistral. Finally the Chilean government made her the principal of a school in Santiago. In 1922 José Vasconcelos, then Mexican minister of education, passed through Santiago after representing his country at the Brazilian centenary of independence in Rio de Janeiro. Vasconcelos offered her a two-year contract to supervise the establishment of rural schools in Mexico. About the same time a volume of her verses, *Desolación*, was brought out in New York and reëdited in Santiago.

Through this volume Gabriela Mistral first became known outside of her native country. Her poetry, because of its self-revelations, belongs to the romantic type. Her verses are the cry of the deceived woman whose lover has left her. "Her whom you love the clouds paint above my house. Go like a thief to kiss her, but when you caress her you find my face. God does not wish you to have sunlight, unless you walk with me. God does not wish you to drink, unless I tremble in the water; nor consent that you sleep, except among my tresses."

Not all the poems are maledictions; many are prayers, conversations with Christ, a trait that lends them a peculiar individuality. "Snatch him, Lord, from those fatal hands or plunge him in the long sleep you can give."

And when, strangely enough, the long sleep does come to the faithless one, her prayers intercede for his repose. "I tell thee, Lord, he was good. . . . Understand, I loved him, loved him. And loving (Thou knowest it well) is bitter exercise."

Her great regret is that he left her no child. "A son, a son, a son! I wanted a son of yours and mine. A son with the big eyes of Christ." The frankness of this *Poema del hijo* has scarcely been surpassed.

˙ The mother-love which fills her soul is transferred to the school children in her care. In them she finds "the brilliance of God." Her most admired pieces are those inspired by some incident or emotion of school life, *Planting the tree*, *Hymn to the tree*, *Prayer for the nest*, *Rondels for children*. Only in these songs has her poetry much lyric quality. In others she is too concerned with the expression of an intense emotion to seek for a rhyme. The thought therefore gains in her prose, as in her *Oración de la maestra*. "Lord, Thou who hast taught, pardon me for teaching; for bearing the name of teacher, which Thou borest on earth. Give me love solely for my school that not even the scorch of beauty be capable of stealing away from it my tenderness at all times. Grant me to be more a mother than the mothers; to be able to love and protect as they do what is not flesh of my flesh, etc."

At the conclusion of her stay in Mexico, via New York she returned to Chile, but did not long remain. Being pensioned by the Chilean government, she visited Buenos Aires and Uruguay on her way to Europe. Residing in Paris she contributes to Spanish American periodicals journalistic articles written in an attractive style. Among them are frequent flings at the United States. The accounts of her visits to Juana de Ibarbourou and Alfonsina Storni are very entertaining.

Chileans are extremely proud of **Gabriela Mistral** and her work has many admirers.

CHAPTER XVI

NOVELS

THAT form of literature which has flourished best in Spanish America since the outbreak of the great European war has been prose fiction. Fortunately authors for the most part have been wise enough to lay their plots among local scenes. The production of novels has not been limited to any one country but has been greatest in Chile and Argentina.

For Venezuela, Rufino Blanco Fombona has upheld his country's literary tradition and his own. In 1916 he published *El hombre de oro*, one of the best written of Spanish American novels and a delightful satire on the ways of politicians. His *Máscara heroica*, 1924, was a thinly veiled attack on President Gómez, so diaphanous that at his instance, the Spanish government seized the edition in the interest of good morals. In *La mitra en la mano*, 1927, the author attacks the influence of the clergy in family life and their part in supporting dictatorships.

In Cuba Arturo Montori in *El tormento de vivir* and Francisco López Leiva in *Los vidrios rotos* have revealed many aspects of Cuban life and customs. As a forceful novelist, however, Carlos Loveira has excelled all other Cubans. His life itself has been a novel on which he has drawn liberally for the scenes and episodes of his books.

Loveira, left an orphan at an early age, was brought to New York by a Cuban family. He grew up practically in the streets. When sixteen he joined a filibustering expedition of Cuban volunteers, returning in this way to his native island. After the close of the Spanish American war, he served the United States army of occupation as interpreter. Then he became a locomotive fireman and engineer, first on the Central Cuban railway and later in Panama and Costa Rica. As a representative of Spanish American workingmen, he was sent to New York to one of the meetings of the American Federation of labor. Samuel Gompers, recognizing his ability, sent him on a mission of labor propaganda through Central and South America. Later he spent five years in Yucatan.

His first writings were articles and pamphlets connected with his labor activities. In 1919 he wrote his first novel, *Los inmorales*. The title is ironic. The story concerns the misadventures of a man and woman who have left their legitimate consorts and live together, first in Cuba and then in Panama. The "immoral ones" are not this couple but other people who refuse them social recognition and subject them to ostracism or persecution. The author used his knowledge of Panama to draw a picture of life in the Canal Zone during the construction of the canal, such as cannot be found elsewhere.

Generales y doctores attacks the vice of the political situation in Cuba where the electorate is too often dazzled by titles, either military or civil. The book opens with a description of life in a country town. Then follows what must be an autobiographical account of the adventures of a young Cuban in New York, as well as the description of the sailing of the filibustering expedition of General Lacret just before the outbreak of the Spanish American war, and its subsequent participation in the revolution.

In *Los ciegos* Loveira uses his knowledge of life at the great sugar centrals. Hauling the cane and tending the fire under the boiling juice was work originally performed by negro slaves driven by the whip. Treatment of workmen apparently retains something of the tradition. The title of the book, "The Blind," is the adjective that the author applies to his characters. Don Ricardo, the capitalist, is blind both toward the state of things on his property and in his private life when his pride of caste refuses to allow his daughter to marry the man of her choice. The anarchist among the workmen is blind when he imagines he can better conditions by acts of violence. Don Ricardo's wife is blind when she permits an intriguing priest to break up her home. The novel is extremely anticlerical as well as socialistic. The theses of the book can be pardoned because the love affair between Adolfina, the rich man's daughter, and Alfonso Valdés, the labor agitator, is full of interest.

Loveira's novels undoubtedly portray real life in Cuba. They have found a large number of readers and will always remain documents for the student of social conditions in the island at the period when they were written.

In Mexico, too, several good novels have been written in recent years. Cayetano Rodríguez Beltrán, in several volumes of *Cuentos* and his novel *Un ingenio*, depicts types, manners and family life in his native state of Vera Cruz.

A notable novel is *La fuga de la quimera* by Carlos González Peña. A business man of sixty marries his ambitious young woman secretary with dreadful results. As the action takes place at the end of the Diaz régime and during that of Madero, the disorder in social life is partly a reflection of the disorder in politics.

The causes of revolutions as they lie deep in social conditions are well illustrated in *Fuertes y débiles* by José López-Portillo y Rojas. Life on a great ranch is sketched in this novel, with all the details, including the owner's free manners with the wives of his helpless tenants. When the revolution comes, the ranch is besieged, but only feebly defended because the men have either run away or have joined the insurrectionists. Bolaños, the owner, is captured and condemned to death. Some friends secure a reprieve. Chance, however, makes an injured husband the bearer of the message. Knowing its importance because he had been told he must arrive by daybreak, the man takes his time, sleeping for hours under a tree. He reaches his destination long after the firing squad has done its work.

In 1916 in Chile a group of writers under the leadership of Pedro Prado formed an organization which they named "Los Diez." Its purpose was to find by means of a literary magazine a market for their literary productions, chiefly collections of short stories and novels. Subscribers received each month either a book or a copy of the magazine. The enterprise was successful in stimulating sales, with the consequence that the next few years witnessed a revival of prose fiction. Most excellent stories of Chilean country life were published. Especially worthy of mention are the volumes *Días de campo* by Federico Gana, *En la montaña* by "F. Santiván," pseudonym of

Fernando Santibáñez, *Hojas al viento* by "Clary," pseudonym of Clarisa Polanco de Hoffmann, *La pampa trágica* by V. D. Silva, and *La lámpara maravillosa* by Amanda Labarca Hubertson. The last named has been called by the great Chilean critic, J. T. Medina, "the one that carries off the palm of all books of the kind which have been written by women in Chile." A noteworthy characteristic of these years has been the amount of literature produced by women in Chile.

Of novels an outstanding example is *La hechizada* by Santiván. The bewitched girl is a charming type of country maiden, who, despite her wooing by a city man, prefers the rustic bully who terrifies the people about him. Some unusual customs and individuals distinguish the pages of this book. Moreover, it shows the advance toward the delineation of character which marks the renascence of the Chilean novel.

In this respect Eduardo Barrios has won the reputation of being the greatest novelist. His tale, *El niño que enloqueció de amor*, first attracted attention to his work. It is the story of precocious love in a boy of eight. Psychological interest again predominates in *El hermano asno*, a book with continental fame, helped thereto because it is totally devoid of regionalistic interest. As the action takes place in a Franciscan monastery, it would fit any Spanish-speaking country. The story is told by Fray Lázaro in autobiographical style, and in matter is the simple recital of the daily life of the brothers and their manias, especially of those of Fray Rufino, who does such things as teach the Brethren Mice to eat out of the same dish with the cats; who gives away to a beggar the gala garment acquired for use on a certain image in an approaching festival; who calls his body, Brother Ass, mortifying the flesh unduly. The dénouement comes when Fray Rufino, at an early morning interview with a young woman, lays hands upon her. He dies of the excitement. To avoid the scandal which would besmirch the greatest saint of the community, the sin is assumed by Fray Lázaro, who, for the common good, is sent to a distant province. The narrative is skilfully written, with great humor. A later novel, *Un perdido*, studies the development of a man's character under the influence of army life. It contains many pictures of Chilean life.

While Chile is a homogeneous country in landscape and population, Argentina on the other side of the Andes is very diverse. While the pampa is its distinctive feature, in the north there are provinces with their backs against the mountains and others bordering on the great rivers, the Paraná and the Uruguay, whose confluence forms the Rio de la Plata. Here is situated Buenos Aires, one of the largest cities in the world and perhaps the most cosmopolitan in respect to the character of its population.

The differences in human types created by the environment and by historical development began to be a topic for writers of sketches of manners about 1900 and is still a fertile field. Poets too, led by Lugones with his *Odas seculares*, have been drawing inspiration from reality. Baldomero Fernández Moreno and Manuel Gálvez have presented the sights of provincial towns with a sentimental touch. Juan Burghi has interpreted farm labor; Evaristo Carriego, the humbler dwellers of the great city.

Miguel A. Camino brought the novelty of the distant and high Andes with their Indian men and women.

One of the first novels to exploit the manners and customs of the provinces was *La maestra normal* by Manuel Gálvez. Raselda, its heroine, was born for motherhood rather than to be a schoolmistress in the old and semi-colonial city of La Rioja. Her nature makes her a rather easy victim of a journalist from Buenos Aires who is spending his days there in an effort to regain his health, broken by dissipation. Through the eyes of these outsiders the reader sees the life of all the social circles of the city: the different groups of men who gather nightly in its cafés or at the druggist's; the home of the exclusive and aristocratic old maids, unable to find husbands of suitable rank; the *ranchería* on the outskirts of the town where poverty and vice rub elbows; the Indians who come into town to celebrate a religious festival with a procession and native songs.

Gálvez was not satisfied to draw sketches of manners but desired to write psychological novels. But the psychological element is never quite as interesting, nor as well done, as the descriptive. *La sombra del convento* is almost a guide book to the customs and the places of historical or picturesque interest in Córdoba, surnamed "the learned city," on account of its being the seat of the Jesuit university, founded in 1613 with the consequent effect on the population. *El mal metafísico* is the sad story of an artist ruined by drink. *Nacha Regules* is a woman of the streets, redeemed by the idealist Monsalvat. The penalty which society exacts of this man is well worked out. In *La tragedia de un hombre fuerte*, the hero wastes his time and energy in love affairs with different types of women. *La pampa y su pasión* studies the native love of horses and horse racing, with attendant gambling evils. In all these books there are pages of realism that make them worth reading.

That the pampa should be a source of perpetual interest in Argentina is natural. *Los caranchos de La Florida* by Benito Lynch is a powerful novel from which the reader gets an impression of the moral atmosphere of the pampa not likely to be forgotten. La Florida is a ranch where live father and son so similar in character and so harsh in their treatment of dependents that a halfwit whom young don Panchito had beaten for grinning, called them "vultures." From their violence of character springs the tragedy. The son kills his father and is put to death over his father's body by a peon whom he had once beaten with a riding whip. In *El inglés de los güesos* the interest of the book derives from the primitive love of a daughter of the pampa for an English scientist who is studying fossils and is therefore contemptuously known to the natives as "the Englishman of the bones." Though the Englishman is entirely innocent, he extricates himself from the situation with difficulty.

The real psychological novelist of the Rio de la Plata region is the Uruguayan Carlos Reyles. His best novel, *El Terruño*, relates the fortunes of an interesting family with special reference to the mother, Mamagela, and the husband of the second oldest daughter, Temístocles Pérez y González, familiarly known as Tocles. Mamagela is the mother of six children. In the opening chapter the author presents her rising at three in the morning to pre-

pare the food for her birthday celebration. Her strength
is matched by her shrewd practical sense. The oldest
daughter inherits the strength but is little more than a
husky animal whose inclinations bring about a personal
tragedy. The second daughter, being mentally bright,
was sent to a normal school and became a teacher. Falling in with Tocles she was fascinated by his brilliant
schemes and gift of talk. But these schemes, whether
social, literary or political, all go astray because people
in general do not have sense enough to understand or to
realize their value. With the birth of a child it becomes
necessary for the couple to seek refuge from dire necessity
on the mother's ranch. All goes well for a couple of years
though Tocles' big ideas for the uplift of the country
people meet with no success. Then a revolution sweeps
away the cattle and the fences as well as his last idealistic
hopes. Tocles saddles his horse to leave for the city, but
after a while yields to Mamagela's pleading and hard practical sense. He remains and finds a measure of happiness
working under his mother-in-law's suggestions for the
restoration of the ranch property. Mamagela's practical
sense thus finally wins.

In Uruguay, which maintains its characteristics as cattle
country, the population retains its creole blood with little
admixture of European through immigration. In consequence it is a fertile field for writers of prose and verse
who devote their attention to the modernized gaucho.
Of all the story tellers, either Argentine or Uruguayan,
none has equalled Javier de Viana (1872–1926). He first
won recognition by novels, *Campo*, 1896, and *Gaucha*, in
1899, which were distinguished by their realism. Other

novels followed, but the short story became and remained
Viana's specialty. When collected in volumes he gave
them titles suggestive of rural life, *Yuyos*, "Weeds,"
Leña seca "Firewood." Were it not that his stories depend so much on the setting, Viana would be numbered
among the world's great masters of the short story. Other
Uruguayans who have attempted to rival him in the delineation of rural character are Otto Miguel Cione, D. A.
Caillava, A. Montiel Ballesteros and Victor Pérez Petit.
The latter's novel, *Entre los pastos*, is practically an ampli-
fication of one of Viana's stories.

Verse, too, has been industriously cultivated in Uruguay. The gaucho verses of Elías Regules are among the
best in this genre. The great city of Montevideo has
been the theme of Emilio Frugoni in *Poemas montevidea-
nos* and other volumes.

The most original of writers of fiction in the region of
the Rio de la Plata is Horacio Quiroga. He has deliber-
ately sought the strange, unusual and fantastic, at times
the morbid. On the other hand, having lived in the
Argentine territory of Misiones, a tropical garden of
Paradise, guarded by a hostile climate and subject to
terrific inundations, he found a virgin realm to exploit.
Nature is really the chief personage in his stories. It is
she who defeats man and beast in their struggle for existence. Quiroga has made even snakes and birds pro-
tagonists of his tales. *Anaconda*, the serpent, who leads
a rebellion of the reptiles against man, the intruder, by
attacking his servants, the mules, comes to grief through
the same overpowering force of the river in flood that
carries away the enemies' feeble structures. Borne down

stream on a floating mass of vegetation, she falls victim to a bullet. One of Quiroga's most widely reprinted stories is that of the tame parrot, nearly killed by a tiger, on which the parrot takes vengeance by leading hunters to his lair.

The most popular and most prolific Argentine novelist is "Hugo Wast," pseudonym of Gustavo Martínez Zuviría. Of his early work, *Flor de durazno*, more copies have been sold than of any other Argentine book. The cine helped materially in establishing this record for it is said that it required seven years to sell the first thousand. It is a story whose setting is the great summer playground, the Sierra de Cordoba. Here a youth from Buenos Aires whiles away his leisure making love to a daughter of the land with the logical tragedy. Despite the popularity of the story it is by no means the best of the twenty or more from his pen.

Writing so rapidly he gets ahead of the literary critics who are prone at times to dismiss his latest book with the statement, "another of Hugo Wast's." Of least value perhaps are those whose plots are derived from historical events, though *La corbata celeste*, introducing episodes of Rosas' tyranny, makes an interesting contrast to Mármol's *Amalia*. It is a trifle difficult to think of a young woman of those heroic times doing such a sentimental and even so dangerous a thing as presenting her departing lover with a skyblue necktie for a keepsake when the color alone would betray him, were he to fall into his enemy's hands.

Valle negro, laid in the province of Cordoba, has the much-used situation of lovers kept apart by parents who dispute about land. But the action opens when the lovers are passing middle age and concerns two children, a boy and a girl. They are well drawn as well as a certain old woman, La Pichana, with fame as a witch. The interest lies in the customs of the country.

La Casa de los cuervos is considered by some the author's best novel. It has a revolutionary background in certain disturbances in the province of Santa Fe about the year 1877, a country well known to the author. There is much action, much fighting, much bloodshed with an intensely tragic situation. Insúa, a leader of one of the parties, kills in self defence two men, brothers-in-law, by the name of Jarque and Borja. Wounded severely he is obliged to take refuge in a manor house known as "the house of the crows." Here lives Gabriela, widow of Jarque, with her mother-in-law. Her marriage had not been one of love. The women receive Insúa and nurse him back to life without at first knowing his identity. Gabriela falls deeply in love with her sick guest. The mother is the first to learn the facts, but she hasn't the heart to inform Gabriela that she has fallen in love with the man who killed both her husband and brother. A parish priest advises her not to do so. Many events occur before Gabriela learns. After a last battle, Insúa dies in the hut of a fisherman whose daughter had also loved the dashing captain.

Buenos Aires, or rather a cross section of society in the *Ciudad turbulenta, ciudad alegre*, is studied in the novel with that title. By weaving the story around the fortunes of two aristocratic families with all their relatives and dependents, the author reaches from the highest circles to the dregs of the city. In fact the canvas is overcrowded. The complex multiplicity of illicit love affairs, leading in some cases to crimes, is perplexing. The satire on politicians and the impecunious, intriguing journalist are no doubt reminiscences of the author's days as a member of Congress.

El desierto de piedra is advertised by Hugo Wast as the novel "which he most desired to write." One can easily understand why it is his favorite. He is describing the people among whom he lives. His literary strength lies in the facile narrative of occurrences he has witnessed, not in complication of plot nor the development of great passions.

The title is the name of a tract of land situated at the upper end of a great ranch near the top of a mountain zone in the Sierra de Cordoba. The old and childless owner of the ranch has received in his home a nephew, whose daughter of twenty, Marcela, is the heroine of the story, which relates her struggles to make a success of maintaining the property. There is of course a love story and an attempted crime to salt and pepper the narrative for those who need the condiments. The interest, both for the author and the reader, springs from the characterization of the different individuals who appear in its pages: the old man who keeps his jug of wine suspended by a cord down a well of water famous for leagues around,—how the water tastes he doesn't know, but it keeps the wine as cold as ice; the grandmother who sings ballads in the winter evenings; the vigorous masculine housekeeper Leopolda and her fat and lazy husband Difunto, the overseer; and in general the contrast between the fatalistic creole indolence and the industrious activity of the Spanish immigrant family, whom the creoles contemptuously call the "gallego." Beside the people, there are episodes to arrest attention, such as the lion hunt; or the great rodeo arranged by Marcela to drive the cattle during a period of drought to the upper reaches of the mountain where they could find water and pasturage (creole indifference would have allowed them to die of hunger).

The critics have never been very well disposed toward Hugo Wast, which is not difficult to understand. In these days when thrill and complexity are considered essentials of literary art, his romantic situations and denoucments seem old-fashioned. But he has won the reading public. It likes his humorous caricatures of odd types of people and his life-like portraits of children — his own large family affords him plenty of opportunity to study their ways. The jury which decided the Argentine prize for the best prose work published in 1925 awarded its thirty thousand pesos to *El desierto de piedra*.

BIBLIOGRAPHY

The names of only those books most useful to the student are given here. In many cases the best sources for more detailed study are the periodicals mentioned in the text. For an incomplete but working list of authors and their productions, see Coester, Alfred. *A Bibliography of Spanish-American Literature* in *Romanic Review*, Vol. III, No. 1.

For a general review of Spanish-American literature, consult the following books:

Menéndez y Pelayo, Marcelino. *Historia de la poesía hispanoamericana*, Madrid, 1913. This is a revision by the author of his introduction to the *Antología de poetas hispanoamericanos, edición de la Academia española*, Madrid, 1893. (This history and anthology cover all Spanish America; but as the author admitted consideration of only those poets who died before the year 1892 with scant mention of works in prose, the book, despite its indispensability, is unsatisfactory.)

Torres Caicedo, José María. *Ensayos biográficos*, 3 vols., Paris, 1863 and 1868. (These are useful and interesting sketches of authors prominent before the date of publication with extracts from their works.)

Valera, Juan. *Cartas americanas* (two series), Madrid, 1889, 1890. (Criticisms of Spanish-American literature contemporary with the date of publication.)

Sosa, Francisco. *Escritores y Poetas sud-americanos*, Mexico, 1890.

García Calderón, Francisco. *Les Democraties latines de l'Amerique*, Paris, 1912. English translation entitled, *Latin America; its rise and progress*, London, 1913. (The best brief account of political conditions in Spanish America during the nineteenth century.)

"Lauxar." *Motivos de crítica hispano-americanos*, Montevideo, 1914.

C. Oyuela. *Antología poética hispano-americana*, 5 vols., Buenos Aires, 1919.

CHAPTER I

Ercilla y Zúñiga, Alonso. *La Araucana. Morceaux choisis* par J. Ducamin, Paris, 1900.

Medina, José Toribio. *Historia de la literatura colonial de Chile.* Santiago, 1882.

Hills, E. C. *The Quechua Drama Ollantá.* In *Romanic Review*, Vol. V, No. 2.

Gutiérrez, Juan María. *Estudios biográficos y críticos sobre algunos poetas anteriores al Siglo XIX*, Buenos Aires, 1865.

CHAPTER II

García Velloso, Enrique. *Historia de la literatura argentina*, Buenos Aires, 1914.

El cancionero popular in the *Revista de Derecho, Historia, y Letras*, Vols. I to XIV, Buenos Aires, 1898 ff.

Gutiérrez, Juan María. Various articles in *La Revista de Buenos Aires*, and *La Revista del Rio de la Plata*.

Piñeyro, Enrique. *Biografías americanas*, Paris.

Amunátegui, Miguel Luis. *La alborada poética en Chile*, Santiago, 1892.

Amunátegui, Miguel Luis. *La vida de don Andrés Bello*, Santiago, 1882.

Cañete, Manuel. *Escritores hispano-americanos*, Madrid, 1884. (About Olmedo.)

Blanco Fombona, Rufino. *Autores americanos juzgados por españoles*, Paris, 1912. (Contains reprint of Cañete's essay on Olmedo and extracts from Menéndez y Pelayo.)

Blanco Fombona, Rufino. *Cartas de Bolívar*, Paris, 1913.

CHAPTER III

Heredia, José María de. *Poesías*, New York, 1875. Edition with introductory study by A. Bachiller y Morales.

Chacón y Calvo, José María. *José María Heredia,* in *Cuba contemporánea* for June and July, 1915.
Pimentel, Francisco. *Historia crítica de la literatura en Mexico,* Mexico, 1883.
González Obregón, Luis. *José Joaquín Fernández de Lizardi. Poetas yucatecos y tabasqueños,* Mexico, 1861.
Urbina, Luis G. *La literatura mexicana durante la guerra de la independencia,* Madrid, 1917.
Urbina, Henriquez Ureña. *Antología del centenario,* 2 vols., Mexico, 1910.

CHAPTER IV

Nuestro Parnaso, colección de poesías argentinas, 4 vols., ed. by E. Barreda, Buenos Aires, 1914.
García Velloso, Enrique. *Historia de la literatura argentina,* Buenos Aires, 1914.
García Merou, Martín. *Recuerdos literarios,* Buenos Aires, 1891.
Groussac, Pablo. *El Viaje intelectual,* Madrid, 1904.
"   "   Editor of *La Biblioteca,* 1896–98, Buenos Aires.
Oyuela, Calixto. *Apuntes de literatura argentina,* Buenos Aires, 1889.
Page, F. M. English translation of *Fausto* in *Publications of Mod. Lang. Association,* Vol. XI, pp. 1–62.
Quesada, Ernesto. *Reseñas y Críticas,* Buenos Aires, 1893.
Rojas, Ricardo. *Historia de la literatura argentina,* 4 vols., Buenos Aires, 1917–18. 2nd edit., Madrid, 8 vols., 1924.
Leavitt, Sturges E. *Bibliography of Argentine Literature,* Univ. of No. Car., 1924.
Bianchi, Alfredo A. *Teatro nacional,* Buenos Aires, 1920.
Noé, Julio. *Antología de la poesía argentina moderna (1900–1925),* Buenos Aires, 1926.

CHAPTER V

Roxlo, Carlos. *Historia crítica de la literatura uruguaya,* Montevideo, 1912.
Bauzá, Francisco. *Estudios literarios,* Montevideo, 1885.

Bustamente, R.   *El parnaso oriental,* Montevideo, 1905.
Zum Felde, Alberto.   *Crítica de la literatura uruguaya,* Montevideo, 1921.
Leavitt, S. E.   *Bibliography of Uruguayan Literature,* in *Hispania,* Vol. V, 2, 3.
García, Calderón V. and Barbagelata, H. D.   *La literatura uruguaya,* in *Revue hispanique,* Tome XL.
Falcao Espalter, M.   *Antología de poetas uruguayas, 1807–1921,* Montevideo, 1922.

Chapter VI

Antología Chilena.   Col. by P. P. Figueroa, Santiago, 1908.
Antología de poetas chilenos.   Col. by E. Donoso, Madrid, 1910.
Amunátegui, M. L., opera citata : also
   Las primeras representaciones dramaticas en Chile, Santiago, 1888.
   Don José Joaquín de Mora, Santiago, 1888.
   Juicio crítico de algunos poetas hispano-americanos, Santiago, 1859.
   Ensayos biográficos, Santiago, 1893–96.
   Don Salvador Sanfuentes, Santiago, 1892.
Eliz, Leonardo.   *Siluetas líricas y biográficas,* Santiago, 1889.
Figueroa, P. P.   *Diccionario biográfico,* Santiago, 1892.
Huneeus Gana, Jorge.   *Cuadro histórico de la producción intelectual de Chile,* Santiago, 1912.
Lastarria, José Victorino.   *Recuerdos literarios,* Santiago, 1878.
Peña, Nicolas.   *Teatro dramático nacional,* Santiago, 1913.
Silva, L. Ignacio.   *La novela en Chile,* Santiago, 1910.
Donoso, Armando.   *Los nuevos (La joven literatura chilena),* Valencia, 1912.
Medina, J. T.   *La literatura feminina en Chile,* Santiago, 1923.
Amunátegui Soler, Domingo.   *Bosquejo histórico de la literatura chilena,* Santiago, 1920.
Leavitt, S. E.   *Bibliography of Chilean Literature* in *Hispanic American Historical Review,* Vol. V.

Chapter VII

García Calderón, Ventura. *Del Romanticismo al Modernismo*, Paris, 1910.

Poetas Bolivianos. Col. by P. Molina and E. Finot.

Leavitt, S. E. *Bibliography of Peruvian Literature (1821–1919)*, in *Romanic Review*, Vol. XIII, No. 2.

Beltroy, Manuel. *Las cien mejores poesías líricas peruanas*, Lima, 1921.

Alarcón, Abel. *Literatura boliviana*, in *Revue hispanique*, Tome XLI.

Chapter VIII

Antología ecuatoriana. Col. by the Academía del Ecuador, Quito, 1892.

Mera, Juan León. *Ojeada histórico-crítica sobre la poesía ecuatoriana*, Quito, 1868.

Chapter IX

Antología colombiana. Col. by E. Isaza, Paris, 1895.

Parnaso colombiano. Col. by J. Añez with preface by J. Rivas Groot, Bogotá, 1886.

Laverde Amaya, I. *Apuntes sobre bibliografía colombiana con muestras escogidas*, Bogotá, 1889.

Arboleda, Julio. *Poesías*, with introduction by M. A. Caro, New York, 1883.

Gutiérrez González, Gregorio. *Poesías*, with introduction by S. Camacho Roldán, R. Pombo and others, Paris, 1908.

Vergara y Vergara, J. M. *Historia de la literatura en Nueva Granada, 1538–1820*, Bogotá, 1867.

Gómez Restrepo, A. *Literatura colombiana*, in *Revue hispanique*, Tome XLIII.

Vargas Tamayo, J. *Las cien mejores poesías líricas colombianas*, 2nd ed., Madrid, 1924.

CHAPTER X

Parnaso venezolano. 12 vols. pub. by J. Calcaño, Caracas, 1892.
Picón Febres, Gonzalo. *La literatura venezolana en el Siglo XIX*, Caracas, 1906.

CHAPTER XI

Antología de poetas mexicanos. Pub. by the Academía mex., Mexico, 1894.
Conferencias del Ateneo de la Juventud, Mexico, 1910.
Biblioteca de autores mexicanos, about 75 volumes, various dates, in which may be found articles on literature in the works of V. Agüeros, I. Altamirano, J. M. Roa Bárcena and the introductions of others.
González Obregón, Luis. *Novelistas mexicanos en el Siglo XIX.*
Starr, Frederick. *Readings from Modern Mexican Authors*, Chicago, 1904.
Las cien mejores poesías (líricas) mejicanas, Mexico, 1914.
Urbina, Luis G. *La vida literaria de Mexico*, Madrid, 1917.
Iguiniz, Juan B. *Bibliografía de novelistas mexicanos*, Mexico, 1926.
Lutrell, Estelle. *Mexican writers. A catalogue of books in the University of Arizona library with synopses and biog. notes.* Tucson, Ariz., 1920.
Estrada, Genaro. *Poetas nuevos de Mexico*, Mexico, 1916.

CHAPTER XII

Arpas cubanas. La Habana, 1904.
Parnaso cubano. Col. by A. López Prieto, 1881.
Bachiller y Morales, A. *Apuntes para la historia de las Letras y de la Instrucción pública en Cuba*, La Habana, 1859.
Calcagno, Francisco. *Diccionario biográfico cubano*, La Habana, 1878.
Calcagno, Francisco. *Poetas de Color*, H. 1887.
Mityans, Aurelio. *Estudio sobre el movimiento científico y literario de Cuba*, H. 1890.

Piñeyro, Enrique. *Vida y Escritos de Juan Clemente Zenea,* Paris, 1901.

Piñeyro, Enrique. *Biografías americanas,* Paris.

Piñeyro, Enrique. *Hombres y Glorias de America,* Paris.

Chacón y Calvo, J. *Literatura cubana. Ensayos críticos,* Madrid, 1922.

Chacón y Calvo, J. *Las cien mejores poesías cubanas,* Madrid, 1922.

Lizaso, F. and Fernández de Castro, J. A. *La poesía moderna en Cuba (1882–1925),* Madrid, 1926.

Remos, Juan J. *Historia de la literatura cubana,* Havana, 1925.

CHAPTER XIII

Antología dominicana. Col. by P. Henríquez Ureña and M. F. Cestero, New York.

Henríquez Ureña, Pedro. *Horas de estudio,* Paris, 1909.

Hostos, Eugenio M. *Meditando,* Paris.

Antología puertorriqueña. Col. by M. Fernández Juncos, New York, 1907.

Fernández Juncos, Manuel. *Semblanzas puertorriqueños,* P. R. 1888.

Lira costarricense. Col. by M. Fernández, San José, C. R. 1890.

Honduras literaria. Col. by R. E. Durón, Tegucigalpa, 1896.

Guirnalda salvadoreña. Col. by R. Mayorga Rivas, San Salvador, 1879.

Lugareñas, antología. Col. by C. A. Imendia, San Salvador, 1895.

Batres Jáuregui, A. *Literatos guatemaltecos,* Guatemala, 1896.

Sotela, Rogelio. *Valores literarios de Costa Rica,* San José, C. R., 1919.

CHAPTER XIV

Blanco Fombona, Rufino. *Letras y Letrados de Hispano-America,* Paris, 1908.

Blanco Fombona, Rufino. In *La Revista de America,* Paris, 1912 ff., various articles.

González Blanco, Andrés. *Estudio preliminar* to the *Obras escogidas* of Rubén Darío, 3 vols., Madrid, 1910.

González Blanco, Andrés. Introduction to *Fiat Lux*, select poems of J. S. Chocano, Paris, 1908.

Gutiérrez Nájera, Manuel. *Poesías* with introduction by Justo Sierra, Paris, 1896.

Meza, Ramón. *Julian del Cacal*, Estudio biográfico, Habana, 1910.

Goldberg, Isaac. *Studies in Spanish American Literature*, New York, 1920.

Coester, Alfred. *Anthology of the modernista movement in Spanish America*, Boston, 1924.

Chapter XV

Barbagelata, H. D. *Rodó y sus críticos*, Paris, 1920.

"Lauxar." *Rubén Darío y José Enrique Rodó*, Montevideo, 1924.

Parra del Riego, Juan. *Antología de poetisas americanos*, Montevideo, 1923.

Chapter XVI

Consult *Cuba Contemporánea, Nosotros, Hispania, Repertorio Americano,* and other journals.

INDEX

(In this index names of periodicals are printed in Italics; pen names, popular titles, catchwords, et cetera, are indicated by quotation marks.)